Preservation
YELLOW PAGES

Preservation
YELLOW PAGES

The Complete Information Source
for Homeowners, Communities,
and Professionals

Revised Edition

National Trust
for Historic Preservation

Julie Zagars
Editor

PRESERVATION PRESS

John Wiley & Sons, Inc.
New York • Chichester • Weinheim • Brisbane • Singapore • Toronto

A cooperative publication with the National Trust for Historic Preservation,
Washington, D.C., chartered by Congress in 1949 to encourage the preservation of sites,
buildings, and communities significant in American history and culture.

This text is printed on acid-free paper.

Library of Congress Cataloging-in-Publication Data
Preservation Yellow pages : the complete information source for
    homeowners, communities and professionals / National Trust for
    Historic Preservation ; Julie Zagars, editor, — Rev. ed.
        p.   cm.
    Published simultaneously in Canada.
    This revised edition was built upon the success of the 1993
edition of the Landmark Yellow Pages.
    Includes bibliographical references (p.   ) and index.
    ISBN 0-471-19183-3 (paper : alk. paper)
    1. Historic preservation—United States—Handbooks, manuals, etc.
2. Historic preservation—United States—Societies, etc.—
Directories.   I. Zagars, Julie.   II. National Trust for Historic
Preservation in the United States.   III. Landmark yellow pages.
E159.P73   1997
363.6'9'0973—dc21   97-7456

Printed in the United States of America

10   9   8   7   6   5   4   3   2   1

Contents

Acknowledgments   vii

Section One: **Introduction**   1
                     How To Use This Book   3
                     Why Preserve?   4
                     Preservation Primer   8

Section Two: **Preservation Topics**   15
                     Overview   17
                     Architectural Styles   18
                     National Register of Historic Places   27
                     Secretary of the Interior's Standards for Rehabilitation   30
                     Historic Rehabilitation Tax Credit   32
                     Introduction to Historic Preservation Law   36
                     Degree Programs in Historic Preservation   43
                     Glossary   50
                     Resources and Readings   56
                     Chronology: Preservation in America   78

Section Three: **Preservation Partners**   81
                     Overview   83
                     National Park Service   85
                     National Trust for Historic Preservation   88
                     Advisory Council on Historic Preservation   97
                     Federal Programs   100
                     National and Regional Organizations   106
                     International Programs   111

Section Four:

Preservation Phone Book

119

State and Local Contacts 121

Alabama	123	Nebraska	201
Alaska	125	Nevada	203
Arizona	127	New Hampshire	204
Arkansas	129	New Jersey	206
California	131	New Mexico	209
Colorado	138	New York	211
Connecticut	141	North Carolina	218
Delaware	144	North Dakota	222
District of Columbia	146	Ohio	223
Florida	149	Oklahoma	227
Georgia	153	Oregon	229
Hawaii	157	Pennsylvania	231
Idaho	159	Rhode Island	237
Illinois	161	South Carolina	239
Indiana	166	South Dakota	241
Iowa	169	Tennessee	243
Kansas	171	Texas	246
Kentucky	173	Utah	251
Louisiana	175	Vermont	253
Maine	177	Virginia	255
Maryland	180	Washington	259
Massachusetts	184	West Virginia	262
Michigan	189	Wisconsin	264
Minnesota	192	Wyoming	267
Mississippi	195	Puerto Rico	268
Missouri	197	U.S. Virgin Islands	269
Montana	199		

Index 271

Acknowledgments

The National Trust for Historic Preservation was established in a collaborative effort among dedicated preservationists—from organizations as diverse as the National Park Service, National Gallery of Art, American Historical Association, American Institute of Architects, and the American Scenic and Historic Preservation Society—congressional leaders, who passed the National Trust's charter, and President Harry S Truman, who signed the legislation on October 26, 1949. That spirit of partnership remains an important part of the preservation movement and is exemplified by this edition of the *Preservation Yellow Pages*.

The concept for the directory began with *The Brown Book: A Directory of Preservation Information*, published in 1983. That work was updated and enlarged by the U.S. Committee, International Council on Monuments and Sites (US/ICOMOS), and published in 1990 as Part I of the first edition of the *Landmark Yellow Pages*. The second edition of the *Landmark Yellow Pages* was published in 1993. That edition forms the basis for this updated volume; the series continues to evolve with expanded listings and reformatted sections.

The editor wishes to thank the many staff members of the National Trust for Historic Preservation who shared their preservation knowledge and proofreading abilities, and all who took the time to offer their thoughts. This is truly a product of the whole staff, as this project touched all corners of the organization. Special thanks to:

Katherine Adams and Byrd Wood, for their help in conceptualizing, shaping, and compiling this revised edition. Their expertise and ideas were simply invaluable.

Wesley Smith, for lending knowledge and experience at a crucial time.

Pat Flowe, Melissa Ford, Rhonda Jones, Stephen Kidd, and Tara Evans Shimberg, for their tireless typing and keen fact-checking.

Dwight Young, for his enlightening, thoughtful writings.

Margaret Welsh, for sharing her wealth of knowledge, and to her ever-informed (and ever-willing) staff, David Arthur and Valerie Carter.

Paul Edmondson and Laura Nelson, for recrafting and writing.

Brian Noyes, for designing the book's cover.

Jeffrey Harris, for researching images and illustrations.

Kathy Cox, for her support and quiet guidance.

Vin Cipolla and J. J. Pryor, for their support and patience.

Paul Vitali, for guidance, wisdom, and humor throughout every step.

Thanks, also, to our friends, colleagues, and partners across the country:

Michael Tomlan at Cornell University, for bibliographical data on his favorite preservation books.

Carol Shull and Carol Fox at the National Park Service, for providing vital data on organization structure.

Carol Highsmith, for the beautiful photography;

Jan Cigliano, and the staff at John Wiley & Sons, Inc., New York, for putting it all together.

Finally, thanks to the personal support team:

Mom and Dad, for encouragement from a distance.

Marty Dobrow and Amy Bowles-Reyer, for the inspiration.

Joe Dobrow, for the sustenance.

SECTION ONE

Introduction

How To Use This Book

Welcome to the *Preservation Yellow Pages*! *Preservation Yellow Pages* builds upon the 1993 *Landmark Yellow Pages,* updating topical issues and expanding national to local contact listings. This revised edition offers *the* most complete and current guide to preservation sources and information locally, statewide, and nationally. From identifying a building's architectural style to establishing a local historic district, from federal standards that regulate renovation of historic buildings and communities to precedent-setting legal cases in land-use law, from federal agencies you may need to know to your local preservation organization you want to know more about, you will find an encyclopedia of resources in these pages.

The **Preservation Primer** in Section One provides an overview, a field guide if you will, of the preservation world, including an explanation of why it is important to list a historic property in the National Register of Historic Places and when a building or district may be eligible for tax incentives or many other preservation grants and loans. Section Two, **Preservation Topics,** offers an overview of major areas and disciplines in preservation today, with an explanation of how each interrelates within the context of the overall field. Brief essays on each topic identify issues within specific disciplines.

Section Three, **Preservation Partners,** contains an explanation of the structure of preservation agencies and organizations, and of regulatory and practical relationships among public and private entities, as well as background and contact information for those organizations. Section Four is the ultimate state-by-state **Phone Book** of preservation-related organizations. New and updated listings are streamlined to help you to get in touch with the agency or organization you need.

Note: All the information contained in these pages is up to date and correct at the time of publication. Names, addresses, and phone numbers may change without notice.

Why Preserve?

The question may be asked: Why preserve? The following text has been adapted from a speech given at San Antonio in September 1990 by Dwight Young, Senior Communications Associate for the National Trust for Historic Preservation.

All over the country there are people who remember October 17, 1989, in a very particular way: It was the day of the San Francisco earthquake. For me, the date has another significance: It was the day I went back to the LBJ Ranch.

I had been there once before. It was 1960, in the summer; probably in July. I was there with my grandmother and my great-grandmother, and we had come for a celebration. You see, my great-grandmother was Lyndon Johnson's first cousin, and she wanted to be at the ranch to welcome him home from Los Angeles, where the Democratic Convention had just nominated him for vice president. So we went to the ranch that summer evening, and there was a big crowd and a band, I think, and some short speeches and lots of flashbulbs. LBJ gave my great-grandmother a bear-hug, and he shook my hand. I was sixteen years old, and I've never forgotten it.

The next day we went to visit some other relatives out in the country near Johnson City. It was hot, so we spent most of the day just sitting in the shade of the porch. Late in the afternoon, we piled into an old pickup truck and drove down to the Pedernales to wade. As we were bumping down a dirt track through the woods, we came upon four or five deer; they were so startled to see us that they jumped completely over the bed of the pickup where I was sitting. I've never forgotten that, either.

That was a long time ago—more than thirty years. By the time I went back to the LBJ Ranch in October of 1989, LBJ, my grandmother, and my great-grandmother were all gone, and that sixteen-year-old kid was gone, too. But what amazed and moved me was the fact that the *place* was still there: the ranch, the hills and woods, the little towns and the farms, and the deer moving down to the river in the dusk. The events of 1960 had become part of the history of the place—and because I had been there, I had become part of that history myself, part of a centuries-long stream of names and dates and events that make that a *special* place, a place worthy of preservation.

That word makes me a little uneasy sometimes. "Preservation" has become such a buzzword that I'm afraid we've forgotten that it describes a simple activity that all of us engage in every day—and for some very simple reasons. Let me give you some examples.

When I lived in Charleston, South Carolina, I had a neighbor who was a real Charleston lady. In the dining room of her 18th-century house, sitting on a fine 18th-century sideboard, is a fine 18th-century silver tea service. She's very proud of it. She shows it off to her guests, even pours tea out of it on very special occasions. That lady has held on to that silver tea service—she has *preserved* it—simply because it is good to look at. She knows that it represents a sense of style and craftsmanship that is difficult to duplicate nowadays. She preserves it because it is beautiful.

In somewhat the same sense, my grandparents up in Plainview, Texas, drove a Model T Ford well into the 1940s. One of my strongest childhood memories is of being driven around town in that car, which even then was old enough to attract considerable attention. Now, my grandparents didn't keep on driving that Model T because it was beautiful. No, they held on to it—they *preserved* it—because it did what they expected a car to do: It took them where they wanted to go, with a minimum of fuss and bother. They preserved that car because it worked.

Finally, in my mother's house in Lubbock, Texas, up on a shelf in the closet in my sister's old room, there is a scrapbook that my sister kept all during the time she was in high school. On one of the pages of that scrapbook is all that's left of a corsage that she wore to some dance or other. My sister has held on to that corsage—she has *preserved* it—not because it's beautiful (it isn't) and not because it works (it isn't good for anything, really). Rather, she has preserved it because it reminds her of an event that she doesn't want to forget. She knows that as long as she preserves what's left of that flower, she has a tangible link with a part of herself that she wants to keep.

So, when you strip away all the rhetoric, that's all "preservation" really is: just having the good sense to hang on to something because it's good to look at, because it works, because it links us with a past that we need to remember.

That's what we preservationists are all about. It's our job. It's a big job, because what we seek to preserve is more than a single building; it's whole communities. And it's a *tough* job, too, particularly for those of us who come from communities that are not like the LBJ Ranch or Charleston or Boston or San Francisco. The fact is, many of us come from "ordinary" places that most people have never heard of, but that are, nonetheless, eminently worth preserving.

My reason for so confidently saying that about so-called ordinary places has much to do with the nature of history. We make a grave mistake, I believe, when we equate history with fact, for they really are two very different things. When it comes to history, the facts really don't speak for themselves; rather, the historian

Apartment entrance on the Upper East Side, New York City, New York. *(Carol M. Highsmith Photography)*

makes them speak, just as a violinist determines what sounds will come out of his or her instrument. History is an interpretation of the facts of the past. It is a reflective, evaluative, and largely subjective statement about the meaning of the past. Historians who persist in thinking that they are merely reporting the past as it really was, therefore, fail to understand what they are about.

Recently we have begun to realize that our interpretation of the past has some major gaps in it. It focuses on politics and war, the cataclysmic and the unique, and pays scant attention to the broad and ordinary flow of commonplace human experience. As an illustration of this tendency, think about what you know about ancient Rome. I'm willing to bet that it has mostly to do with the intrigues of the Caesars, the long wars all over the Empire, the spectacles in the Colosseum.

Now carry that image forward. If a student far in the future wanted to know about life in our own time, think what a skewed vision he or she would get if the only history available dealt exclusively with Margaret Thatcher and Madonna, bloody civil strife in South Africa, and the birth of the first test-tube baby. While those may have been important people and events in the grand scheme of things, I think you'll agree with me that our lives—yours and mine—have proceeded along other, quieter paths and were only slightly affected by those big names and big deals. And it is just these quieter paths, these places where you and I live and work, these aspects of our lives that affect us most deeply and every day, that are conspicuously absent in most history as we are taught it. Our hometowns—the places that no one has ever heard of—are worth saving because they are exceptions to the general tendency to overlook or ignore the overwhelming importance of the ordinary in history.

I live now in a city of monuments. You can hardly turn a corner in Washington, D.C., without bumping into a statue of a general on horseback or a politician striking a pose, their arms sweeping out in dramatic gestures of determination, heroism, or pomposity. The other monuments—our "ordinary" communities—speak of other achievements. Think of a Kansas town's Main Street, or its treeshaded old neighborhoods. Chances are, no battles were fought there, except for the hard-fought struggle to make a living out of dirt. Chances are, no ringing oratory was uttered there, only the jokes and curses and quiet front-porch-swing conversations of men and women and children making lives for themselves in a new, raw place. Chances are, no empires were won or lost there, except in the gradual pushing-back of limits that heralded the passing of the frontier, the making of a nation. Seen in those terms, "monument" doesn't seem too far-fetched a description for such an "ordinary" community.

This quote from the 19th-century English artist and critic John Ruskin says it best: "Great nations write their autobiographies in three manuscripts, the book of their deeds, the book of their words, and the book of their art. Not one of these books can be understood unless we read the two others, but of the three the only trustworthy one is the last."

I think that our ordinary communities are important entries in that book of the nation's art that Ruskin describes. Think of a New England

county seat. I think that such a place—an assemblage of front yards and storefronts and signboards and brick pavements, a low-rise skyline of church steeples and chimneys and courthouse domes—can be very good to look at. What makes these communities particularly intriguing to me is the fact that they are largely unconscious art, the same sort of art that Horatio Greenough was speaking of a hundred years ago when he said that the most beautiful things America had produced were the clipper ship and the trotting-wagon. It is an art that begins with a job to be done, and through conscientious workmanship and happy juxtaposition winds up with a form that embodies just enough of whatever it takes to get the job done. The brick and wood and flower beds of those communities have a great power to make real for me the people who were responsible for their being there. And the appreciation I feel for that human presence is constant, whether I see it in the stonework of a pasture fence, the careful matching of grain in a wood-paneled parlor, or the arrangement of windows and porches on the facade of a Victorian house. Seen in those terms, "outdoor art gallery" is a pretty good label for our "ordinary" communities, too. Whatever we call them, these places are very good things to have around. They are worth saving, and I hope you feel a tremendous sense of satisfaction in being involved in that effort.

But preservation isn't easy, and there have been many times when you ask yourself, "Why bother?" Why strain your brain trying to forge relationships and alliances among preservationists and shopkeepers and city managers who seem to have been

born with blinders on? Why go to the trouble of identifying and inventorying the cultural resources of your community and developing plans to protect and enhance them? Why bother? Fortunately, I don't have to make up an answer to that question; it's been answered often and eloquently many times.

Perhaps because I grew up in an area with its share of dust storms, I've always felt a special affection for John Steinbeck's dust bowl novel *The Grapes of Wrath*. One of the most moving passages in that book comes when the women of the Joad family sit in their house, poring over their possessions. You see, the Joads are leaving the next morning in search of a better life in California, and they have to decide which of their treasures can be taken along and which must be left behind. Here's how the passage goes:

> . . . the women sat among doomed things, turning them over and looking past them and back. "This book, my father had it. He liked a book. *Pilgrim's Progress.* Used to read it. Got his name in it, right here. Why, here's his pipe—it still smells rank. And this picture—an angel. I looked at it before the first three children were born. Didn't seem to do much good. Think we could get this china dog in? Aunt Sadie brought it from the St. Louis fair. See—it says right on it. No, I guess we can't take that. Here's a letter my brother wrote the day before he died. Here's an old-time hat. These feathers—I never got to use them. No, there isn't room . . . . How can we live without our lives? How will we know it's us without our past?"

It's important to note that the women in that scene aren't members of any local historical society or planning commission. They're just people facing the imminent loss of their own heritage. The anguish of their experience should teach us once and for all that our heritage is not the sole property of our historians. It belongs to all of us.

A sense of place can grow by being shared, but it also can be lost. As historian Sidney Hyman has pointed out, a place can fall victim to amnesia. It can lose the memory of what it was, and thereby lose touch with what it is, what it wants to be. That loss of community memory happens most dramatically in the destruction of familiar landmarks and landscapes that are tangible manifestations of who we were, what we believed, what shaped us.

When we preserve, we strengthen the perpetual partnership that, if maintained unbroken, makes for orderly growth in the life and appearance of our communities: the perpetual partnership among the past, present, and future. The terms of that partnership guarantee to each generation the right to express itself in its own style and to meet its needs in its own way. But experience has taught us that each generation shapes its environment most wisely when it maintains a healthy respect for the handiwork of nature and of preceding generations.

One of the most profound statements about preservation was made more than a century ago by John Ruskin. Actually, he was writing about architecture, but his remarks apply beautifully to preservation, too:

> When we build, let us think that we build forever. Let it not be for present delight, not for present use alone; let it be such work as our descendants will thank us for; and let us think . . . that a time is to come when men will say, "See! This our fathers did for us."

Just as we learn about our fathers—who they were, what they believed, how they lived—from the buildings and landscapes they left for us, our children will learn about us in the same way. It is entirely proper for us to say, as Ruskin suggested, "See! This our fathers did for us: they found a land of subtle beauty and richness, they built solidly and simply, with a respect for materials and an innate sense of style, and they created ornaments in harmony with the land." And if you here do your job well, you make it possible to hope that our children will say, "See! This our fathers did for us: they saw the beauty of this landscape and the worth of these buildings, they protected and nurtured them, and they passed them on to us—alive."

Any real community almost seems to have a heart of its own. Working with the help of sensitive outsiders and learning from the example of others who have succeeded at what you're attempting, you as homefolks have the opportunity—and the awesome responsibility—to see that that heart keeps beating. People far down the future will need that heart beating strong and true just as much as we need it now.

Preservation Primer

*Adapted from a presentation by Dwight Young at the National Trust's Preservation
Conference in Fort Worth, Texas, in October 1995.*

This chapter presents an overview of some of the major players and elements in the preservation community: the National Historic Preservation Act of 1966, the National Register of Historic Places, National Historic Landmarks, local preservation ordinances, and tax incentives for preservation.

THE NATIONAL HISTORIC PRESERVATION ACT OF 1966

By the mid-1960s, there was growing concern about the rate at which America's heritage was disappearing. That period marked the heyday of several federal programs that did enormous amounts of damage to America's historic resources.

One of these was a program called Urban Renewal. The main idea behind Urban Renewal was that the best way to revitalize America's inner cities was to demolish blighted neighborhoods—"blighted" being the federal government's favorite word to describe a neighborhood that needed a new coat of paint—so that vacant land then could be offered to developers who would build shiny new office towers, hotels, and housing in the inner cities. The first part of the program worked: The demo-

lition was a complete success. The second part didn't work so well: The rebuilding didn't always occur either at the speed or with the quality that had been intended. The result is that, even now, the scars of Urban Renewal are all too visible in many communities.

At the same time, construction of the interstate highway system was in full swing. In passing through big cities and small towns alike, these highways naturally took the route of least resistance—namely, through the middle of older neighborhoods where land values were depressed. For a while in the 1960s, it seemed likely that any historic building or neighborhood that wasn't demolished in the name of Urban Renewal stood a very good chance of being demolished in the name of interstate highway construction.

Alarmed by the devastation caused by these and other programs, the U.S. Conference of Mayors in 1965 appointed a special committee to find a way to strengthen the federal government's commitment to and involvement in historic preservation. The committee promptly traveled to Europe, believing that the European experience in preservation must have some lessons for the United

States. After a couple of months traveling around Europe, talking to public- and private-sector leaders in preservation, committee members came back to this country and issued their report. If any one document can legitimately be called the "Bible" of the modern preservation movement, it is this report, which is entitled *With Heritage So Rich*.

There are two aspects of that report that are particularly impressive. First, it is beautifully and thoughtfully written—not the sort of thing you might expect from a committee report. It presents a candid overview of the state of preservation at that time, as well as an eloquent and compelling statement of why preservation is important. The second impressive thing about the report is that it accomplished just what its authors hoped it would: Within a few years, every one of the major recommendations included in *With Heritage So Rich* was enacted into law.

In 1966, acting partly in response to *With Heritage So Rich*, Congress passed the **National Historic Preservation Act (NHPA)**. While it has been amended a few times, this is the federal preservation law under which we still operate today. NHPA accomplished four things of enormous importance to preservationists.

First, it created the **National Register of Historic Places**, the federal government's official list of properties worthy of preservation.

Second, it led to the appointment, in every state and territory, of a **State Historic Preservation Officer (SHPO)** with responsibility for encouraging and assisting preservation efforts at the state level. A major part of each SHPO's responsibility is to see that significant properties in his or her state are nominated to the National Register.

Third, the legislation established a program of **grants in aid of preservation** whereby the federal government provides funds to help the states carry out the preservation responsibilities mandated to them by NHPA. Today, the work of the SHPOs is still supported in part by a federal appropriation from the Department of the Interior.

Fourth, NHPA created an independent federal agency called the **President's Advisory Council on Historic Preservation**. The role of the Advisory Council is spelled out in Section 106 of the Act. Section 106 says that whenever a federal agency (or any other agency using federal funds or acting under a federal license) is going to do something that will impact a property listed in the National Register of Historic Places, it must give the Advisory Council the opportunity to review and comment on the proposed undertaking. It is important to note that Section 106 gives

Freemason Street Baptist Church, Norfolk, Virginia. *(Carol M. Highsmith Photography)*

the Advisory Council the power to "review and comment" only; the Council does not have the power to refuse permission for a proposed project. Note also that the protection provided by Section 106 is invoked *only* when the historic resources affected are listed in the National Register *and* when the proposed project is being undertaken by a federal agency or involves the use of federal funds.

Here's an illustration of how Section 106 works: If a state highway department, using federal highway funds, is planning to widen a highway that runs through a historic district that is listed on the National Register, the highway department may not carry out the project until it gives the Advisory Council the op-

portunity to review and issue comments on it. If the Advisory Council's review indicates that the road-widening project will have an adverse impact on the historic district, the Council will work with the highway department and other interested parties (such as the SHPO and local preservationists, for instance) to work out some form of mitigation.

One major recommendation of *With Heritage So Rich* was not included in the 1966 legislation—but it was enacted into law ten years later. In 1976 Congress passed the Tax Reform Act, which provided tax incentives for the rehabilitation of historic buildings. While the 1976 legislation itself was relatively ineffectual, it eventually led to the adoption of tax-incentive laws (most notably the Economic Recovery Tax Act of 1982) that had a major impact on historic preservation.

THE NATIONAL REGISTER OF HISTORIC PLACES

The National Register of Historic Places is the foundation upon which our preservation activities are based. The National Register is the federal government's official list of properties worthy of historic preservation. When the federal government puts a property on the National Register, it is saying, in effect, "This property is important enough to be preserved." It does not say, "This property *must* be preserved" or, "This property *will* be preserved" or, "We are prepared to offer financial help to ensure that it will be preserved." It says only that the property is of sufficient importance to us as Americans that it *should* be preserved.

We tend to think of the National Register as a list of buildings, but in fact it includes ships, grain elevators, engineering structures of all kinds, dams, bridges, locomotives, mine headframes in Butte, Montana, and the cable car system in San Francisco. The Register is far more than just buildings.

As a major part of his or her responsibility, the SHPO in each state is responsible for seeing that all of the state's significant properties are nominated to the National Register. Obviously, that's an enormous job, a job that will never be fully completed—particularly if properties have to be nominated one by one. Fortunately, it is possible to streamline the nomination process so that groups of properties can be added to the Register all at once.

The most common form of multiple-property nomination is the **historic district**. A historic district nomination draws a boundary around a portion of a community or a group of buildings and nominates everything within that boundary to the National Register, all at once. The historic district recognizes the fact that a group of buildings may have a significance greater than the significance of any single building in the group. The historic district of Charleston, to cite an example, extends over several square blocks. Some of the buildings in the district are very impressive landmarks, while others are not so impressive. But what makes the place really significant is that it presents a context that makes the indi-

vidual buildings less important than the whole collection.

The second form of multiple-property nomination, called a **multiple resource nomination**, simply provides a way of adding all of a community's historic resources to the National Register at once. A multiple resource nomination may include some historic districts as well as individual historic buildings.

The third form of multiple listing, a **thematic group nomination**, provides a means of adding to the Register several properties that share some feature or quality in common. Perhaps they were all designed by the same architect, for instance, or they are all made of the same material, or they were all built at roughly the same time. Whatever the quality or feature, it provides a link among individual properties—and this link makes it possible to add them all to the National Register in a single nomination.

How does the nomination process work? Since this is a federal government program, the first step in nominating a property to the National Register of Historic Places is filling out an official form. The nomination process is fully democratic: Anybody can nominate anything to the National Register, assuming that he or she is willing to fill out the form and do the research or knows the history that is required to justify the property's eligibility for the Register. The completed forms are reviewed by the SHPO in the state where the property is located.

The SHPO also notifies the owner of the property—who might not have been involved in the process up to this point—that the nomination is being reviewed. The owner, if he or

she does not want the property listed in the Register, can object to the nomination. If the owner does object, the property will not be listed in the Register. If the owner does not object, he or she is presumed to have concurred, and the nomination will proceed. In the case of a historic district, or any of the multiple listings, every property owner concerned must be notified. In the case of a historic district, they all must be given the opportunity to object; if a simple majority of them object, the nomination will not go forward.

There is a process by which, even if an owner refuses to allow a property to be put on the National Register, the property may still be declared eligible for the Register if it meets the criteria. This declaration of eligibility is important because, generally speaking, the benefits of National Register listing are also extended to properties that have been declared *eligible* for the Register.

Next, the nomination goes before a state review board. These review boards go by various names—the National Register Review Board, the State Architecture Review Board, and the like. Typically, members of the board are appointed by the governor; the actual makeup of the board—at least one architect, at least one historian, and so on—may be specified by state statute. The board meets at intervals—every month in a few states, quarterly in others—to review National Register nominations against the evaluation criteria.

If the review board feels that the property meets the criteria, the nomination form goes to the SHPO for signature. Then the form is forwarded to the National Register staff in Washington, where it is reviewed once more. If the nomination is found to be in order, it is signed by the keeper of the National Register, and the owner receives a formal letter of notification.

Once a property is listed, it generally cannot be removed from the Register unless something happens—a catastrophic fire, for instance, or an ill-considered and extensive "remodeling"—to destroy or compromise the significance that made it eligible for listing in the first place. If a building is listed in the Register because of its outstanding design features and an owner eliminates or changes those features, is there a penalty? No. But if the alteration is severe enough that it destroys the property's significance, the property may be removed from the Register (or "de-listed"). But since there are no "National Register police" to wander the country and keep an eye on these properties, delisting generally occurs only when someone takes the time to notify the SHPO or the National Register that a property's status should be reviewed. Simple change in ownership does not affect a property's National Register status, even if a new owner objects to the listing.

The federal government does not provide an official marker for properties listed in the Register. A number of private firms do manufacture plaques that identify National Register properties, and owners are free to purchase them and attach them to their properties if they wish.

There are three primary criteria that determine a property's eligibility for the National Register for Historic Places. The first of these is **significance**. The nomination form must demonstrate that this property is sufficiently significant in some way to justify being placed on the National Register. This means, generally speaking, that the property is associated with a person or event of significance in history; or that it exhibits distinctive characteristics or high artistic values, or is the work of a master; or that it is likely to be of help in the discovery of important information at some time in the future.

It is important to note that the property only has to satisfy one of these criteria for significance. It may, for instance, be a great piece of architecture in which nothing historically significant ever happened. It is also important to note that the National Register is intended to include properties of *local* as well as *national* significance. This means that association with a person or event of local significance may be sufficient to justify a property's listing in the National Register.

The second major criterion is **integrity**. Think of it this way: What-

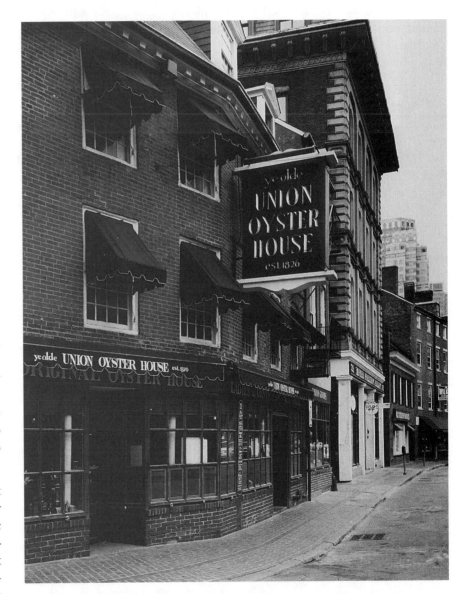

Union Oyster House, Boston, Massachusetts. *(Carol M. Highsmith Photography)*

ever it is that makes a property significant, is there still enough of it present—in terms of location, design, materials, and so on—to justify its being listed in the National Register? The issue of integrity may arise in the case of a property that has been moved from its original location, to cite a single example. If the property's significance is primarily architectural, its integrity may not have been destroyed by the relocation; however, if the property's significance is primarily historical (if, for instance, it is the house where an important event took place), its relocation may be thought to have destroyed its integrity and rendered it ineligible for the Register insofar as that criterion is concerned.

The third criterion is **age** of the property. Generally speaking, properties are not eligible for the National Register if they have achieved significance within the past fifty years. There are exceptions, of course, and there are a number of properties in the National Register that are not yet fifty years old. For instance, Washington's Dulles Airport, which is much less than fifty years old, is listed in the National Register because it is the work of a master architect and demonstrates an innovative approach to the challenge of getting people off the ground and into the air.

What are the benefits that accrue to the owner once a property is added to the National Register of Historic Places? The first benefit is extremely important yet frequently overlooked. Listing in the National Register is an honorific designation. Property owners should take justifiable pride in the fact that the federal government has acknowledged the significance of their property by listing it in the

Register. Second, listing in the National Register is the basic criterion of eligibility for whatever preservation funds may be available. Granted, there aren't many funds currently available; money for preservation is difficult to come by these days. But every source of preservation funding that *is* available requires that the property be listed in the National Register. Third, tax incentives for the preservation or rehabilitation of historic buildings are restricted to properties listed in the National Register. And finally, as mentioned earlier, properties listed in the National Register enjoy a measure of protection through Section 106 of the National Historic Preservation Act.

Many people believe that there are severe restrictions associated with being listed in the Register. They're wrong. Listing imposes no restrictions on private property rights. That simple fact is so important—and so frequently misunderstood—that it's worth repeating: Listing in the National Register imposes no restrictions on an owner's right to do anything to his or her property that local law allows. When people object to having their properties listed in the Register, it is almost always because they don't understand this fact. Any restriction that is imposed on an owner's private property rights is the result of local law, not the provisions of the National Register.

NATIONAL HISTORIC LANDMARKS

Some historic properties—a relatively small number—are designated National Historic Landmarks. These are properties of exceptional significance; think of them as the cream of the crop of America's historic and cultural resources. National Historic

Landmark (NHL) designation, unlike National Register nomination, is a process in which the general public plays no direct part; it is essentially an in-house function of the Department of the Interior.

NHLs enjoy somewhat greater measure of protection than other properties listed in the National Register of Historic Places. Every year the National Park Service issues a list of threatened and endangered NHLs (called the Section 8 Report) in order to call attention to these landmarks in jeopardy and spur local efforts to ensure their preservation. The major difference between NHLs and other National Register properties is their level of significance, which the National Park Service commemorates with a plaque that identifies a given property as a National Historic Landmark.

LOCAL ORDINANCES

The first local preservation ordinance was enacted in Charleston, South Carolina, in 1931. For the first time, the Charleston ordinance designated a portion of the city as a historic district and imposed restrictions on what owners could do to their properties in that district. Charleston's example has been widely emulated: Today there are approximately 2,000 communities across the country that employ preservation ordinances of one kind or another.

It is important to note that in most cases there is no correlation between being listed in the National Register of Historic Places and being protected by a local preservation ordinance. In Charleston, for example, there is a historic district that is listed in the Register. There is also a historic district that was created by the local preservation ordinance. While these districts occupy the same general area, their boundaries are not identical, which means that a particular house may be in the National Register but not protected by the local ordinance, or vice versa, or it may be covered by both.

Generally, these ordinances create a review board of local residents that has the power to approve or disapprove an owner's application to do certain things to his or her property. In short, the ordinance simply imposes an additional level of regulation with which a property owner must deal before carrying out certain kinds of work. In most cases, the ordinance says that any work that requires a building permit must be approved by the review board before the building permit can be issued; this means, obviously, that work not requiring a building permit—routine maintenance, for example—can be done without the review board's approval. Beyond this generalization, the specific provisions of local ordinances vary enormously from community to community. Typically, ordinances say that: (1) if the owner of a protected building wants to tear the building down, the review board's approval must be obtained before a demolition permit can be granted; (2) if the owner wants to make certain alterations to a protected building, the review board must approve before the work is undertaken; and (3) if a property owner wants to put up a new building in a protected historic district, the review board must approve the plans before the new building can be constructed.

Relatively few ordinances give the review board the power to prohibit demolition outright. More com-

Ship Captain's "Steamboat House," New Orleans, Louisiana. *(Carol M. Highsmith Photography)*

monly, the ordinance empowers the review board to impose a delay on the issuance of the demolition permit. Ideally, local preservationists will utilize the delay period to find a way to save the building from demolition—but if no such solution has been devised by the end of the delay period, the owner may proceed with demolition. In dealing with proposed alterations to protected buildings, review boards generally have control over exterior alterations, although a few ordinances do impose design-review controls over significant interiors as well. In a further limitation of their powers, many review boards have jurisdiction only over exterior alterations that will be visible from the public right-of-way. In dealing with the proposed construction of a new building in a protected historic district, review boards generally seek to ensure that the new building will be

compatible with the historic architecture that characterizes the rest of the district. This is a thorny issue, since it is perilously easy to allow matters of personal taste to become mixed up in the definition of "compatible" design, so most well-drafted ordinances establish clear and specific criteria by which new designs will be evaluated.

There is no way to generalize further about what local ordinances say. Some ordinances regulate paint color; some do not. Others regulate such features as architectural styles, signage, landscaping, and the placement of satellite dishes. Obviously, the only way to know what a particular local ordinance specifies is to obtain a copy and read it.

In many respects, the benefits of local ordinance protection are the same as those of listing in the National Register of Historic Places. For many homeowners, living in a locally designated historic district is a distinct honor and privilege. Moreover, in some states, owners of properties located in historic districts that are protected by a local ordinance are eligible for certain tax benefits (to find out whether such benefits are available in a particular state, contact the SHPO). Over the years, a significant body of evidence has demonstrated conclusively that the imposition of controls in a historic district does not lower property values, as some alarmists have claimed, but in fact has the opposite effect. In any number of communities where these studies have been carried out, property values in districts protected by local ordinances have at the very least remained stable and, much more commonly, have risen at a higher rate than property values outside the historic district.

The legality of local preservation ordinances has been upheld consistently by courts all the way up to and including the United States Supreme Court. Perhaps the most important landmark preservation case involved New York's Grand Central Station: A developer who wanted to build a skyscraper above the station was refused permission to do so by the city's Landmarks Preservation Commission. The ensuing lawsuit went all the way to the Supreme Court, which ruled in 1978 that New York's ordinance was constitutional and went on to affirm a community's right "to enhance the quality of life by preserving the character and desirable aesthetic features of a city."

TAX INCENTIVES FOR PRESERVATION

In 1976, the federal government first put in place a system of tax incentives for the rehabilitation of historic buildings. After subsequent changes to these incentives in the 1980s, the Historic Rehabilitation Tax Credit fueled the biggest boom ever in preservation, encouraging and facilitating the rehabilitation of some of the most important historic buildings in dozens of communities across the country. Union Station in Washington, D.C., was rehabilitated under the provisions of this credit, as was the Willard Hotel on Pennsylvania Avenue, which had been closed for a decade. Hundreds of smaller "mom-and-pop" projects were also carried out because of this credit.

Unfortunately, the law has been changed so that the tax credit is no longer as attractive as it once was, but it is still on the books. In summary, the law says that the owner of a certified historic building (which, in this case, means a building that is listed in the National Register or located in a locally designated historic district that meets National Register criteria) who rehabilitates it according to the Secretary of the Interior's Standards for Rehabilitation is entitled to a tax credit—not a deduction, a *credit*—equal to 20 percent of the rehabilitation expenditures. In order to qualify, the property must be depreciable, income-producing property; owner-occupied residences do not qualify. Also, the rehabilitation must be "substantial," which means that rehab expenditures must total either $5,000 or the basis in the building, whichever is greater. The "basis in the building" is an amount reached by adding to the purchase price of the building the value of any improvements made and then subtracting the cost of the land on which the building stands and any depreciation already taken.

Changes to the law in the 1980s limit its applicability. Individuals with an adjusted gross income greater than $250,000 generally cannot use the credit, and in most cases, individuals with an adjusted gross income below $200,000 can utilize no more than $8,000 to $9,000 of the credit per year. This means, of course, that the credit is no longer so attractive as a tax shelter as it once was—but for small to medium-size projects such as the rehabilitation of a modest Main Street commercial building, the availability of a tax credit of this amount may still provide an attractive incentive to the property owner.

That, in a nutshell, is preservation, at least procedurally. The remainder of this book explains the organizations and processes in greater detail, and highlights the contacts—the people—and resources available to you to make preservation happen.

Section Two

Preservation Topics

Overview

Here is a preview of major topics and subject areas covered in this section.

Architectual Styles—identify the period design of your house or commercial building with this reference guide to architectual design trends, historical building periods, and major building types.

National Register of Historic Places—facts and sources for this National Park Service program, including details about how to nominate a property or district to the National Register.

Secretary of the Interior's Standards for Rehabilitation—to plan a rehabilitation or renovation project, these established regulatory *Standards* define areas of compliance to enable a preservation project to be eligible for tax credits or other incentives.

Historic Rehabilitation Tax Credit—through a series of worksheets, this section provides the formula to calculate a historic property's eligiblity for federal assistance.

Historic Preservation Law—an introduction to preservation law and public policy, with information on federally administered and government-related preservation programs, relevant court cases, and legislative acts governing heritage resources, historic land use, and state and local preservation.

Degree Programs in Historic Preservation—a complete list of professional and undergraduate and graduate academic programs in preservation and related fields of architectural design and planning.

Glossary—definitions for some of the most often used terms in preservation practice.

Resources and Readings—a bibliography of preservation topics and a list of subscription periodicals.

Chronology: Preservation in America—a timeline of influential events and turning points.

Detail of a building in the French Quarter, New Orleans, Louisiana.
(Carol M. Highsmith Photography)

Architectural Styles

Architectural styles help define a building's time and place. In the United States, building styles have been influenced by dominant cultural forces, influential architectural designers, and evolving aesthetic tastes. American building styles embody both grand ideas that have swept across the nation and small ideas that have grown within a region or locale; all styles reflect the skills and outlooks of their architects or builders. The geographical extent of the country's various architectural styles has depended on the spread of ideas through transportation routes, the media, and migration.

The architectural styles outlined in this chapter represent well-documented designs that have influenced American buildings. Each style is defined by its basic building form, framing system, roof line, materials, floor plan, other constructional methods, and ornamentation.

Many significant American buildings represent pure examples of particular architectural styles. But most American buildings either represent local or regional interpretations of national styles, illustrate hybrids of style, or cannot be categorized by any particular style. In many areas, architectural styles have grown out of local conditions, such as readily available building materials or climatic factors.

From the austerity of New England colonials, through the ornate extravagance of Second Empire, to the streamline shapes of Art Deco, every architectural style possesses its own special characteristics of structure and ornament. This survey of twenty influential styles of American architecture celebrates a rich cultural heritage, representing four centuries of creativity. The text is adapted from the book *What Style Is It? A Guide to American Architecture* (John Poppeliers. Preservation Press/John Wiley & Sons. 112 pages, paper. ISBN 0-471-14434-7.).

EARLY ENGLISH COLONIAL

1600s–1700

The term "late medieval" perhaps best describes 17th-century English colonial architecture in America. Residences were modeled after the ample but plain houses built in England in the late 1500s, in which medieval forms predominated: steeply pitched roofs, massive chimneys, and small windows with leaded casements. In New England, where

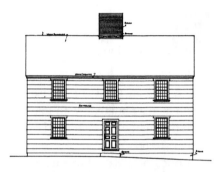

Old Ogden House, Fairfield, Connecticut. *(W. Schomburg, HABS)*

hardwoods were plentiful, the substantial half-timbered house was almost universal, with clapboard covering, low ceilings, and small rooms to conserve heat in winter. In the southern colonies, airier one-story brick houses were built throughout the 1600s. Settlers from other parts of the world—France, Holland, Germany, Scandinavia, and Africa—also brought their own building traditions to America.

New England Colonial

- medieval half-timbered construction with clapboard covering
- steeply pitched gable roof
- tall, massive, central chimney
- small leaded casement windows
- often a "saltbox" silhouette
- second-story overhangs

Southern Colonial

- brick or timber-frame construction
- steeply pitched gable roof
- massive chimneys at ends of houses
- narrow plan, often only one room deep
- patterned, bonded brickwork

SPANISH COLONIAL

1565–1850

From Florida to California and the Southwest, the Spanish left a lasting architectural tradition rivaled only by that of the English. In addition to grid street plans, the most important remaining examples of Spanish colonial architecture in the United States are the mission churches of the Southwest; these were frontier versions of the exuberant baroque style of 16th- and 17th-century Spain, especially as it had developed in Mexico. Missionary priests reproduced the baroque style with whatever materials and labor were at hand. The New Mexico missions, strongly influenced by the building techniques of the Pueblo Indians, are the most austere. Elsewhere, artisans trained in Europe and Mexico produced more elaborate structures.

The Spanish colonial style was revived beginning in the 1890s and into the early 20th century, particularly in California, Florida, and the Southwest.

- adobe or stone construction, often coated with lime wash or plaster
- massive, unadorned, windowless walls
- flat or red tile roof
- projecting roof timbers, sometimes supported by decorative brackets
- twin bell towers
- Spanish baroque ornament applied to bare walls
- curved gable

GEORGIAN

1700–1776

Named for the kings who ruled England for most of the 1700s, the Georgian style reflected Renaissance architectural forms made popular in England by the architect Sir Christopher Wren (1632–1723). Wren's work was based on Italian architecture of the 1500s, especially that of Andrea Palladio (1508–80), who freely adapted Roman classical forms. In America, Georgian buildings had a symmetrical, axial composition enriched with classical detail.

The Revolutionary War brought a halt to construction projects and effectively ended the Georgian style in America, although conservative builders continued to use it into the 1800s. The style was revived at the time of the 1876 Centennial, when architects were moved by patriotic zeal to look to the American past for models.

- symmetry in plan and exterior design
- symmetrical arrangement of building parts on an axis
- geometrical proportions

Dr. Upton Scott House, Annapolis, Maryland. *(J. Waite, HABS)*

- hipped roof
- main entrances emphasized with columns, pilasters, and broken pediment
- sash windows
- Palladian windows
- classical decorative details

FEDERAL

1780–1820

By 1776 a new style created in Britain by the Adam brothers had surpassed Georgian Palladianism in popularity. The Adamesque style combined Renaissance and Palladian forms, the delicacy of French rococo, and features from recently excavated houses and villas of ancient Rome. In America it was called the

Amory Tickner House, Boston, Massachusetts. *(J. Dudley, HABS)*

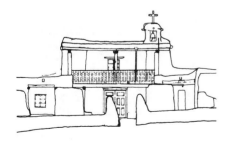

Mission Church, Santa Anna Pueblo, New Mexico. *(J. Schafer, K. Ahn, HABS)*

Federal style because it flowered in the early decades of the new nation.

The Federal style differs most strikingly from the Georgian in its interior design and use of pastel colors. Many rooms were oval, circular, or octagonal in shape. Mantels, cornices, doorways, and ceilings were decorated with delicate rosettes, urns, swags, and garlands. Federal-style buildings are found especially throughout the cities and towns of the eastern seaboard.

- low-pitched roof
- smooth facade
- large window panes
- exterior decoration confined to porch or entrance, such as fanlight over doorway
- delicate columns and molding
- louvered shutters
- circular, oval, or octagonal rooms
- interior wall decoration of garlands, swags, urns, and rosettes
- pastel colors

JEFFERSONIAN

1790–1830

In the 1780s the state of Virginia asked Thomas Jefferson to find an architect to design a new state capitol. Instead, Jefferson designed the

Pavilion II, University of Virginia, Charlottesville, Virginia. *(M.D. Sullivan, HABS)*

building himself. Inspired by the Maison Carrée, a Roman temple at Nîmes in southern France, he created the first pure temple form in American architecture. For Jefferson, the Roman orders symbolized Rome's republican form of government, which he saw being revived in the New World. Jefferson's architectural theories can be found in many red brick houses and courthouses in Virginia and places where Virginians settled.

- red brick construction
- raised first floor
- slender columns with smooth shafts
- pedimented portico
- classical moldings left plain and painted white
- lunette enclosed in pediment

GREEK REVIVAL

1820–1860

The Greek Revival style symbolized for many the idea that America, with its democratic ideals, was the spiritual successor of ancient Greece. By the mid-1840s the Grecian motifs were used throughout the country for churches, banks, courthouses, and other public buildings as well as for houses.

The most easily identified features are the columns and pedimented porch resembling a Greek temple. (Not every Greek Revival structure had these features, however.) Because ancient Greek buildings did not use arches, Greek Revival architects abandoned the arched entrances and fan windows so common in the Federal and Jeffersonian styles.

- pared-down simplicity
- columns (often fluted) and capitals

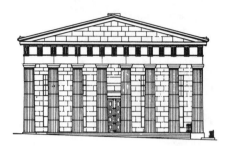

United States Sub-Treasury, New York, New York. *(T. Rachelle, HABS)*

- pedimented roof
- tall first-floor windows
- heavy cornice
- rectangular transom over entrance
- plain frieze

GOTHIC REVIVAL

1830–1890

The Gothic Revival was fostered by literature's Romantic movement of the late 1700s and early 1800s, which glorified the medieval past and was brought to America from England. By the 1830s a growing taste for the romantic—coupled with dissatisfaction with the restraints of classical architecture—turned the Gothic Revival into a popular movement.

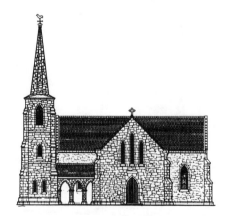

Christ Episcopal Church, Raleigh, North Carolina. *(G. Small, P. Wilday, E. Jenkins, HABS)*

It was an enduring style. The invention of the jigsaw made possible the fanciful wooden scrollwork known as Carpenter Gothic. After the Civil War, architects produced the eclectic High Victorian Gothic style, which drew on Italian and German as well as English Gothic models. In the late l9th century more authentic Gothic designs emerged in Collegiate Gothic, which left its stamp on many college campuses. Gothic Revival remained the most influential style for churches well into the 1900s.

- steep gabled roof
- pointed arches
- picturesque silhouette
- towers and battlements
- bay and oriel windows
- leaded stained glass
- crenellation
- "gingerbread" trim on eaves and gable ends

ITALIANATE

1830–1880

The architecture of Italy inspired this building style, which enjoyed immense popularity in the 1850s. Also known as the Tuscan, Lombard, round, bracketed, and even the American style, the Italianate could be as picturesque as Gothic

Public Square, Nashville, Tennessse.
(R. Dunay, HABS)

or as restrained as the classical. In the 1850s it was very nearly America's national style.

The development of cast-iron and pressed metal technology in the mid-1800s permitted the mass production of such decorative features as bracketed cornices and window moldings. These features were applied to a variety of commercial buildings and urban row houses. New York, St. Louis, and Portland, Oregon, had districts of cast-iron buildings in the Italianate style. Towns across America still boast stores with cast-iron fronts masquerading as Italian palaces.

- low-pitched or flat roof
- round arches
- heavily decorated, bracketed cornices and eaves
- scroll-shaped brackets
- tall first-floor windows
- hood moldings over windows
- cupola
- ample porches or verandas
- cast-iron facades on some commercial buildings

EXOTIC REVIVALS

1830–1930

Reflecting the period's romantic turn of mind, 19th-century architects explored exotic historic styles in search of appropriate forms. The Egyptian Revival was inspired by French archeological work in Egypt. This massive style, with its heavy sense of permanence, was considered appropriate for prisons, mausoleums, cemetery gates, churches, and monuments. In the 1920s the style was revived once more for movie theaters.

Near-Eastern architectural forms were adopted in the Moorish Revival style, chiefly for garden kiosks,

Oriental Greek Orthodox Church, Jacksonville, Florida. *(R. Moje, HABS)*

clubs, hotels, theaters, and a few ostentatious mansions. In the mid-1800s the style was also associated with the Jewish Reform movement in America and was used in the design of synagogues.

Egyptian Revival

- battered sloping walls
- battered window and door frames
- columns topped with palm or lotus capitals
- concave cornice
- winged-disk motif

Moorish Revival

- Moorish arches
- domes of various sizes and shapes
- minaret-like spire
- intricate surface decoration, including mosaics and tiles

SECOND EMPIRE

1860–1890

Picturesqueness, asymmetry, and eclecticism marked the architecture of the mid- to late l9th century. Architects borrowed freely from a variety of styles, placing great emphasis on character and a sense of permanence.

The Second Empire style takes its name from French designs built dur-

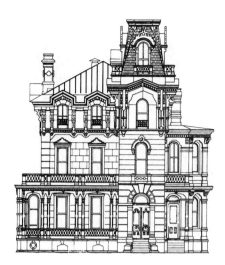

Goyer-Lee House, Memphis, Tennessee.
*(M. P. Frederickson, D. K. Pattison,
HABS)*

ing the reign of the emperor Napoleon III (1852–70). The hallmark of the Second Empire style is the mansard roof, adopted from the 17th-century French architect François Mansart (1598–1666). The style, which aspired to a monumental and ornate look, was used widely for public buildings and many houses.

- mansard roof
- prominent projecting and receding surfaces
- paired columns
- projecting central bay
- classical pediments and balustrades
- windows flanked by columns or pilasters
- arched windows with pediments and molded surrounds
- tall first-floor windows

STICK STYLE

1860–1890

The Stick Style evolved from the Carpenter Gothic to flourish in the mid- to late 1800s. Embodying the idea that architecture should be truthful, Stick Style houses expressed the

John Griswold House, Newport, Rhode Island. *(J. Chimura, HABS)*

building's inner structure through its exterior ornament. A series of boards was applied over the clapboard surface—most often on gable ends and upper stories—to symbolize the structural skeleton. Sometimes diagonal boards were incorporated to resemble Tudor-style half-timbering.

- wood construction
- vertical, horizontal, or diagonal boards applied over clapboard siding
- angularity, asymmetry, verticality
- roof composed of steep intersecting gables
- large veranda or porch
- simple corner posts, roof rafters, brackets, porch posts, and railings

QUEEN ANNE

1880–1900

Eclecticism is the keynote of the Queen Anne style. The name was coined in England to describe buildings that grafted classical ornament onto medieval forms. The style is varied and decoratively rich, with picturesque and asymmetrical silhouettes shaped by turrets, towers, gables, and bays. First floors were often brick or stone, while upper floors were of stucco, clapboard, or decorative shingles. The picturesque effects were best employed in sprawling, freestanding residences, but the Queen Anne style also had a major

John Houghton House, Austin, Texas.
(D. Yturralde, HABS)

impact on the urban row house. The typical projecting bay front topped by a gable or pinnacle roof is found in cities from Boston to San Francisco.

- rambling, asymmetrical silhouette
- corner towers or turrets
- steep gable or hipped roof with dormers
- huge "medieval" chimneys
- verandas and balconies
- contrasting materials and colors
- second-story overhangs
- gable ends decorated with half-timbering or stylized relief decoration
- molded bricks as decorative accents
- stained-glass window accents

SHINGLE STYLE

1880–1900

A completely American style that grew out of the Queen Anne, the Shingle Style was born in New England. It reflected the post-Centennial interest in American colonial architecture, especially the shingle architecture of coastal towns that were being rediscovered as fashionable resorts.

Isaac Bell House, Newport, Rhode Island. *(T. Schubert, HABS)*

Less ornate and more horizontal than the Queen Anne house, the Shingle Style house is a rambling two- or three-story structure entirely covered with unpainted wooden shingles. The first examples of the fully developed style appeared in the 1880s. Among the most important practitioners were H. H. Richardson, Bruce Price, and McKim, Mead and White. Some of Frank Lloyd Wright's earliest work was in the Shingle Style.

- unpainted wood shingles entirely covering the exterior
- prominent roofs, either steeply pitched or with long slopes
- rough-surfaced stone or field rubble used as contrasting materials
- turrets and verandas integrated into the overall design
- eaves close to walls
- reduced ornament

RICHARDSONIAN ROMANESQUE

1870–1900

Architects had experimented with the Romanesque Revival for public buildings in the 1840s and 1850s, borrowing round arches and other features from the pre-Gothic architecture of Europe. As interpreted by H. H. Richardson (1836–86), however, Romanesque became a different and uniquely American style.

First Presbyterian Church, Salisbury, North Carolina. *(G. Anastes, E. Mills, HABS)*

Richardsonian Romanesque was favored for churches, university buildings, train stations and courthouses. Although Richardson produced few houses in this style, elements of his work found their way into many residences of the period.

- massiveness
- stone construction with rock-faced finish
- broad round arches
- towers (often a single massive tower)
- broad roof planes
- eyebrow dormers
- deep-set windows; bands of windows
- cavernous door openings
- doors and windows defined by contrasting color or short, robust columns
- eaves close to walls
- little carved or applied ornament

BEAUX ARTS

1890–1920

Les beaux arts (the fine arts) refers to the aesthetic principles of the Ecole des Beaux-Arts in Paris. American architects who studied at the Ecole or who were trained by its graduates were influenced by the school's academic design principles, which emphasized the study of Greek and Roman structures, composition, and symmetry.

Beaux Arts architecture is characterized by large and grandiose symmetrical classical compositions with a wealth of exuberant detail and a variety of stone finishes. American Beaux Arts designs generally were for colossal public buildings. About 1900, however, such designs gave way to more sedate forms, which were used for the town houses and country and resort villas of the wealthy.

- grandiose composition
- imposing stairway
- large arched openings
- variety of stone finishes
- projecting facades or pavilions
- monumental columns
- classical ornament
- enriched entablature topped with a tall parapet, balustrade, or attic story
- pronounced cornice
- decorative swags, medallions, cartouches, and sculpture

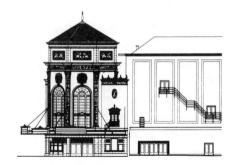

Grand Riviera Theatre, Detroit, Michigan. *(C. Morrison, HABS)*

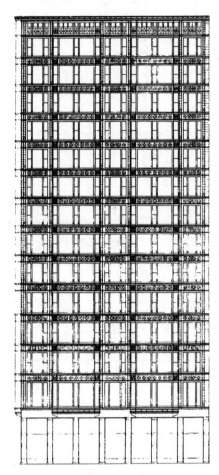

Reliance Building, Chicago, Illinois, in the Chicago Style. *(P. Borchers, N. Clouten, HABS)*

CHICAGO STYLE

1875–1910

In the late 1800s Chicago-based architects and engineers exploited new construction technologies to produce the tall commercial buildings that would transform cities around the world. Until then, building height had been limited by the ability of masonry walls to support upper stories. By using a cast-iron or wrought-iron skeleton frame—coupled with improvements in fireproofing, wind bracing, and foundation technology, and the invention of the elevator—Chicago architects began to create commercial buildings of six to twenty stories.

The best-known architect of this school was Louis Sullivan (1856–1924). His buildings are easily identified by their distinctive low-relief decoration of intricately interwoven leaf designs around the entranceway, cornice, and windows.

- tall rectangular buildings of six to twenty stories
- three-part construction: one- or two-story base with large display windows; shaft housing
- identical floors of offices; elaborate cornice
- gridlike exterior mimicking the steel skeleton
- large areas of glass, terra cotta, or other nonsupporting material
- vertical piers between windows, emphasizing height
- stripped, no-nonsense exterior

PRAIRIE STYLE

1900–1920

About 1900, another group of Chicago architects developed a distinctive midwestern residential style, known as the Prairie Style. Their acknowledged leader was Frank Lloyd Wright (1867–1959). Rejecting the currently popular revivals of historic styles, they sought to create buildings that harmonized with the midwestern prairie. The Prairie Style house had a strongly horizontal appearance, emphasized by porches, walls, and terraces extending from the main structure. Windows were arranged in horizontal ribbons and often featured stained glass in stylized floral or geometric patterns.

Interiors were as innovative as exteriors; Prairie School architects often designed furnishings for their houses. The style had its greatest influence in the Chicago area, but examples can be found as far afield as Rochester, New York, the West Coast, and Puerto Rico.

- low, horizontal silhouette
- wide overhanging eaves
- porches, walls, and terraces extending from the main house to emphasize horizontal lines
- broad, low-pitched roof
- large, low, plain rectangular chimney
- walls of light-colored brick or stucco and wood
- horizontal ribbons of casement windows; stained-glass accents in stylistic floral or geometric designs
- walls at right angles; no curves

CLASSICAL REVIVAL

1900–1920

The later, more refined stage of the Beaux Arts style influenced the last, or 20th-century, phase of the Classical Revival in the United States. In the late 1800s and early 1900s com-

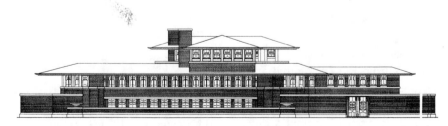

Frederick C. Robie House, Chicago, Illinois, in the Prairie style. *(J. J. Erins, HABS)*

Bank of San Mateo, Redwood City, California. *(A. Weinstein, HABS)*

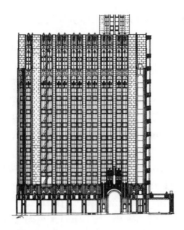

Richfield Oil Building, Los Angeles, California. *(R. Giebner, HABS)*

Design for a modern house. (The Modern House, *New York, 1933; adapted and delineated by S. Bauer)*

missions for public buildings and grand houses generally went to architects trained in the Beaux Arts tradition, who produced designs based on classical and Renaissance models.

Less theatrical than Beaux Arts, the Classical Revival style is based more on Greek than Roman architectural orders. Consequently, the arch is not often used, and highly decorated moldings are rare. The style was used primarily to create massive public buildings on a grand scale.

- monumental size
- symmetry
- giant columns
- Greek and some Roman classical forms
- smooth or polished stone surface
- unadorned entablature and roof line

ART DECO

1925–1940

Art Deco took its name from the Exposition Internationale des Arts Decoratifs et Industriels Modernes, held in Paris in 1925 as a showcase for works of "new inspiration and real originality." Art Deco and its deriva-

tion, Art Moderne (also called Streamline Moderne or Modernistic) were the first popular styles in the United States to break with the tradition of reviving historical styles.

Art Deco consciously strove for modernity, an artistic expression of the machine age, and the suggestion of motion. Its forms were simplified and streamlined. Essentially, Art Deco was a style of decoration and was applied to jewelry, clothing, furniture, and handicrafts as well as buildings. At its best, Art Deco architecture was a harmonious collaboration of architects, painters, sculptors, and designers.

Art Deco

- surfaces of concrete, stucco, or smooth-faced stone
- vertical emphasis
- facades often arranged in a stepped series of setbacks
- hard-edged, low-relief geometrical designs and stylized figures or floral motifs; multicolored, often vivid, designs
- accents in terra cotta, glass, and colored mirror

Art Moderne

- surfaces of concrete, stucco, or metal
- horizontal emphasis
- facades asymmetrically composed
- accents in terra cotta, glass block
- curved corners and other details suggesting motion

INTERNATIONAL STYLE

1920–1945

The hallmarks of the International Style are stark simplicity, vigorous functionalism, and flexible planning, all based on modern structural principles and materials. Whereas Chicago School architects merely revealed skeleton-frame construction, International Style architects reveled in it.

Ribbons of windows became an important design feature, creating a horizontal feeling even in high-rise buildings. Artificial symmetry was studiously avoided, but balance and regularity were fostered. Mundane building components such as elevator shafts and air-conditioning machinery became highly visible aspects of design. Many of the most famous architects working in 20th-century America—such as Walter Gropius, Ludwig Mies van der Rohe, Richard Neutra, and Marcel Breuer—designed in the International Style.

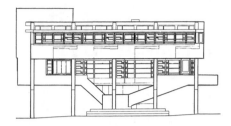

Lovell Beach House, Newport Beach, California. *(R.H. Nagata, S.A. Westfall, HABS)*

- concrete, glass, and steel construction
- complete absence of ornamentation
- asymmetrical but balanced composition
- horizontal emphasis
- flat roof
- smooth and uniform wall surface
- mundane building components incorporated into the visual design
- horizontal bands of windows
- corner windows
- windows set flush to the wall

VERNACULAR ARCHITECTURE

As preservationists across the country expand architectural and historical surveys of buildings to small communities and rural areas, new architectural terminology has evolved to depict local building practices that do not conform to well-known styles. In such instances, buildings may be classified as "vernacular." Vernacular architecture has been described as common, ordinary buildings or landscapes fashioned by anonymous people for functional purposes. While vernacular architecture may

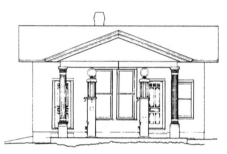

Rockfish Service Station, Augusta County, Virginia. *(D. Donovan, HABS)*

incorporate one or more styles, it is not a style in itself. Rather, it is a classification or a way of studying a building, a group of buildings, or a landscape. Vernacular buildings result from (1) commonly agreed upon forms and elements that are passed among generations; (2) practices learned from the Old World; (3) community or group tastes rather than those of an individual designer or architect; or (4) use of locally available building materials. To analyze vernacular architecture one must study social history, folklore, cultural geography, and anthropology to provide insight into the ethnic roots and lifeways of the designers and occupants of these buildings. Early vernacular studies focused on the analysis of farmhouses and related buildings. More recently, vernacular studies have expanded to include rural schoolhouses, tract houses, urban dwellings, field patterns, town plans, factories, and commercial strips.

National Register of Historic Places

National Register of Historic Places
National Register, History and Education
National Park Service
U.S. Department of the Interior
P.O. Box 37127
Washington, DC 20013-7127
(202) 343-9500 (general)
(202) 343-8012 (for publications and information)

The National Register of Historic Places is the official list of the nation's historic and cultural resources worthy of preservation. The National Register was authorized by the National Historic Preservation Act of 1966 and is part of the national effort to identify, evaluate, and protect our historic and archeological resources. The program is administered by the National Park Service (see separate listing) under the secretary of the interior. Properties listed in the National Register include buildings, structures, sites, districts, and objects significant in American history, architecture, archeology, engineering, and culture.

NATIONAL REGISTER NOMINATION PROCESS

1. Nominations may be prepared by property owners, interested citizens, preservation organizations, or state historic preservation officers (SHPOs). Federal agencies submit nominations for their properties through their agency preservation officers. Eligible properties include districts, sites, buildings, structures, and objects of local, state, and national significance. Nominations may also be made for multiple historic resources, a flexible and efficient means of registering a number of significant properties linked by a common historical context or property type.

2. Standard National Register forms, including computer templates, are available from the SHPO or the National Park Service. Standard forms must be used and submitted to the SHPO, which reviews the nomination against the National Register evaluation criteria. Certified local governments may also review nominations prior to submission to the SHPO.

3. The SHPO notifies property owners and local officials thirty to seventy-five days in advance that the state will present a nomination to a state review board. If a property meets the evaluation criteria, the board recommends it for nomination. The nomination form is signed by the SHPO and forwarded to the National Register office in Washington, D.C. The SHPO may also send the nomination for further consideration even if it has been rejected by the board.

4. Private property owners, including owners in a historic district, have the opportunity to concur with or object to National Register nominations. If the owner of an individual property or the majority of owners in a historic district object to listing by means of notarized letters, the property will not be listed but may be determined eligible for listing. Properties eligible for the National Register receive the same review by the Advisory Council on Historic Preservation as accorded to listed properties.

5. The staff of the National Register reviews nominations submitted by the SHPO. Provided the documentation is adequate and all procedures have been followed in accordance with federal regulations, a decision must be made on the eligibility of the property within forty-five days of receipt. If found acceptable, the nomination form is signed and a notice is sent to members of Congress and the SHPO.

NATIONAL REGISTER EVALUATION CRITERIA

The quality of significance in American history, architecture, archeology,

Saint Charles Avenue mansions, New Orleans, Louisiana. *(Carol M. Highsmith Photography)*

and culture is present in districts, sites, buildings, structures, and objects that possess integrity of location, design, setting, materials, workmanship, feeling, and association, and:

1. That are associated with events that have made a significant contribution to the broad pattern of our history; or
2. That are associated with the lives of persons significant in our past; or
3. That embody the distinctive characteristics of a type, period, or method of construction, or that represent the work of a master, or that possess high artistic values, or that represent a significant and distinguishable entity whose components may lack individual distinction; or
4. That have yielded, or may be likely to yield, information important in prehistory or history.

Ordinarily, cemeteries, birthplaces, or graves of historical figures, properties owned by religious institutions or used for religious purposes, structures that have been moved from their original locations, reconstructed historic buildings, properties primarily commemorative in nature, and properties that have achieved significance within the last fifty years shall not be considered eligible for the National Register. However, such properties will qualify if they are integral parts of a district that do meet the criteria or if they fall within the following categories:

1. A religious property deriving primary significance from architectural or artistic distinction or historical importance; or
2. A building or structure removed from its original location but which is significant primarily for architectural value, or which is

the surviving structure most importantly associated with a historic person or event; or

3. A birthplace or grave of a historical figure of outstanding importance if there is no other appropriate site or building directly associated with his or her productive life; or
4. A cemetery that derives its primary significance from graves of persons of transcedent importance, from age, from distinctive design features, or from association with historic events; or
5. A reconstructed building when accurately executed in a suitable environment and presented in a dignified manner as part of a restoration master plan, and when no other building or structure with the same association has survived; or
6. A property primarily commemorative in intent if design, age, tradition, or symbolic value has invested it with its own historical significance; or
7. A property achieving significance within the past fifty years if it is of exceptional importance.

All historic areas in the National Park System are automatically listed in the National Register. Three nationally significant properties were exempted under the 1966 act: the White House, the U.S. Supreme Court, and the U.S. Capitol.

BENEFITS OF NATIONAL REGISTER LISTING

1. Recognition that a property is of significance to the nation, state, or community.
2. Consideration in the planning for federally assisted projects, including review by the Advisory

Council on Historic Preservation under Section 106 of the National Historic Preservation Act of 1966.

3. Eligibility for certain federal tax benefits, such as the investment tax credit for rehabilitation of income-producing buildings and the charitable deductions for donation of easements.

4. Qualification for federal preservation grants when funding is available.

5. Consideration in the issuance of surface coal mining permits.

NATIONAL HISTORIC LANDMARKS

Certain National Register properties are designated as National Historic Landmarks by the Secretary of the Interior. They represent the nation's most important historic and cultural resources. National Historic Landmarks include buildings, sites, structures, and objects that possess exceptional value or quality in American history, architecture, archeology, engineering, and culture.

FURTHER READING

How to Complete the National Register Registration Form. National Register Bulletin 16A.

How to Complete the National Register Multiple Property Documentation Form. National Register Bulletin 16B.

How to Apply the Register Criteria for Evaluation. National Register Bulletin 15.

Researching a Historic Property. National Register Bulletin 39.

You may obtain these and other National Register bulletins by mail, by writing to:

National Register of Historic Places
National Register, History and Education
National Park Service
U.S. Department of the Interior
P.O. Box 37127, Mail Stop 2280
Washington, DC 20013-7127

To order National Register bulletins by e-mail, send a message to the following address:

nr_reference@nps.gov

Bulletins 16A, 15, and 39 can be downloaded from the World Wide Web at the following site:

www.cr.nps.gov/nr/nrpubs.html

The following are available from Preservation Press of John Wiley & Sons, Inc., 605 Third Avenue, New York, NY 10158-0012 (or call 1-800-225-5945):

The National Register of Historic Places 1966 to 1994, a cumulative list of buildings, districts, sites, structures, and objects listed on the National Register of Historic Places. ISBN 0-471-14403-7.

African-American Historic Places, containing brief descriptions of more than 800 National Register properties in forty-two states and two U.S. territories that are significant in African-American history. Also included are eight essays on the African-American experience. ISBN 0-471-14345-6.

Secretary of the Interior's Standards for Rehabilitation

The Secretary of the Interior is responsible for establishing standards for all programs under departmental authority and for advising federal agencies on the preservation of historic properties listed or eligible for listing in the National Register of Historic Places. In partial fulfillment of this responsibility, the Secretary of the Interior's Standards for Historic Projects have been developed to guide work undertaken on historic buildings—there are separate standards for acquisition, protection, stabilization, preservation, rehabilitation, restoration, and reconstruction.

The *Standards for Rehabilitation*, originally published in 1977 and revised in 1990, appear in Title 36 of the Code of Federal Regulations, Part 68, which governs alterations to buildings listed in the National Register of Historic Places. "Rehabilitation" is defined as "the process of returning a property to a state of utility, through repair or alteration, which makes possible an efficient contemporary use while preserving those portions and features of the property which are significant to its historic, architectural, and cultural values."

Initially developed by the Secretary of the Interior to determine the appropriateness of proposed project work on registered properties within the Historic Preservation Fund grant-in-aid program, the *Standards for Rehabilitation* have been widely used over the years—particularly to determine if a rehabilitation qualifies as a Certified Rehabilitation for federal tax purposes. In addition, the Standards have guided federal agencies in carrying out their historic preservation responsibilities for properties in federal ownership or control; and state and local officials in reviewing both federal and nonfederal rehabilitation proposals. They have also been adopted by historic district and planning commissions across the country.

The intent of the Standards is to assist the long-term preservation of a property's significance through the preservation of historic materials and features. The Standards pertain to historic buildings of all materials, construction types, sizes, and occupancy and encompass the exterior and interior of the construction. To be certified for federal tax purposes, a rehabilitation project must be determined by the Secretary to be consistent with the historic character of the structure(s) and, where applicable, the district in which it is located. In addition to the Standards, the Department of the Interior also issues "Guidelines for Rehabilitating Historic Buildings," which contains recommended (and not recommended) treatments commonly used in restoration and rehabilitation projects.

THE SECRETARY OF THE INTERIOR'S STANDARDS FOR REHABILITATION

The following Standards are to be applied to specific rehabilitation projects in a reasonable manner, taking into consideration economic and technical feasibility.

1. A property shall be used for its historic purpose or be placed in a new use that requires minimal change to the defining characteristics of the building and its site and environment.

2. The historic character of a property shall be retained and preserved. The removal of historic materials or alteration of features and spaces that characterize a property shall be avoided.

3. Each property shall be recognized as a physical record of its time,

place, and use. Changes that create a false sense of historical development, such as adding conjectural features or architectural elements from other buildings, shall not be undertaken.

4. Most properties change over time; those changes that have acquired historic significance in their own right shall be retained and preserved.

5. Distinctive features, finishes, and construction techniques or examples of craftsmanship that characterize a historic property shall be preserved.

6. Deteriorated historic features shall be repaired rather than replaced. Where the severity of deterioration requires replacement of a distinctive feature, the new feature shall match the old in design, color, texture, and other visual qualities and, where possible, materials. Replacement of missing features shall be substantiated by documentary, physical, or pictorial evidence.

7. Chemical or physical treatments, such as sandblasting, that cause damage to historic materials shall not be used. The surface cleaning of structures, if appropriate, shall be undertaken using the gentlest means possible.

8. Significant archeological resources affected by a project shall be protected and preserved. If such resources must be disturbed, mitigation measures shall be undertaken.

9. New additions, exterior alterations, or related new construction shall not destroy historic materials that characterize the property. The

Delaware Block building, now a hotel in Leadville, Colorado. *(Carol M. Highsmith Photography)*

new work shall be differentiated from the old and shall be compatible with the massing, size, scale, and architectural features to protect the historic integrity of the property and its environment.

10. New additions and adjacent or related new construction shall be undertaken in such a manner that if removed in the future, the essential form and integrity of the historic property and its environment would be unimpaired.

As stated in the definition, the treatment "rehabilitation" assumes that at least some repair or alteration of the historic building will be needed in order to provide for an efficient contemporary use; however, these repairs and alterations must not damage or destroy materials, features or finishes that are important in

defining the building's historic character. For example, certain treatments—if improperly applied—may cause or accelerate physical deterioration of historic buildings. This can include using improper repointing or exterior masonry cleaning techniques, or introducing insulation that damages historic fabric. In almost all of these situations, use of these materials and treatments will result in a project that does not meet the Standards. Similarly, exterior additions that duplicate the form, material, and detailing of the structure to the extent that they compromise the historic character of the structure will fail to meet the Standards.

FURTHER READING

The National Park Service, U.S. Department of the Interior, conducts a variety of activities to guide federal agencies, states, and the general public in historic preservation project work. In addition to establishing standards and guidelines, the Service develops, publishes, and distributes technical information on appropriate preservation treatments, including Preservation Briefs, case studies, and Preservation Tech Notes.

A catalog of historic preservation publications with stock numbers, prices, and ordering information may be obtained by writing: Preservation Assistance Division, Technical Preservation Services, P.O. Box 37127, Washington, DC 20013-7127.

Historic Rehabilitation Tax Credit

This explanation of the historic rehabilitation tax credit was reproduced from A Guide to Tax-Advantaged Rehabilitation *published in 1986 and revised in 1994 by the National Trust for Historic Preservation. This self-help text was prepared by Donovan D. Rypkema. To order the complete* Guide, *contact: Information Series, National Trust for Historic Preservation, 1785 Massachusetts Avenue, N.W., Washington, DC 20036; phone (202) 588-6286. The current cost per booklet is $6 with a 50 percent discount for orders of 10 or more booklets.*

Rehabilitation of a historic structure can provide the investor with a sizable tax credit. A tax credit is a dollar-for-dollar reduction of income tax liability. Qualifying investors in historic rehabilitation projects are eligible for a tax credit equal to 20 percent of the rehabilitation expenditures.

For a project to qualify for the historic tax credit, certain criteria must be met:

1. The building must be a "certified historic structure." A certified historic structure is one that is: (a) individually listed in the National Register of Historic Places; or (b) is a contributing building in a historic district listed in the National Register of Historic Places; or (c) is a contributing building in a designated local historic district that has been certified as substantially meeting the criteria for listing in the National Register.
2. The project must constitute a "substantial rehabilitation." Substantial rehabilitation is the greater of $5,000 or the basis in the building.
3. The building must be a depreciable property held for use in trade or business or as an investment property. One's own personal residence does not qualify.
4. The project must be certified by the National Park Service as having been rehabilitated according to the *Secretary of the Interior's Standards for Rehabilitation.*

The passive activity loss limitations restrict the amount of the tax credit an individual taxpayer can use in any given year. If adjusted gross income is less than $200,000, the taxpayer may use the tax credit to offset taxes due on active income (wages, salaries, business income). The amount that may be used is calculated by multiplying the taxpayer's marginal tax rate by $25,000. Thus an individual in the 36 percent tax bracket could use $9,000 of the credit each year under this exception ($25,000 × .36). Additionally, the credit can be used to offset any tax liability generated from passive investments (i.e., real estate).

For individuals with an adjusted gross income greater than $250,000, this exception to passive loss rules does not apply. For those with incomes between $200,000 and $250,000, the exception amount is phased out. Corporate taxpayers ordinarily are not subject to passive activity loss limitations. Any tax credits not used in the first year can be carried forward until the entire benefit has been received.

The historic rehabilitation tax credit program is administered by the National Park Service in the Department of the Interior. For more information or to obtain the necessary certification forms, contact your state historic preservation office. To find the office that serves your state, refer to the listing for your state in Section Four of this book or contact the National Conference of State Historic Preservation Officers at (202) 624-5465.

Can I Use the 20% Historic Rehabilitation Tax Credit?

1. Am I a corporation?

   ___ Yes ___ No

   If "yes," passive activity loss limitations probably do not apply.

   Go to Question 5 and omit Question 14. Other tax provisions may apply, however, so consult your tax or accounting advisor. If "no," go to Question 2.

2. Am I an individual taxpayer with an adjusted gross income greater than $250,000?

   ___ Yes ___ No

   If "yes," your use of the tax credit will be severely limited. Go to Question 5. If "no," go to Question 3.

3. Am I an individual taxpayer with an adjusted gross income between $200,000 and $250,000?

   ___ Yes ___ No

   If "yes," you may be eligible for part of the credit. See your tax or accounting advisor. Go to Question 5. If "no," go to Question 4.

4. Am I an individual taxpayer with an adjusted gross income less than $200,000?

   ___ Yes ___ No

   If "yes," you probably can use the credit. Continue to the next question.

5. Is the building listed in the National Register of Historic Places?

   ___ Yes ___ No

   ___ I don't know

   If "yes," the building should qualify for the credit. Go to Question 8. If "no," go to Question 6. If "I don't know," contact the state historic preservation office.

6. Is the building a contributing structure in a National Register historic district or a qualifying local historic district?

   ___ Yes ___ No

   ___ I don't know

   If "yes," the building should qualify for the credit. Go to Question 8. If "no," go to Question 7. If "I don't know," contact the state historic preservation office.

7. If not yet a certified historic structure, is the property eligible to be so designated?

   ___ Yes ___ No

   ___ I don't know

   If "yes," the building may qualify for the credit. Go to the next question. If "no," the building will not qualify for the credit. If "I don't know," contact the state historic preservation office.

8. What is the adjusted basis of the building?

Purchase price	$_____
Less: amount attributable to land	– $_____
Plus: capital improvements	+ $_____
Less: depreciation taken	– $_____
Adjusted basis of the building	= $_____

   A quick look at your most recent tax return or a call to your accountant may provide this information as well.

9. What is the proposed budget for the project, including construction, architect, developer, and consultant fees; but excluding acquisition, landscaping, and site improvements?

   $ _____

10. Does the amount in Question 9 exceed the adjusted basis of the building (Question 8)?

    ___ Yes ___ No

    If "yes," the substantial rehabilitation test has been met.

    If "no," the substantial rehabilitation test has not been met and the project must be revised in order to qualify for the credit.

11. Is the property your personal residence?

    ___ Yes ___ No

    If "yes," the property is not eligible for the credit.

    If "no," go to the next question.

12. Is the property going to be used in your trade or business or held for investment?

    ___ Yes ___ No

    If "yes," the property should be eligible for the credit.

    If "no," the property probably is not eligible. See your accountant or tax advisor.

13. How much tax credit will I receive?

Rehabilitation budget (Question 9)	$ _____
× 20 percent	× .20
Amount of tax credit	= $_____

14. How much of the tax credit can I take each year?

    Marginal tax rate
    (see your accountant)   ____ %
    × $25,000   × $25,000
    ————————————————————————————————

    Amount usable under
    passive loss exception $_____
    Plus: amount of tax
          liability on
          "passive
          income" (see
          accountant)   + $_____
       Total credit
       available each year = $_____

15. What will be the depreciable basis of the rehabilitated property?

    Pre-rehabilitation
    basis of the building $ _____
    Plus: rehabilitation
          expenditure   + $ _____
    Less: tax credit
          allowed   − $ _____
       Depreciable basis
       of the building   = $ _____

16. What will my depreciation be?

    Depreciable basis
    (Question 15) $ _____
    Depreciable life (39
    years or 27.5 years)   ÷ $ _____
       Annual
       depreciation   = $ _____

SAMPLE PROJECT

Acquisition price	$100,000
Land portion	+ $ 20,000
Building portion	+ $ 80,000
Rehabilitation expenditures	$200,000

(greater than $80,000, therefore meets the substantial rehabilitation test)

Amount of tax credit	$40,000 ($200,000 × 20%)
Investor's marginal tax rate	36%
Annual credit allowable	$9,000 ($25,000 × 36%)

(this falls within the passive loss exception)

Depreciable Basis Calculation

Acquisition cost of building	$ 80,000
Plus: rehabilitation	+ $200,000
Less: tax credit	− $ 40,000
Depreciable basis	$240,000
Depreciable life	÷ 39

(39 years under current law)

Annual depreciation	$ 6,154

Loan amount	$200,000 (8%, 25 years)
Annual payments	$ 18,524

FIVE-YEAR OPERATING STATEMENT

	Year				
	1	*2*	*3*	*4*	*5*
Net Operating Income[a]	$27,500	$28,325	$29,175	$30,049	$30,951
Depreciation	$ 6,154	$ 6,154	$ 6,154	$ 6,154	$ 6,154
Interest	$15,906	$15,686	$15,452	$15,198	$14,916
Taxable Income[b]	$ 5,440	$ 6,485	$ 7,569	$ 8,697	$ 9,881
Tax Rate	36%	36%	36%	36%	36%
Taxes[c]	$ 1,958	$ 2,335	$ 2,725	$ 3,131	$ 3,557
Usable Credit[d]	$ 9,000	$ 9,000	$ 9,000	$ 5,982	$ 0
Usable Credit[e]	$ 1,958	$ 2,335	$ 2,725	$ 0	$ 0
Accumulated Credit Used	$10,958	$22,293	$34,018	$40,000	$40,000

FIVE-YEAR CASH FLOW STATEMENT

	Year				
	1	*2*	*3*	*4*	*5*
Net Operating Income[a]	$27,500	$28,325	$29,175	$30,049	$30,951
Debt Service[f]	$18,524	$18,524	$18,524	$18,524	$18,524
Before-Tax Cash Flow[g]	$ 8,976	$ 9,801	$10,651	$11,525	$12,427
Taxes	$ 1,958	$ 2,335	$ 2,725	$ 3,131	$ 3,557
After-Tax Cash Flow[b]	$ 7,018	$ 7,466	$ 7,926	$ 8,394	$ 8,870
Usable Tax Credit[e]	$10,958	$11,335	$11,725	$ 5,982	$ 0
After Credit Cash Flow[i]	$17,976	$18,801	$19,651	$14,376	$ 8,870

[a]Income increasing at 3% per year.

[b]Net operating income less depreciation and interest.

[c]Taxable income times tax rate.

[d]This is the amount of credit the owner is entitled to under the passive loss exception provision.

[e]This is the amount of the credit usable to offset passive gains.

[f]Principal and interest payment.

[g]Net operating income less debt service.

[b]Before-tax cash flow less taxes.

[i]After-tax cash flow plus useable tax credit.

Introduction to Historic Preservation Law

This chapter is a summary of the various legal approaches to preservation—the web of federal, state, and local laws that help to protect America's heritage. It is intended to serve as a refresher for those well-versed in preservation law, and as a basic overview for the uninitiated, who may benefit by a simple, yet comprehensive, look at preservation laws.

Historic preservation may be accomplished in several ways, including direct acquisition of historic properties by organizations and governmental entities; land use and preservation regulation (or procedural protections) at the federal, state, and local levels; and private investment in historic resources spurred by tax incentive programs. No single approach works in every situation, and in many cases it may be necessary to draw from, and rely on, a blend of private and regulatory solutions to accomplish preservation goals.

PRIVATE AND PUBLIC OWNERSHIP

For many years historic resources within the United States have been protected through voluntary efforts accomplished primarily by acquisition. Often limited to places associated with important people or significant historic events, these resources are purchased by governmental entities or nonprofit organizations and generally operated as house museums. While this approach to preservation has merit, the purchase and restoration of historic properties on an ad hoc basis often proves to be a prohibitively costly solution and is justifiable only in situations where funding is available and no other alternative exists. Thus, over time, historic preservation techniques have become far more sophisticated, relying on a complex array of regulatory and incentive programs. Through relatively small amounts of public investment, large numbers of historically significant resources can realize lasting protection.

PROPERTY IDENTIFICATION AND LISTING

The first step in developing preservation programs, under either a regulatory or incentive approach, is to identify what properties are considered to be "historic or cultural resources." In most cases, this is accomplished through an official process of identification that lists buildings, structures, districts, objects, and sites as resources based on specific criteria.

Historic or cultural resources may be listed in any of three types of registers: the National Register of Historic Places; a state register of historic places; or a local listing of historic landmarks and districts. To be eligible for listing, properties must meet certain statutory criteria generally based on historical, architectural, archaeological, or cultural significance. Properties tend to be listed on historic registers only after they have been researched, photographed, and evaluated by a preservation professional (such as an architectural historian or archaeologist).

NATIONAL REGISTER OF HISTORIC PLACES

Established under the Historic Sites Act of 1935 (16 U.S.C. §§ 461 et. seq.) and expanded by the National Historic Preservation Act of 1966, as amended (16 U.S.C. §§ 470a et. seq.), the National Register is the official list of historic and cultural resources at the national level and serves as a primary resource for significant historical, architectural, and archaeological resources today. The Register includes districts, sites, buildings, structures, and other objects that are significant in American history, architecture, archaeology, engineering, and culture.

Designed primarily as a planning tool for federal agencies, the National Register's principal purpose is to identify the historical and cultural resources of our nation. While listing on the National Register does not regulate the private use of land, the National Register plays a central role in the federal protection scheme (which is largely procedural), enables property owners to qualify for federal tax benefits, and often helps to trigger protection at the state and local level as well.

The National Register of Historic Places is maintained by the secretary of the interior through the National Park Service. The Keeper of the National Register within the Park Service is responsible for actually listing and determining eligibility for listing in the National Register. A cumulative listing of the National Register of Historic Places is published every several years. The National Park Service also publishes an annual compilation of newly listed National Register properties in the Federal Register.

STATE REGISTERS

Several states maintain a state register of historic places that may be more or less inclusive than the National Register of Historic Places. In many cases, the composition of a state register has more to do with a particular state's commitment toward historic preservation than with differences in criteria for nomination. As with the National Register, listing on a state register is primarily honorific. However, in some cases, it may trigger regulatory or procedural

Statues at the Museum of Science and Industry, Chicago, Illinois. *(Carol M. Highsmith Photography)*

protections or govern whether a property owner may qualify for favorable tax treatment.

LOCALLY DESIGNATED LANDMARKS AND HISTORIC DISTRICTS

Properties may also be designated as individual landmarks or as contributing structures within a historic district pursuant to a local historic preservation ordinance. Unlike listing on the National Register, designation under local ordinances generally serves as a means of identifying properties subject to regulations governing the issuance of permits for demolitions, alterations, removals, or new construction. In some cases, properties designated under local ordinances may be eligible for significant tax benefits, including federal tax benefits, if the local government program has been "certified" by the federal

government. (See I.R.C. § 48(g)(3)(A) and 36 C.F.R. Part 67.)

REGULATION AND PROCEDURAL PROTECTIONS

The identification and listing (or designation) of properties is central to all regulatory schemes governing historic properties. Owners of properties identified as historic or cultural resources may be prevented from taking actions that would adversely affect those properties until they receive approval from a preservation review board or other administrative body. However, the degree and nature of the restrictions imposed on such properties vary widely. In some cases, historic preservation controls are essentially "advisory," while in other cases such controls afford historic resources meaningful protection.

FEDERAL PRESERVATION LAWS

The National Historic Preservation Act of 1966, amended in 1980, and again in 1992 (NHPA), established a national preservation program and a system of procedural protections, which together encourage both the identification and protection of historic and cultural resources at the federal, state, and local levels through the use of a federal–state–local partnership. In addition to providing for the systematic identification of historic resources through the National Register of Historic Places, the NHPA also encourages their protection by requiring federal agencies to consider the potential impact proposed actions may have on such resources.

The key statutory tool for protecting historic and cultural resources under the NHPA is the Section 106 review process. **Section 106 of the NHPA,** codified at 16 U.S.C. § 470f, directs federal agencies to consider the effects of their activities on properties that are listed or are eligible for listing in the National Register. No federal agency may proceed with a proposed activity adversely affecting any such properties until the agency has taken into account the effects of its actions, consulted with the State Historic Preservation Officer (SHPO) and other interested parties to identify measures that would mitigate any harm, and afforded the Advisory Council on Historic Preservation an opportunity to comment on the undertaking. (See 36 C.F.R. Part 800.) In the vast majority of cases, the Section 106 review process culminates in the execution of a Memorandum of Agreement, a legally binding document, that identifies specific measures an agency will undertake to

mitigate or avoid harm to historic or cultural resources.

Other major tools for protecting historic and cultural resources at the national level include the **National Environmental Policy Act (NEPA)** and **Section 4(f) of the Department of Transportation Act** (42 U.S.C. §§ 4321–4347; 49 U.S.C. § 303). NEPA is broader in scope than the NHPA in that it protects all aspects of the environment—not just historic properties. It requires that federal agencies consider the harmful impact of "major federal actions" on the environment. Section 4(f) governs actions undertaken by the Department of Transportation that affect historic and cultural properties, as well as parklands, recreational areas, and wildlife and waterfowl refuges. The secretary may not proceed with a project unless "there is no feasible and prudent alternative" and then only if the project "includes all possible planning to minimize harm to such . . . historic site resulting from such use."

Together the NHPA, NEPA, and Section 4(f) are helpful in compelling federal agencies to identify and consider the impact of their actions on historic or cultural resources. They provide a useful and sometimes critical mechanism for developing workable solutions that accomplish both agency and preservation objectives. Nonetheless, it is important to recognize that these laws are simply procedural safeguards that do not guarantee that historic resources will be protected. The NHPA and NEPA require federal agencies to consider the impact of their actions on historic or cultural properties; however, they do not *mandate* that such properties be protected. While Section 4(f) provides stronger protection for

historic or cultural resources in that it prohibits harm to such properties unless there is no reasonable alternative, it applies only to Department of Transportation actions. In addition, none of these federal laws has any effect on private actions in the absence of *some* degree of federal involvement, such as funding or licensing. The strongest measures for ensuring the protection of historic properties from state, local, and private actions are substantive regulatory controls found at the state and local levels.

Several other federal laws provide protection for historic and cultural resources. Among these are the **Reservoir Salvage Act**, 16 U.S.C. §§ 469–469c-1; the **Archaeological Resource Protection Act** of 1979, 16 U.S.C. §§ 470aa–470mm (discussed below); the **Surface Mining Control and Reclamation Act** of 1977, 30 U.S.C. § 1272; the **Abandoned Shipwreck Act**, 43 U.S.C. §§ 2101–2106 (discussed below); and the **Public Buildings Cooperative Use Act**, 40 U.S.C. §§ 601–606.

STATE PRESERVATION LAWS

State involvement in historic preservation activities historically has concentrated on the administration of federal government programs. Pursuant to the NHPA, each state has established a State Historic Preservation Office for the purpose of administering federal preservation programs, such as nominating properties for listing on the National Register of Historic Places or reviewing projects seeking certification for federal tax benefits. However, an increasing number of states have expanded their role in historic preservation by adopting a comprehensive preservation program that includes regulatory protection for historic and cultural resources, rehabilitation incentives, and educational and technical support.

The regulation of historic properties at the state level varies considerably. Most states have enacted enabling laws that grant specific powers and authority to local governments to pass ordinances for the protection and preservation of historic structures. Unless a local government operates under home rule authority, the degree of protection afforded to historic resources by an enabling act can be critical to the extent that the act defines the regulatory scope of a local preservation ordinance. An increasing number of states also regulate governmental actions affecting historic and cultural property through state environmental protection laws and other laws specific to historic preservation. For example, the California Environmental Quality Act (CEQA), Cal. Pub. Res. Code § 21000 et. seq., requires state agencies to consider the impact of their actions in making decisions that could adversely affect the environment, including historical resources; and the Alaska Coastal Management Program (ACMP), Alaska Stat. § 46.40.040-210, sets forth specific requirements agencies must follow to protect environmental and cultural resources within Alaska's coastal zone. Other states have enacted laws patterned after the Section 106 review process under the NHPA and Section 4(f) of the Department of Transportation Act. For example, the Minnesota Environmental Rights Act, Minn. Stat. § 116B.02, prohibits the demolition of a historic resource unless there is "no prudent and feasible alternative site," and the New Mexico Prehis-

Colorado State Historic Society building (formerly the courthouse), Colorado Springs, Colorado. *(Carol M. Highsmith Photography)*

toric and Historic Sites Preservation Act, New Mex. Stat. Annot. § 18-8-1–18-8-8, requires "all possible planning to preserve and protect and to minimize harm" to historic resources.

LOCAL PRESERVATION LAWS

It is at the *local* level—not federal or state—that preservation laws are more likely to regulate private actions affecting privately owned historic property. Through historic preservation ordinances, local jurisdictions regulate changes to historic resources that would otherwise irreparably change or destroy their character. Today, an estimated 2,000 historic preservation ordinances have been enacted across the country.

Preservation ordinances vary widely from jurisdiction to jurisdiction depending on a number of factors rang-

ing from limitations on permissible regulatory action imposed at the state level to the degree of support for preservation within a given community. Most local historic preservation laws empower historic preservation commissions to review and deny requests to alter, demolish, or remove property designated as a historic landmark or included in historic districts. Other jurisdictions confer ultimate regulatory authority to a zoning board of appeals or, in some cases, a legislative body, limiting the authority of the preservation commission to making recommendations to the decision-making body.

Most jurisdictions designate both historic districts and individual landmarks. While designations generally include entire historic structures, many communities extend protection only to the exteriors of such properties and, in a few cases, only to facades visible from a public way; however, some communities protect both the interior and exterior of historic properties.

Although the scope of protection afforded to individual structures varies among jurisdictions, most jurisdictions regulate both proposed alterations and demolitions of historic structures and new construction within a historic district. Many communities allow for the demolition of historic properties only in cases where a property owner establishes "economic hardship" or the property poses a safety threat to the community. Some communities only regulate alterations, allowing property owners to demolish historic properties after a waiting period, during which private preservation groups may attempt to purchase the property. An increasing number of communities also impose affirmative maintenance requirements on property owners to prevent structural damage through "demolition by neglect" provisions, and authorize preservation commissions to make limited repairs to landmarked properties and recoup expenses through the imposition of liens, when necessary.

In addition to "standalone" preservation ordinances, local zoning and planning laws are increasingly used to meet broader preservation goals, often through the inclusion of specific preservation elements in the local land-use regulatory scheme. Many jurisdictions are also developing preservation plans, either as a standalone measure or in conjunction with the comprehensive planning process, to ensure citywide consistency in preservation policy.

OTHER LAWS AFFECTING THE REGULATION OF HISTORIC AND CULTURAL PROPERTIES

In addition to historic preservation laws, there are a number of laws that focus on specific types of resources or a specific aspect of preservation, such as the **Archaeological Resources Protection Act** (ARPA) (16 U.S.C. § 470aa–mm) and the **Abandoned Shipwreck Act** (43 U.S.C. §§ 2102–2106 (1988)).

ARPA prohibits the removal, excavation, or alteration of any archaeological resource from federal or Indian lands, in the absence of a permit issued by the Department of the Interior. The law also prohibits the selling, purchasing, exchanging, transporting, and trafficking of archaeological resources illegally removed from private lands, as well as from public and Indian lands. Violators are subject to civil and criminal penalties.

The Abandoned Shipwreck Act clarifies the authority of states to enact—and enforce—laws and regulations to protect historic shipwrecks found in state territorial waters (generally defined as three miles from the coast or islands off the coast of the state). The act governs abandoned shipwrecks that are: (1) embedded in submerged lands of a state; (2) embedded in coralline formations protected by a state on submerged lands of a state; or (3) on submerged lands of a state and included in, or determined eligible for inclusion in, the National Register.

There are also a number of other laws that may or may not address historic preservation matters per se, but nonetheless affect historic resources in significant ways. Laws falling within this category include

transportation laws, such as the **Intermodal Surface Transportation Efficiency Act** of 1991 (ISTEA) (23 U.S.C. §133-35), which focuses on transportation planning requirements. (Regulations implementing ISTEA may be found at 23 C.F.R. § 450.) Other laws that affect historic resources include aesthetic regulations such as sign control and scenic highway laws, state and local environmental laws, land use and planning laws, certain nonregulatory programs that can be used to encourage historic resource preservation in specific situations, such as land banking, and laws governing what accommodations must be made to meet the needs of the disabled, such as the **Americans with Disabilities Act** (ADA) (42 U.S.C. § 12204).

TAX INCENTIVES FOR THE REHABILITATION OF HISTORIC PROPERTY

Tax incentive programs generally address three important objectives: (1) they provide financial benefits to owners otherwise burdened by preservation laws; (2) they counter private and public land-use policies favoring demolition and new construction; and (3) they encourage the rehabilitation of historic structures. While no single incentive program accomplishes all three objectives, meaningful tax incentives have been adopted at the federal, the state, and, increasingly, the local level.

Federal Rehabilitation Tax Credit

Perhaps the best known incentive to preserve historic property is the rehabilitation tax credit. This incentive gives property owners either a 10 percent or 20 percent tax credit on rehabilitation expenses, depending on the classification of the building at issue. Certified historic structures are eligible for a 20 percent credit while noncertified, nonresidential properties placed in service before 1936 are eligible for a 10 percent credit (I.R.C. §§ 46(b); 48(g)).

Several specific conditions must be satisfied to qualify for the credit, including: the use of the building—it must be income-producing, not an owner-occupied residence; rehabilitation costs must exceed the adjusted basis of the building or $5,000; and the work performed must meet preservation standards. The National Park Service administers the tax certification process. (See I.R.C. § 48(g) and Treas. Reg. §§ 1.46 et. seq. It should be noted that, since 1986, passive activity loss rules have restricted the amount of the tax credit an individual taxpayer can use in any given year.) See the previous chapter, entitled "Historic Rehabilitation Tax Credit," for a detailed discussion.

Federal Tax Benefits Relating to Preservation Easements

Owners of historic properties who donate preservation easements to qualified preservation organizations also may be eligible for a charitable contribution deduction under Section 170 of the Internal Revenue Code (I.R.C. § 170(h); I.R.C. §§ 2055(f) and 2522; and Treas. Reg. § 1.170A et. seq.). Among other requirements, eligibility entails the relinquishment of rights to demolish or alter a property and the gift of such rights, in perpetuity, to a qualified historic preservation organization. Thereafter, the property owner and all subsequent owners will not be able to alter or demolish the property without the express permission of the recipient organization.

The value of the easement is the difference between the property's fair market value before donation of the easement and its fair market value afterward. In order to obtain the charitable deduction, the taxpayer must retain a qualified appraiser to value the donated easement if its value exceeds $5,000.

State and Local Incentives for Rehabilitation

Several states and local jurisdictions provide special incentives to encourage the maintenance and rehabilitation of historic properties, typically in the form of property tax freezes or income tax credits on rehabilitation expenditures. Georgia, for example, provides an eight-year freeze on property tax assessments of substantially rehabilitated buildings, and Rhode Island permits owners of historic residential property to claim a 10 percent credit against state income taxes. San Antonio provides a ten-year property tax freeze at prerehabilitation levels to taxpayers who substantially rehabilitate residential historic structures. Owners of rehabilitated commercial historic buildings may qualify for a five-year city property tax exemption, and then a property tax freeze at half the property's value during the subsequent five-year period.

LEGAL ADVOCACY

At its most effective, preservation law involves both incentives and regulatory (or procedural) protections. The effectiveness of such tools—particularly regulatory tools— often depends on the willingness of individuals and organizations to use the courts to enforce the law.

The National Trust for Historic Preservation plays a leading role in historic preservation advocacy by directly intervening in legal controversies and in assisting local groups in planning legal strategy and finding local counsel, and by providing research and expertise. Through its Legal Defense Fund, the National Trust has taken an increasingly active role in advocating historic preservation as a fundamental value in programs and policies at all levels of government through litigation and other legal action. A small but experienced staff of attorneys, working with the voluntary, or pro bono, assistance of lawyers from across the country, has helped many local organizations and municipalities win important preservation battles in their own communities. In more than 100 court cases to date, the National Trust has helped municipalities and preservation commissions defend against legal challenges to local preservation laws, and has worked directly with federal, state, and local government agencies on disputes involving publicly funded, licensed, or approved projects. In many cases, the Trust is able to encourage cooperative solutions to these disputes without resorting to enforcement in the courts. In other cases, however, the National Trust—joined by local and state preservation organizations—has found it necessary to either bring suit or join in litigation as a "friend of the court," or *amicus curiae*, to ensure compliance with federal and state preservation laws and to protect threatened historic resources.

The National Trust also publishes the *Preservation Law Reporter*, a monthly journal that provides information on legal developments in historic preservation. This publication serves lawyers, preservation commissions, local organizations, and developers engaged in historic rehabilitation projects.

CONTACTS

Legal Defense Fund, National Trust for Historic Preservation, 1785 Massachusetts Avenue, N.W., Washington, DC 20036 (202-588-6035).

Center for Preservation Policy Studies

Legislative Hotline, National Trust for Historic Preservation, 1785 Massachusetts Avenue, N.W., Washington, DC 20036 (1-800-765-NTHP).

FURTHER READING

The *Preservation Law Reporter* should be consulted for further information on each of the topics previously discussed, or for a summary of recent legal developments in legislation and litigation. Information on the *Preservation Law Reporter* may be obtained by contacting the National Trust's Department of Law and Public Policy, at (202) 588-6035

or 1-800-944-NTHP (e-mail: law@nthp.org).

For a list of law-related publications, refer to the "Resources and Readings" chapter later in this section. Relevant information is available under these particular headings: Accessibility, Archaeology, Downtown Revitalization, Easements, Economic Revitalization, Growth Management, Incentives, Land Use Planning, Legal Issues, Legislation, Local Historic Preservation Ordinances, National Register, Planning, Property Rights, Rural Preservation, State Historic Preservation Laws, and Transportation.

Degree Programs in Historic Preservation

UNDERGRADUATE PROGRAMS IN HISTORIC PRESERVATION

Alabama

Shelton State Community College
Tuscaloosa, AL 35405
Katherine Alexander
Skyland Campus
Certificate in Historic Preservation
27 Credit Hours
American Architectural History;
Preservation Law; Research;
Documentation; Theory and History
of Historic Preservation; Crafts and
Technical Training
NCPE Member

Missouri

Southeast Missouri State University
Cape Girardeau, MO 63701
Bonnie Stepenoff, Coordinator
Historic Preservation Program
Department of History
c526huh@semovm.semo.edu
B.S. in Historic Preservation and
M.A. in History, Historic
Preservation Emphasis
Average enrollment: 75 in B.S.,
8–10 in M.A.
57 Semester Hours B.S. and 36
Semester Hours M.A.
Internship and Thesis
Museum and Site Management;

Preservation Administration;
Archives; Local History
NCPE Member

Ohio

Belmont Technical College
St. Clairsville, OH 43950
David R. Mertz, Coordinator
Building Preservation Technology
BTCBPR@ovnet.com
A.A.S. in Building Preservation
Technology
Average enrollment: 80–100
99 Quarter Hours
Internship Option
Materials Conservation; Traditional
Skills; Building Analysis; Hands-on
Restoration
NCPE Member

Pennsylvania

Bucks County Community College
Newtown, PA 18940
Lyle L. Rosenberger, Director
Historic Preservation Program
Certificate in Historic Preservation
Average enrollment: 60–70
24 Credits
Internship Option
Documentation and Building
Analysis
NCPE Member

Harrisburg Area Community
College
Harrisburg, PA 17110
Linda Lefevre
Technical Institute
Diploma in Historic Preservation
Average enrollment: 12–15
21 Credits
General Preservation; Research
Methods; Legal, Theoretical, and
Practical Issues; Practicum
NCPE Member

Rhode Island

Roger Williams University
Bristol, RI 02809
Michael R. H. Swanson
Center for Historic Preservation
mrhs@alpha.rwu.edu
B.S. in Historic Preservation
Average enrollment: 85–95
64 Credits
Internship, Thesis, Study Abroad,
Semester in England
Preservation Planning/Architectural
Conservation; Research;
Philosophy; Documentation; Law
NCPE Member

Virginia

Mary Washington College
Fredericksburg, VA 22401
Gary W. Stanton
Department of Historic Preservation

gstanton@mwc.edu
B.A. in Historic Preservation
Average enrollment: 120
39 Credits
Internship Recommended
Theory; Architectural Conservation;
Historic Preservation Planning;
Documentation; Material Culture;
Management
NCPE Member

GRADUATE PROGRAMS IN HISTORIC PRESERVATION
(some also offer undergraduate programs)

Georgia

Georgia State University
Atlanta, GA 30303
Timothy Crimmins, Director
Master of Heritage Preservation
Program
histjc@gsusgi2.gsu.edu
M.A. in Heritage Preservation
Average enrollment: 40
70 Quarter Hours
Internship and Optional Thesis
History; Folklore; Building
Materials; Historic Interiors
NCPE Member

University of Georgia
Athens, GA 30602
John C. Waters, Director
Graduate Studies in Historic
Preservation
Caldwell Hall
JCWATERS@uga.cc.uga.edu
M.A. in Historic Preservation,
Certificate in Historic Preservation
and J.D./M.A. in Historic
Preservation
Average enrollment: 36
90 Quarter Hours
Internship and Thesis
Preservation Planning;
Environmental Conservation;
Building Materials; Historic
Landscape; Historic Interiors;

Documentation; Management; Law;
Research
NCPE Member

Savannah College of Art and
Design
Savannah, GA 31401
Robert C. Dickensheets
Historic Preservation Department
B.F.A. and M.F.A.
Average enrollment: 80 B.F.A. and
25 M.F.A.
180 Quarter Hours B.F.A. and
90–105 Quarter Hours M.F.A.
Internship and Thesis
Technology; Interpretation; Law;
Economics; Design; Preservation
Construction
NCPE Member

Illinois

School of the Art Institute of
Chicago
37 South Wabash
Chicago, IL 60603
Don Kalec, Director
Historic Preservation Program
M.S. in Historic Preservation
Average enrollment: 30
60 Credits
Internship and Thesis
Restoration Design; Materials
Conservation and Building
Technology; Preservation Planning;
History; Interiors; Landscape

Indiana

Ball State University
Muncie, IN 47306
James A. Glass, Director
Historic Preservation Program
College of Architecture and
Planning
OOJAGLASS@bsuvc.bsu.edu
M.S. in Historic Preservation
Average enrollment: 20
55 Semester Hours
Internship and Thesis
Preservation; Documentation;

Architectural History; Technology;
Law; Economics; Planning
NCPE Member

Maryland

Goucher College
Baltimore, MD 21204
Richard Wagner, Director
Historic Preservation Program
B.A. and M.A. in Historic
Preservation
Average enrollment: 45
36 Credits
Comprehensive Exam and Thesis
Historic Preservation; Limited
Residency Urban Issues; Traditional
Skills
NCPE Member

Massachusetts

Boston University
226 Bay State Road
Boston, MA 02215
Richard M. Candee, Director
Preservation Studies Program
M.A. in Historic Preservation,
M.A./J.D.
Average enrollment: 20-24
48 Credits
Internship and Optional Thesis
Architectural History; Preservation
Management; Building
Conservation; Research; Building
Documentation; Law;
Neighborhoods
NCPE Member

Michigan

Eastern Michigan University
Ypsilanti, MI 48197
Marshall McLennan, Director
Historic Preservation Program
Department of Geography
M.S. in Historic Preservation
Certificate in Historic Preservation
Studies
Average enrollment: 65
36 Credit Hours

5 Course Certificate
Project and Optional Internship
General Preservation; Preservation
Planning; History Administration;
Heritage Interpretation/Tourism;
Cultural Landscapes
NCPE Member

New York

Columbia University
400 Avery Hall
New York, NY 10027
Robert A. M. Stern, Director
Historic Preservation Program
M.S. in Historic Preservation
Average enrollment: 60
60 Points
Internship and Thesis
Conservation; Design; Planning;
History
NCPE Member

Cornell University
106 West Sibley Hall
Ithaca, NY 14853
Michael Tomlan, Director
Graduate Program in Historic
Preservation Planning
mat4@cornell.edu
M.A. and Ph.D. in Historic
Preservation Planning
Average enrollment: 20–24
60 Semester Hours
Thesis and Optional Internship
Planning; Conservation; Research;
Documentation
NCPE Member

Oregon

University of Oregon
Eugene, OR 97403
Donald L. Peting, Director
Historic Preservation Program
M.S. in Historic Preservation
Average enrollment: 20
70 Quarter Hours
Internship and Thesis
Administration; Documentation;

Yale University tower, New Haven, Connecticut. *(Carol M. Highsmith Photography)*

Interpretation and Technology of
Buildings; Interiors; Landscapes
NCPE Member

Pennsylvania

University of Pennsylvania
115 Meyerson Hall
Philadelphia, PA 19104
David G. De Long, Chair
Graduate Program in Historic
Preservation

M.S. and Ph.D. in Architecture and
City Planning, Historic Preservation
Certificate
Average enrollment: 50
48 Credit Hours
Internship and Thesis
Documentation; Material
Conservation; Technology;
Planning; Site Management;
Landscape
NCPE Member

Tennessee

Middle Tennessee State University
Murfreesboro, TN 37132
Andrew Gulliford, Director
Public History/Preservation
History Department
M.A. and D.A. in Historic
Preservation
Average enrollment: 50
M.A. 36 Credits
D.A. 60 Credits
Internship and Thesis
Preservation Administration; Public
History; Cultural Resources;
Museum Management
NCPE Member

Vermont

University of Vermont
213 Wheeler House
Burlington, VT 05405
Thomas D. Visser, Interim Director
Historic Preservation Program
Thomas.Visser@uvm.edu
M.S. in Historic Preservation
Average enrollment: 20
36 Credits
Internship and Optional Thesis
Preserving the Built Environment;
Building Conservation;
Administration; Economics; Rural
Preservation
NCPE Member

GRADUATE PROGRAMS IN ALLIED DISCIPLINES WITH A SPECIALIZATION IN PRESERVATION

Arizona

Northern Arizona University
Flagstaff, AZ 86011
Charles Hoffman
Department of Anthropology
M.A. in Anthropology
Average enrollment: 12

24 Credits Thesis and 45 Credits
Applied Internship
Field Work; Historic Preservation;
CRM; Historical Archeology; Ruins
Stabilization; Life Histories;
Ethnographic Research Method
NCPE Member

Arkansas

University of Arkansas at Little Rock
Little Rock, AR 72204
Stephen Recken, Coordinator
Public History Program
SLRECKEN@ualr.edu
M.A. in Public History, Historic
Preservation Specialization
Average enrollment: 10
39 Semester Credit Hours
Internship and Thesis
Material Culture; Research;
Resource Management
NCPE Member

California

University of California
Riverside, CA 92521
Piotr Gorecki, Director
History Department
M.A. in History, Historic
Preservation Specialization
Average enrollment: 12
36 Credit Hours
Thesis
History; Museum Curatorship;
Historic Preservation Management;
Archival Management
NCPE Member

University of California
Santa Barbara, CA 93106
Otis Graham, Jr., Director
Public History Program
M.A. and Ph.D. in Public History
Average enrollment: 5–10
5 Quarters M.A.
History; Public History; Research

Colorado

Colorado State University
Fort Collins, CO 80523
Liston E. Leyendecker
Department of History
lleyendecker@vines.colostate.edu
M.A. in History, Historic
Preservation Specialization
Average enrollment: 15
33 Semester Hours
History; History of Architecture;
Historic Interiors; Construction
Management; Preservation
Administration
NCPE Member

Delaware

University of Delaware
Newark, DE 19716
David L. Ames, Director
Center for History of Architecture
and Engineering
M.A. and Ph.D., Historic
Preservation Specialization
Average enrollment: 8–10 M.A. and
2 Ph.D.
36 Semester Hours M.A. and 48
Semester Hours Ph.D.
History of Architecture and
Landscapes; Material Culture;
Planning; Documentation;
Advocacy
NCPE Member

District of Columbia

George Washington University
Washington, DC 20052
Richard Longstreth, Director
Graduate Program in Historic
Preservation
M.A. and Ph.D. in History of
American Civilization, Historic
Preservation Specialization
Average enrollment: 15
36 Credit Hours M.A. and 72 Credit
Hours Ph.D.

History of Architecture and Urbanism; Surveys; Material Culture; Folklife; Preservation Management; Documentation
NCPE Member

Florida

University of Florida
Gainesville, FL 32611
Herschell Shepard, Director
Department of Architecture
M.A. in Architecture
Average enrollment: 24
52 Semester Hours
Architecture; Preservation Technology; Documentation
NCPE Member

Georgia

Armstrong State College
Savannah, GA 31419
Christopher Hendricks
Public History Program
Chris_Hendricks@mailgate.Armstrong.edu
M.A. in History, Public History Specialization
Average enrollment: 15
60 Quarter Hours
Internship and Thesis
Historic Preservation; Museums; Historical Archeology; Archives; Oral History
NCPE Member

Hawaii

University of Hawaii–Manoa
Honolulu, HI 96822
William Chapman, Director
Historic Preservation Program
Moore 324
wchapman@hawaii.edu
Certificate in Historic Preservation and M.A. and Ph.D. in American Studies, Historic Preservation Specialization
Average enrollment: 35

33 Credit Hours M.A., 48 Credit Hours Ph.D., and 15 Credit Hours Certificate
American Studies; Preservation Management; Surveys; Material Culture; Documentation
NCPE Member

Illinois

University of Illinois, Urbana–Champaign
Urbana, IL 61801
Eliza Steelwater, Coordinator
Historic Preservation Concentration
Urban and Regional Planning
B.A., M.A., and Ph.D. in Urban Planning, Preservation Certificate
Average enrollment: 6–8 B.A. and 8–10 M.A.
48 Credit Hours B.A., 48 Credit Hours M.A. and 60 Credit Hours Ph.D.
Urban Planning; Research; Documentation
NCPE Member

Kansas

Kansas State University
Manhattan, KS 66506
Wayne Charney, Coordinator
Graduate Studies in Historic Preservation
Department of Architecture
M.A. in Architecture, M.L.A., and M.R.C.P., Preservation Specialization
Average enrollment: 7–10
30 Credits M.A. in Architecture, 31–34 Credits M.L.A., and 51 Graduate Units M.R.C.P.
Architecture; Regional Planning and Design; Documentation
NCPE Member

Kentucky

Western Kentucky University
Bowling Green, KY 42101

Larry Danielson, Director
Graduate Program in Folk Studies
Department of Modern Languages
M.A. in Folk Studies with Specialization
Average enrollment: 25
36 Credit Hours
Folk Studies; Planning; Cultural Resources
NCPE Member

Louisiana

University of New Orleans
New Orleans, LA 70148
Jane Brooks, Coordinator
Historic Preservation Concentration
College of Urban and Public Affairs
cupa@uno.edu
M.U.R.P., M.S., M.P.A., and Ph.D. in Urban Studies, Certificate in Historic Preservation
Average enrollment: 25–30
45 Credit Hours M.U.R.P., 33 Credit Hours M.S., 42 Credit Hours M.P.A./Ph.D., and 15 Credit Hours Historic Preservation Certificate
Urban Studies; Preservation Planning; Urban Anthropology
NCPE Member

Maryland

University of Maryland
College Park, MD 20742
David P. Fogel, Director
HISP Program
School of Architecture
Graduate Certificate, Degree in Participating Department
Average enrollment: 30
24 Semester Hours
American Studies; Anthropology; Architecture; Geography; History; Horticulture and Landscape; Urban Studies and Planning; National Trust Library
NCPE Member

Michigan

Michigan State University
East Lansing, MI 48824
Richard L. Graham
Department of Human Environment
and Design
M.A. in Interior Design and
Facilities Management, Historic
Preservation Specialization
Average enrollment: 5–10
30–34 Semester Hours
Interior Preservation; Adaptive Use;
Material Culture; Archival Research
and Documentation
NCPE Member

Miriam Rutz, Urban and Regional
Planning Program
M.U.P., Historic Preservation
Specialization
Average enrollment: 10–12
30 Credits
Optional Internship
History and Philosophy; Historic
Preservation Planning; Field Work
NCPE Member

Missouri

University of Missouri
Columbia, MO 65211
Howard W. Marshall
Department of Art History and
Archeology
M.A. in Art History, History, and
Environmental Design
Average enrollment: 6–10
30 Semester Hours
Internship and Thesis
History of Architecture; Public
History; Folklife Studies;
Archeology; Material Culture
NCPE Member

Nevada

University of Nevada
Reno, NV 89557
Don Fowler, Director
Historic Preservation Program

hp@scs.unr.edu
B.A. and M.A., Historic Preservation
Specialization
Average enrollment: 15
18 Credit Hours B.A. and 9–12
Credit Hours M.A.
Anthropology; Surveys;
Documentation
NCPE Member

Ohio

Kent State University
Kent, OH 44242
Daniel Vieyra, Director
Historic Preservation Graduate
Program
M.A. in Architecture, Historic
Preservation Specialization
Average enrollment: 7–10
54 Credit Hours
Architecture; Environmental Design;
Planning
NCPE Member

Ohio State University
Columbus, OH 43210
Judith Kitchen
Department of Architecture
190 West Seventeenth Avenue
M.A. in Architecture
Average enrollment: 3-5
90 Quarter Hours
Architecture Design; Historic
Buildings
NCPE Member

University of Cincinnati
Cincinnati, OH 45221
Bruce Goetzman, Chair
Historic Preservation Certificate
Committee
B.A., M.A., and Ph.D. in Discipline,
Historic Preservation Certificate
Average enrollment: 15–20
30 Credit Hours
Internship
Urban Historic Preservation;
Prehistorical and Classical
Archeology
NCPE Member

Oklahoma

Oklahoma State University
Stillwater, OK 74078
Bill Bryans, Coordinator
Applied History Program
501-H Life Sciences West Building
M.A. in History, Historic
Preservation Specialization
Average enrollment: 5
33 Semester Hours
Cultural Resources; Surveys;
History; Preservation Administration
NCPE Member

South Carolina

University of South Carolina
Columbia, SC 29208
Robert Weyeneth, Co-Director
Applied History Program
weyeneth@scarolina.edu
M.A. in Applied History and Ph.D.
in History
Average enrollment: 35–40
36 Semester Hours
History; Public History; Preservation
Law and Philosophy; Archives;
Museums; Documentation
NCPE Member

Tennessee

University of Tennessee
Knoxville, TN 37996
J. S. Rabun
School of Architecture
B.A. in Architecture, M.A. in Interior
Design, and M.A. in Community
Planning
Average enrollment: 9–12 in Design
and 36 in Community Planning
27 Credits B.A. in Architecture, 36
M.A. in Interior Design and 46 M.A.
in Community Planning
Architecture; Anthropology;
Planning; Interior Design
NCPE Member

Texas

Texas A & M University
College Station, TX 77843
David G. Woodcock
College of Architecture
woodcock@archone.tamu.edu
M.A. in Architecture, M.L.A., M.U.P.,
and M.S.
Average enrollment: 25
52 Credits M.A. in Architecture, 40
Credits M.L.A., 48 Credits M.U.P., 32
Credits M.S. Architecture;
Documentation; Preservation
Technology; Law; Historical and
Cultural Landscapes
NCPE Member

Texas Tech University
Lubbock, TX 79409
John P. White
School of Architecture
M.A. in Architecture and Historic
Preservation
Average enrollment: 3–5
36 Credit Hours
Architecture; Documentation;
Restoration; Conservation
NCPE Member

University of Texas
Austin, TX 78713
Lance Tatum, Director
School of Architecture, Historic
Preservation
Goldsmith Hall
M.A. in Architecture, M.S. in
Architecture, and M.A. in Urban
Planning
Average enrollment: 15
52 Hours M.A. in Architecture, 32
Hours M.S. in Architecture, and 48
Hours M.A. in Urban Planning
Thesis
Architecture; Documentation;
Building Technology; Measured
Drawing; Design
NCPE Member

Utah

University of Utah
Salt Lake City, UT 84112
Robert A. Young
Graduate School of Architecture
Room 235 AAC
young@arch.utah.edu
M.S. in Historic Preservation
Average enrollment: 10
54 Quarter Hours
Project Administration;
Documentation; Interpretation;
Planning; Building Technology;
Community and Service-Based
Projects
NCPE Member

Virginia

University of Virginia
Charlottesville, VA 22903
Daniel Bluestone, Director
Historic Preservation Program
School of Architecture
Campbell Hall
dblues@virginia.edu
Historic Preservation Certificate
with Participating Programs
Average enrollment: 25
25 Credit Hours
History of Architecture;
Preservation Theory; Preservation
Design; Urbanism

Washington

University of Washington
Seattle, WA 98195
Nelie Graham, Program Coordinator
Preservation Planning and Design
Program
Nelie@u.washington.edu
M.A. in Architecture, M.L.A., M.U.P.,
Ph.D., Preservation Planning and
Design Certificate
Average enrollment: 30
30 Credit Hours
Architecture; History of
Architecture; Planning; Landscape;
Design
NCPE Member

Wisconsin

University of Wisconsin
Madison, WI 53706
William H. Tishler
Department of Landscape
Architecture
25 Agricultural Hall
M.S. and M.A. in Landscape
Architecture
Average enrollment: 6–8
34 Credits
Landscape Architecture; Planning
and Design; Resource Management
NCPE Member

Glossary

Adaptive use The process of converting a building to a use other than that for which it was designed, for example, changing a factory into housing. Such conversions are accomplished with varying degrees of alterations to the building.

Advisory Council on Historic Preservation An independent federal agency established in 1966 through the Historic Preservation Act. The Advisory Council advises the president and Congress on national historic preservation matters, reviews federally licensed properties listed in or eligible for the National Register of Historic Places, and issues the president's Historic Preservation Awards.

Amenity A building, object, area, or landscape feature that makes an aesthetic contribution to the environment, rather than one that is purely utilitarian.

Amicus curiae Friend of the court (Latin). A party that may be allowed to present a brief on an issue before a court, frequently one with relevant, special expertise.

Architect Generally, one who designs and supervises the construction of buildings; legally, only professionals who are licensed by a state, territory, or the District of Columbia to practice architecture.

Architecture The art and science of design and construction of buildings; also refers to particular periods, styles, or methods of construction, as in Victorian architecture.

Assessed value Economic value of land or buildings for tax purposes determined by location, use, improvements, and other factors.

Background buildings Buildings that may lack exemplary character or significance but that are nonetheless essential to maintain a sense of place.

Building code Standards adopted by local governments regulating methods and materials of construction, egress, and accessibility and other factors affecting the construction of safe and sanitary buildings. Federal, state, territorial, and the District of Columbia governments also issue building codes used for government or government-funded buildings.

Building occupancy Classification of buildings by use in building codes; used to determine methods and materials of construction, egress, and other requirements.

Certificate of appropriateness A document awarded by a preservation commission or architectural review board allowing an applicant to proceed with a proposed alteration, demolition, or new construction in a designated area or site, following a determination of the proposal's suitability according to applicable criteria.

Certified historic structure For the purposes of the federal preservation tax incentives, any structure subject to depreciation as defined by the Internal Revenue Code that is listed individually in the National Register of Historic Places or located in a registered historic district and certified by the secretary of the interior as being of historical significance to the district.

Certified rehabilitation Any rehabilitation of a certified historic structure that the secretary of the interior has determined is consistent with the historical character of the property or the district in which the property is located.

Code compliance Ensuring that a building is built in agreement with the appropriate building code.

Code enforcement Local regulation of building practices and enforcement of safety and housing code provisions; a principal tool to ensure neighborhood upkeep.

Commercial archeology The study of structures and artifacts created in connection with popular commercial activity, such as diners, motels, gasoline stations, and signs.

Conservation archeology A field of archeology concerned with limiting excavations to a minimum consistent with research objectives and with preserving archeological sites for future scientific investigation.

Contingency budget Unassigned construction funds set aside to pay for unexpected expenses or changes to the contract documents. A typical restoration or rehabilitation project should have a contingency budget of 10 percent.

Contract documents Detailed plans, known as working drawings, and instructions and materials lists, known as specifications, concerned with the construction of a building.

Cultural resource A building, structure, district, site, object, or document that is of significance in American history, architecture, archeology, or culture.

Demolition by neglect The destruction of a building through abandonment or lack of maintenance.

Demolition delay A temporary halt or stay in the planned razing of a property, usually resulting from a court injunction obtained by preservationists to allow a period of negotiation.

Design development Phase of the design process when plans, elevations, and sections of a building are fully developed, when materials and methods of construction are determined, and when preliminary cost estimates are generated.

Design guidelines Criteria developed by preservation commissions and architectural review boards to identify design concerns in an area and to help property owners ensure that rehabilitation and new construction respect the character of designated buildings and districts.

Design process Method by which buildings are designed. The process typically has the following phases: determining the requirements of the owner and the proposed use; researching applicable codes and other legal requirements; analyzing the existing building, in the case of preservation projects; schematic design; design development; contract documents; bidding; site observation; and cost-occupancy evaluation.

Design review The process of ascertaining whether modifications to historic and other structures, settings, and districts meet standards of ap-propriateness established by a government or advisory review board.

Dismantling Taking apart a structure piece by piece, often with the intention of reconstructing it elsewhere.

Displacement The movement of individuals, businesses, or industries from property or neighborhoods because of real estate activities.

Easement A less-than-fee interest in real property acquired through donation or purchase and carried as a deed restriction or covenant to protect important open spaces, building facades, and interiors.

Egress Term used in building codes for exiting a building; egress requirements are designed to allow occupants to exit safely in the event of fire or other disaster.

Eminent domain The power of a government to acquire private prop-

Round barn, Hancock Shaker Village near Pittsfield, Massachusetts. *(Carol M. Highsmith Photography)*

erty for public benefit after payment of just compensation to the owner.

Enabling legislation Federal or state laws that authorize governing bodies within their jurisdictions to enact particular measures or delegate powers, such as enactment of local landmarks and historic district ordinances, zoning, and taxation.

Energy audit Analysis of a building's energy consumption for heating, cooling, lighting, and so forth. The purpose of an audit is to determine means to reduce energy consumption by improving the thermal performance of foundations, walls, doors, windows, roofs, and other exterior surfaces and the efficiency of heating, cooling, and lighting systems.

Extended use Any process that increases the useful life of an old building, for example, adaptive use or continued use.

Fabric The physical material of a building, structure, or city, connoting an interweaving of component parts.

Facadism The retention of only the facade of a historic building during conversion while the remainder is severely altered or destroyed to accept the new use.

Fenestration Openings in an external wall such as doors and windows.

Financial incentives Grants, low-interest loans, tax deductions and credits, easements, and other monetary inducements that improve the financial feasibility of a building project.

Found space Old buildings or spaces within them that have been retrieved from near oblivion for rehabilitation or adaptive use after

having been abandoned or "lost."

Gentrification British term for the process by which young professionals or "gentry" buy into inner-city areas as part of a neighborhood preservation trend.

Historical archeology The study of the cultural remains of literate societies, including excavated material as well as aboveground resources such as buildings, pottery, weapons, tools, glassware, cutlery, and textiles.

Historic district A geographically definable area with a significant concentration of buildings, structures, sites, spaces, or objects unified by past events, physical development, design, setting, materials, workmanship, sense of cohesiveness, or related historical and aesthetic associations. The significance of a district may be recognized through listing in a local, state, or national landmarks register and may be protected legally through enactment of a local historic district ordinance administered by a historic district board or commission.

Homesteading Programs under which abandoned buildings are made available at little or no cost in return for an agreement to rehabilitate and occupy them for a specified period of time. Similar programs to recycle commercial structures may be called shopsteading.

House museum A museum whose structure itself is of historical or architectural significance and whose interpretation relates primarily to the building's architecture, furnishings, and history.

Human scale A combination of qualities in architecture or the landscape that provides an appropriate rela-

tionship to human size, enhancing rather than diminishing the importance of people.

Industrial archeology The study of the history and development of industry as revealed by industrial buildings and artifacts such as bridges, transportation systems, and other engineering landmarks.

Infiltration Movement of air between the interior of a building and the exterior. Eliminating gaps around windows, doors, and their joints in a building's exterior surfaces reduces infiltration and increases the building's thermal performance.

Landmarks register A listing of buildings, districts, and objects designated for historical, architectural, or other special significance that may carry protection for listed properties.

Landscape The totality of the built or human-influenced habitat experienced at any one place. Dominant features are topography, plant cover, buildings or other structures, and their patterns.

Landscape architecture A design profession accommodating human uses and needs to the land in a manner that is aesthetically pleasing and respectful of the natural environment. Landscape architects, university-trained professionals, work with the siting of structures and facilities; the design of parks, public spaces, and gardens; environmental management and reclamation of the environment; and the planning of communities, transportation, and industrial facilities in harmony with the natural environment.

Leverage The use of a small amount of funding to attract additional money to provide project capital; also, the use of fixed-cost funds to acquire a property that is expected to produce a higher rate of return through income or appreciation.

Life-safety code Sections of a building code dealing with egress, fire separation, and other aspects of occupant safety; also a specialized code dealing with safety in buildings.

Maintenance program Specific methods, procedures, and schedule to maintain and repair a building.

Massing Composition of a building's volumes and surfaces that contribute to its appearance; for example, many classical-style buildings have a central mass or pavilion, flanked by subordinate masses or wings.

Material culture Tangible objects used by people to cope with the physical world, such as utensils, structures, and furnishings, all of which provide evidence of culturally determined behavior.

Methods of construction Systems and types of construction usually related to the types of structural materials used. For example, the balloon frame method of construction used in most single-family homes employs light structural wood members (twelve-by-fours, two-by-sixes, etc.) nailed together; a poured-in-place method of construction uses concrete poured into forms, reinforced with steel bars.

Mixed use A variety of authorized activities in an area or a building, as distinguished from the isolated uses and planned separatism prescribed by many zoning ordinances.

National Historic Landmark An official designation awarded by the National Park Service to National Register properties which, because of

their exceptional value or quality, are considered the nation's most important cultural resources.

National Register eligibility Formal determination that a property meets the criteria for listing in the National Register of Historic Places even though it is not officially listed. Generally, properties determined eligible for the National Register receive the same protection and benefits as listed properties.

National Register listing Formal inclusion of a property in the National Register of Historic Places.

National Register of Historic Places The nation's official list of historic and cultural resources worthy of preservation. Created by the National Historic Preservation Act of 1966 and maintained by the National Park Service, the National Register includes buildings, structures, sites, districts, and objects significant in American history, architecture, archeology, engineering, and culture.

Outdoor museum A restored, re-created, or replica village site in which several or many structures have been restored, rebuilt, or moved and whose purpose is to interpret a historical or cultural setting, period, or activity.

Planning office The department of local, and sometimes state, government responsible for analyzing and formulating policy regarding land use, housing, economic development, open-space preservation, transportation, infrastructure, and historic preservation.

Police power The inherent right of a government to restrict individual conduct or use of property to protect the public health, safety, and welfare; it must follow due processes of

the law but, unlike eminent domain, does not carry the requirement of compensation for any alleged losses. Police power is the basis for such regulations as zoning, building codes, and preservation ordinances.

Preservation Generally, saving from destruction or deterioration old and historic buildings, sites, structures, and objects, and providing for their continued use by means of maintenance, restoration, rehabilitation, or adaptive use. Specifically, "the act or process of applying measures to sustain the existing form, integrity, and material of a building or structure, and the existing form and vegetative cover of a site. It may include stabilization work, where necessary, as well as ongoing maintenance of the historic building materials" (Secretary of the Interior's Standards for Rehabilitation).

Preservation commission A generic term for an appointed municipal or county board that recommends the designation of, and regulates changes to, historic districts and landmarks. It may be called a historic district review board or commission, architectural or design review board, or landmarks commission; the latter's authority may be limited to individual buildings.

Proportions The relative size of two or more dimensions of a building; many architectural styles use highly developed mathematical proportions to determine the composition of facades and volumes of interior spaces.

Reconstruction "The act or process of reproducing by new construction the exact form and detail of a vanished building, structure, or object, or a part thereof, as it appeared at a specific period of time" (Secretary of the Interior's Standards for Rehabilitation).

Redlining A practice among financial institutions and insurance companies of refusing to provide services to certain supposedly high-risk geographical areas, regardless of the merits of individual applicants; derived from the red line that the institutions may draw around the area on a map.

Redundant building British term for a building or site no longer in demand for its original or current use. In the United States the terms *endangered property* and *surplus property* are most often used.

Rehabilitation "The act or process of returning a property to a state of utility through repair or alteration that makes possible an efficient contemporary use while preserving those portions or features of the property significant to its historical, architectural, and cultural values" (Secretary of the Interior's Standards for Rehabilitation).

Reinvestment The channeling of public and private resources into declining neighborhoods in a coordinated manner to combat disinvestment.

Renovation Modernization of an old or historic building that may produce inappropriate alterations or eliminate important features and details.

Restoration "The act or process of accurately recovering the form and details of a property and its setting as it appeared at a particular period of time by means of the removal of later work or by the replacement of missing earlier work" (Secretary of the Interior's Standards for Rehabilitation).

Revolving fund Funding source that makes loans accomplish some preservation purpose, for example, purchase and rehabilitation of an endangered property. The loans are repaid to maintain the fund for other projects.

Salvage archeology Rescue of archeological materials and data threatened by damage or destruction.

Schematic design Preliminary plans, elevations, and sections showing the approximate sections and sizes of rooms, composition of the facade, and other aspects of a building project. Typically, a number of schematic designs are developed for each project to study alternative solutions.

Section 106 The provision of the National Historic Preservation Act of 1966 that requires the head of a federal agency financing or licensing a project to make a determination of the effect of the project on property in, or eligible for, the National Register of Historic Places.

Seismic code Building code governing structural design and methods and materials of construction to prevent the collapse of a building during an earthquake.

Sense of place The sum of attributes of a locality, neighborhood, or property that give it a unique and distinctive character.

Setback Distance between the facade of a building and the property line. Setback requirements are usually found in zoning codes.

Site coverage Percentage of a site covered by buildings.

Site observation Services provided by an architect during construction to ensure that the building is being constructed according to the contract documents.

Sprawl Development that is spread out, low-density, and land-consumptive; located at the outer fringes of cities, towns, or suburbs; characterized by segregated land uses; and dominated by, and dependent on, the automobile.

Stabilization "The act or process of applying measures designed to reestablish a weather-resistant enclosure and the structural stability of unsafe or deteriorated property while maintaining the essential form as it exists at present" (Secretary of the Interior's Standards for Rehabilitation).

Standing to sue The doctrine stating that cases presented to a court must be concrete controversies between parties with a real stake in the dispute, such as a financial injury. In environmental matters, other parties may gain the right to sue.

State Historic Preservation Officer The SHPO in each state and U.S. territory carries out the nation's historic preservation program under the National Historic Preservation Act of 1966 by nominating properties to the National Register of Historic Places; reviewing applications for tax act certifications, which can qualify certified historic building rehabilitations for certain tax benefits; reviewing federal actions to determine their effect on historic properties; surveying and evaluating the state's architectural, archeological, historical, and cultural resources; and when funds are available, administering state or federal matching grants programs. The term "SHPO" often refers to the state office as well.

Statewide The statewide not-for-profit preservation organization that exists in most states. This organization has a volunteer board of directors and is usually a 501(c)(3) organization. The Statewide is to be distinguished from the State Historic Preservation Office, a public entity within state government.

Street furniture Municipal equipment placed along streets, including light fixtures, fire hydrants, police and fire call boxes, signs, benches, and kiosks.

Streetscape The distinguishing character of a particular street as created by its width, degree of curvature, paving materials, design of the street furniture, and forms of surrounding buildings.

Style A type of architecture distinguished by special characteristics of structure and ornament and often related in time; also, a general quality of distinctive character.

Sweat equity The investment of property owners' or occupants' own labor in rehabilitation work as a form of payment.

Taking The appropriation by government of private property, for example, condemnation through eminent domain for public use with just

Entrance, Howard University Divinity School (former Franciscan seminary), Washington, D.C.
(Carol M. Highsmith Photography)

compensation. A "taking issue" arises when the use of the police power appears to diminish the value of affected property, such as a decision under a preservation ordinance.

Tax incentive A tax reduction designed to encourage private investment in historic preservation and rehabilitation projects.

Thermal performance The ability of wall, roof, foundation, and other external building surfaces to regulate the exchange of heat or cold between the interior and exterior. Thermal performance is determined by the materials used as well as methods of construction.

Townscape The relationship of buildings, shapes, spaces, and textures that gives a town or area its distinctive visual character or image.

Underwater archeology A field of archeology concerned with the identification, analysis, and documentation of sites and properties submerged under water, for example, shipwrecks.

Vernacular buildings Buildings designed and built without the aid of an architect or trained designer; buildings whose design is based on ethnic, social, or cultural traditions rather than on an architectural philosophy.

Visual pollution Anything that, because of its placement or intrinsic nature, is offensive to the sense of sight, for example, garbage dumps and billboards.

Zoning code Local government regulation governing the use of land and buildings, setbacks, site coverage, and other aspects of land development.

Resources and Readings

This section provides reference information for publications and other works, listed by topic.

Ordering and contact information appears at the end of this section; in instances where materials are out of print or are otherwise unavailable, you are advised to check your local library.

Please note: all information contained in these pages is up to date and correct at the time of publication. Addresses, prices, and availability may change without notice.

ACCESSIBILITY

Accessibility and Historic Preservation: Entrances to the Past
Historic Windsor, Inc., 1993
VHS
$13.00
(To order, write: Historic Windsor, Inc., P.O. Box 1777, Windsor, VT 05089, or call (802) 674-6752.)

The Accessible Museum: Model Programs of Accessibility for Disabled and Older People
American Association of Museums, 1992
184 pages, Paper
Order Number YAX221

$40.00
ISBN: 0-931201-16-0

Everyone's Welcome: Universal Access in Museums
American Association of Museums, 1996
VHS
Order Number YUD217
$45.00
ISBN: 0-931201-32-2

The Impact of the Americans with Disabilities Act on Historic Structures
National Trust for Historic Preservation, 1991
Paper
Order Number 2155
$6.00
ISBN: 0-89133-328-2

Manual for Signs and Labels in the Metropolitan Museum of Art
American Association of Museums, 1996
56 pages, Paper
Order Number XRA849
$34.00
ISBN: 0-931201-37-3

Museums Without Barriers: A New Deal for the Disabled
Routledge, 1992
240 pages, Paper

Order Number YSA318
$30.00
ISBN: 0-415-06994-7

Preservation Briefs 32: Making Historic Properties Accessible
Thomas C. Jester and Sharon C. Park
National Trust for Historic Preservation, 1993
14 pages, Paper
GPO Stock Number 024-005-01121-8
$1.50

What Museum Guides Need to Know: Access for Blind and Visually Impaired Visitors
Gerda Groff and Laura Gardner
American Foundation for the Blind, 1989
62 pages, Paper
AAM Order Number YVA782
$17.00
ISBN: 0-89128-158-4

ADAPTIVE USE

BARN AGAIN! A Guide to Rehabilitation of Older Farm Buildings
National Trust for Historic Preservation, 1988
18 pages, Paper
Order Number 2BAR
$6.00

Curtain Up: New Life for Historic Theaters
National Trust for Historic Preservation, 1993
24 pages, Paper
Order Number 2I72
$6.00
ISBN: 0-89133-385-1

New Life for White Elephant Buildings
National Trust for Historic Preservation, 1996
24 pages, Paper
Order Number 2I95
$6.00
ISBN: 0-89133-366-5

Using Old Farm Buildings
National Trust for Historic Preservation, 1989
16 pages, Paper
Order Number 2I46
$6.00
ISBN: 0-89133-384-1

ADVOCACY

Successful State Advocacy
National Trust for Historic Preservation, 1996
16 pages, Paper
Order Number 2I52
$6.00
ISBN: 0-89133-366-5

APPRAISING

Appraising Historic Properties
National Trust for Historic Preservation, 1994
24 pages, Paper
Order Number 2I87
$6.00
ISBN: 0-89133-369-X

ARCHEOLOGY

Archeological Resource Protection
Sherry Hutt
Preservation Press/John Wiley & Sons, Inc., 1992

Detail of statue of lion in front of the New York Public Library, Manhattan, New York. *(Carol M. Highsmith Photography)*

176 pages, Paper
$19.95
ISBN: 0-471-14353-7

Archeology and Historic Preservation
National Trust for Historic Preservation, 1995
24 pages, Paper
Order Number 2I86
$6.00
ISBN: 0-89133-371-1

Protecting Archaeological Sites on Private Land
S. Henry
Interagency Resources Division, National Park Service, 1993

A Survey of State Statutes Protecting Archaeological Resources
Carol L. Carnett

National Trust for Historic Preservation, 1995
86 pages, Paper
$5.00

ARCHITECTURE

Architects House Themselves
Michael Webb
Preservation Press/John Wiley & Sons, Inc., 1994
224 pages, Cloth
$39.95
ISBN: 0-471-14356-1

Architectural Follies in America
Gwyn Headly
Preservation Press/John Wiley & Sons, Inc., 1996
224 pages, Paper
$19.95
ISBN: 0-471-14362-6

Curious Architecture
Preservation Press/John Wiley & Sons, Inc., 1995
20 full-color postcards
$7.95
ISBN: 0-471-14375-8

Discover America's Favorite Architects
Patricia Brown Glenn and Joe Stites
Preservation Press/John Wiley & Sons, Inc., 1996
80 illustrations
120 pages, Paper
$19.95
ISBN: 0-471-14354-5

Frank Lloyd Wright Domestic Architecture and Objects
Preservation Press/John Wiley & Sons, Inc., 1991
20 full-color postcards
$8.95
ISBN: 0-471-14501-7

Frank Lloyd Wright Remembered
Patrick J. Meehan
Preservation Press/John Wiley &
Sons, Inc., 1995
265 pages, Cloth
$29.95
ISBN: 0-471-14383-9

**Identifying American Architecture:
A Pictorial Guide to Styles and
Terms, 1600–1945**
John Blumenson
AltaMira Press/American
Association for State and Local
History, 1990
128 pages, Paper
$12.95
ISBN: 0-393-30610-0

**Main Street to Miracle Mile:
American Roadside Architecture,
Reprint Edition**
Chester H. Liebs
Johns Hopkins University Press,
1995
262 pages, Paper
$24.95
ISBN: 0-801-85095-9

**The National Trust Guide to Art
Deco in America**
David Gebhard
Preservation Press/John Wiley &
Sons, Inc., 1996
304 pages, Paper
$19.95
ISBN: 0-471-14386-3

**Understanding Architectural
Drawings**
John J. Cullinane
Preservation Press/John Wiley &
Sons, Inc., 1995
130 pages, Paper
$24.95
ISBN: 0-471-14429-0

**Usonia: Frank Lloyd Wright's
Design for America**
Alvin Rosenbaum
Preservation Press/John Wiley &
Sons, Inc., 1995

216 pages, Cloth
$29.95
ISBN: 0-471-14430-4

**What Style Is It?: A Guide to
American Architecture**
John Poppeliers
Preservation Press/John Wiley &
Sons, Inc., 1995
112 pages, Paper
$8.95
ISBN: 0-471-14434-7

BATTLEFIELDS

**The Dollars and Sense of Battlefield
Preservation**
Francis M. Kennedy
Preservation Press/John Wiley &
Sons, Inc., 1995
96 pages, Paper
$14.95
ISBN: 0-471-14378-2

BUILDING CODES

**Safety, Building Codes and Historic
Preservation**
National Trust for Historic
Preservation, 1996
16 pages, Paper
Order Number 2I57
$6.00
ISBN: 0-89133-366-5

CHILDREN'S LITERATURE

Archabet: An Architectural Alphabet
Balthazar Korab
Preservation Press/John Wiley &
Sons, Inc., 1995
64 pages, Cloth
$15.95
ISBN: 0-471-14351-0

**Archabet: An Architectural Alphabet
Postcard Book**
Balthazar Korab
Preservation Press/John Wiley &
Sons, Inc., 1995
26 postcards, Paper
$8.95

ISBN: 0-471-14352-9

Architects Make Zigzags
Roxie Munro
Preservation Press/John Wiley &
Sons, Inc., 1986
64 pages, Paper
48 illustrations
$9.95
ISBN: 0-471-14357-X

Architecture Animals
Michael J. Crosbie, Steve Rosenthal
Preservation Press/John Wiley &
Sons, Inc., 1995
12 photographs
$6.95
ISBN: 0-471-14358-8

Architecture Colors
Michael J. Crosbie, Steve Rosenthal
Preservation Press/John Wiley &
Sons, Inc., 1993
22 pages, Paper
$6.95
ISBN: 0-471-14359-6

Architecture Counts
Michael J. Crosbie, Steve Rosenthal
Preservation Press/John Wiley &
Sons, Inc., 1993
22 pages, Cloth
12 photographs
$6.95
ISBN: 0-471-14361-8

Architecture Shapes
Michael J. Crosbie, Steve Rosenthal
Preservation Press/John Wiley &
Sons, Inc., 1993
26 pages, Cloth
12 photographs
$6.95
ISBN: 0-471-14366-9

Bridges Go from Here to There
Forrest Wilson
Preservation Press/John Wiley &
Sons, Inc.
88 pages, Cloth
80 drawings
$16.95

ISBN: 0-471-14369-3

Daily Life in a Victorian House
Laura Wilson
Preservation Press/John Wiley &
Sons, Inc., 1993
48 pages, Cloth
100 photographs
$16.95
ISBN: 0-471-14377-4

**Discover America's Favorite
Architects**
Patricia Brown Glenn and Joe Stites
Preservation Press/John Wiley &
Sons, Inc., 1996
120 pages, Paper
80 illustrations
$19.95
ISBN: 0-471-14354-5

**The Great American Landmarks
Adventure**
Kay Weeks
National Park Service, 1992
48 pages, Paper
GPO Stock Number 024-005-01105-6
$3.25

I Know That Building!
Jane D'Alelio
Preservation Press/John Wiley &
Sons, Inc., 1995
88 pages, Paper
200 illustrations
$14.95
ISBN: 0-471-14396-0

Old House, New House
Herbert Camburn
Preservation Press/John Wiley &
Sons, Inc., 1995
56 pages, Paper
48 illustrations
$16.95
ISBN: 0-471-14408-8

Under Every Roof
Patricia Brown Glenn and Joe Stites
Preservation Press/John Wiley &
Sons, Inc., 1995
112 pages, Paper
170 drawings

$17.95
ISBN: 0-471-14428-2

What It Feels Like to Be a Building
Forrest Wilson
Preservation Press/John Wiley &
Sons, Inc., 1995
112 pages, Paper
76 illustrations
$10.95
ISBN: 0-471-14433-9

CONSERVATION

Conservation of Historic Buildings,
Revised Edition
Bernard M. Feilden
Butterworth Architecture
Paper
$59.95
ISBN: 0-750-61739-X

**Conserving Buildings: A Guide to
Techniques and Materials**
Martin E. Weaver and F. M. Matero
John Wiley & Sons, Inc., 1997
288 pages, Cloth
$74.95
ISBN: 0-471-50945-0

Essentials of Conservation
American Association of Museums
55 pages, Paper
AAM Order Number CCC198
$10.00

**Twentieth-Century Building
Materials: History and Conservation**
Thomas C. Jester
National Park Service, Preservation
Assistance and McGraw-Hill, 1995
$50.00

CULTURAL DIVERSITY

African American Historic Places
Beth L. Savage
623 pages, Paper
$25.95
ISBN: 0-471-14345-6

**America's Architectural Roots:
Ethnic Groups That Built America**
Dell Upton

Preservation Press/John Wiley &
Sons, Inc., 1986
196 pages, Paper
$10.95
ISBN: 0-471-14349-9

**Cultural and Ethnic Diversity in
Historic Preservation**
National Trust for Historic
Preservation, 1992
40 pages, Paper
Order Number 2I65
$6.00
ISBN: 0-89133-330-4

**Fostering Appreciation for Cultural
Diversity** (Featuring plenary
speakers from the 46th National
Preservation Conference in Miami)
National Trust for Historic
Preservation, 1992
Order Number 2VID
VHS
$25.00

DESIGN REVIEW

Building Improvement File
National Trust for Historic
Preservation, 1995
32 pages, Paper
Order Number MD-41
$28.00

**Design and Development: Infill
Housing Compatible with Historic
Neighborhoods**
National Trust for Historic
Preservation
Paper
Order Number 2I41
$6.00
ISBN: 0-89133-361-4

Design Review in Historic Districts
National Trust for Historic
Preservation, 1994
16 pages, Paper
Order Number 2I85
$6.00
ISBN: 0-89133-357-6

Developing Downtown Design Guidelines
National Trust for Historic Preservation, 1988
52 pages, Paper
Order Number MR-42
$18.00

Factory-Built Housing: Finding a Home in Historic Neighborhoods
National Trust for Historic Preservation
Paper
Order Number 2I43
$6.00
ISBN: 0-89133-360-6

Guiding Design on Main Street: Buildings
National Trust for Historic Preservation, 1994
120 pages, Paper
60 Slides
Order Number MD-40
$78.00
ISBN: 0-16-035979-1

Illustrated Guidelines for Rehabilitating Historic Buildings and the Secretary of the Interior's Standards for Rehabilitation
National Trust for Historic Preservation
120 pages, Paper
Order Number MR-50
$18.00

Main Street Guidelines: Design
National Trust for Historic Preservation
75 pages, Paper
Order Number MD-44
$40.00

Master Builders
Roger K. Lewis
Preservation Press/John Wiley & Sons, Inc., 1985
204 pages, Paper and VHS
$10.95
ISBN: 0-471-14402-9

DIRECTORIES

1996 Directory of Private Nonprofit Statewide Preservation Organizations
National Trust for Historic Preservation, 1996
Order Number 2I81
36 pages, Paper
$6.00
ISBN: 0-89133-364-9

1995 Directory of Staffed Local Preservation Organizations
National Trust for Historic Preservation, 1995
48 pages, Paper
Order Number 2I91
$6.00
ISBN: 0-89133-368-1

University and College Museums, Galleries, and Related Facilities: A Descriptive Directory
Victor J. Danilov
Greenwood Press, 1996
692 pages, Cloth
AAM Order Number RUC793
$99.50
ISBN: 0-313-28613-2

DISASTERS

Controlling Disaster: Earthquake-Hazard Reduction for Historic Buildings
National Trust for Historic Preservation, 1992
16 pages, Paper
Order Number 2I61
$6.00
ISBN: 0-89133-333-9

Hurricane Readiness Guide for Owners and Managers of Historic Resources
National Trust for Historic Preservation, 1997
24 pages, Paper
Order Number 2I97
ISBN: 0-89133-390-8

1991 Disaster Preparedness Seminar Proceedings
Pamela Meister
Southeastern Museums Conference, 1991
165 pages, Paper
AAM Order Number SSS335

PREP: Planning for Response and Emergency Preparedness
Mary Candee and Richard Casagrande
Texas Association of Museums, 1993
334 pages
AAM Order Number SPR772
$40.00
ISBN: 0-9352600-4-X

Protecting the Past from Natural Disasters
Carl Nelson
Preservation Press/John Wiley & Sons, Inc., 1991
192 pages, Paper
$174.95
ISBN: 0-471-14416-9

Treatment of Flood-Damaged Older and Historic Buildings
National Trust for Historic Preservation, 1993
12 pages, Paper
Order Number 2I82
$6.00

DOCUMENTATION

Introduction to Photographing Historic Properties
National Trust for Historic Preservation, 1988
15 pages, Paper
Order Number 2I42
$6.00
ISBN: 0-89133-337-1

Photogrammetric Recording of Cultural Resources
Perry E. Borchers
U.S. Department of Commerce,

National Technical Information
Service, 1977
38 pages
National Technical Information
Service Order Number PB85-180792
$17.50

Recording Historic Structures
John E. Burns
AIA Press, 1989
246 pages, Cloth
Order Number R743P
$19.95
ISBN: 1-558-35018-7
(To order, call: 1-800-365-2724)

**Rectified Photography and Photo
Drawings for Historic Preservation**
J. Henry Chambers
U.S. Department of Commerce,
National Technical Information
Service, 1973
38 pages
National Technical Information
Service Order Number PB87-232146
$17.50

**Using Photogrammetry to Monitor
Materials Deterioration and
Structural Problems on Historic
Buildings: Dorchester Heights
Monument, A Case Study**
J. Henry Chambers
U.S. Department of Commerce,
National Technical Information
Service, 1985
National Technical Information
Service Order Number PB87-232146
$17.50

DOWNTOWN
REVITALIZATION

**America's Downtowns: Growth,
Politics, and Preservation**
Richard C. Collins, Elizabeth B.
Waters, and Anthony Bruce Dotson
Preservation Press/John Wiley &
Sons, Inc., 1991
162 pages, Paper
$14.95
ISBN: 0-471-14499-1

Gingerbread house with simulated thatched roof, Tyringham, Massachusetts. *(Carol
M. Highsmith Photography)*

Building the Streetscape: Slide Show
National Trust for Historic
Preservation, 1996
40 slides
Order Number MS-14
$48.00

**Creative Promotion Ideas for Main
Street**
National Trust for Historic
Preservation, 1995
32 pages, Paper
Order Number MD-30
$32.00

**Fill-in-the-Blank Business
Recruitment: A Workbook for
Downtown Business Development**
National Trust for Historic
Preservation, 1995
102 pages, Paper
Order Number MD-82
$40.00

The Living City
Roberta Brandes Gratz

Preservation Press/John Wiley &
Sons, Inc., 1994
448 pages, Paper
$16.95
ISBN: 0-471-14425-8

**Living on Main Street: Lessons in
Livability from Oregon's Downtown
Districts**
National Trust for Historic
Preservation, 1994
44 pages, Paper
Order Number MR-86
$25.00

**Local Businesses: Exploring Their
History**
K. Austin Kerr, Amos J. Loveday,
and Mansel G. Blackford
AltaMira Press/American
Association for State and Local
History, 1990
128 pages, Paper
$16.95
ISBN: 0-9420630-9-0

The Main Street Approach: Slide Show
National Trust for Historic Preservation, 1996
78 Slides
Order Number MS-16
$70.00

Main Street at Work: Video Set
National Trust for Historic Preservation, 1985
VHS
Order Number MD-17
$55.00

Main Street Success Stories
National Trust for Historic Preservation, 1996
100 pages
Order Number MS-01
$58.00

Marketing an Image for Main Street
National Trust for Historic Preservation, 1995
114 pages, Paper
Order Number MD-31
$32.00

Public Markets and Community Revitalization
National Trust for Historic Preservation, 1995
128 pages, Paper
Order Number MR-63
$28.00

Public Places: Exploring Their History
Gerald A. Danzer
AltaMira Press/American Association for State and Local History, 1987
152 pages, Paper
$16.95
ISBN: 0-9100508-8-0

Revitalizing Downtown
National Trust for Historic Preservation, 1996
200 pages, Paper
Order Number MS-10
$40.00

Signs of a Successful Main Street: Slide Show
National Trust for Historic Preservation, 1996
40 slides
Order Number MS-21
$48.00

Step-by-Step Market Analysis: A Workbook for Downtown Business Development
National Trust for Historic Preservation, 1995
76 pages
Order Number MD-81
$40.00

EASEMENTS

Appraising Easements: Guidelines for Valuation of Historic Preservation and Land Conservation Easements
National Trust for Historic Preservation and Land Trust Alliance, 1990
82 pages, Paper
$17.00
(To order, write: 1319 F Street, N.W. Suite 501, Washington, DC 20004)

The Conservation Easement Handbook: Managing Land Conservation and Historic Preservation Easement Programs
J. Diehl and T. Barrrett
Land Trust Exchange and Trust for Public Land, 1988
269 pages, Paper
$35.00
(To order, write: 1319 F Street, N.W. Suite 501, Washington, DC 20004)

The Conservation Easement Stewardship Guide: Designing, Monitoring, and Enforcing Easements
B. Lind
Land Trust Alliance and Trust for New Hampshire Lands, 1991

107 pages, Paper
$16.00
(To order, write: 1319 F Street, N.W. Suite 501, Washington, DC 20004)

Establishing an Easement Program to Protect Historic, Scenic and Natural Resources
National Trust for Historic Preservation, 1995
20 pages, Paper
Order Number 2I25
$6.00
ISBN: 0-89133-338-X

The Federal Tax Law of Conservation Easements
Stephen Small
The Land Trust Exchange, 1986
Supplement, 1989
437 pages, Cloth
$69.00
(To order, write: 1319 F Street, N.W. Suite 501, Washington, DC 20004)

ECONOMIC REVITALIZATION

The Economics of Historic Preservation: A Community Leader's Guide
National Trust for Historic Preservation, 1994
130 pages, Paper
Order Number 2ECO
$20.00
ISBN: 0-89133-388-6

The Economics of Rehabilitation
National Trust for Historic Preservation, 1991
24 pages, Paper
Order Number 2I53
$6.00
ISBN: 0-89133-326-6

ENVIRONMENTAL ISSUES

In Search of Collaboration: Historic Preservation and the Environmental Movement
National Trust for Historic Preservation, 1992

16 pages, Paper
Order Number 2I71
$6.00
ISBN: 0-89133-340-1

FUNDRAISING

Achieving Excellence in Fund Raising: A Comprehensive Guide to Priciples, Strategies, and Methods
Henry A. Rosso and Associates
Jossey-Bass Inc., 1991
319 pages, Cloth
AAM Order Number DDD300
$43.00
ISBN: 1-55542-387-6

The Big Book of Museum Grant Money
American Association of Museums, 1995
2000 pages
AAM Order Number DDR845
$125.00

The Board Member's Guide to Fund Raising: What Every Trustee Needs to Know About Raising Money
Fisher Howe
Jossey-Bass, Inc., 1991
168 pages, Cloth
AAM Order Number DGD664
$26.00
ISBN: 1-55542-322-1

Don't Just Applaud—Send Money!
Alvin Reiss
Theatre Communications Group, 1995
146 pages, Paper
AAM Order Number DDJ760
$16.00
ISBN: 1-55936-105-0

Fund Raising and the Nonprofit Board Member
Fisher Howe
National Conference for Nonprofit Boards, 1988
13 pages, Paper
AAM Order Number DGD794

$11.00
ISBN: 0-925299-02-0

Fundraising for Non-Profits: How to Build a Community Partnership
HarperPerennial, 1990
214 pages, Paper
Order Number MS-12
$18.00
ISBN: 0-06-273205-6

Fund-Raising Fundamentals: A Guide to Annual Giving for Professionals and Volunteers
James M. Greenfield
John Wiley & Sons, Inc., 1994
416 pages, Paper
AAM Order Number DFD3306
$25.00
ISBN: 0-471-59534-9

Grant Proposals That Succeed
Virginia White
Plenum Press, 1983
240 pages, Cloth
AAM Order Number DDD748
$35.00
ISBN: 0-3-6-40873-2

The "How To" Grants Manual: Successful Grant Seeking Techniques for Obtaining Public and Private Grants
David G. Bauer
American Council on Education/Oryx Press, 1995
248 pages, Cloth
AAM Order Number DDD3304
$30.00
ISBN: 0-89774-801-8

Keep the Money Coming: A Step-by-Step Strategic Guide to Annual Fund-Raising
Christine Graham
Pineapple Press, Inc., 1992
127 pages, Paper
AAM Order Number DDD381
$19.00
ISBN: 1-56164-025-5

Main Street Fund-Raising Kit
National Trust for Historic Preservation
Order Number MR-22
$54

Membership Development: A Guide for Nonprofit Preservation Organizations
National Trust for Historic Preservation, 1996
16 pages, Paper
Order Number 2I49
$6.00
ISBN: 0-89133-349-5

Proposal Planning and Writing
Lynn E. Miner and Jerry Griffith
Oryx Press, 1993
153 pages, Paper
AAM Order Number DDD3304
$29.50
ISBN: 0-89774-726-7

Quest for Funds Revisited: A Fund-Raising Starter Kit
National Trust for Historic Preservation, 1993
32 pages, Paper
Order Number 2I75
$6.00
ISBN: 0-89133-346-0

Share Your Success: Fund-Raising Ideas
National Trust for Historic Preservation, 1993
20 pages, Paper
Order Number 2I80
$6.00
ISBN: 0-89133-344-4

Speaking of Money: A Guide to Fund Raising for Non-Profit Board Members
National Center for Non-Profit Boards, 1996
VHS
AAM Order Number DSM773
$59.00

Successful Fundraising: A Complete
Handbook for Volunteers and
Professionals
Contemporary Books, 1993
295 pages, Paper
Order Number MS-11
$18.00
ISBN: 0-8092-4090-4

Where the Money Is: A Fund
Raiser's Guide to the Rich
Helen J. Bergan
BioGuide Press, 1992
257 pages, Paper
AAM Order Number DDD358
$30.00
ISBN: 0-9615277-6-5

GAMING

High Stakes Decision Making:
Understanding the Choices Your
Community Can Make
National Trust for Historic
Preservation, 1992
61 pages, Paper
Order Number 2I08
$20.00

GROWTH MANAGEMENT

Back Against the Wall
Co-sponsored by the Preservation
Trust of Vermont and the Vermont
Natural Resources Council, 1994
Order Number 2WAL
VHS
$10.00

How Superstore Sprawl Can Harm
Communities (And What Citizens
Can Do About It)
National Trust for Historic
Preservation, 1997
120 pages, Paper
Order Number 2SUP
$15.00
ISBN: 0-89133-392-4

Smart States, Better Communities
Constance E. Beaumont

National Trust for Historic
Preservation, 1996
394 pages, Paper
$30.00
ISBN: 0-89133-356-8

Up Against the Wal-Marts: How
Your Business Can Prosper in the
Shadow of the Retail Giants
National Trust for Historic
Preservation, 1994
260 pages, Paper
Order Number MR-72
$22.00

GUIDEBOOKS

Guide to New York City Landmarks
New York City Landmarks
Preservation Commission
Preservation Press/John Wiley &
Sons, Inc., 1992
256 pages, Paper
$9.95
ISBN: 0-471-14391-X

The National Trust Guide to Historic
Bed & Breakfasts, Inns, and Small
Hotels, Fourth Edition
National Trust for Historic
Preservation
Preservation Press/John Wiley &
Sons, Inc., 1996
576 pages, Paper
$18.95
ISBN: 0-471-14973-X

The National Trust Guide to New
Orleans
Roulhac Toledano
Preservation Press/John Wiley &
Sons, Inc., 1996
208 pages, Paper
$17.95
ISBN: 0-471-14404-5

Old Greenwich Village: An
Architectural Portrait
Steve Gross
Preservation Press/John Wiley &
Sons, Inc., 1995

128 pages, Paper
$24.95
ISBN: 0-471-14406-1
128 pages, Cloth
$39.95
ISBN: 0-471-14405-3

HAZARDOUS MATERIALS

Coping with Contamination: A
Primer for Preservationists
National Trust for Historic
Preservation, 1993
28 pages, Paper
Order Number 2I70
$6.00
ISBN: 0-89133-325-8

Preservation Briefs 37: Appropriate
Methods of Reducing Lead-Paint
Hazards in Historic Housing
Sharon C. Park and Douglas C.
Hicks
National Park Service, 1995
16 pages, Paper
GPO Stock Number 024-005-01149-8
$1.75

HERITAGE CORRIDORS

Regional Heritage Areas:
Approaches to Sustainable
Development
National Trust for Historic
Preservation, 1994
48 pages, Paper
Order Number 2I88
$6.00
ISBN: 0-89133-372-X

HISTORIC DISTRICTS

Design Review in Historic Districts
National Trust for Historic
Preservation
16 pages, Paper
Order Number 2I85
$6.00
ISBN: 0-89133-357-6

Maintaining Community Character:
How to Establish a Local Historic
District
National Trust for Historic
Preservation, 1996
27 pages, Paper
Order Number 2I58
$6.00
ISBN: 0-89133-358-4

Reviewing New Construction
Projects in Historic Areas
National Trust for Historic
Preservation, 1992
24 pages, Paper
Order Number 2I62
$6.00
ISBN: 0-89133-359-2

Saving Face: How Corporate
Franchise Design Can Respect
Community Identity
National Trust for Historic
Preservation
70 pages
Order Number MR-54
$24.00

Sign Regulations for Small
Communities
National Trust for Historic
Preservation, 1989
42 pages
Order Number MR-53
$24.00

HISTORIC HOMES

Appraising Historic Properties
National Trust for Historic
Preservation, 1994
24 pages, Paper
Order Number 2I89
$6.00
ISBN: 0-89133-373-8

The *New* Old House Starter Ket
National Trust for Historic
Preservation, 1997
20 pages, Paper
Order Number 2I96

$6.00
ISBN: 0-89133-391-6

Inspecting an Old House Before You
Buy
National Trust for Historic
Preservation
Preservation Press/John Wiley &
Sons, Inc., 1994
VHS
$29.95
ISBN: 0-471-14397-9

INCENTIVES

Affordable Housing Through
Historic Preservation: A Case Study
Guide to Combining the Tax Credits
Susan Escheric and William Delvac
National Park Service, 1994
74 pages, Paper
GPO Stock Number 024-005-01148
$3.50
ISBN: 0-16045-258-9

A Guide to Tax-Advantaged
Rehabilitation
National Trust for Historic
Preservation, 1996
12 pages, Paper
Order Number 2I89
$6.00
ISBN: 0-89133-370-3

Historic Preservation Certification
Application
National Park Service, Preservation
Assistance Division
(To order, write: National Park
Service, Preservation Assistance
Division, P.O. Box 37127,
Washington, DC 20013.)
No charge

Local Incentives for Historic
Preservation
Constance E. Beaumont
National Trust for Historic
Preservation, 1991
20 pages, Paper
No charge

Preservation Tax Incentives for
Historic Buildings: Current Fiscal
Analysis
National Park Service, Preservation
Assistance Division
(To order, write: National Park
Service, Preservation Assistance
Division, P.O. Box 37127,
Washington, DC 20013.)
No charge

Preservation Tax Incentives for
Rehabilitating Historic Buildings
National Park Service, Preservation
Assistance Division
(To order, write: National Park
Service, Preservation Assistance
Division, P.O. Box 37127,
Washington, DC 20013.)
No charge

Preserving and Revitalizing Older
Communities: Sources of Federal
Assistance
Leslie Slavitt
National Park Service, 1993
161 pages
GPO Stock Number 024-005-01129-3
$11.00

Protecting and Preserving
Communities: Preservation
Revolving Funds
Office of Financial Services,
National Trust for Historic
Preservation, 1994
No charge

Tax Incentives for Rehabilitating
Historic Buildings: Current Fiscal
Year Analysis
National Park Service, Preservation
Assistance Division
(To order, write: National Park
Service, Preservation Assistance
Division, P.O. Box 37127,
Washington, DC 20013)
No charge

Using the Community Reinvestment
Act in Low-Income Historic
Neighborhoods
National Trust for Historic
Preservation, 1992
24 pages, Paper
Order Number 2I59
$6.00
ISBN: 0-89133-336-3

INDUSTRIAL SITES

Great American Bridges and Dams
Donald C. Jackson
Preservation Press/John Wiley &
Sons, Inc., 1988
360 pages, Paper
$19.95
ISBN: 0-471-14385-5

INSPECTION

**X-Ray Examination of Historic
Structures**
David M. Hart
U.S. Department of Commerce,
National Technical Information
Service, 1975
24 pages
National Technical Information
Service Order Number PB85-180800
$17.50

LANDSCAPES

**American Landscape Architecture:
Designers and Places**
William H. Tishler
Preservation Press/John Wiley &
Sons, Inc., 1995
240 pages, Paper
$10.95
ISBN: 0-471-14348-0

**Landscapes and Gardens for Historic
Buildings: A Handbook for
Reproducing and Creating
Authentic Landscape Settings**
Rudy J. Favretti and Joy Putnam
Favretti

AltaMira Press/American
Association for State and Local
History, 1991
212 pages, Paper
$24.95
ISBN: 0-942063-10-4

**The Landscape Universe: Historic
Designed Landscapes in Context**
Charles A. Birnbaum
National Park Service, 1994
113 pages
$16.95
(To order, write: Wave Hill, Catalog
of Landscape Records, 675 West
252nd Street, Bronx, NY 10471)

**Preservation Briefs 36: Protecting
Cultural Landscapes: Planning,
Treatment, and Management of
Historic Landscapes**
Charles A. Birnbaum
National Park Service, 1994
16 pages, Paper
GPO Stock Number 024-005-01144-7
$1.50

LAND-USE LAWS AND PRESERVATION

Aesthetics and Land Use Controls
C. Duerkson
American Planning Association PAS
Report No. 399, 1986

**Coordination of Historic
Preservation and Land-Use Controls:
New Directions in Historic
Preservation Regulation.**
Reprinted from *Preservation Law
Reporter*
J. Miller
National Trust for Historic
Preservation, 1986–87

**Transferrable Development Rights
Programs: TDRs and the Real Estate
Marketplace.**
C. Ingrahm
American Planning Association PAS
Report No. 401, 1987

LAND-USE PLANNING

**Participation Tools for Better Land-
Use Planning**
National Trust for Historic
Preservation
38 pages
Order Number MS-19
$20.00

**The Practice of Local Government
Planning, Second Edition**
Frank S. So and Judith Getzels
International City/County
Management Association
Cloth
$39.95
ISBN: 0-873-26077-5

LEGAL ISSUES

**Avoiding Takings Challenges While
Protecting Historic Properties from
Demolition**
Thomas W. Logue
Stetson Law Review
Summer 1990
30 pages, Paper

**Hunting for Quarks: Constitutional
Takings, Property Rights, and
Government Regulation**
Jerold S. Kayden
Journal of Urban and Contemporary
Law, Volume 50, 1996
15 pages, Paper

**Legal Considerations in Establishing
a Historic Preservation Organization**
National Trust for Historic
Preservation, 1994
24 pages, Paper
Order Number 2I14
$6.00

LEGISLATION

**Federal Historic Preservation Case
Law: A Special Report**
Charlotte R. Bell
Advisory Council on Historic
Preservation, 1985

88 pages, Paper
GPO Stock Number 479-803-8143250-4

Federal Historic Preservation Laws
Sara K. Blumenthal and Emogene A. Bevitt
National Park Service, 1993
96 pages
Order Number 024-005-01124-2
$3.00

A Handbook on Historic Preservation Law
Christopher Duerksen, Editor
Conservation Foundation
Paper
$30.00
ISBN: 0-891-64079-7

Local Government and Historic Preservation
National Trust for Historic Preservation
Order Number 2LOC
$10.00

Preparing a Historic Preservation Ordinance
Richard J. Roddewig
American Planning Association, 1983
Paper
$26.00
ISBN: 9-994-63353-8

Successful State Advocacy
National Trust for Historic Preservation, 1996
Paper
Order Number 2I52
$6.00
ISBN: 0-89133-366-5

Takings Law in Plain English
National Trust for Historic Preservation, 1994
45 pages, Paper
Order Number 2TAK
$24.00

LOCAL HISTORIC PRESERVATION ORDINANCES

A Citizen's Guide to Protecting Historic Places: Local Preservation Ordinances
Contance E. Beaumont
National Trust for Historic Preservation, 1992
21 pages, Paper

Preparing a Preservation Ordinance
R. Roddewig
American Planning Association PAS Report No. 374, 1983

Preparing a Preservation Plan
B. White and R. Roddewig
American Planning Association PAS Report No. 450, 1994

MAINTENANCE

Adhesives and Coatings (The Science for Conservators Series, Volume 3)
Routledge, 1992
140 pages, Paper
AAM Order Number CCC376
$20.00
ISBN: 0-415-07163-1

Boats: A Manual for Their Documentation
Paul Lipke, Peter Spectre, and Benjamin A. G. Fuller
AltaMira Press/American Association for State and Local History, 1993
415 pages, Paper
$39.95
ISBN: 0-942063-17-1

The Care of Antiques and Historical Collections
A. Bruce MacLeish
AltaMira Press/American Association for State and Local History, 1985
250 pages, Paper
$16.95

Care of Collections
Simon Knell
Routledge, 1994
304 pages, Paper
AAM Order Number CCC715
$30.00
ISBN: 0-415-11285-0

Caring for Your Old House: A Guide for Owners and Residents (Respectful Rehabilitation)
Judith L. Kitchen
Preservation Press/John Wiley & Sons, Inc., 1991
208 pages, Paper
$16.95
ISBN: 0-471-14371-5

Cleaning (The Science for Conservators Series, Volume 2)
Routledge, 1992
136 pages, Paper
AAM Order Number CCC376
$20.00
ISBN: 0-415-07163-1

The Complete Sourcebook: A Comprehensive Guide to Building and Decorating Resources
Jay Fruin
Microtronics, 1995
$29.95
ISBN: 0-9645594-0-4

Cyclical Maintenance for Historic Buildings
J. Henry Chambers
U.S. Department of Commerce, National Technical Information Service, 1976
125 pages
National Technical Information Service Order Number PB87-118659
$27.00

Dictionary of Building Preservation
Ward Bucher
Preservation Press/John Wiley & Sons, Inc., 1996
500 pages, Cloth
$39.95
ISBN: 0-471-14413-4

Epoxies for Wood Repairs in Historic Buildings
Morgan W. Phillips and Judith E. Selwyn
U.S. Department of Commerce, National Technical Information Service, 1978
72 pages
National Technical Information Service Order Number PB85-180834
$19.50

Exterior Woodwork No. 4: Protecting Woodwork Against Decay Using Borate Preservatives
Ron Sheetz and Charles Fisher
National Park Service, Preservation Assistance Division, 1993
No charge
(To order, write: National Park Service, Preservation Assistance Division, P.O. Box 37127, Washington, DC 20013)

Gaslighting in America: A Guide to Historic Preservation
Denys Peter Myers
Dover Publications
279 pages
$16.95
(To order, write: 31 East Second Street, Mineola, NY 11051)

A Glossary of Historic Masonry Deterioration Problems and Preservation Treatments
Anne E. Grimmer
U.S. Department of Commerce, National Technical Information Service, 1984
68 pages
Order Number PB92-147172
$19.50

An Introduction to Materials (The Science for Conservators Series, Volume 1)
Routledge, 1992
120 pages, Paper
AAM Order Number CCC374
$20.00
ISBN: 0-415-07167-4

Keeping It Clean: Removing Dirt, Paint, Stains, and Graffiti from Historic Exterior Masonry
Anne E. Grimmer
National Park Service, 1987
45 pages
GPO Stock Number 024-005-01035-1
$2.50

Maintaining Your Old House
National Trust for Historic Preservation
Preservation Press/John Wiley & Sons, Inc., 1995
VHS
$29.95
ISBN: 0-471-14400-2

Masonry: How to Care for Old and Historic Brick and Stone
Mark London
Preservation Press/John Wiley & Sons, Inc., 1988
208 pages, Paper
$12.95
ISBN: 0-471-14401-0

Masonry No. 3: Water-Soak Cleaning of Historic Limestone
Robert Powers
National Park Service, Preservation Assistance Division, 1992
No charge
(To order, write: National Park Service, Preservation Assistance Division, P.O. Box 37127, Washington, DC 20013)

Metals in America's Historic Buildings: Uses and Preservation Treatments
Margot Gayle, David W. Look, and John G. Waite
National Park Service, 1992
168 pages
GPO Stock Number 024-005-01108-1
$10.00

Moisture Problems in Historic Masonry Walls: Diagnosis and Treatment
Baird M. Smith
National Park Service, 1984

48 pages, Paper
GPO Stock Number 024-005-00872-1
$2.25

Moving Historic Buildings
John Obed Curtis
International Association of Structural Movers, 1991
50 pages, Paper
$2.50
(To order, write: Carl Tuxill, IASM, P.O. Box 1213, Elbridge, NY 13060)

The 1996 Old-House Journal Restoration Directory
Old-House Books
Dovetail Publishers, 1995
274 pages, Paper
$14.95
ISSN: 1077-2332

Preservation Briefs 24: Heating, Ventilation, and Cooling Historic Buildings: Problems and Recommended Approaches
Sharon C. Park
National Park Service, 1991
14 pages, Paper
GPO Stock Number 024-005-01090-4
$1.00

Preservation Briefs 25: The Preservation of Historic Signs
Michael J. Auer
National Park Service, 1991
12 pages, Paper
GPO Stock Number 024-005-01086-6
$1.00

Preservation Briefs 26: The Preservation and Repair of Historic Log Buildings
Bruce L. Bomberger
National Park Service, 1991
14 pages, Paper
GPO Stock Number 024-005-01087-4
$1.00

Preservation Briefs 27: The Maintenance and Repair of Architectural Cast Iron
John G. Waite
National Park Service, 1991

12 pages, Paper
GPO Stock Number 023-005-01088-2
$1.00

**Preservation Briefs 28: Painting
Historic Interiors**
Sara B. Chase
National Park Service, 1992
16 pages, Paper
GPO Stock Number 024-005-01089-1
$1.00

**Preservation Briefs 29: The Repair,
Replacement, and Maintenance of
Slate Roofs**
Jeffrey S. Levine
National Park Service, 1992
16 pages, Paper
GPO Stock Number 024-005-01109-9
$1.25

**Preservation Briefs 30: The
Preservation and Repair of Historic
Clay Tile Roofs**
Anne E. Grimmer and Paul K.
Williams
National Park Service, 1992
16 pages, Paper
GPO Stock Number 024-005-01110-2
$1.25

**Preservation Briefs 31: Mothballing
Historic Buildings**
Sharon C. Park
National Park Service
14 pages, Paper
GPO Stock Number 024-005-01120-0
$1.50

**Preservation Briefs 33: The
Preservation and Repair of Stained
and Leaded Glass**
Neal A. Vogel and Rolf Achilles
National Park Service, 1993
16 pages, Paper
GPO Stock Number 024-005-01122-6
$1.50

**Preservation Briefs 34: Applied
Decoration for Historic Interiors:
Preserving Historic Composition
Ornament**

Jonathan Thornton and William
Adair
National Park Service, 1994
16 pages, Paper
GPO Stock Number 024-005-01137-4
$1.50

**Repairing Old and Historic
Windows**
New York Landmarks Conservancy
Preservation Press/John Wiley &
Sons, Inc., 1992
208 pages, Paper
$24.95
ISBN: 0-471-14418-5

**Respectful Rehabilitation: Answers
to Your Questions About Old
Buildings**
Kay D. Weeks and Diane Maddex
Preservation Press/John Wiley &
Sons, Inc., 1982
200 pages, Paper
$14.95
ISBN: 0-471-14419-3

**Temporary Protection No. 2:
"Specifying Temporary Protection
of Historic Interiors During
Construction and Repair**
Dale Frens
National Park Service, Preservation
Assistance Division, 1993
Paper
No charge
(To order, write: National Park
Service, Preservation Assistance
Division, P.O. Box 37127,
Washington, DC 20013)

**Walls and Molding: How to Care for
Old and Historic Buildings**
Natalie Shivers
Preservation Press/John Wiley &
Sons, Inc., 1990
198 pages, Paper
$16.95
ISBN: 0-471-14432-0

**The Window Handbook: Successful
Strategies for Rehabilitating
Windows in Historic Buildings**

Charles Fisher, Editor
National Park Service and the
Center for Architectural
Conservation, Georgia Institute of
Technology
$30.00
(To order, write: The Window
Handbook, HPEF, P.O. Box 27080,
Central Station, Washington, DC
20038)

MARITIME

Great American Lighthouses
F. Ross Holland
Preservation Press/John Wiley &
Sons, Inc.
350 pages, Paper
$19.95
ISBN: 0-471-14387-1

Great American Ships
James P. Delgado
Preservation Press/John Wiley &
Sons, Inc., 1991
312 pages, Paper
$19.95
ISBN: 0-471-14384-7

MILITARY INSTALLATIONS

**Base Closures and Historic
Preservation: A Guide for
Communities**
National Trust for Historic
Preservation, 1996
19 pages, Paper
Order Number 2I92
$6.00
ISBN: 0-89133-363-0

**A Moment of Silence: Arlington
National Cemetery**
Owen Andrews and Cameron
Davidson
Preservation Press/John Wiley &
Sons, Inc., 1994
64 pages, Cloth
$14.95
ISBN: 0-471-14367-7

MUSEUM PROPERTIES

Conservation in Context: Finding a Balance for the Historic House Museum
Wendy Claire Jessup
National Trust for Historic Preservation, 1995
84 pages, Paper
Check your library

Historic House Museums: A Practical Handbook for Their Care, Preservation, and Management
Sherry Butcher-Younghans
Oxford University Press, 1996
269 pages, Paper
AAM Order Number CSM628
$17.00
ISBN: 0-19-510660-1

History for Hire: Using Cultural Resources as Film Locations
National Trust for Historic Preservation, 1995
23 pages, Paper
Order Number 2I93
$6.00
ISBN: 0-89133-367-3

Interpretation of Historic Sites
William T. Alderson and Shirley Payne Low
AltaMira Press/American Association for State and Local History, 1985
202 pages, Paper
$19.95
ISBN: 0-761991-62-X

NATIONAL REGISTER

Guidelines for Completing National Register of Historic Places Forms.
U.S. Department of the Interior, National Park Service, Interagency Resources, 1991
National Register of Historic Places, 1966–1994
National Park Service
Preservation Press/John Wiley & Sons, Inc.

926 pages, Paper
$98.00
ISBN: 0-471-14403-7

NEIGHBORHOOD REVITALIZATION

Houses and Homes: Exploring Their History
Barbara J. Howe, Dolores A. Fleming, Emory L. Kemp, and Ruth Ann Overbeck
AltaMira Press/American Association for State and Local History, 1987
168 pages, Paper
$16.95
ISBN: 0-9100508-4-8

Houses by Mail
Katherine Cole Stevenson
Preservation Press/John Wiley & Sons, Inc., 1995
368 pages, Paper and VHS
$24.95
ISBN: 0-471-14394-4

The *New* Old House Starter Kit
National Trust for Historic Preservation, 1997
20 pages, Paper
Order Number 2I96
$6.00
ISBN: 0-89133-391-6

Saving the Neighborhood: You *Can* Fight Developers and Win
Peggy Robin
Preservation Press/John Wiley & Sons, Inc., 1990
428 pages, Paper
$16.95
ISBN: 0-471-14420-7

Using the Community Reinvestment Act in Low-Income Historic Neighborhoods
National Trust for Historic Preservation, 1992
24 pages, Paper
Order Number 2I56
$6.00
ISBN: 0-89133-336-3

ORAL HISTORY

Oral History: An Interdisciplinary Anthology
David K. Dunaway and Willa K. Baum
AltaMira Press/American Association for State and Local History, 1996
432 pages, Cloth
$22.95
ISBN: 0-761991-88-3

Oral History for the Local Historical Society
Willa K. Baum
AltaMira Press/American Association for State and Local History, 1987
80 pages, Paper
$12.95
ISBN: 0-761991-33-6

Recording Oral History: A Practical Guide for Social Scientists
Valerie Raleigh Yow
AltaMira Press/American Association for State and Local History, 1994
284 pages, Paper
$21.95
ISBN: 0-803955782

Transcribing and Editing Oral History
Willa K. Baum
AltaMira Press/American Association for State and Local History, 1991
128 pages, Paper
$14.95
ISBN: 0-9100502-6-0

ORGANIZATIONAL DEVELOPMENT

Building on Experience: Improving Organizational Capacity to Handle Devleopment Projects
National Trust for Historic Preservation, 1985
15 pages, Paper
Order Number 2I39

$6.00

**Building Support Through Public
Relations: A Guide for Nonprofit
Preservation Organizations**
National Trust for Historic
Preservation, 1992
24 pages, Paper
Order Number 2163
$6.00
ISBN: 0-89133-378-9

**The Good Guide: A Source-Book for
Interpreters, Docents and Tour
Guides**
Alison L. Grinder and E. Sue McCoy
Ironwood Publishing, 1985
163 pages, Paper
AAM Order Number VPA784
$16.00
ISBN: 0-932541-00-3

**A Guide to Effective Volunteer
Management**
National Trust for Historic
Preservation, 1995
20 pages, Paper
Order Number 2137
$6.00
ISBN: 0-89133-342-8

**Leadership and Management of
Volunteer Programs: A Guide for
Volunteer Administrators**
James C. Fisher and Kathleen M.
Cole
Jossey-Bass, Inc., 1993
208 pages, Cloth
AAM Order Number VHV389
$24.00
ISBN: 1-55542-531-3

**Personnel Issues for Preservation
Nonprofit Organizations**
National Trust for Historic
Preservation, 1994
24 pages, Paper
Order Number 2179
$6.00
ISBN: 0-89133-345-2

Ironwork entrance lights at the Boston Public Library, Copley Square, Boston,
Massachusetts. *(Carol M. Highsmith Photography)*

**A Primer for Local Historical
Societies**
Laurence R. Pizer
AltaMira Press/American
Association for State and Local
History, 1991
122 pages, Paper
$19.95
ISBN: 0-942063-12-0

**Recruiting and Retaining a Diverse
Staff**
American Association of Museums,
1995
100 pages, Paper
AAM Order Number HHT834
$25.00

**Rescuing Historic Resources: How
to Respond to a Preservation
Emergency**
National Trust for Historic
Preservation, 1991
20 pages, Paper
Order Number 2151

$6.00
ISBN: 0-89133-327-4

**Risk Management and Liability
Insurance for Nonprofit
Preservation Organizations**
National Trust for Historic
Preservation, 1995
20 pages, Paper
Order Number 2190
$6.00
ISBN: 0-89133-343-6

**A Self-Assessment Guide for
Community Preservation
Organizations**
National Trust for Historic
Preservation, 1989
20 pages, Paper
Order Number 2145
$6.00
ISBN: 0-89133-375-4

Six Keys to Recruiting, Orienting, and Involving Nonprofit Board Members
National Trust for Historic Preservation, 1996
63 pages, Paper
Item Number MS-09
$40.00
ISBN: 0-925299-64-2

Steering Nonprofits: Advice for Boards and Staff
National Trust for Historic Preservation, 1991
16 pages, Paper
Order Number 2I54
$6.00
ISBN: 0-89133-348-7

Strategic Planning for Nonprofit Organizations
National Trust for Historic Preservation, 1992
24 pages, Paper
Order Number 2I66
$6.00
ISBN: 0-89133-347-9

Using Professional Consultants in Preservation
National Trust for Historic Preservation, 1994
24 pages, Paper
Order Number 2I26
$6.00
ISBN: 0-89133-377-0

Volunteer Program Administration: A Handbook for Museums and Other Cultural Institutions
John Kuyper with Ellen Hirzy and Kathleen Huftalen
American Council for the Arts and American Association for Museum Volunteers, 1993
160 pages, Paper
AAM Order Number VVV354
$17.00
ISBN: 0-915400-95-2

PLANNING

Innovative Tools for Historic Preservation
(PAS Report Number 348)
Co-American Planning Association and the National Trust for Historic Preservation, 1986
Order Number 2INN
$24.00

Place Notes
National Trust for Historic Preservation, 1995
Order Number 2IPN
$10.00

Preparing a Historic Preservation Plan
(PAS Report Number 450)
American Planning Association and the National Trust for Historic Preservation, 1994
Order Number 2PRE
$24.00

Saving Place: A Guide and Report Card for Protecting Community Character
National Trust for Historic Preservation, 1991
Order Number 2I07
$15.00

PRESERVATION PHILOSOPHY

American Mosaic: Preserving a Nation's Heritage
Robert E. Stipe and Antoinette J. Lee
National Trust for Historic Preservation
Paper
$19.95
ISBN: 0-89133-140-9

The Beginnings of a New National Historic Preservation Program, 1957 to 1969
James A. Glass
Altamira Press/American Association for State and Local History, 1990

96 pages, Paper
$19.95
ISBN: 0-910-05098-8

A Complex Fate: Gustav Stickley and the Craftsman Movement
Barry Sanders
Preservation Press/John Wiley & Sons, Inc., 1996
256 pages, Cloth
$24.95
ISBN: 0-471-14392-8

The Geography of Nowhere
James Kunstler
Sheed and Ward, 1994
302 pages, Paper
Order Number MS-31
$11.00
ISBN: 1-556127-16-2

Historic Preservation: Curatorial Management of the Built World
James M. Fitch
University Press of Virginia, 1992
443 pages, Paper
$17.50
ISBN: 0813912725

Nearby History: Exploring the Past Around You
AltaMira/American Association for State and Local History, 1982
300 pages, Paper
$22.95
ISBN: 0-761991-58-1

Past Meets Future: Saving America's Historic Environments
Antoinette J. Lee
Preservation Press/John Wiley & Sons, Inc., 1992
384 pages, Cloth
$25.95
ISBN: 0-471-14412-6

They All Fall Down
Richard Cahan
Preservation Press/John Wiley & Sons, Inc., 1994
284 pages, Cloth
$24.95
ISBN: 0-471-14426-6

Truth Against the World
Patrick J. Meehan
Preservation Press/John Wiley &
Sons, Inc., 1992
496 pages, Paper
$24.95
ISBN: 0-471-14427-4

PROPERTY RIGHTS

**Procedural Due Process in Plain
English: A Guide for Preservation
Commissions**
National Trust for Historic
Preservation, 1994
24 pages, Paper
Order Number 2I14
$5.00

Takings Law in Plain English
National Trust for Historic
Preservation, 1994
45 pages, Paper
Order Number 2TAK
$24.00

RAILROADS

Great American Railroad Stations
Janet Greenstein Potter
Preservation Press/John Wiley &
Sons, Inc., 1996
496 pages, Paper
$29.95
ISBN: 0-471-14389-8

REFERENCE

**Accessibility and Historic
Preservation Resource Guide**
Historic Windsor, Inc., 1993
600 pages, Paper
$50.00
Out of print. Check your library.

America Restored
Carol M. Highsmith
Preservation Press/John Wiley &
Sons, Inc., 1994
320 pages, Cloth
$45.00
ISBN: 0-471-14347-2

Basic Preservation Procedures
National Trust for Historic
Preservation, 1995
16 pages, Paper
Order Number 2I48
$6.00
ISBN: 0-89133-329-0

A Bibliography on History-Making
Lois Silverman
American Association of
Museums/Center on History-Making
in America, 1993
75 pages, Paper
AAM Order Number TRP837
$12.00

**The Culture Vulture: A Guide to
Style, Period, and Ism**
Carol Dunlap
Preservation Press/John Wiley &
Sons, Inc., 1994
320 pages, Paper
$19.95
ISBN: 0-471-14423-1

Dictionary of Building Preservation
Ward Bucher
Preservation Press/John Wiley &
Sons, Inc., 1996
500 pages, Cloth
$39.95
ISBN 0-471-14413-4

**Historic Preservation Forum Index,
Volumes 1–10: 1987–1995**
National Trust for Historic
Preservation
Paper
Order Number 2IND
$6.00

**Landmark Yellow Pages, Second
Edition**
National Trust for Historic
Preservation
Preservation Press/John Wiley &
Sons, Inc., 1993
395 pages, Paper
$22.95
ISBN: 0-471-14398-7

**Making Educated Decisions: A
Landscape Preservation
Bibliography**
Charles A. Birnbaum and Cheryl
Wagner
National Park Service, 1994
160 pages, Cloth
GPO Stock Number 024-005-01142-1
$5.50
ISBN: 0-160451-45-0

Of Houses and Time
William Seale
Harry N. Abrams, Inc., 1992
240 pages, Cloth
$49.50
ISBN: 0-8109-3671-2

Old House Dictionary
Steven J. Phillips
Preservation Press/John Wiley &
Sons, Inc., 1994
235 pages, Paper
$12.95
ISBN: 0-471-14407-X

**Pioneers of American Landscape
Design: An Annotated Bibliography**
Charles A. Birnbaum and Lisa
Crowder
National Park Service, 1993
150 pages, Paper
GPO Stock Number 024-005-01127-7
$10.00
ISBN: 0-788104-67-5

**Preservation of Library and Archival
Materials: A Manual**
American Association of Museums,
1992
155 pages, Cloth
AAM Order Number CPL813
$54.50
ISBN: 0-9634685-0-2

**Sturgis' Illustrated Dictionary of
Architecture and Building: An
Unabridged Reprint of the 1901–2
Edition, 3 volumes**
Russell Sturgis
Dover Publishing, 1989
Paper
$16.95 per volume
Vol. 1: ISBN: 0-486-26025-9; Vol. 2:

ISBN: 0-486-26026-7; Vol. 3: ISBN:
0-486-26027-5

Terminology for Museums
D. Andrew Roberts
Museum Documentation
Association, 1990
623 pages, Cloth
AAM Order Number CRC690
$85.00
ISBN: 0-905963-62-8

RELIGIOUS PROPERTIES

**Conservation of Urban Religious
Properties**
National Trust for Historic
Preservation, 1990
16 pages, Paper
Order Number 2I47
$6.00
ISBN: 0-89133-380-0

**Places of Worship: Exploring Their
History**
James P. Wind
AltaMira Press/American
Association for State and Local
History, 1990
145 pages, Paper
$16.95
ISBN: 0-9420630-4-X

**The Preservation of Churches,
Synagogues, and Other Religious
Structures**
National Trust for Historic
Preservation, 1996
35 pages, Paper
Order Number 2I17
$6.00

Stained Glass in Houses of Worship
National Trust for Historic
Preservation, 1993
28 pages, Paper
Order Number 2I84
$6.00
ISBN: 0-89133-382-7

**Strategies for the Stewardship and
Active Use of Older and Historic
Religious Properties**

National Trust for Historic
Preservation, 1996
35 pages, Paper
Order Number 2I17
$6.00
ISBN: 0-89133-379-7

**Systems in Houses of Worship: A
Guide to Heating, Cooling,
Ventilation, Electrical and Lighting
Protection Systems**
National Trust for Historic
Preservation, 1992
24 pages, Paper
Order Number 2I64
$6.00
ISBN: 0-89133-381-9

RESTORATION

**Fabrics for Historic Buildings,
Revised Edition**
Jane C. Nylander
Preservation Press/John Wiley &
Sons, Inc., 1990
304 pages, Paper
$19.95
ISBN: 0-471-14379-0

**Floor Coverings for Historic
Buildings**
Helene Von Rosenstiel
Preservation Press/John Wiley &
Sons, Inc., 1988
284 pages, Cloth
$19.95
ISBN: 0-471-14382-0

Lighting for Historic Buildings
Roger W. Moss
Preservation Press/John Wiley &
Sons, Inc., 1988
192 pages, Paper
$16.95
ISBN: 0-471-14399-5

New Life for Old Houses
George Stephen
Preservation Press/John Wiley &
Sons, Inc., 1989
257 pages, Paper
Out of print. Check your library.
ISBN: 0-89133-149-2

Paint in America
Roger W. Moss
Preservation Press/John Wiley &
Sons, Inc., 1994
320 pages, Paper
$19.95
ISBN: 0-471-14411-8
320 pages, Cloth
$39.95
ISBN: 0-471-14410-X

**Wallpapers for Historic Buildings,
Revised Edition**
Richard C. Nylander
Preservation Press/John Wiley &
Sons, Inc., 1992
224 pages, Paper
$19.95
ISBN: 0-471-14431-2

**The Window Workbook for Historic
Buildings**
Charles Fisher
National Park Service/Historic
Preservation Education Foundation,
1986
368 pages
$45.00
(To order, write: HPEF, P.O. Box
77160, Central Station, Washington,
DC 20013)

REVOLVING FUNDS

Preservation Revolving Funds
National Trust for Historic
Preservation, 1993
24 pages, Paper
Order Number 2I78
$6.00
ISBN: 0-89133-374-6

RURAL PRESERVATION

Rural Conservation
National Trust for Historic
Preservation, 1993
24 pages, Paper
Order Number 2I77
$6.00
ISBN: 0-89133-341-X

Saving America's Countryside: Guide to Rural Conservation
Samuel N. Stokes and Elizabeth A. Watson
Johns Hopkins University Press, 1989
320 pages, Cloth
$47.50
ISBN: 0-801-83695-6

Views from the Road: A Community Guide for Assessing Rural Historic Landscapes
David H. Copps
Island Press, 1995
Paper
$25.00
ISBN: 1-55963-412-X

SCENIC BYWAYS/HISTORIC TRAILS

The Protection of America's Scenic Byways
National Trust for Historic Preservation, 1996
19 pages, Paper
Order Number 2I68
$6.00
ISBN: 0-89133-339-8

SPECIAL STRUCTURE TYPES

BARN AGAIN! A Guide to Rehabilitation of Older Farm Buildings
National Trust for Historic Preservation, 1988
17 pages, Paper
Order Number 2BAR
$6.00

Curtain Up: New Life for Historic Theaters
National Trust for Historic Preservation, 1993
24 pages, Paper
Order Number 2I72
$6.00
ISBN: 0-89133-385-1

A Graveyard Preservation Primer
Lynette Strangstad
AltaMira Press/American Association for State and Local History, 1988
126 pages, Paper
$19.95

Great American Lighthouses
F. Ross Holland
Preservation Press/John Wiley & Sons, Inc., 1995
350 pages, Paper
$19.95
ISBN: 0-471-14387-1

Great American Railroad Stations
Janet Greenstein Potter
Preservation Press/John Wiley & Sons, Inc., 1996
496 pages, Paper
$29.95
ISBN: 0-471-14389-8

Great American Ships
James P. Delgado
Preservation Press/John Wiley & Sons, Inc., 1991
312 pages, Paper
$19.95
ISBN: 0-471-14384-7

Local Schools: Exploring Their History
Ronald E. Butchart
Alta Mira Press/American Association for State and Local History, 1986
136 pages, Paper
$16.95
ISBN: 0-910050-82-1

The National Trust Guide to Great Opera Houses in America
Karyl Lynn Zietz
Preservation Press/John Wiley & Sons, Inc., 1996
256 pages, Paper
$29.95
ISBN: 0-471-14421-5

Preservation of Historic Burial Grounds
National Trust for Historic Preservation, 1995
24 pages, Paper
Order Number 2I76
$6.00
ISBN: 0-89133-331-2

Preserving Historic Bridges
National Trust for Historic Preservation, 1995
28 pages, Paper
Order Number 2I36
$6.00
ISBN: 0-89133-383-5

Railroad Depot Acquisition and Development
National Trust for Historic Preservation, 1991
16 pages, Paper
Order Number 2I44
$6.00
ISBN: 0-89133-386-X

Using Old Farm Buildings
National Trust for Historic Preservation, 1989
24 pages, Paper
Order Number 2I46
$6.00
ISBN: 0-89133-384-3

STATE HISTORIC PRESERVATION LAWS

Smart States, Better Communities
National Trust for Historic Preservation, 1997
408 pages, Paper
Order Number 2SMA
$30.00
ISBN: 0-89133-356-8

State Tax Incentives for Historic Preservation: A State-by-State Summary
Constance Beaumont
National Trust for Historic Preservation, 1992

18 pages, Paper
ISBN: 0-891-331337-9

TECHNOLOGY

Interactive Multimedia in American Museums
Stephanie Koester
Archives and Museum Informatics, 1993
137 pages, Paper
AAM Order Number EMC3302
$20.00
ISBN: 1-885626-04-5

Museums and Technology Selected Source List
American Association of Museums, 1996
14 pages, Paper
AAM Order Number EMT853
$4.00

Where the Information Is: A Guide to Electronic Research for Nonprofit Organizations
Helen Bergan
BioGuide Press, 1996
257 pages, Paper
AAM Order Number EWI3001
$30.00
ISBN: 0-9615277-2-2

The Wired Museum: Emerging Technology and Changing Paradigms
Katherine Jones-Garmil
American Association of Museums, 1996
250 pages, Paper
AAM Order Number EWM230
$35.00
ISBN: 0-931201-36-5

TOURISM

Getting Started: How to Succeed in Heritage Tourism: Preserving Our Past . . . Building Our Future
National Trust for Historic Preservation, 1993

48 pages, Paper and VHS
Order Number 2I05
$25.00

Heritage Tourism: Partnerships and Possibilities
National Trust for Historic Preservation, 1994
12 pages, Paper
Order Number 2TOU
$6.00

Touring Historic Places
National Tour Association and the National Trust for Historic Preservation, 1995
18 pages, Paper
Order Number 2THP
$10.00

TRANSPORTATION

Building on the Past, Traveling to the Future
I Me Chan
National Trust for Historic Preservation and Federal Highway Administration, 1995
80 pages, Paper
(To order, write: National Transportation Enhancements Clearinghouse, 1506 21st Street, N.W., Suite 210, Washington, DC 20036)

TWENTIETH-CENTURY ARCHITECTURE

Contemporary Architecture in Washington, D.C.
Claudia D. Kousoulas
Preservation Press/John Wiley & Sons, Inc., 1995
512 pages, Paper
$24.95
ISBN: 0-471-14374-X

Getting to Know Your 20th Century Neighborhood
National Trust for Historic Preservation, 1996

20 pages, Paper
Order Number 2I94
$6.00
ISBN: 0-89133-362-2

Preservation and the Recent Past
National Trust for Historic Preservation, 1993
24 pages, Paper
Order Number 2I69
$6.00
ISBN: 0-89133-335-5

Twentieth-Century Building Materials: History and Conservation
Thomas C. Jester, Editor
McGraw-Hill, 1996
352 pages, Cloth
$55.00
ISBN: 0070325731

URBAN ENVIRONMENTS

The Challenge of Livable Communities Revitalizing Urban Environments Through Historic Preservation
National Trust for Historic Preservation
Order Number 2VSE
VHS
$40.00

Conservation of Urban Religious Properties
National Trust for Historic Preservation, 1990
16 pages, Paper
Order Number 2I47
$6.00
ISBN: 0-89133-380-0

The Living City
Roberta Brandes Gratz
Preservation Press/John Wiley & Sons, Inc., 1994
448 pages, Paper
$16.95
ISBN: 0-471-14425-8

To order a National Trust publication with an order number that begins with "2," write to Information Series, National Trust for Historic Preservation, 1785 Massachusetts Avenue, N.W., Washington, DC 20036, or call (202) 588-6286. A reduced cost is available for bulk orders of 10 or more.

To order a National Trust publication with an order number that begins with "M," write to Main Street, National Trust for Historic Preservation, 1785 Massachusetts Avenue, N.W.

Washington, DC 20036, or call (202) 588-6219.

For items published by or carried by the American Association of Museums (AAM), write to American Association of Museums, P.O. Box 4002, Washington DC 20042, or call (202) 289-9127.

To order a publication from AltaMira Press, write to AltaMira, 2455 Teller Road, Thousand Oaks, CA 91320, or call (805) 499-9774.

To order a publication from the National Park Service or the U.S. Department of Commerce National Technical Information Service, indicate GPO order number and write to Superintendent of Documents, P.O. Box 371954, Pittsburgh, PA 15250, or call (202) 512-1800.

To order a publication from John Wiley & Sons, Inc., write to John Wiley & Sons, Inc., 1 Wiley Drive, Somerset, NJ 08875, or call 1-800-CALL-WILEY.

Chronology: Preservation in America

1812 First national historical organization, the American Antiquarian Society, is founded in Worcester, Massachusetts.

1816 Philadelphia purchases Independence Hall to save it from demolition.

1828 Touro Synagogue in Newport, Rhode Island, is the nation's first restoration.

1850 New York legislature purchases the Hasbrouck House, George Washington's headquarters in Newburgh, and opens it to the public as the nation's first historic house museum.

1853 Ann Pamela Cunningham initiates efforts to save Mount Vernon; her Mount Vernon Ladies' Association of the Union is chartered in 1856, and restoration of Mount Vernon begins in 1859.

1856 Tennessee legislature authorizes purchase of The Hermitage, Andrew Jackson's home near Nashville.

1872 Yellowstone is named America's—and the world's—first national park.

1876 Old South Meeting House in Boston is rescued from demolition.

1888 Association for the Preservation of Virginia Antiquities is formed as the nation's first statewide preservation organization.

1889 America's first National Monument designation is awarded to Casa Grande, near Coolidge, Arizona.

1890 Chickamauga Battlefield in Georgia becomes the first National Military Park.

1891 Trustees of Public Reservations is incorporated in Massachusetts, and becomes a model for the English (1894) and American (1949) national trusts.

1896 In *United States v. Gettysburg Electric Railway Company*, the U.S. Supreme Court hears its first case involving preservation.

1906 Antiquities Act, the first major federal preservation legislation, is passed to preserve archeological sites.

1909 Essex Institute opens America's first outdoor museum of historic buildings in Salem, Massachusetts.

1910 Society for the Preservation of New England Antiquities is incorporated as America's first regional preservation organization.

1916 National Park Service is created, taking over nine existing national monuments.

1926 Greenfield Village, Henry Ford's collection of historic buildings and artifacts in Dearborn, Michigan, opens to the public.

Restoration of Williamsburg, Virginia, begins under a plan formulated by W. A. R. Goodwin, with funding from John D. Rockefeller, Jr.

1931 America's first municipal preservation ordinance is passed in Charleston, South Carolina.

Moore House at Yorktown, Virginia, is the first National Park Service restoration.

1933 Responsibility for operation and maintenance of battlefields and other historic federal property is transferred to the National Park Service.

Historic American Buildings Survey is begun.

1935 National Historic Sites Act is passed, authorizing the U.S. Department of the Interior to survey historic sites under a National Historic Landmarks Program and to acquire historic properties for public use.

1936 Louisiana state constitution is amended to create a commission to preserve the Vieux Carré in New Orleans.

1938 First National Historic Site designation is awarded to Salem Maritime National Historic Site in Massachusetts.

1940 Society of Architectural Historians and the American Association for State and Local History are founded.

1944 *This Is Charleston* is published in Charleston, South Carolina, representing the nation's first attempt at a citywide inventory of historic buildings.

1947 National Council for Historic Sites and Buildings, the first nationwide private preservation organization and predecessor of the National Trust for Historic Preservation, is formed.

1949 National Trust for Historic Preservation in the United States is chartered by Congress.

1951 National Trust acquires Woodlawn Plantation in Virginia as its first museum property.

1952 First issue of *Historic Preservation* magazine published.

1954 National Council for Historic Sites and Buildings merges with the National Trust.

1959 College Hill Demonstration Study in Providence, Rhode Island, is the first urban renewal study to address preservation concerns.

1960 A limited register of nationally significant landmarks, predecessor of the National Register of Historic Places, is initiated by the National Park Service.

Mount Vernon Ladies' Association of the Union is named the first winner of the National Trust's Crowninshield Award.

1961 First issue of *Preservation News* published.

1963 Despite widespread public outcry and celebrity picket lines, the demolition of New York's Pennsylvania Station begins.

1964 Columbia University School of Architecture offers the first graduate-level course in historic preservation.

1966 *With Heritage So Rich* is published.

National Historic Preservation Act is passed, establishing an expanded National Register of Historic Places, an Advisory Council on Historic Preservation, and matching grants-in-aid to the states and the National Trust.

Department of Transportation Act declares a national policy of preservation of natural and historic sites on highway routes.

Demonstration Cities and Metropolitan Development Act redirects urban renewal to recognize and fund preservation projects.

1967 First state historic preservation officers and the first keeper of the National Register are appointed.

1968 Association for Preservation Technology is founded.

New York City enacts the nation's first ordinance allowing transfer of development rights.

1969 U.S. Department of the Interior makes the first preservation grants to the states.

National Environmental Policy Act stresses federal preservation respon-

Ukrainian church, Chicago, Illinois.
(Carol M. Highsmith Photography)

sibility and creates environmental impact statements.

Historic American Engineering Record is established, and its first site-recording project is carried out at Great Falls Canal and Locks in Virginia.

Proposed Vieux Carré elevated expressway in New Orleans becomes the first interstate highway stopped for environmental reasons.

1970 First Earth Day is celebrated.

1971 Executive Order (1593) directs federal agencies to preserve, restore, and maintain their cultural properties.

National Trust opens a Western Regional Office in San Francisco as the first of six regional offices.

Society for Industrial Archeology is established.

1972 Congress authorizes transfer of surplus significant federal property to local public agencies for preservation.

1973 First National Historic Preservation Week is celebrated.

New York City's Landmarks Preservation Commission is authorized to designate historic interiors.

Nation's first urban homesteading program is launched in Wilmington, Delaware.

1974 Preservation Action is formed as a national citizens' lobby.

1976 Celebration of the Bicentennial of the American Revolution strengthens interest in preservation.

Tax Reform Act of 1976 provides the first major preservation tax incentives for the rehabilitation of certified historic income-producing properties.

Public Buildings Cooperative Use Act encourages restoration and adaptive use of historic buildings for federal use.

1977 National Trust's Main Street Project, forerunner of the National Main Street Center, is launched in Galesburg, Illinois; Hot Springs, South Dakota; and Madison, Indiana.

1978 U.S. Supreme Court rules in its first major preservation case, involving Grand Central Terminal, that New York City's preservation ordinance is constitutional.

1979 Miami Beach becomes the site of the first National Register historic district made up entirely of 20th-century buildings.

1980 Amendments to the National Historic Preservation Act are passed directing federal agencies to nominate and protect historic federal properties, broadening participation of local governments, and requiring owner consent for National Register listing.

1981 Economic Recovery Tax Act provides significant new investment tax credits for rehabilitation.

1982 Zero preservation funding proposed by the Reagan administration is fought, and funding is restored after an intensive nationwide campaign.

1983 Congress approves restoration rather than extension of the West Front of the U.S. Capitol.

1984 National Trust acquires Montpelier, the 2,677-acre Virginia home of President James Madison.

1985 McDonald's announces plans to store the first roadside stand built by Ray Kroc in 1955 in Des Plaines, Illinois.

San Francisco adopts a downtown master plan with the strongest design controls yet devised in an American city, including the protection of more than 250 landmark buildings.

1986 Nationwide campaign helps save the rehabilitation tax credits in the Tax Reform Act of 1986.

Centennial and restoration of the Statue of Liberty are celebrated on July 4.

1987 International Council on Monuments and Sites (ICOMOS) holds its 8th General Assembly in Washington, D.C., its first such meeting in the Western Hemisphere.

1988 Federal Abandoned Shipwrecks Act protects significant shipwrecks and authorizes state management of them.

Manassas National Battlefield Park in Virginia is saved from adjacent shopping mall development.

National Trust issues its first "11 Most Endangered Historic Places" list.

1989 Jobbers Canyon warehouse area of Omaha is demolished, the largest National Register historic district lost to date.

1990 President Bush's 1991 budget proposal reinstates preservation funding, ending a decade in which preservation had been "zeroed out" every year. The budget document states that "the preservation, understanding and passing on of the best of [our] local heritage is essential if Americans are to know what it means to be 'American'."

1991 In two separate cases, the U.S. Supreme Court affirms the right of localities to designate religious properties as landmarks.

Pennsylvania Supreme Court, stating that landmark designation without owner consent represents a "taking," rules Philadelphia's preservation ordinance unconstitutional.

Enactment of the Intermodal Surface Transportation and Enhancements Act (ISTEA) provides a significant source of funding for historic preservation projects.

1994 In the face of widespread public concern over the threat of sprawl, the Walt Disney Company abandons plans for a theme park and related development in the historic Virginia countryside near Washington, D.C.

1995 Action by Congress initiates a three-year phaseout of the National Trust's federal appropriation.

1996 Executive Order 13006 directs federal agencies to give first consideration to historic properties within historic districts when locating government offices.

SECTION THREE

Preservation Partners

Overview

This section explains the structure and relationships of the public and private organizations that carry out and/or impact historic preservation, as well as background information and listings for these organizations.

Public offices and organizations are federal, national, state, or municipal government entities. Public offices' mandates come from the government; leadership positions in these organizations are generally by appointment. Private groups also may be national, statewide, or local in scope, yet are privately held and funded. They exist to support the mandated preservation efforts and to foster and initiate a more far-reaching understanding, appreciation, and application of preservation and related endeavors and practices.

Preservation Resources

Public	*Private*
FEDERAL/NATIONAL	
National Park Service	National Trust for Historic Preservation
Advisory Council on Historic Preservation	Preservation Action
	National Trust Regional Offices
STATE	
State Historic Preservation Officers (SHPO)	Statewide Preservation Organizations
LOCAL	
Historic District Commissions	Local Preservation Organizations
Certified Local Governments	

Louisiana State Museum Cabildo, New Orleans, Louisiana. *(Carol M. Highsmith Photography)*

The *National Park Service* chapter explains the directives of the organization and includes pertinent phone numbers for particular programs.

The *National Trust for Historic Preservation* chapter details some of the larger programs offered by the Trust and includes a listing of Regional Offices and Historic Sites.

For information on the workings of the *Advisory Council on Historic Preservation*, look to its chapter, which also includes relevant contact information.

Federal Programs and Agencies lists contact information for government-affiliated organizations.

National and Regional Organizations, like the Federal Programs and Agencies chapter, lists various groups with broad scopes and central offices.

The *International Programs* chapter primarily lists programs that are based in the United States, but affect preservation interests internationally. The International and Territory listings of the Phone Book complement the Programs chapter.

National Park Service

The National Park Service (NPS) is the principal federal agency responsible for historic preservation. Part of the Department of the Interior, NPS administers the national park system and is responsible for a number of programs that assist privately held historic resources.

National Park Service
P.O. Box 37127
Washington, DC 20013-7127
(202) 208-4621

Associate Director for Cultural Resources
Stewardship and Partnership
(202) 208-7625

ARCHEOLOGY AND ETHNOGRAPHY

The Archeology and Ethnography Program provides national leadership and coordination for archeology and ethnography. It encourages and supports the protection, preservation, and interpretation of America's archeological resources inside the National Park System and beyond. It identifies, protects, and interprets cultural and natural resources that have traditional value for contemporary communities within existing and proposed units of the National Park System. Several programs are carried out in the context of seven functional areas headed by team leaders: Applied Ethnography; Communications; Native American Graves Protection and Repatriation; Protection and Enforcement; Public Education and Outreach; Resource Information Management; and Resource Management Assistance.

Chief Archeologist and
Departmental Consulting
Archeologist
(202) 343-4101

MUSEUM MANAGEMENT PROGRAM

The Museum Management Program supports development and coordination of servicewide policies, standards, and procedures for managing museum collections, including natural, cultural, archival, and manuscript materials. The program provides staff advice, technical assistance, and professional development pertaining to museum collections acquisitions, documentation, preservation, protection, use, and disposal for the National Park Service. It provides similar services to Department of the Interior bureaus. The program develops and maintains a servicewide catalog and other statistics on museum collections.

Chief Curator
(202) 343-8138

HISTORIC AMERICAN BUILDINGS SURVEY/HISTORIC AMERICAN ENGINEERING RECORD

The Historic American Buildings Survey (HABS) and the Historic American Engineering Record (HAER) reflect the general government's commitment to preserve important architectural, engineering, and industrial properties through programs that document outstanding examples of this country's heritage. Project teams produce measured drawings, large format photography, and written histories. These documents are available to the public through HABS/HAER collections housed, serviced, and maintained by the Prints and Photographs Division of the Library of Congress in Washington, D.C. For more information, call (202) 707-6394.

Historic American Buildings Survey
(202) 343-4227

Historic American Engineering Record
(202) 343-4237

Fieldhouse in Garfield Park, Chicago, Illinois. *(Carol M. Highsmith Photography)*

Local Programs; and Technical Preservation Services.

Heritage Preservation Services
(202) 343-9509

NATIONAL REGISTER, HISTORY, AND EDUCATION

The National Register, History, and Education Program promotes the recognition, preservation, and appreciation of historic places nationwide. It provides leadership throughout the National Park System and beyond through a variety of activities that include the identification, evaluation, documentation, and interpretation of these places. Its programmatic responsibilities are implemented within the following functional areas: Administrative History; National Historic Landmarks Survey; National Maritime Initiative; National Register of Historic Places; Park History (research, education, and park planning); and Teaching with Historic Places.

National Register, History and
Education Program
(202) 343-8167

National Register of Historic Places
(202) 343-9504

PARK HISTORIC STRUCTURES AND CULTURAL LANDSCAPES

This program is responsible for providing support for the development of policies and prepares guidelines, standards, techniques, methods, and technical information for inventory, documentation, planning, treatment, management, and use of historic and prehistoric structures and cultural landscapes in the National Park System. It develops and maintains management inventories and information systems for these resources

HERITAGE PRESERVATION SERVICES

HPS provides diverse educational and assistance tools to help our nation's citizens and communities identify, protect, and preserve historic properties for future generations. It provides a broad range of products and services, financial assistance and incentives, guidance, and technical information in support of this mission. Its programmatic responsibilities are implemented within the following functional areas: Mapping and Information Technologies; Preservation Initiatives; State, Tribal, and

and provides professional advice and assistance.

Chief Historical Architect
(202) 343-8146

NATIONAL PARK SERVICE REGIONS

Alaska Area
2525 Gambell Street
Anchorage, AK 99503
(907) 257-2690
FAX (907) 257-2533

Northeast Area
U.S. Custom House, Third Floor
200 Chestnut Street, Room 306

Philadelphia, PA 19106
(215) 597-7013
FAX (617) 223-5199

Midwest Area
1709 Jackson Street
Omaha, NE 68102
(402) 221-3431
FAX (402) 341-2039

National Capital Area
1100 Ohio Drive, S.W.
Washington, DC 20242
(202) 619-7223
FAX (202) 619-7062

Intermountain Area
P.O. Box 25287
12795 West Alameda Parkway

Denver, CO 80225-0287
(303) 969-2503
FAX (303) 969-2785

Southeast Area
100 Alabama Street, N.W.
1924 Building
Atlanta, GA 30303
(404) 331-4998
FAX (404) 563-3263

Pacific West Area
600 Harrison Street
Suite 600
San Francisco, CA 94107-1362
(415) 427-1304
FAX (415) 427-1485

National Trust for Historic Preservation

National Trust for Historic Preservation
l785 Massachusetts Avenue, N.W.
Washington, DC 20036
(202) 588-6000
TTY: (202) 588-6200
http://www.nthp.org

The National Trust, a private, non-profit corporation, is the only national preservation organization chartered by Congress (in 1949) to encourage public participation in the preservation of sites, buildings, and objects significant in American history and culture. The National Trust acts as a clearinghouse of information on all aspects of preservation, assists in co-ordinating efforts of preservation groups, provides professional advice on preservation, conducts conferences and seminars, maintains twenty historic sites as museums, administers grant and loan programs, and issues a variety of publications. Seven regional and field offices provide localized preservation advisory services and represent the National Trust in their regions. A board of trustees directs the organization's policies and a board of advisors representing the states helps implement programs.

Financial support for National Trust programs comes from membership dues, endowment funds, contributions, and matching grants from federal agencies, including the U.S. Department of the Interior, National Park Service, under the National Historic Preservation Act of 1966. The National Trust's Washington office is in the McCormick Apartments, a National Historic Landmark (1915–17, Jules Henri de Sibour) in Washington, D.C.

OFFICES, PROGRAMS, AND SERVICES

During the past forty years, the scope of programs at the National Trust has expanded dramatically to include downtown revitalization, support for state and local preservation organizations, litigation, advocacy, tourism, growth management, and rural preservation. The organization has rallied to save Civil War battlefields; testified on Capitol Hill to protect underwater shipwrecks; marched in South Pasadena, California, to protest construction of a freeway; sent emergency assistance to disaster-stricken Charleston, St. Croix, and northern California; charted the future of James Madison's home, Montpelier; funded inner-city housing; argued in court to halt a proposed elevated highway along the historic waterfront of Mobile, Alabama; and much more.

With such a diversity of activities, it can be difficult to determine which office to call with your preservation questions. This listing of offices, programs, and services will help direct you to the right place. Each entry includes the appropriate phone number for the Washington office. The best place to start in most instances, however, is with your regional office. Staff members there can help direct your inquiry to the appropriate office or program. Regional offices advise state and local preservation organizations on preservation issues; organize field visits, workshops, and seminars of interest to the region; and conduct special projects focusing on regional historic preservation resources and issues.

Advertising: To place an ad in *Preservation* magazine, call (202) 588-6083. To advertise in the National Preservation Conference brochure, call (202) 588-6100.

Advisors: See **Board of Advisors**.

Advocacy: See **Center for Preservation Policy Studies**.

Award Programs: See **BARN AGAIN!** Awards, Crowninshield Award, Honor

Awards, and Great American Home Awards.

BARN AGAIN!: Award program co-sponsored by the National Trust and *Successful Farming* magazine to encourage farmers to restore and adapt their barns to new agricultural uses. For information, call (303) 623-1504.

Bed and Breakfasts: *The National Trust Guide to Historic Bed & Breakfasts, Inns, and Small Hotels*, fourth edition, published in 1996 by Preservation Press/John Wiley & Sons, Inc., lists more than 500 historic bed-and-breakfast inns. To order copies of the book, call 1-800-225-5945.

Bequests: See **Planned Giving**.

Board of Advisors: The Board of Advisors was established in 1966 to increase the National Trust's direct contact and communication with state and local constituents through the creation of a nationwide network of 106 volunteer preservation leaders (two per state, plus the District of Columbia, Puerto Rico, and the U.S. Virgin Islands). Call your National Trust Regional Office or (202) 588-6122, or e-mail: boards@nthp.org for more information.

Board of Trustees: The National Trust is governed by a Board of Trustees elected by the membership at the annual membership meeting. For information, call (202) 588-6171, or e-mail: boards@nthp.org.

Books: See **Preservation Press**.

Bookstore: See **Decatur House Shop**.

Center for Preservation Policy Studies: Provides research and testimony on pending federal legislation, advocacy of preservation issues, coordination of a national lobbying network, and research on preservation policy issues. For informa-

tion, call (202) 588-6254, or e-mail: policy@nthp.org. See also **Legislative Information Hotline**.

COEP: See **Community Preservation Organization Effectiveness Program**.

Commercial Buildings: See **National Main Street Center**.

Communications: The National Trust's Office of Communications carries out media-relations programs to promote National Trust activities, coordinates Preservation Week activities, and provides information to National Trust members. For information, call (202) 588-6141, or e-mail: pr@nthp.org.

Community Preservation Organization Effectiveness Program (COEP): National Trust program that helps preservation organizations increase their effectiveness to better achieve their preservation goals. Call your National Trust Regional Office for more information.

Computer Network: See **PreserveLink**.

Conferences: The National Trust offers a variety of educational conferences, seminars, workshops, and outreach programs including the annual National Preservation Conference. For information, call 1-800-944-6847. For information on regional and state preservation conferences, call your National Trust Regional Office. Upcoming Conferences: October 13–19, 1997, Santa Fe, NM; October 20–25, 1998, Savannah, GA; October 4–10, 1999, Washington, DC; November 1–4, 2000, Los Angeles, CA.

Congressional Liaison: See **Center for Preservation Policy Studies**.

Critical Issues Fund (CIF): The Critical Issues Fund supports innovative

research and model projects that examine the most serious issues facing the historic preservation movement today. The program's goal is to integrate preservation values into public policy at the local, state, and national levels. Call (202) 588-6255 for information.

Crowninshield Award: Named for Louise DuPont Crowninshield, this is the National Trust's highest recognition for superlative lifetime achievement in the preservation movement, including interpretation of the nation's historic, architectural and maritime heritage. Winners are selected by the preservation committee of the National Trust's Board of Trustees. Although there is no formal nomination process, the committee chairperson welcomes candidate suggestions. For information, call (202) 588-6039.

Decatur House Shop: The National Trust's Washington, D.C., book and gift shop is located at Decatur House, 1600 H Street, N.W., in downtown Washington. Preservation Press publications are available along with an extensive selection of books and gifts relating to preservation, architecture, and history. For information on shop hours, call (202) 842-1856.

Deferred Gifts: See **Planned Giving**.

Design Competition: See **Student Competitions**.

Disaster Relief: The National Trust has provided technical assistance and emergency funding when natural disasters threaten or destroy historic sites. Call your National Trust Regional Office for information.

Downtown Revitalization: See **National Main Street Center**.

Montpelier, Orange, Virginia. *(Carol M. Highsmith Photography)*

Easements: The National Trust helps organizations initiate and administer preservation easement programs along with other protection tools. The National Trust also maintains its own active easement program and holds preservation easements on more than seventy properties. For information, call (202) 588-6035.

Educational Supplement: A list of historic preservation degree programs in colleges, universities, and preservation training centers is published annually in *Preservation* magazine. To receive a copy, call (202) 588-6164. See also the Degree Programs in Historic Preservation chapter in the **Preservation Topics** section of this book.

Employment: See **Human Resources**.

Endangered Places: The National Trust maintains a list of the nation's "11 Most Endangered Historic Places." The list is revised and updated annually. Call the National Trust's Office of Communications at (202) 588-6141 for more information.

Fax Numbers: Fax numbers most often requested at the Washington office are the following: Main fax number, (202) 588-6038; Publications, (202) 588-6172; President's Office, (202) 588-6082; and Programs, Services and Information, (202) 588-6223.

Funding: See **Critical Issues Fund, Inner-City Ventures Fund, National Preservation Loan Fund, Preservation Services Fund**, or call your National Trust Regional Office.

Gift Shop: The National Trust operates gift shops at each of its historic sites. The shops carry gifts and books relating to the history of the specific site and region. See **Decatur House Shop**.

Grants: See **Critical Issues Fund, Inner-City Ventures Fund, Preservation Services Fund**, or call your National Trust Regional Office.

Great American Home Awards: Annual recognition program for outstanding residential rehabilitation projects in the United States. Winners are announced in *Preservation* magazine. For information and entry forms, call (202) 588-6283.

Heritage Society: National Trust membership program for members who contribute $1,000 or more annually. For information, call (202) 588-6188.

Heritage Tourism: The National Trust's Tourism Program provides technical assistance to states and communities across the country in developing heritage tourism products. The program also offers how-to publications. For information, call (303) 623-1504.

Historic District Commissions: The National Trust works to strengthen state preservation legislation and local preservation ordinances. For information, call (202) 588-6255.

Historic Hotels of America: Membership program for hotels that are distinguished by their historic character and architectural quality. To inquire about membership or obtain a hotel directory, call (202) 588-6267, or e-mail: hotels@nthp.org. To make reservations at participating hotels, call 1-800-678-8946.

Historic Preservation Forum: National Trust membership program designed specifically for preservation professionals and organizations. Benefits include subscriptions to the publications *Historic Preservation Forum Journal, Forum News,* and *Preservation,* participation in financial/insurance assistance programs, technical advice, and substantial discounts on professional conferences and publications. For membership information, call (202) 588-6296, or e-mail: forum@nthp.org.

Historic Preservation News: The last issue of this newspaper was published in March 1995. For back issues, call (202) 588-6388.

Historic Rehabilitation Tax Credit: Federal income tax incentives are available for preservation projects designated by the secretary of the interior as rehabilitations of certified historic structures. For information, call your state historic preservation office or the National Park Service at (202) 343-9573. A National Trust publication, *A Guide to Tax-Advantaged Rehabilitation,* explains how the historic rehabilitation tax credit works. To order a copy, call (202) 588-6286.

Historic Sites: The National Trust owns and operates twenty historic sites across the country. For information, call (202) 588-6151; please call the sites directly for hours of operation. A full listing appears later in this chapter.

Holiday Cards: The National Trust's holiday cards are available exclusively by mail. To order cards, call 1-800-944-6847. To add your name to our mailing list, call (202) 588-6169.

Honor Awards: The National Trust's annual recognition program for organizations and individuals whose projects demonstrate outstanding dedication and commitment to ex-

cellence in historic preservation. Awards are presented at the National Preservation Conference. For information and nomination forms, call (202) 588-6039.

Hotels: See **Historic Hotels of America.**

Human Resources: For information on volunteer opportunities, job openings, careers in preservation, and internships, call (202) 588-6120.

Information Series: National Trust publications that provide concise information on basic and frequently used preservation and organizational development techniques. To order a booklet or request a list of titles, call (202) 588-6286.

Inner-City Ventures Fund: Matching grants and low-interest loans to nonprofit community organizations to help revitalize older historic neighborhoods for the benefit of low- and moderate-income residents. Call your National Trust Regional Office or (202) 588-6054 for more information.

Insurance: Insurance programs available to *Historic Preservation Forum* members include property, employee benefits, health, directors and officers, and maritime insurance. For information, call (202) 588-6296. For information on insurance for private homeowners, call 1-800-899-6004.

Internships: See **Human Resources.**

Investment Tax Credit: See **Historic Rehabilitation Tax Credit.**

Jobs: See **Human Resources.**

Leadership Training: The National Trust offers periodic Preservation Leadership Training Institutes. For information on upcoming programs, call your National Trust Regional Office or (202) 588-6067.

Legal Defense Fund: The only national organization that regularly goes to court to protect America's heritage—defending, enforcing and monitoring preservation laws at the federal, state and local levels to ensure their effectiveness in protecting historic resources. LDF's dedicated staff lawyers advises and educates private and government lawyers, as well as citizen activists around the country, on preservation law and using the tools of legal advocacy, thereby creating a vital network of preservation advocates. For more information, call (202) 588-6035.

Legal Services: The legal department provides education and advice on preservation law and historic districts, zoning, the monitoring of preservation litigation, intervention as an *amicus curiae* (friend of the court) in litigation, and advice on tax incentives and easements. For information, call your National Trust Regional Office or (202) 588-6035.

Legislative Information Hotline: To obtain updates on preservation legislation or to place an order for copies of legislative bills, testimony, fact sheets, and other public policy information, call 1-800-765-NTHP.

Library: The National Trust's collection is operated by and located at the University of Maryland's College Park campus and is maintained as a separate collection in the university's McKeldin Library. For information, call (301) 405-6319.

Licensing: The National Trust's licensing program offers historic reproductions of gifts, accessories, and home furnishings. For information on the licensees and where to find their products, call (202) 588-6118. For information on becoming a licensee, call (202) 588-6096.

Litigation: The National Trust regularly enters court cases throughout the United States in support of local preservation organizations when an issue of national significance is involved. For information, call your National Trust Regional Office or (202) 588-6035.

Loan Programs: See **Inner-City Ventures Fund, National Preservation Loan Fund**.

Lobbying: See **Center for Preservation Policy Studies**.

Mailing Lists: To exchange or purchase mailing lists, contact the following departments: *Preservation Forum,* (202) 588-6296; National Trust Membership, (202) 588-6184; National Main Street Network, (202) 588-6219.

Mail Order: To order books and gifts seen in advertisements or catalogs, call 1-800-274-3694, or in the Washington, DC, area, call (202) 588-6118.

Main Street: See **National Main Street Center**.

Main Street Certification Institute: Advanced, professional certification program for Main Street managers. For information, call (202) 588-6219.

Main Street Network: See **National Main Street Network**.

Main Street News: Monthly newsletter of the National Main Street Center. For information, call (202) 588-6219.

Media Relations: See **Communications**.

Membership Inquiries: For questions concerning new membership, renewals, or change of address, call (202) 588-6166; for questions concerning membership in *Preservation Forum,* call (202) 588-6296; for ques-

tions concerning National Main Street Network membership, call (202) 588-6219; or e-mail: members@nthp.org.

Museum Properties: See **Historic Sites**.

National Main Street Center: National Trust program aimed at stimulating the economic revitalization of business districts in the context of historic preservation. The center conducts training courses, provides technical assistance to states, towns, and cities, and helps build business and government partnerships. For information, call (202) 588-6219, or e-mail: mainst@nthp.org.

National Main Street Network: Organizational membership program through which communities receive current information on business district revitalization techniques and activities. Members receive the monthly newsletter, *Main Street News,* technical advice, and referrals on issues of local concern. For information, call (202) 588-6219, or e-mail: mainst@nthp.org.

National Preservation Conference: Annual conference organized by the National Trust that includes educational sessions, affinity group meetings, tours, the annual meeting of the National Trust and special events. Future National Preservation Conferences will be held in Santa Fe (1997), Savannah (1998), Washington, DC (1999), and Los Angeles (2000). For information, call 1-800-944-6847.

National Preservation Loan Fund: Below-market-rate loans to nonprofit organizations and public agencies to help preserve properties listed, or eligible for listing, in the National Register of Historic Places. For information, call your National

Trust Regional Office or (202) 588-6054.

National Preservation Week: See **Preservation Week**.

National Town Meeting: Annual conference of Main Street revitalization professionals and volunteers. For information, call (202) 588-6219.

Neighborhood Business Districts: See **National Main Street Center**.

Personnel: See **Human Resources**.

Planned Giving: The National Trust welcomes donations in the form of real estate, cash, securities, personal property, and bequests. For information, call (202) 588-6176.

Preservation: Bimonthly magazine published by the National Trust. Calendar listings are published without charge, space permitting. Send items to *Preservation,* Calendar, National Trust for Historic Preservation, 1785 Massachusetts Avenue, N.W., Washington, DC 20036. For back issues, call (202) 588-6388, or e-mail: preservation@nthp.org. To place an ad, call (202) 588-6083.

Preservation Law Reporter: Legal periodical on federal, state, and local preservation legislation and administrative decisions. Includes reports on recent legislative developments, comprehensive model ordinances, and easement provisions. Reduced rates for National Trust Forum members. For information, call (202) 588-6035, or e-mail: law@nthp.org.

Preservation Press: For general information, call John Wiley & Sons, Inc., at 1-800-225-5945.

Preservation Services Fund: Small matching grants to nonprofit organizations, universities, and public agencies to initiate preservation projects. For more information, call your Regional Office or (202) 588-6197.

Preservation Week: Celebrated the second full week in May, Preservation Week is a nationwide celebration of our local, state, and national heritage and efforts to preserve them. For a Preservation Week kit, call (202) 588-6141.

PreserveLink: Membership in Preservation Forum provides computer access to information at the National Trust's password-protected website, and allows local, state, and national preservation organizations to network together. For information, call (202) 588-6067, or e-mail: plink@nthp.org.

Public Relations: See **Communications**.

Railroad Depots: The National Trust's Mountains/Plains Regional Office offers technical assistance for organizations or individuals interested in preserving historic railroad depots. For information, call (303) 623-1504.

Regional Offices: See the list that appears later in this chapter.

Rural Preservation: The National Trust's rural heritage initiative offers support to rural communities on preservation issues and public policy. Call your National Trust Regional Office for information or (202) 588-6037.

Seminars: See **Conferences**.

Study Tours: The National Trust hosts study tours throughout the world focusing on architecture and historic preservation. Open to members and nonmembers. For information, call (202) 588-6300, or e-mail: tours@nthp.org.

Tax Credits: See **Historic Rehabilitation Tax Credit**.

Tourism: See **Heritage Tourism**.

Tours: See **Study Tours**.

Volunteers: See **Human Resources** or call the individual National Trust historic sites listed later in this chapter.

Workshops: See **Conferences**.

Zoning: See **Legal Services**.

EXECUTIVE STAFF

Richard Moe, President

Peter Brink, Vice President, Department of Programs, Services and Information

Greg Coble, Vice President, Department of Finance, Human Resources and Information Technology

Betty J. Marmon, Vice President, Department of Resources Development

Edward M. Norton, Jr., Vice President, Department of Law and Public Policy

J.J. Pryor, Vice President, Department of Marketing and Communications

Frank E. Sanchis, Vice President, Department of Stewardship of Historic Sites

REGIONAL OFFICES

Mid-Atlantic Regional Office
One Penn Center at Suburban Station, Suite 1520
1617 John F. Kennedy Boulevard
Philadelphia, PA 19103-1815
(215) 568-8162
FAX (215) 568-9251
E-mail: maro@nthp.org
Web Site: http://www.nthp.org
Patricia Wilson Aden, Director
Delaware, District of Columbia, Maryland, New Jersey, Pennsylvania, Puerto Rico, Virginia, Virgin Islands, West Virginia

Midwest Regional Office
53 West Jackson Boulevard
Suite 1135
Chicago, IL 60604
(773) 939-5547
FAX (773) 939-5651
E-mail: mwro@nthp.org
Web Site: http://www.nthp.org
James Mann, Director and Associate General Counsel for State Policy
Illinois, Indiana, Iowa, Michigan, Minnesota, Missouri, Ohio, Wisconsin

Mountains/Plains Regional Office
910 16th Street, Suite 1100
Denver, CO 80202
(303) 623-1504
FAX (303) 623-1508
E-mail: mpro@nthp.org
Web Site: http://www.nthp.org
Barbara Pahl, Director
Colorado, Kansas, Montana, Nebraska, North Dakota, South Dakota, Wyoming

Northeast Regional Office
Seven Faneuil Hall Marketplace
Boston, MA 02109
(617) 523-0885
FAX (617) 523-1199
E-mail: nero@nthp.org
Web Site: http://www.nthp. org
Wendy Nicholas, Director
Connecticut, Maine, Massachusetts, New Hampshire, New York, Rhode Island, Vermont

Southern Regional Office
456 King Street
Charleston, SC 29403
(803) 722-8552
FAX (803) 722-8652
E-mail: sro@nthp.org
Web Site: http://www.nthp.org
David Brown, Director
Alabama, Arkansas, Florida, Georgia, Kentucky, Louisiana, Mississippi, North Carolina, South Carolina, Tennessee

Southwest Field Office
500 Main Street, Suite 1030
Fort Worth, TX 76102
(817) 332-4398
FAX (817) 332-4512
E-mail: swro@nthp.org
Web Site: http://www.nthp.org
Jane Jenkins, Director
Texas, New Mexico, Oklahoma

Western Regional Office
One Sutter Street, Suite 707
San Francisco, CA 94104
(415) 956-0610
FAX (415) 956-0837
E-mail: wro@nthp.org
Web Site: http://www.nthp.org
Elizabeth Goldstein, Director
Alaska, Arizona, California, Guam,
Hawaii, Idaho, Micronesia, Nevada,
Oregon, Utah, Washington

HISTORIC SITES

Belle Grove
P.O. Box 137
Middletown, VA 22645
(540) 869-2028
FAX (540) 869-9638
Web Site: http://www.nthp.org
Elizabeth McClung, Director

Brucemore
2160 Linden Drive, S.E.
Cedar Rapids, IA 52403
(319) 362-7375
FAX (319) 362-9481
E-mail: mail@brucemore.org
Web Site: http://www.brucemore.org
Peggy Whitworth, Director

Chesterwood
P.O. Box 827
4 Williamsville Road
Stockbridge, MA 01262-0827
(413) 298-3579
FAX (413) 298-3973
E-mail: mail@brucemore.org
Web Site:
http://www.brucemore.org
Paul Ivory, Director

Cliveden
6401 Germantown Avenue
Philadelphia, PA 19144
(215) 848-1777
FAX (215) 438-2892
E-mail: cliveden@nthp.org
Web Site: http://www.nthp.org
Jennifer Esler, Director

Cooper-Molera Adobe
525 Polk Street
Monterey, CA 93940
(408) 649-7172
FAX (408) 647-6236
Web Site: http://www.nthp.org
Hayden Sohm, Director

Decatur House
748 Jackson Place, N.W.
Washington, DC 20006
(202) 842-0920
FAX (202) 842-0030
E-mail: Decatur_House@nthp.org
Web Site: http://www.nthp.org
Paul Reber, Director

Drayton Hall
3380 Ashley River Road
Charleston, SC 29414
(803) 766-0188
FAX (803) 766-0878
E-mail: Drayton_Hall@nthp.org
Web Site: http://www.nthp.org
George McDaniel, Director

Filoli
Canada Road
Woodside, CA 93940
(415) 364-8300
FAX (415) 366-7836
Web Site: http://www.nthp.org
Anne Taylor, Director

Frank Lloyd Wright Home and Studio
951 Chicago Avenue
Oak Park, IL 60302
(708) 848-1976
FAX (708) 848-1248
Web Site: http://www.nthp.org
Joan Mercuri, Director

Gaylord Building
200 West 8th Street
Lockport, IL 60441
(815) 838-0328
Web Site: http://www.nthp.org
Ann Hintze, Director

Kykuit (Pocantico Conference Center)
200 Lake Road
Tarrytown, NY 10591
(914) 524-6500
FAX (914) 524-6550
For tours: (941) 631-9491
Web Site: http://www.nthp.org
Charles Granquist, Director

Lyndhurst
635 South Broadway
Tarrytown, NY 10591
(914) 631-0046
FAX (914) 631-5634
E-mail: Lyndhurst@nthp.org
Web Site: http://www.nthp.org
Susanne Brendel-Pandich, Director

Montpelier
P.O. Box 67
11407 Constitution Highway
Montpelier Station, VA 22957
(540) 672-2728
FAX (540) 672-0411
E-mail: montpelier@nthp.org
Web Site: http://www.nthp.org
Kathleen Mullins, Director

Oatlands
20805 Oatlands Plantation Lane
Leesburg, VA 20175
(703) 777-3174
FAX (703) 777-4427
Web Site: http://www.nthp.org
Linda Cox Glidden, Director

Robie House
5757 South Woodlawn Avenue
Chicago, IL 60637
(708) 848-1976
FAX (708) 848-1248
Web Site: http://www.nthp.org

Shadows-on-the-Teche
317 East Main Street
New Iberia, LA 70562
(318) 369-6446
FAX (318) 365-5213
E-mail: shadows@nthp.org
Web Site: http://www.nthp.org
Patricia Kahle, Acting Director

Woodlawn Plantation and **Frank Lloyd Wright's Pope-Leighey House**
P.O. Box 37
900 Richmond Highway
Mount Vernon, VA 22309
(703) 780-4000
FAX (703) 780-8509
E-mail: woodlawn@nthp.org
Web Site: http://www.nthp.org
Susan Olsen, Director

Woodrow Wilson House
2340 S Street, N.W.
Washington, DC 20008
(202) 387-4062
FAX (202) 483-1466
E-mail: wilson_house@nthp.org
Web Site: http://www.nthp.org
Michael Sheehan, Director

BOARD OF TRUSTEES
(as of February 1997)

Nancy N. Campbell, Chairman
Former President, Preservation
League of New York
New York, NY

William B. Hart, Jr., Vice Chairman
The Dunfey Group
Portsmouth, NH

Camille J. Strachan, Esq., Vice Chairman
Barkan, Conner and Strachan
New Orleans, LA

Robert C. Allen
Duke Power Company
Charlotte, NC

Michael Andrews, Esq.
Vinson and Elkins L.L.P.
Washington, DC

Garden District home, New Orleans, Louisiana. *(Carol M. Highsmith Photography)*

John W. Baird
Baird and Warner, Inc.
Chicago, IL

Richard D. Baron
McCormack Baron and Associates
St. Louis, MO

Claire W. Bogaard
Community Volunteer
Pasadena, CA

Lovida H. Coleman
Community Volunteer
McLean, VA

D. Ronald Daniel
McKinsey & Company, Inc.
New York, NY

Katharine H. Dickenson
Chair, Historic Palm Beach County
Preservation Board
Boca Raton, FL

Susan Guthrie Dunham
Capstone Financial Group
Oklahoma City, OK

Elinor K. Farquhar
Community Volunteer
Washington, DC

Terry Goddard, Esq.
Law Offices of Terry Goddard
Phoenix, AZ

Tony Goldman
Goldman Properties, Inc.
New York, NY

Graham Gund
Graham Gund Architects, Inc.
Cambridge, MA

Dealey Decherd Herndon
Herndon, Stauch and Associates
Austin, TX

Susan L. Howard
Vice President, Corporate
Community Development, Bank of
America
San Francisco, CA

Lily Rice Kendall
Nonprofit Consultant
South Hamilton, MA

Advisory Council on Historic Preservation

Advisory Council on Historic Preservation
1100 Pennsylvania Avenue, N.W.
Suite 809
Washington, DC 20004
(202) 606-8503
FAX (202) 606-8672
E-mail: achp@achp.gov

The Advisory Council on Historic Preservation is an independent federal agency that provides a forum for influencing federal policies, programs, and activities affecting cultural resources in communities across the nation. Primary policy advisor to the president and Congress on historic preservation matters, the Council is the only entity—public or private—with the legal responsibility to balance historic values with federal project requirements. Its main function is to review and comment on federal and federally assisted and licensed projects that affect properties eligible for, or listed in, the National Register of Historic Places, as provided under Section 106 of the National Historic Preservation Act of 1966.

Under Section 106, federal agencies must identify and assess the effects of planned actions on historic resources and consult with state and local officials, Native American tribes, and members of the public to lessen or avoid adverse impacts. Projects proceed only after agreement has been reached among the Council, the affected parties, the State Historic Preservation Officer, and the agency. Section 106 is applicable when two thresholds are met: A historic property is present and a federal or federally sponsored action is planned.

In addition to overseeing the Section 106 review process, the Council offers training, guidance, and public information to help the review process operate smoothly and ensure citizen involvement. It publishes an annual report to the president and Congress, coordinates U.S. membership in the International Centre for the Study of the Preservation and Restoration of Cultural Property (ICCROM), and presents a three-day training program, "Introduction to Federal Projects and Historic Preservation Law," throughout the country, among its other activities.

Mediating conflicts between federal projects and local historic preservation goals, the Council provides an invaluable service to state, tribal, and local governments, in addition to businesses, property owners, and concerned citizens.

For additional information, contact the Council at the above address.

A brief look at Section 106 review

The standard Section 106 review process is spelled out in regulations issued by the Council. Entitled "Protection of Historic Properties," the regulations appear in the U.S. Code of Federal Regulations at 36 CFR Part 800. The process involves several basic steps.

1. *Determine undertaking and area of potential effects.* The responsible federal agency first determines whether it has an undertaking subject to Section 106 that could result in changes in the character or use of historic properties, defined as properties that are included in, or that meet, the criteria for the National Register of Historic Places. If an agency has such an action under its jurisdiction or control, it must decide on the geographic area within which such changes could occur.

2. *Identify and evaluate historic properties.* Based on the nature of the undertaking and the area of potential effects, the agency identifies the historic properties that the undertaking may affect. Depending on what is already known of the area,

Randolph-Macon College building, Lynchburg, Virginia.
(Carol M. Highsmith Photography)

the agency reviews background information, consults with the State Historic Preservation Officer (SHPO) and others, and conducts additional studies including field surveys. Districts, sites, buildings, structures, and objects listed in the National Register are considered; if previously unevaluated properties are found, the agency evaluates them in consultation with the SHPO against the National Park Service's published criteria. If questions arise about the eligibility of a given property, the agency may seek a formal determination of eligibility from the secretary of the interior. Section 106 review gives equal consideration to properties that have already been included in the National Register as well as those that are eligible for inclusion.

3. *Assess effects.* If historic properties, that is, properties included in, or eligible for, inclusion in the National Register, are found, the agency then assesses what effect its undertaking will have on them. Again the agency works with the SHPO and considers the views of others. The agency makes its assessment based on criteria found in the Council's regulations and can make one of three determinations:

- **no effect**: the undertaking will not affect historic properties;
- **no adverse effect**: the undertaking will affect one or more historic properties, but the effect will not be harmful; or
- **adverse effect**: the undertaking will harm one or more historic properties.

4. *Consultation.* If an adverse effect will occur, the agency consults with the SHPO and others in an effort to find ways to make the undertaking less harmful. Others who are consulted, under various circumstances, may include local governments, Native American tribes, permit or license applicants, property owners, other members of the public, and the Council. Consultation is designed to result in a Memorandum of Agreement (MOA), which outlines agreed-upon measures that the agency will take to reduce, avoid, or mitigate the adverse effect. In some cases the consulting parties may agree that no such measures are available but that the adverse effects must be accepted in the public interest. If consultation proves unproductive, the agency or the SHPO, or the Council itself, may terminate consultation. The agency must submit appropriate documentation to the Council and request the Council's written comments.

5. *Council comment.* The Council may comment by participating in consultation and signing the resulting MOA. Otherwise, the agency obtains Council comment by submitting the MOA to the Council for review and acceptance. The Council can accept the MOA, request changes, or opt to issue written comments. If consultation was terminated, the Council issues its written comments directly to the agency head, as the agency had requested.

6. *Implementation.* If an MOA is executed, the agency proceeds with its undertaking under the terms of the MOA. In the absence of an MOA, the agency head must take into account the Council's written comments in deciding whether and how to proceed.

7. *Alternative approaches.* Section 106 regulations also spell out several alternative means of complying with Section 106. These include:

- **programmatic agreements** among an agency, the Council, one or more SHPOs and others;
- **counterpart procedures** developed by an agency and approved by the Council;
- **an agreement between the Council and a state**, which substitutes a state review system for the standard Section 106 review process; and
- **an agreement between the Council and a tribe**, which substitutes use of tribal regulations for those of the Council on tribal land.

A.C.H.P. Regional Offices

Washington Office
Old Post Office Building
1100 Pennsylvania Avenue, N.W.
Suite 809
Washington, DC 20004
(202) 606-8503
FAX (202) 606-8647
E-mail: achp@achp.gov
Web site: www.achp.gov

Denver Office
12136 West Bayaud Avenue,
Suite 330
Lakewood, CO 80226
(303) 969-5110
FAX (303) 969-5115

Publications of Interest

Available from the Advisory Council

Fact Sheet: Council Members
Fact Sheet: Professional Staff
Fact Sheet: A Five-Minute Look at Section 106 Review
Protection of Historic Properties [36 CFR Part 800]
Section 106, Step-by-Step
Federal Historic Preservation Case Law, 1966-1996: Thirty Years of the National Historic Preservation Act

Federal Programs

In addition to the National Park Service (see separate listing), a number of federal programs and agencies affect historic preservation in the United States. The principal programs and agencies are listed below.

EXECUTIVE BRANCH

U.S. Department of Agriculture
Farm Service Agency
Environmental Activities Branch
P.O. Box 2415
Washington, DC 20013
(202) 720-6303
FAX (202) 720-4619

Forest Service
Recreation Division
P.O. Box 96090
Washington, DC 20090-6090
(202) 205-1760
FAX (202) 205-1145

Rural Utilities Service
Electric Staff Division
1400 Independence Avenue, S.W.
Room 1246
Washington, DC 20240
(202) 720-1255
FAX (202) 720-7491
Web Site: http://www.usda.gov/
rus/home/home.htm

Natural Resources Conservation
Service
Resource Economic, and Social
Sciences Division
P.O. Box 2890
Washington, DC 20013-2890
(202) 720-3210
FAX (202) 720-1564
Web Site: http://www.ncg.nrcs.
asda.gov/

U.S. Department of Commerce
Building and Fire Research
Laboratory
National Institute of Standards and
Technology
Building 226, Room B-216
Gaithersburg, MD 20899
(301) 975-5900
FAX (301) 975-4032
Web Site: http://www.bfrl.nist.gov

Economic Development
Administration
14th Street and Constitution
Avenue, N.W., Room 7804
Washington, DC 20230
(202) 482-5081
FAX (212) 273-4781

National Oceanic and Atmospheric
Administration
Office of Ocean and Coastal
Resource Management
1305 East–West Highway
SSMC-4, 10414

Silver Spring, MD 20910
(301) 713-3115
FAX (301) 713-4012

U.S. Department of Defense
U.S. Air Force
Office of Air Force History
HQ USAF/CHO
Bolling Air Force Base
Building 5681
Washington, DC 20330
(202) 767-5764
FAX (202) 767-5527

U.S. Army
Center of Military History Museum
Division
1099 14th Street, N.W.
Washington, DC 20005
(202) 761-5373
FAX (202) 761-5444

U.S. Army
Corps of Engineers
20 Massachusetts Avenue, N.W.
Washington, DC 20314
(202) 761-0660
FAX (202) 761-1373

U.S. Marine Corps
History and Museums Division
HD, Building 58
Washington Navy Yard
Washington, DC 20374-0580
(202) 443-3914
(202) 433-3840

U.S. Navy
Navy Museum
901 M Street, S.E.
Washington Navy Yard
Washington, DC 20374-5060
(202) 433-4882
FAX (202) 433-8200

U.S. Department of Education
400 Maryland Avenue, S.W.
Washington, DC 20202
(202) 708-5366

U.S. Department of Energy
1000 Independence Avenue, S.W.
Washington, DC 20585
(202) 586-5000
FAX (202) 586-5049
Web Site: http://www.doe.gov

**U.S. Department of Housing and
Urban Development**
451 7th Street, S.W.
Washington, DC 20410
(202) 708-1422
Web Site: http://www.hud.gov

Capitol pillars at the National Arboretum, Washington, D.C.
(Carol M. Highsmith Photography)

Community Development Block
Grants
(202) 708-3587
FAX (202) 401-2044

Historic Preservation Information
(202) 708-2300
FAX (202) 708-1300

Section 202: Housing for the Elderly
and Assisted Housing
(202) 708-2866
FAX (202) 708-3104

Section 221: Homeowners
Assistance for Low and Moderate
Housing
(202) 708-2700

Section 312: Rehabilitation Loans
(202) 708-1367
FAX (202) 708-1744

Title I: Property Improvement Loan
Program
(202) 708-6396

Urban Homesteading Program
(202) 708-0324
FAX (202) 708-1744

U.S. Department of the Interior
Assistant Secretary for Fish and
Wildlife and Parks
(202) 208-4416
FAX (202) 208-4684

National Park Service
18th and C Streets, N.W.
Washington, DC 20840
(202) 208-4621
FAX (202) 208-7889

Associate Director for Cultural
Resources
(202) 208-7625
FAX (202) 273-3237

Assistant Director for Cultural
Resources, Stewardship and
Partnership Programs
(202) 343-3379

Assistant to the Associate Director
(202) 343-3411
FAX (202) 343-5260

International Liaison Officer for
Cultural Resources
(202) 343-7069
FAX (202) 343-5260

Office of International Affairs
(202) 565-1294
FAX (202) 565-1290

U.S. Department of Labor
Employment and Training
Administration
200 Constitution Avenue, N.W.
Washington, DC 20210
(202) 219-6666
Web Site: http://www.doleta.gov

U.S. Department of Transportation
Coast Guard
Aids to Navigation Office
2100 2nd Street, S.W.
Washington, DC 20593
(202) 267-0980
FAX (202) 267-4427
Web Site: http://www.hsc.comdt.
uscg.mil/

Federal Highway Administration
Environmental Analysis Division
400 7th Street, S.W.
Washington, DC 20590
(202) 366-2060
FAX (202) 366-3409

Federal Railroad Administration
Office of Policy
400 7th Street, S.W., Room 8300
Washington, DC 20590
(202) 632-3147

Federal Transit Administration
400 7th Street, S.W., Room 9301
Washington, DC 20590
(202) 366-0096

U.S. Department of the Treasury
Bureau of the Mint
United States Mint
633 3rd Street, N.W.
Washington, DC 20220
(202) 874-6000
FAX (202) 874-4083

Comptroller of the Currency
250 E Street, S.W.
Washington, DC 20219
(202) 874-5000
FAX (202) 874-5263
Web Site: http://www.occ.treas.gov

Internal Revenue Service
500 North Capitol Street
Washington, DC 20001
(800) 829-1040

INDEPENDENT AGENCIES

Advisory Council on Historic Preservation
1100 Pennsylvania Avenue, N.W.
Suite 809
Washington, DC 20004
(202) 606-8503
FAX (202) 606-8647

Amtrak
National Railroad Passenger
Corporation
60 Massachusetts Avenue, N.E.
Washington, DC 20002
(202) 906-3000
Web Site: http://www.amtrak.com

Commission of Fine Arts
441 F Street, N.W., Room 312
Washington, DC 20001
(202) 504-2200
FAX (202) 504-2195

Council on Environmental Quality
722 Jackson Place, N.W.
Washington, DC 20503
(202) 395-5750
FAX (202) 456-6546

Federal Emergency Management Agency
500 C Street, S.W., Room 713
Washington, DC 20472
(202) 646-3807
FAX (202) 646-3147
Web Site: http://www.fema.gov

General Services Administration
Public Buildings Service
7th and D Streets, S.W.
Washington, DC 20407
(202) 708-5891
FAX (202) 708-8801

National Archives and Records Administration
National Historical Publications and
Records Commission
8th and Pennsylvania Avenue, N.W.
Washington, DC 20408
(202) 501-5600
FAX (202) 501-5601

Web Site: http://www.nara.gov/
nara/nhprc

National Foundation on the Arts and Humanities
Institute of Museum and Library
Services
1100 Pennsylvania Avenue, N.W.
Suite 510
Washington, DC 20506
(202) 606-8539
FAX (202) 606-8591
Web Site: http:www.ims.fed.us

National Endowment for the Arts
1100 Pennsylvania Avenue, N.W.
Washington, DC 20506
(202) 682-5442
FAX (202) 682-5721
Web Site: http:www.arts.endow.gov

National Endowment for the
Humanities
1100 Pennsylvania Avenue, N.W.
Room 503
Washington, DC 20506
(202) 606-8438
FAX (202) 606-8240
Web Site: http://www.neh.fed.us

Neighborhood Reinvestment Corporation
1325 G Street, N.W., Suite 800
Washington, DC 20005
(202) 376-2400
FAX (202) 376-2600
Web Site: http://www.nw.org

Small Business Administration
409 3rd Street, S.W.
Washington, DC 20416
(202) 205-6605
FAX (202) 205-6802

Smithsonian Institution
National Institute for Conservation
of Cultural Property
3299 K Street, N.W., Suite 602
Washington, DC 20007-4415
(202) 625-1496
FAX (202) 625-1485
Web Site: http://www.nic.org

Tennessee Valley Authority
Cultural Resources Program
17 Ridgeway Road
Norris, TN 37828
(423) 632-1585
FAX (423) 632-1795
Web Site: http://www.tva.gov

LEGISLATIVE BRANCH

Architect of the Capitol
U.S. Capitol Building
Washington, DC 20515
(202) 224-3121
FAX (202) 228-1893

Library of Congress
101 Independence Avenue, S.E.
Washington, DC 20540
(202) 707-5000
FAX (202) 707-5844
Web Site: http://www.lcweb.loc.
gov

FEDERAL PRESERVATION OFFICERS

U.S. Department of Agriculture
Farm Service Agency
Mail Stop 0513
1400 Independence Avenue, S.W.
Washington, DC 20250-0513
(202) 720-6825
FAX (202) 720-4619
E-mail: mlinsenb@wac.fsa.usda.gov
Michael Linsenbigler, Preservation
Representative

Forest Service
P.O. Box 96090
Washington, DC 20090-6090
(202) 205-1427
Evan De Bloois, Preservation
Officer

Natural Resources Conservation
Service
Economic and Social Service
Division
P.O. Box 2890
Washington, DC 20250-2890
(202) 720-2171

FAX (202) 720-6473
Peter Smith, Director

Rural Development
Mail Stop 0705
1400 Independence Avenue, S.W.
Washington, DC 20250-0705
(202) 720-6903
FAX (202) 690-0311
Susan Wieferich, Senior
Environmental Specialist

Rural Utilities Service
Engineer and Environmental Staff
Mail Stop 1571
1400 Independence Avenue, S.W.
Washington, DC 20250
(202) 720-5093
FAX (202)720-5093
Lawrence R. Wolfe, Senior
Environmental Protection Specialist

U.S. Department of Commerce
Economic Development
Administration
14th Street and Constitution
Avenue N.W., Room 7019
Washington, DC 20230
(202) 482-2710
FAX (202) 482-0995
Frank Monteferrante, Senior
Environmental Officer

National Oceanic and Atmospheric
Administration
Office of Ocean and Coastal
Resource Management
1305 East–West Highway, SSMC-4
Room 10414
Silver Spring, MD 20910
(301) 713-3115
FAX (301) 713-4012
Jeff Benoit, Director

Office of Real Estate Policy and
Major Programs
14th Street and Constitution
Avenue, N.W., Room 1040
Washington, DC 20230
(202) 482-3580
FAX (202) 482-1969
James Andrews, Director

U.S. Department of Defense
U.S. Air Force
1660 Air Force Pentagon
Washington, DC 20330-1660
(703) 614-2884
Thomas W. L. McCall Jr., Deputy
Assistant Secretary of the Air Force
Federal Preservation Officer

U.S. Army
110 Army Pentagon
Washington, DC 20310-0110
(703) 695-7824
FAX (703) 693-8149
Raymond J. Fatz, Deputy Assistant
Secretary of the Army Environment,
Safety and Occupational Health
Federal Preservation Officer

U.S. Navy and U.S. Marine Corps
Department of the Navy
Office of the Assistant Secretary
Installations and Environment
1000 Navy Pentagon
Washington, DC 20350-1000
(703) 695-3221
Dr. Bernard Murphy, Federal
Preservation Officer

U.S. Department of Energy
Federal Energy Regulatory
Commission
888 1st Street, N.E.
Washington, DC 20426
(202) 208-0400
FAX (202) 208-2268
Web Site:
http://www.federal.gov/ferd/
ferdhgm/
Lois D. Cashell, Secretary

**U.S. Department of Health and
Human Services**
330 Independence Avenue, S.W.
Room 4700
Washington, DC 20201
(202) 619-0426
FAX (202) 619-1407
E-mail: swaldman@us.dhhs.gov
Scott Waldman, Historic
Preservation Officer

U.S. Department of Housing and Urban Development
Office of Community Viability
451 7th Street, S.W., Room 7240
Washington, DC 20410
(202) 708-2894
FAX (202) 708-3363
E-mail: richard_broun@hud.gov
Richard H. Broun, Director

U.S. Department of the Interior
Bureau of Indian Affairs
Office of Trust Responsibilities
1849 C Street, N.W., Room 4516
Washington, DC 20240
(202) 208-3606
FAX (202) 208-1605
Don Sutherland, Chief Archeologist

Bureau of Land Management
1849 C Street, N.W., Room 3360
Washington, DC 20240
(202) 208-3353
John G. Douglas, Senior
Archeologist

Fish and Wildlife Service
Refuges and Wildlife
18th and C Street, N.W.
Washington, DC 20240
(202) 208-5333
FAX (202) 208-3082
E-mail: robert_streeter@fns.gov
Dr. Robert Streeter, Assistant
Director

Minerals Management Service
Branch of Environmental Assesment
381 Elden Street
Herndon, VA 20170-4817
(703) 787-1736
FAX (703) 787-1010
E-mail: melanie.stright@mms.gov
Melanie Stright, Archeologist
Federal Preservation Officer

National Park Service
History Division
P.O. Box 37127
Washington, DC 20013-7127
(202) 343-8167

Katherine Stevenson, Associate
Director for Cultural Resources,
Stewardships and Partnerships

Office of Surface Mining
Office of the Director
1951 Constitution Avenue, N.W.
Washington, DC 20240
(202) 208-2700

U.S. Geological Survey
Environmental Affairs Program
122201 Sunrise Valley Drive
Mail Stop 423
Reston, VA 20192
(703) 648-6828
FAX (703) 648-4530
Norman Wingard, Federal
Preservation Officer

U.S. Department of Justice
Real Property and Management
Services
1331 Pennsylvania Avenue, N.W.
Suite 1060
Washington, DC 20530
(202) 307-1873
FAX (202) 307-1915
Lisa Harris, Assistant Director

U.S. Department of Labor
Division of Administrative Services
200 Constitution Avenue, N.W.
Room N-4659
Washington, DC 20210
(202) 219-5468
FAX (202) 219-7842
Michael O'Malley, Architect

U.S. Department of Transportation
Office of Environment, Energy and
Safety
P-14, 400 7th Street, S.W.
Room 9217
Washington, DC 20590
(202) 366-4866
E-mail: stephen.shapiro@ost.dot.gov
Stephen M. Shapiro, Historic
Preservation Officer

Federal Aviation Administration
Office of Environment and Energy
800 Independence Avenue, S.W.
Room 902
Washington, DC 20591
(202) 493-4018
FAX (202) 267-5594
E-mail: ann.hooker.faa.dot.gov
Dr. Ann Hooker, Federal
Preservation Officer

Federal Highway Administration
Natural and Cultural Resources
Team
400 7th Street, S.W.
Room 3240
Washington, DC 20590
(202) 366-5004
FAX (202) 366-3409
Web Site: http://www.fhua.dot.gov
Fred Bank, Team Leader

Federal Railroad Administration
Office of Policy and Program
Development
400 7th Street, S.W.
Washington, DC 20590
(202) 632-3134
Marilyn Klein

U.S. Department of the Treasury
Treasury Annex, Room 6140
Washington, DC 20220
(202) 622-0043
FAX (202) 622-1468
E-mail: william mcgovern@
treas.sprint.com
William McGovern, Environment
and Energy Programs Officer

U.S. Department of Veterans Affairs
Historic Preservation Office
810 Vermont Avenue, N.W.
Washington, DC 20420
(202) 565-5680
Karen Tupek, Historic Preservation
Officer

INDEPENDENT AGENCIES

Environmental Protection Agency
Office of Federal Activities
401 M Street, S.W. (2252A)
Washington, DC 20460
(202) 564-7152
FAX (202) 504-0070
Pat Haman, Federal Preservation
Officer

Federal Communications Commission
1919 M Street, N.W., Room 222
Washington, DC 20554
(202) 418-0300
Bill Caton, Acting Secretary

Federal Deposit Insurance Corporation
Division of Supervision
550 17th Street, N.W.
Washington, DC 20429
(202) 898-8510
FAX (202) 898-3638
Nicholas J. Ketcha Jr., Director

Riggs Bank Building, Georgetown, Washington, D.C.
(Carol M. Highsmith Photography)

General Service Administration
Public Buildings Service
Office of Portfolio Management
7th and D Streets, S.W., Room 7600
Washington, DC 20407
(202) 708-5334
FAX (202) 708-7671
Art Torowski, Director, Arts and
Historic Preservation

National Aeronautics and Space Administration
Facilities Management and
Securities
300 E Street, S.W.
Washington, DC 20546
(202) 358-1293
FAX (202) 358-3096
Annie O'Donoghue, Chief

National Capital Planning Commission
Technical Planning Services
Division
801 Pennsylvania Avenue, N.W.
Suite 301
Washington, DC 20576
(202) 482-7239
FAX (202) 482-7272
Nancy Witherell, Historic
Preservationist

Nuclear Regulatory Commission
Office of State Programs
11555 Rockville Pike
Rockville, MD 20852
(301) 415-1219
Rosetta Virgilio, Inter-Governmental
Programs Officer

Small Business Administration
Borrower and Lender Servicing
409 3rd Street, S.W., Suite 8300
Washington, DC 20416
(202) 205-6481
FAX (202) 205-7519
Annie McCluney, Analyst Specialist

Federal Agency Area Offices
Listed in local telephone directories
by agency under "State
Government."

Federal Information Centers
Listed in local telephone directories
under "Federal Information Center,
United States Government" and
connected to other agencies by toll-
free lines.

National and Regional Organizations

American Association for State and Local History
530 Church Street, Suite 600
Nashville, TN 37219
(615) 255-2971
FAX (615) 255-2979
E-mail: aaslh@nashville.net
Web Site: http://www.
nashville.net/~aaslh

American Association of Museums
1575 I Street, N.W., Suite 400
Washington, DC 20005
(202) 289-1818
FAX (202) 289-6578
Web Site: http://www.aam~us.org

American Historical Association
400 A Street, S.E.
Washington, DC 20003
(202) 544-2422
FAX (202) 544-8307
Web Site: http://www.
gmu.edu/chnm/aha

American Institute for Conservation of Historic and Artistic Works
1717 K Street, N.W., Suite 301
Washington, DC 20006
(202) 452-9545
FAX (202) 452-9328
E-mail: infoaic@aol.com

American Institute of Architects
1735 New York Avenue, N.W.
Washington, DC 20006

(202) 626-7300
FAX (202) 626-7426
E-mail: aia@aia.org
Web Site: http://www.aia.org

   Committee on Historic Resources
   Regional Urban Design
   Assistance Teams
   (202) 626-7589

American Planning Association
122 South Michigan Avenue
Suite 1600
Chicago, IL 60603
(312) 431-9100
FAX (312) 431-9985
Web Site: http://www.planning.org

   Urban Design and Preservation
   Division
   (312) 431-9100

American Society of Civil Engineers
Committee on History and Heritage
of American Civil Engineering
1015 15th Street, N.W., Suite 600
Washington, DC 20005
(202) 789-2200
FAx (202) 289-6797
Web Site: http://www.asce.org

American Society of Interior Designers
Historic Preservation Committee
608 Massachusetts Avenue, N.E.
Washington, DC 20002
(202) 546-3480

E-mail: network@asid.noli.com
Web Site: http://www.aisd.org

American Society of Landscape Architects
4401 Connecticut Avenue, N.W.
Fifth Floor
Washington, DC 20008-2369
(202) 686-2752
FAX (202) 686-1001
Web Site: http://www.asla.
org/asla/

American Society of Mechanical Engineers
History and Heritage Program
345 East 47th Street
New York, NY 10017-2392
(212) 705-8159
FAX (202) 705-8676
Web Site: http://www.asme.org

America the Beautiful Fund
1511 K Street N.W., Suite 611
Washington, DC 20005
(202) 638-1649

Archaeological Conservancy
5301 Central Avenue, N.E.
Suite 1218
Albuquerque, NM 87108-1517
(505) 266-1540
E-mail:
104017.3526@compuserve.com
Web Site: http://www.gorp.com/
archcons/

Archeological Institute of America
656 Beacon Street, Fourth Floor
Boston, MA 02215-2010
(617) 353-9361
FAX (617) 353-6550
E-mail: aia@bu.edu
Web Site: http://www.csaws.
brynmar.edu:443/aia.html/

Association for Living Historical Farms and Agricultural Museums
c/o Judith Sheridan, Secretary-Treasurer
Brownwood Farm
8774 Route 45 N.W.
North Bloomfield, OH 44450-9701
(216) 685-4410

Association for Preservation Technology International
904 Princess Anne Street
P.O. Box 8178
Fredericksburg, VA 22404
(540) 373-1621, 373-1622

Association of American Geographers
1710 16th Street, N.W.
Washington, DC 20009
(202) 234-1450
FAX (202) 234-2744
Web Site: http://www.aag.org

Council of American Maritime Museums
c/o Chesapeake Bay Maritime Museum
P.O. Box 636
St. Michaels, MD 21663-0636
(301) 745-2916
FAX (410) 745-6088
Web Site: http://www.cbmm.org

Council of Planning Librarians
114 North Aberdeen
Chicago, IL 60607
(312) 409-3349
FAX (312) 666-3681

Decorative Arts Society
c/o Brooklyn Museum
200 Eastern Parkway

Brooklyn, NY 11238
(718) 638-5000
FAX (718) 638-3731
Web Site: http://wwar.com/
brooklyn_museum/index.html

Environmental Action Foundation
6930 Carroll Avenue, Suite 600
Takoma Park, MD 20912
(301) 891-1100

Environmental Defense Fund
257 Park Avenue, South
New York, NY 10010
(212) 505-2100
FAX (212) 505-2375
E-mail: members@edf.org

Environmental Law Institute
1616 P Street, N.W., Suite 200
Washington, DC 20036
(202) 939-3800
FAX (202) 939-3868
E-mail: eli@eli.org
Web Site: http://www.eli.org

Friends of Cast-Iron Architecture
235 East 87th Street, Room 6C
New York, NY 10128-3236
(212) 369-6004

Friends of the Earth
1025 Vermont Avenue, N.W.
Washington, DC 20005
(202) 783-7400
FAX (202) 783-0444

Friends of Terra Cotta
c/o Susan Tunick
771 West End Avenue, 10E
New York, NY 10025
(212) 932-1750

Great Lakes Lighthouse Keepers Association
c/o Henry Ford Estate
4901 Evergreen Rd.
Deerborn, MI 48128-1491
(313) 436-9150

Henry Reed Classical America
227 East 50th Street
New York, NY 10022
(212) 753-4376

Institute for Urban Design
47 Barrow Street
New York, NY 10014
(212) 741-2041

Institute of Early American History and Culture
P.O. Box 8781
Williamsburg, VA 23187
(757) 221-1110
FAX (757) 221-1047

International Downtown Association
915 15th Street, N.W., Suite 600
Washington, DC 20005
(202) 783-4963
FAX (202) 347-2161
E-mail: ida@atlantech.net
Web Site: http://www.ida-downtown.org

League of Historic American Theaters
34 Market Place, Suite 320
Baltimore, MD 21202
(410) 659-9533
FAX (410) 837-9664

Lighthouse Preservation Society
4 Middle Street
Newburyport, MA 01950
(508) 499-0011, 1-800-727-BEAM
FAX (508) 499-0026

National Alliance of Preservation Commissions
c/o Pratt Cassity
P.O. Box 1605
Athens, GA 30603
(706) 542-4731
E-mail: pcassity@sed.uga.edu

National Alliance of Statewide Preservation Organizations
c/o Landmarks Foundation of Indiana, Southern Regional Office
113 West Chestnut
Jeffersonville, IN 47130
(812) 284-4534
FAX (812) 285-9923
E-mail: sregion@unix.adcpt.net

National Association for
Olmsted Parks
7315 Wisconsin Avenue,
Suite 705E
Bethesda, MD 20814
(202) 362-9511
FAX (301) 469-3841

National Association of
Conservation Districts
509 Capitol Court, N.E.
Washington, DC 20002
(202) 547-6223
FAX (202) 547-6450
Web Site:
http://www.nacdet.org

National Association of
Counties
440 1st Street, N.W.
8th Floor
Washington, DC 20001
(202) 393-6226
FAX (202) 393-2630
Web Site:
http://www.naco.org

National Association of
Housing and Redevelopment
Officials
630 I Street, N.W.
Washington, DC 20001
(202) 289-3500
FAX (202) 289-4961
Web Site: http://www.nahro.org

National Building Museum
401 F Street, N.W.
Washington, DC 20001
(202) 272-2448
FAX (202) 272-2564
Web Site: http://www.nbm.org

National Conference of State
Historic Preservation Officers
444 North Capitol Street, N.W.
Suite 342
Washington, DC 20001-1512
(202) 624-5465
FAX (202) 624-5419

Trinity Church, Chicago, Illinois. *(Carol M. Highsmith
Photography)*

National Council for Preservation
Education
Center for Historic Architecture and
Design
University of Delaware
Newark, DE 19716
(302) 831-1050
FAX (302) 831-3587
E-mail: davames@udcl.edu

National Council of Preservation
Executives
Chestnut Hill Historical Society
8708 Germantown Avenue
Philadelphia, PA 19118
(215) 247-0417
FAX (215) 247-9329

National Institute for the
Conservation of Cultural Property
c/o Smithsonian Institution
900 Jefferson Drive, S.W.
Room 2225

Washington, DC 20560
(202) 357-2295

National Parks and
Conservation Association
1776 Massachusetts
Avenue, N.W., Suite 200
Washington, DC 20036
(202) 223-6722
FAX (202) 659-0650
Web Site: http://www.
npca.org

National Recreation and
Park Association
2775 South Quincy Street,
Suite 300
Arlington, VA 22206
(703) 820-4940
FAX (703) 671-6772
Web Site: http://www.
nrpa.org

National Trust for Historic
Preservation
1785 Massachusetts
Avenue, N.W.
Washington, DC 20036
(202) 588-6000
FAX (202) 588-6038
Web Site: http://www.nthp.org

Natural Resources Defense Council
40 West 20th Street
New York NY 10011
(212) 727-2700
FAX (212) 727-1773
Web Site: http://www.nrdc.org

The Nature Conservancy
1815 North Lynn Street
Arlington, VA 22209
(703) 841-5300
FAX (703) 841-1283
Web Site: http://www.tnc.org

Organ Historical Society
National Office
P.O. Box 26811
Richmond, VA 23261
(804) 353-9226
FAX (804) 358-9266

Organization of American Historians
112 North Bryan Street
Bloomington, IN 47408
(812) 855-7311
FAX (812) 855-0696
E-mail: oah@indiana.edu
Web Site: http://www.indiana.edu/~oah

Partners for Livable Communities
1429 21st Street, N.W.
Washington, DC 20036
(202) 887-5990
FAX (202) 466-4845
E-mail: plcomms@concentric.net

Partners for Sacred Places
1616 Walnut Street, Suite 2310
Philadelphia, PA 19103
(215) 546-1288
FAX (215) 546-1180
Web Site: http://www.sacredplaces.org

Pioneer America Society
c/o Charles F. Calkins
UW Center–Waukesha
Department of Geography
Waukesha, WI 53188
(414) 521-5498
FAX (414) 521-5491

Popular Culture Association
Bowling Green State University
Bowling Green, OH 43403
(419) 372-7865
FAX (419) 372-8095

Preservation Action
1350 Connecticut Avenue, N.W.
Suite 401
Washington, DC 20036
(202) 659-0915
FAX (202) 296-2705
E-mail:
preservationaction@worldnet.att.net
Web Site: http://www.preservenet.cornell.edu/presaction/home.htm

Project for Public Spaces
153 Waverly Place, Fourth Floor
New York, NY 10014

(212) 620-5660
FAX (212) 620-3821
E-mail: pps@pps.org
Web Site: http://www.pps.org

Public Works Historical Society
106 West 11th Street, Suite 1800
Kansas City, MO 64105
(816) 472-6100

Railroad Station Historical Society
430 Ivy Avenue
Crete, NE 68333
(402) 826-3356

Scenic America
21 Dupont Circle, N.W.
Washington, DC 20036
(202) 833-4300
FAX (202) 833-4304

Small Towns Institute
P.O. Box 517
Ellensburg, WA 98926
(509) 925-1830

Smithsonian Institution
Museum Reference Center
Arts and Industries
Room 2235, MRC 427
900 Jefferson Drive, S.W.
Washington, DC 20560
(202) 786-2271
FAX (202) 357-2311
Web Site: http://www.sil.si.edu/mrchp.htm

Society for American Archaeology
900 Second Street, N.E., Suite 12
Washington, DC 20002
(202) 789-8200
FAX (202) 789-0284
Web Site: http://www.saa.org

Society for Commercial Archeology
National Museum of American
History, Room 5010
Washington, DC 20560
(202) 882-5424

Society for Historical Archaeology
P.O. Box 30446
Tucson, AZ 85751

(520) 886-8006
FAX (520) 886-0182
E-mail: sha@azstarnet.com
Web Site: http://www.sha.org

Society for Industrial Archeology
c/o Patrick Martin, Editor of
Industrial Archeology
Department of Social Sciences
Michigan Technological University
1400 Townsen Dr.
Houghton, MI 49931-1295
(906) 487-1889
FAX (906) 487-2468
E-mail: sia@mtu.edu

**Society for the Preservation of New
England Antiquities**
141 Cambridge Street
Boston, MA 02114
(617) 227-3956
FAX (617) 227-9204

**Society for the Preservation of Old
Mills**
c/o Floyd Harwood
Box 5
Hartford, NY 12838
(518) 632-5237

Society of American Historians
c/o Mark C. Carnes
History Department, Barnard
College
Columbia University
415 Lehman Hall
New York, NY 10027
(212) 854-5943
E-mail: mcarnes@barnard.columbia.edu

Society of Architectural Historians
1365 North Astor Street
Chicago, IL 60610-2144
(312) 573-1365
FAX (312) 573-1141
E-mail: L-torrance@nwu.edu
Web Site: http://www.upenn.edu/sah/

Society of Professional Archeologists
Department of Geography and
Anthropology
Louisiana State University
Baton Rouge, LA 70803
(504) 388-6172

Trust for Public Land
116 New Montgomery Street
Fourth Floor
San Francisco, CA 94105
(415) 495-4014
FAX (415) 495-4103
Web Site: http://www.tpl.org/tpl

U.S. Lighthouse Society
244 Kearney Street, Fifth Floor
San Francisco, CA 94108
(415) 362-7255
(415) 362-7464

Urban Land Institute
1025 Thomas Jefferson Street, N.W.
Suite 500 West
Washington, DC 20007
(202) 624-7000
FAX (202) 624-7140
Web Site: http://www.uli.org

The Victorian Society in America
219 South 6th Street
Philadelphia, PA 19106

(215) 627-4252
FAX (215) 627-7221

The Wilderness Society
900 17th Street, N.W.
Washington, DC 20006
(202) 833-2300
FAX (202) 429-2658
E-mail: tws@tws.org

World Wildlife Fund
1250 24th Street, N.W., Suite 500
Washington, DC 20037
(202) 293-4800
FAX (202) 293-9211
E-mail: publicinfo@wwf.us.org
Web Site: http://www.pancke.org

International Programs

Aga Khan Program for Islamic Architecture
School of Architecture
Massachusetts Institute of
Technology, Room 10-390
777 Massachusetts Avenue
Cambridge, MA 02139-4307
(617) 253-1400
FAX (617) 258-8172

L'Association des Vieilles Maisons Francaises
93, rue de l'Universite
75005 Paris, France

   Friends of Vieilles Maisons Francaises
   14 E. 60th Street, Suite 605
   New York, NY 10022
   (212) 759-6846
   FAX (212) 759-9632

Association for Industrial Archeology
Church Hill
Ironbridge
Telford, Salop TF8 7RE, England

Australian Council of National Trusts
C. M. L. Building, 11th Floor
14 Martin Place
Sydney 20 (a), N.S.W., Australia

   Civic Trust
   17 Carlton House Terrace
   London SW 1 Y 5AW, England

Canadian Parks Service
National Historic Sites Directorate
255 Eddy Street
Ottawa, Ontario K1A OH3 Hull,
Quebec
(819) 994-1808

Council of Europe
Directorate for Environment and
Local Authorities
BP431 R6
67006 Strasbourg Cedex, France

English Heritage
Historic Buildings and Monuments
Commission for England
Fortress House
23 Savile Row
London W 1 X 2HE, England

   American Friends of English Heritage
   477 Madison Avenue, Eighth
   Floor
   New York NY 10022
   (212) 243-3853

Environment Canada, Parks
Les Terrasses de la Chaudiere
Ottawa, Ontario K1A lG2, Canada

Heritage Canada Foundation
P.O. Box 1358, Station B
Ottawa, Ontario K1P 5R4, Canada
(613) 237-1066

Historic Houses Association
38 Ebury Street

London SW 1, England

L'Inspection Generale des Monuments Historiques
Direction du Patrimonie
Ministere de la Culture
3, rue de Valois
75042 Paris Cedex 01, France

International Centre for the Study of the Preservation and the Restoration of Cultural Property (ICCROM)
13 Via di San Michele 00153
Rome, Italy (6) 587-90l
39-6-587901
FAX 39-6-58-55-33-49

   U.S. Committee, ICCROM
   c/o Advisory Council on Historic
   Preservation
   1100 Pennsylvania Avenue, N.W.
   Suite 809
   Washington, DC 20004
   (202) 786-0503

International Committee of the American Institute of Architects
1735 New York Avenue, N.W.
Washington, DC 20006
(202) 626-7315

International Congress for the Conservation of the Industrial Heritage
Dramstigen 12
S/16138 Bramma, Sweden

International Council of
Museums (ICOM)
Maison de l'Unesco
l, rue Miollis
75732 Paris Cedex 15,
France

AAM/ICOM
1575 I Street, N.W.,
Suite 400
Washington, DC 20005
(202) 289-1818

International Council on
Monuments and Sites
(ICOMOS)
49-51 rue de la Federation
75015 Paris, France
33-1-45-67-67-70
FAX 33-1-45-66-06-22

U.S./ICOMOS
National Building Museum
401 F Street, N.W.
Room 331
Washington, DC 20001
(202) 842-1862
FAX (202) 842-1861

International Institute for
Conservation of Historic and Artistic
Works (IIC)
6 Buckingham Street
London WC2N 6BA, England

International Union of Architects
51, rue Raynouard
75016 Paris, France

International Union for
Conservation of Nature and Natural
Resources
Avenue du Mont-Blanc CH-1196
Gland, Switzerland

IUCN/US
1400 16th Street, N.W., Suite 502
Washington, DC 20036
(202) 797-5454

Irish Georgian Society
Castletown House
Celbridge
County Kildare, Ireland

Detail, Haughwout Building, lower Broadway, Manhattan,
New York. *(Carol M. Highsmith Photography)*

National Monuments Record
Fortress House
23 Savile Row
London W1X 1AB, England

National Trust for Places of Historic
Interest or Natural Beauty
36 Queen Anne's Gate
London SW1H 9AS, England

Northern Ireland Region
Rowallane House
Saintfield, Ballynahinch
County Down BT24 7LH,
Northern
Ireland

Royal Oak Foundation
285 West Broadway, Suite 400
New York, NY 10013
(212) 966-6565

National Trust for Scotland
for Places of Historic
Interest or Natural Beauty
5 Charlotte Square
Edinburgh EH2 4DU,
Scotland

Organization of American
States
Department of Cultural
Affairs
Cultural Patrimony Division
1889 F Street, N.W.
Washington, DC 20006
(202) 458-3142

Royal Institute of British
Architects
British Architectural Library
66 Portland Place
London W1N 4AD, England

Save Britain's Heritage
68 Battersea High Street
London SW11, England

Scottish Civic Trust
24 George Square
Glasgow G21 1 EF,
Scotland

Scottish Georgian Society
39 Castle Street
Edinburgh EH2 3BH, Scotland

Society for the Protection of Ancient
Buildings
37 Spital Square
London E1 6DY, England

UNESCO
Physical Property Division and the
World
Heritage Centre
1, place de Fontenoy
75352 Paris 07SP, France

Victorian Society
Priory Gardens
Bedford Park
London W4 1TT, England

World Monuments Fund
949 Park Avenue
New York, NY 10028
(212) 517-9367

Members of the ICOMOS Advisory Committee

Carmen Anon, Chairman
Puerto Santa Maria 49
Madrid 28043
Spain
34-1-388-39-57
FAX 34-1-300-34-27

Blanche Weicherding, Vice Chair
21 route de Diekirch
7220 Walferdange
Luxemburg
352-33-88-14

Algeria
Abderrahmane Khelifa
c/o Agence Nationale d'Archeologie
de la Promotion des Sites et
Monuments
2 avenue Mohamed Taleb
Haute Casbah
Algeria
213-257-62-84-44

Angola
Freire
Conseil National de la Culture
C.X. Postal 1223
Luanda

Argentina
Professor Carlos Pernaut
Calilla de Correo 2163
Buenos Aires 1000
54-1-342-45-80
FAX 54-1-811-32-25

Australia
Dr. Sandy Blair
P.O. Box E 303
Queen Victoria Terrace ACT 2600
61-6-270-65-58
FAX 61-6-273-48-25

Austria
Ernst Bacher
Bundesdenkmalamt
Hofburg Saulenstiege
1010 WIEN 1
431-53-41-51-24
431-53-41-52-77
FAX 431-53-41-52-52

Belgium
Michel van der Meerschen
Groot Beginjhof 95
3000 Leuven
32-16-32-17-48
FAX 32-16-32-19-83

Benin
Aime Goncalves
B.P. 03-2103
Cotonou
229-30-32-19
229-30-32-22
FAX 229-30-21-36

Bolivia
Mireya Munoz
P.O. Box 5240
La Paz
591-2-721-145
FAX 591-2-377-709

Brazil
Suzanna Cruz Sampaio
Rua Itapirucu, 369-17
CJ 1709
CEP 05006-000 Sao Paulo
55-11-873-4060
FAX 55-11-873-6796

Bulgaria
Dr. Prof. Todor Krestev
Comite National Bulgare de
I'COMOS
16 Blvd Dondukov
1000 Sofia
359-2-980-56-56
FAX 359-2-980-6050

Burkina Faso
Absoulaye Sankara
Directeur General de l'Office
National

du Tourisme Burkinabe
06 BP 9833
Ouagadougou 06

Cameroon
Mohaman Haman
Secretaire General ICOMOS
Cameroun
38 rue Max Dormoy
75018 Paris
221-255-938
221-255-940
FAX 221-213-735

Canada
Herb Stovel
P.O. Box 737
Station B
Ottawa, ONT K1P 5R4
1-613-749-09-71
1-514-487-01-00
FAX 1-514-487-78-03

Chile
Edwin Binda Compton
Martin de Zamora 4247
Santiago
56-2-228-25-91
FAX 56-2-231-54-89

China
Zhang Bai
The State Bureau of Cultural Relics
29 Wusi Street
Bejing 100009
86-10-640-15-577
86-10-640-15-278
FAX 86-10-640-13-101

Colombia
Rodolfo Ulloa V.
Calle 62 n 7-33 Apto 11-01
Bogota
FAX 571-212-34-47

Costa Rica
Carlos Mesen
Apartado Postal 2348-1002
San Jose
506-258-05-52
FAX 506-233-69-28

Croatia
Tomislav Marasovic
Marasovico 8
21000 Split
385-21-45-566
FAX 385-21-47-798

Cuba
Isabel Rigol
CNCRM
Antigua Convento de Santa Claro
Calle Cuba 610 entre Sol y Luz
Havana 1
53-7-61-37-75
53-7-61-33-35
FAX 53-7-33-56-96

Cyprus
Demos Christou
Director of the Department of
Antiquities
Box 2024
Nicosia
357-2-302-191
FAX 357-2-303-148

Czech Republic
Dr. Dobroslav Libal/Mme Polakova
Valdstejnske namesti 3
11801 Praha 1—Mala Strana
42-2-513-25-92
42-2-513-25-65
FAX 42-2-513-54-96

Denmark
Niels-Knud Liebgott
The National Museum of Denmark
Frederiksholms Kanal 12
DK-1220 Copenhagen K
45-33-47-31-00
FAX 45-33-47-33-12

Dominican Republic
Manuel S. Gautier
Isabel la Catolica n 103
Santo Domingo
1-809-682-01-85
1-809-686-86-57
FAX 1-809-688-69-25

Ecuador
Wilson Herdoiza
Casilla: 17-12-066
Quito
593-2-509-033
593-2-507-690

Egypt
Nur El-Din
Egyptian Antiquities Organization
Ministry of Culture
4d. Fakhri Abdel Nour Street
El Cairo
20-2-836-572

El Salvador
Arch. Carlos A. Hernandez
Avenida don Bosco n 209
Col. Centro Americana
San Salvador
503-25-26-35

Estonia
Kaur Alttoa
Pikk 46
P.O. Box 3141
Tallinn EE0090
372-260-17-39
FAX 372-260-17-39

Ethiopia
Jarra Halle Mariam
P.O. Box 30795
Addis Abeba
251-1-44-56-00
251-1-15-76-30
FAX 251-1-55-31-88

Finland
Maire Mattinen
National Board of Antiquities
Department of Historic Monuments
P.O. Box 187
FIN-00171 Helsinki
35-80-40-501
FAX 35-80-661-132

France
Michel Jantzen
Section Francaise ICOMOS
62 rue Saint Antoine
75004 Paris
33-1-42-78-56-42
FAX 33-1-44-61-21-81

Gabon
Michel Mboumba Kassa
Ministere de la Culture
Directeur de la Conservation du
Patrimoine Culturel
B.P.1007
Libreville
241-724-028

Georgia
Merab Bochoidze
Secretaire General
5 Rezo Tabukashvill str.
Tbilisi 380005
995-32-99-84-47

Germany
Dr. Michael Petzet
ICOMOS—Bayerisches Landesamt
fur Denkmalpflege
Postfach 10 02 03
80076 Munich
49-89-21-14-260
49-89-21-14-275
FAX 49-89-21-14-300

Ghana
Arch. D.S. Kpodo Tay
P.O. Box 523
Teshis—Nungua Estate
Accra
233-21-775-655
FAX 233-21-712-710

Greece
Nikos Agriantonis
Section Hellenique de l'ICOMOS
P.O. Box 30109
Athens 10033
30-1-323-57-79
FAX 30-1-322-97-51

Guatemala
Bianca Nino Norton
Apartado Postal 625A
Zona 9
01909 Guatemala
502-4-730-535

Haiti
Patrick Delatour
BP 15190
Petion Ville
509-57-21-91
FAX 509-57-39-74

Honduras
Gloria Lara Hasemann
Apartado Postal 2933
Tegucigalpa D.C.
504-38-31-98

Hungary
Dr. Andras Roman
P.O. Box 6
H - 1250 Budapest
36-1-1750-763

India
Achala Moulik
Add. Director General
Government of India
Archaeological Survey of India
Janpath
New Delhi 110011
FAX 91-11-30144-56

Indonesia
Frances B. Affandy
Executive Secretary
Jalan Asia Afrika 112
Bandung
West Java 40261
FAX 62-22-436-187

Ireland
M.A.M. Lindsay
School of Architecture
University College
Belfield
Dublin 4
353-1-269-32-44
FAX 353-1-283-77-78

Israel
Glora Solar
The Getty Conservation Institute
1200 Getty Center Drive, Suite 700
Los Angeles, CA 90049-1684
(310) 440-62 45
FAX (310) 440-77 09

Italy
Gian Franco Borsi
Chiesa Trecentesca di Donnaregina
Vico Donnaregina 26
80128 Napoli
39-81-299-101
FAX 39-81-57-88-283

Ivory Coast
Kindo Bouadi
Director de la Conservation, de la
Protection et de la Valorisation du
Patrimoine Culturel
P.B.V. 39
Abidjan
335-21-53-21
FAX 385-21-47-798

Jamaica
Patricia Green
P.O. Box 8949
Kingston CSO
Jamaica, West Indies
809-967-2481
FAX 809-967-3742

Japan
Akira Ishii
c/o Bunkazai Kougaku Kenkyu-sho
3-9-5-113, Ikuba, Shinjuku-ku
Tokyo 169
81-33-200-93-55
FAX 81-33-200-94-23

Jordan
Dr. Ghazi Bisheh
The Hashemite Kingdom of Jordan
Department of Antiquities
P.O. Box 88
Amman
962-6-644-336
962-6-641-275
FAX 962-6-615-848

Korea
Djang Tcheul
Vice Ministre
Ministere de la Culture et des Arats
Pyong Yang

Latvia
Janis Lejnieks

Latvijas Republikas Valsts
M. Pils ila 19
LV—1050 Riga
371-7-22-92-72
FAX 371-7-21-37-57

Lebanon
Joseph Phares
70 rue Saint-Didler
75116 Paris
961-325-688
FAX 961-330-019

Lithuania
Audrone Kasperaviciene
Kulturos Paveldo Centro
The Centre on Cultural Heritage
Pilies 16, Vilnius
Lithuania 2000
370-2-61-94-59
FAX 370-2-22-21-91

Luxembourg
Blanche Weicherding
21 route de Diekirch
7220 Walferdange
352-33-88-14
FAX 352-33-03-70

Macedonia
Lazar Sumanov
Republic Institute for the Protection
of Cultural Monuments
ul. E. Celebija b.b.
P.O. Box 225
91000 Skopje
38-991-116-465
38-991-116-735
FAX 38-991-227-240

Mali
Baba Ismail A. Cisse
B.P. 2001
Bamako
223-22-40-65
FAX 223-22-89-88

Mauritania
Hamar Fall Diagne
B.P. 1970
Nouakchott
FAX 222-50706

Mexico
Carlos Flores-Marini
Mazatlan 190
Col. Condesa
06140 Mexico DF
52-5-51-51-252
52-5-51-51-471
FAX 52-5-27-73-166

The Netherlands
Dr. J. M. Hengeveld
Huis de Pinto
Sint Antoniesbreestraat 69
1011 HB Amsterdam
31-20-627-77-06
FAX 31-20-624-25-36

New Zealand
Jeremy Salmond
P.O. Box 90851
Auckland Mail Centre
Aukland 1001
64-9-445-40-45
FAX 64-9-445-41-11

Norway
Lisen Roll
Riksantikvaren
Postbox 8196 Dep.
N-0034 OSLO 1
47-22-94-04-00
FAX 47-22-94-04-04

Pakistan
Fakir Syed Aijazuddin
Department of Archaeology and
Museums
27A Central
Union Commercial Area
Shaheed E. Millat Road
Karachi 8
92-21-43-06-38
FAX 92-21-43-64-38

Panama
Manuel Choy Garcia
P.O. Box 6-6927
Eldorado
507-64-13-67

Paraguay
Maria Teresa Gaona

Casilla Correo 212
Asuncion
595-21-25-941
FAX 595-21-20-20-04

Peru
Arq. Jose Correa
Jose Quinones 141
Lima 18
51-14-41-20-44
FAX 51-14-41-41-52

Philippines
Jose T. Regalado, Jr.
107 Wison Circle
San Juan
Metro Manila 1500
63-2-701-654
63-2-722-57-45

Poland
Professor Dr. Krzysztof Pawlowski
Chateau Royal
Plac. Zamkowy 4.
00 277 Warsaw
48-22-48-53-53
FAX 48-22-29-37-91
FAX 33-4-67-54-78-27

Portugal
Claudio Torres
Campo Arqueologico
Rua da Republica n 12
7750 Mertola
351-86-62-443
FAX 351-86-61-10-89

Romania
Eugenia Greceaun
Str. Ienachita Vacarescu 16
Sector 4, Of. Postal 53
70528 Bucarest
401-613-70-08
401-615-83-86
FAX 401-312-50-68

Russia
Igor Makovetski
1 Novodevichi per.,119435 Moscow
7-095-246-13-27
FAX 7-095-246-23-24

Senegal
Mamadou Berthe
BP 1982
Dakar
221-255-938
221-255-940
FAX 222-242-285

Slovakia
Jaroslav Kilian
Cesta na ceverny most a
81104 Bratislava
42-7-375-024
FAX 42-7-333-409

Slovenia
Jovo Grobovsek
Institute for Conservation of Natural
and Cultural Heritage
Piecnikov trg 2
P.O. Box 176
61001 Ljubljana
38-66-11-13-012
38-66-11-13-083
FAX 38-66-11-13-120

South Africa
Andrew Hall
c/o National Monuments Council
P.O. Box 4637
Cape Town 8000
27-21-462-45-02
FAX 27-21-462-45-09

Spain
Alvaro Gomez-Ferrer Bayo
President C.N.E. Cons Sup. Col.
Arquitectos
Paseo de la Castellana 12
34-1-435-22-00
FAX 34-1-575-38-39

Sri Lanka
Lakshman Alwis
Central Cultural Funa
212 Baudahaloka Mawatha
Colombo 7
94-1-546-250
FAX 94-1-500-731

Sweden
M. Bjornstad/Nils Ahlberg
Central Board of National
Antiquities
P.O. Box 5405
S-114 84 Stockholm
46-8-783-90-36
FAX 46-8-783-90-13

Switzerland
Hans Rutishauser
Section Nationale Suisse de
l'ICOMOS
Case Postale
Berne 8
41-31-322-36-72
FAX 41-31-324-40-93

Tanzania
Dr. Simon A. C. Waane
Ministry of Education and Culture
Antiquities Unit
P.O. Box 2280
Dar Es Salaam
255-51-28-840
FAX 255-51-28-593

Thailand
Kowit Vorapipatana
Ministry of Education
Rajadamnorm Nok Avenue
Bangkok

Tunisia
Abdelaziz Daoulatli
Institut National d'Archeologie et
d'Art
4 place du Chateau
1008 Tunis
216-1-261-693
216-1-261-622
FAX 216-1-562-452

Turkey
Nevzat Ilhan
Yeldiz Universitesi
Mimarlik Tarhi ve restorasyon
Ogretim
Gorevilsi
Istanbul
90-212-249-61-46
FAX 90-212-249-60-89

Ukraine
Leonid Prybeha
18 G Radianskoyi Ukrainy Avenue,
Apartment 37
252208 Kiev
380-44-434-26-82
FAX 380-44-212-10-48

United States
Ann Webster-Smith
US/ICOMOS
401 F Street, N.W., Room 331
Washington, DC 20001
(202) 842-1859
FAX (202) 842-1861
E-mail: awebster@erols.com

Venezuela
Maria Carlota Ibanez
Apartado 5552
Carmelitas
Caracas 1010-A
58-2-561-55-01
FAX 58-2-574-66-75

Zaire
Zola Kuandi
Institut des Musées Nationaux du
Zaire
B.P. 4249
Kinshasa II

Zambia
Phillip Ziba
National Heritage Commission
P.O. Box 60124
Livingstone
260-33-23-488
FAX 260-33-24-509

Zimbabwe
Dawson Munjeri
P.O. Box CY 1485
Causeway
Harare
263-4-752-876
FAX 263-4-753-085

WORLD HERITAGE CONVENTION

The Convention Concerning the Protection of the World Cultural and Natural Heritage was adopted in 1972 as the most powerful international legal instrument for protecting cultural and natural resources. The United States was the first nation to adopt this treaty, and in 1988 the 100th nation ratified it. In 1991 the World Heritage List included 339 significant cultural and natural properties in sixty-nine countries; seventeen of the properties are in the United States

Participating nations have agreed to inventory, recognize, and protect irreplaceable properties of outstanding international significance. Each country assumes primary responsibility for protecting and interpreting its own properties, while pledging to cooperate with other nations as required. Through a World Heritage Fund, made up of contributions from member nations, the World Heritage Committee provides financial and technical aid to properties and national governments for threatened sites as well as for preparation of new nominations.

Each participating country may nominate a property within its jurisdiction. Cultural properties must meet criteria such as unique artistic achievement, exceptional examples of vanished civilization, or association with events or ideas of universal significance. Natural areas must demonstrate significance in areas such as evolutionary history of the Earth, ongoing geological or biological processes, or exceptional natural phenomena, formations, or scenic or scientific features.

Proposals are evaluated by the twenty-one-member World Heritage Committee, which is assisted by the International Council on Monuments and Sites for cultural areas and by the International Union for Conservation of Nature for natural areas.

In the United States, the U.S. Department of the Interior is responsible for directing and coordinating participation in the World Heritage Convention, through a Federal Interagency Panel for World Heritage and the National Park Service. A U.S. World Heritage Committee also has been established to obtain support from business, conservation, and cultural interests.

U.S. World Heritage Sites

Cultural Sites

Cahokia Mounds State Historic Site, Illinois

Chaco Culture National Historical Park, New Mexico

Independence Hall, Pennsylvania

La Fortaleza and San Juan Historic Site, Puerto Rico

Mesa Verde, Colorado

Monticello and the University of Virginia, Virginia

Statue of Liberty, New York

Natural Sites

Everglades National Park, Florida

Grand Canyon National Park, Arizona

Great Smoky Mountains National Park, North Carolina and Tennessee

Hawaii Volcanoes National Park, Hawaii

Mammoth Cave National Park, Kentucky

Olympic National Park, Washington

Redwood National Park, California

Wrangell–St. Elias National Park, Alaska

Yellowstone National Park, Wyoming

Yosemite National Park, California

Contacts

U.S. Department of the Interior
National Park Service
Federal Interagency Panel for World Heritage
P.O. Box 37127
Washington, DC 20013-7127
(202) 343-7063
Richard Cook, International Cooperation Specialist

U.S. World Heritage Committee
c/o World Wildlife Fund/
The Conservation Foundation
1250 24th Street, N.W.
Washington, DC 20037
(202) 778-9512
Russell E. Train, Chairman

US/ICOMOS (regarding cultural property)
1600 H Street, N.W.
Washington, DC 20006
(202) 842-1866
Terry B. Morton, President

IUCN/US (regarding natural property)
1400 16th Street, N.W.
Washington, DC 20036

UNESCO
World Heritage Committee
7, Place de Fontenoy
75700 Paris, France

FURTHER READING

Historic Preservation in Other Countries, Vol. 2, Austria, Switzerland, the Federal Republic of Germany. Margaret T. Will; Robert E. Stipe, ed. Washington, D.C.: US/ICOMOS, 1984.

Historic Preservation in Other Countries, Vol. 3, Poland. Paul H. Gleye and Waldemar Szczerba; Robert E. Stipe, ed. Washington, D.C.: US/ICOMOS, 1989.

Historic Preservation in Other Countries, Vol. 4, Turkey. Jo Ramsay Liemenstoll; Robert E. Stipe, ed. Washington, D.C.: US/ICOMOS, 1990.

International Membership Directory and Resource Guide. Association for Preservation Technology. 2nd ed. Ottawa, 1988.

Our World's Heritage. Carol Lutyk, ed. Washington, D.C.: National Geographic Society, 1987.

The Yearbook of International Organizations. Brussels: K. G. Saur (rue Washington 40-1050). Annual.

SECTION FOUR

Preservation Phone Book

State and Local Contacts

OVERVIEW

Presented on the following pages are the key organizations and resource centers in the grassroots preservation movement, organized by state or territory. Listings are drawn from the National Trust's Preservation Forum membership, a program aimed at preservation groups, homeowners, and professionals in the fields of historic preservation, architecture, planning, and government.

Following the initial list of state-level key contacts is a listing of local resources, organized alphabetically by city or town.

For additional information on international preservation resources, see "International Programs" in the **Preservation Partners** section of this book.

STATES AND TERRITORIES

Each state or territorial section is introduced by a list of its major preservation contacts. Not all organizations have officers in each state; therefore, the number of preservation contacts listed at the beginning of each state will differ. The following is a brief summary of the work carried out by these offices and individuals. For more information on the relationships of these organizations, refer to the "Overview" of the **Preservation Partners** section.

State Historic Preservation Office

The State Historic Preservation Office (SHPO) in each state and U.S. territory carries out the nation's historic preservation program under the National Historic Preservation Act of 1966 by nominating properties to the National Register of Historic Places; reviewing applications for tax act certifications, which can qualify certified historic building rehabilitations for certain tax benefits; reviewing federal actions to determine their effect on historic properties; surveying and evaluating the state's architectural, archeological, historical, and cultural resources; and when funds are available, administering state or federal matching grants programs.

Statewide Preservation Organization

Private statewide preservation groups serve as the network centers and representatives of local preservation activities within their states. They work with the SHPOs, assist local groups, intervene in preservation issues, advocate state legislative support, provide membership and educational programs, issue publications, engage in real estate and revolving fund programs, and serve as preservation clearinghouses.

National Trust Regional Office

The seven regional and field offices of the National Trust for Historic Preservation represent National Trust programs and services and provide leadership to preservationists within their regions. They work to strengthen local and state preservation organizations, provide on-site technical assistance, advocate preservation positions, respond to inquiries, operate and advise on National Trust financial aid programs, hold conferences, and develop special projects to address key regional preservation issues. Preservationists are encouraged to refer inquiries to their National Trust Regional Office before contacting the Trust's Washington, D.C. office.

National Trust Advisors

A Board of Advisors composed of two members in each state or terri-

Beacon Hill courtyard, Boston, Massachusetts. *(Carol M. Highsmith Photography)*

tory assists the National Trust by advising on preservation concerns and serving as a channel for the expression of local opinions and interests. See the "National Trust" chapter for a listing of officers.

National Park Service Contact

The field directors and superintendents of the National Park Service, U.S. Department of the Interior, listed here are specially designated to handle rehabilitation tax credit applications and similar inquiries involving cultural resources not owned or managed by the National Park Service. Among their responsibilities are certifying the significance of buildings within historic districts, state and local statutes, and rehabilitation applications.

Statewide Main Street Coordinators

In partnership with National Main Street Center staff, coordinators deliver direct technical assistance to demonstration communities taking part in the state or citywide programs. Coordinators play a major role in looking at legislation, public policy, planning issues, and other influences that affect the overall environment for commercial district revitalization in their respective areas. Coordinators also serve as information resources for communities interested in revitalizing their traditional commercial districts.

Alabama

STATE HISTORIC PRESERVATION OFFICE

Alabama Historic Commission
468 South Perry Street
Montgomery, AL 36130-0900
(334) 242-3184
FAX (334) 240-3477
E-mail: lawereoaks@aol.com
Web Site: http://www.
preserveala.org
F. Lawerence Oaks, SHPO

STATEWIDE PRESERVATION ORGANIZATION

Alabama Preservation Alliance
P.O. Box 2228
Montgomery, AL 36102
(334) 434-7281
FAX (334) 434-7966
Devereaux Bemis, President

NATIONAL TRUST REGIONAL OFFICE

Southern Regional Office
456 King Street
Charleston, SC 29403
(803) 722-8552
FAX (803) 722-8652
E-mail: sro@nthp.org
Web Site: http://www.nthp.org
David Brown, Director

NATIONAL TRUST ADVISORS

Douglas C. Purcell
Eufaula, AL

Marjorie L. White
Birmingham, AL

STATEWIDE MAIN STREET COORDINATOR

Alta Cassady, Coordinator
The Alabama Historical
Commission

468 South Perry Street
Montgomery, AL 36130-0900
(334) 242-3184
FAX (334) 240-3477

AMERICAN INSTITUTE OF ARCHITECTS CONTACTS

Mike L. Tapley, Executive Director
Alabama Council AIA
1521 Mulberry Street
Montgomery, AL 36106
(334) 264-3037
FAX (334) 263-6377
E-mail: tapin@taplink.com

Mary Putnam, Executive Director
AIA Birmingham
107 21st Street South
Birmingham, AL 35233
(205) 322-4347
FAX (205) 322-4386

Local Contacts

ANNISTON

Anniston Historic Preservation
Commission
City of Anniston
P.O. Box 670
Anniston, AL 36202

BIRMINGHAM

Sloss Furnaces
National Historic Landmark
P.O. Box 11781
Birmingham, AL 35202
(205) 324-1911

DOTHAN

Dothan Landmarks Foundation, Inc.
P.O. Box 6362
Dothan, AL 36302

(334) 794-3452
FAX (334) 677-7229

FLORENCE

Frank Lloyd Wright Rosenbaum
House Foundation Inc.
601 Riverview Drive
Florence, AL 35630
(205) 764-5274

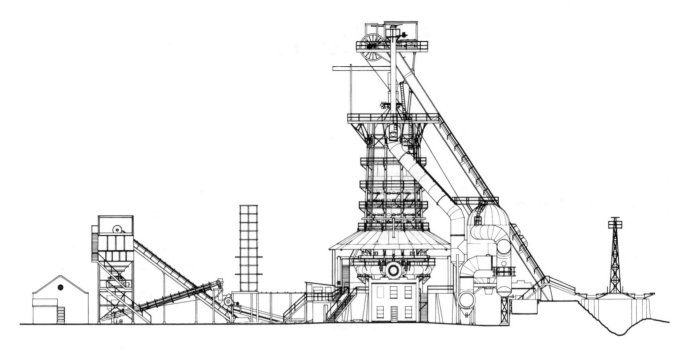

Sloss-Sheffield Steel and Iron Company Furnaces, Birmingham, Alabama. *(J. Y. Hunt, HABS)*

HUNTSVILLE

Alabama Constitution Village and Historic Huntsville Depot
320 Church Street S.W.
Huntsville, AL 35801
(205) 535-6565
FAX (205) 533-1247

Burritt Museum and Park
3101 Burritt Drive, S.E.
Huntsville, AL 35801
(205) 536-2882

LINDEN

City of Linden
211 North Main Street
Linden, AL 36748
(334) 295-5051
FAX (334) 295-0224

MOBILE

Friends of Magnolia Cemetery
P.O. Box 6383
Mobile, AL 36660
(334) 432-8672

Historic Mobile Preservation Society
300 Oakleigh Place
Mobile, AL 36604
(334) 432-6161

Mobile Historic Development Commission
P.O. Box 1827
Mobile, AL 36633
(205) 438-7281

MONTGOMERY

City of Montgomery
Planning Controls Division
P.O. Box 1111
Montgomery, AL 36101
(334) 241-2722
FAX (334) 241-2017

Landmarks Foundation of Montgomery
310 North Hull Street
Montgomery, AL 36104
(334) 240-4500
FAX (334) 240-4519
E-mail: olatown@mont.mindspring.
com

Web Site: http://www.mindspring.
com/olatown

SELMA

Black Heritage Council
3007 North Broad Street
Selma, AL 36701
(334) 872-9985
FAX (334) 872-7746

Olde Towne Association
P.O. Box 728
Selma, AL 36702
(334) 872-3827

Selma Historic Preservation Society
P.O. Box 586
Selma, AL 36702

TUSCALOOSA

Tuscaloosa County Preservation Society
P.O. Box 1665
Tuscaloosa, AL 35403
(205) 758-2238
FAX (205) 758-8163

Alaska

STATE HISTORIC PRESERVATION OFFICE

Division of Parks, Office of History and Archeology
3601 C Street, Suite 1278
Anchorage, AK 99503-5921
(907) 269-8721
FAX (907) 269-8908
E-mail: oha@alaska.net
Judith Bittner, SHPO

STATEWIDE PRESERVATION ORGANIZATION

Alaska Association for Historic Preservation
645 West Third Avenue
Anchorage, AK 99501-2124
FAX (907) 762-2628
Pat Murphy, President
William Coghill, Executive Officer

NATIONAL TRUST REGIONAL OFFICE

Western Regional Office
One Sutter Street, Suite 707
San Francisco, CA 94104
(415) 956-0610
FAX (415) 956-0837
E-mail: wro@nthp.org
Web Site: http://www.nthp.org
Elizabeth Goldstein, Director

NATIONAL TRUST ADVISORS

Judith Bittner
Anchorage, AK

Renee Blahuta
Fairbanks, AK

NATIONAL PARK SERVICE CONTACT

Regional Director
Alaska Region
2525 Gambell Street
Anchorage, AK 99503-2892
(907) 257-2690
FAX (907) 257-2510
E-mail: bob_barbee@nps.gov

AMERICAN INSTITUTE OF ARCHITECTS CONTACT

Bonnie Littlefield, Business Manager
AIA Alaska
P.O. Box 10-3563
Anchorage, AK 99510-3563
(907) 276-2834
FAX (907) 276-5758

Local Contacts

ANCHORAGE

Anchorage Historic Properties, Inc.
645 West Third Avenue
Anchorage, AK 99501-2124
(907) 274-3600
FAX (907) 274-3600

FAIRBANKS

Fairbanks Historical Presevation Foundation
2300 Airport Way
P.O. Box 70552
Fairbanks, AK 99707
(907) 456-8848
FAX (907) 456-6305

Fairbanks North Star Borough
P.O. Box 71267
Fairbanks, AK 99707
(907) 459-1000
FAX (907) 459-1100

Tanana Yukon Historical Society
Box 71336
Fairbanks, AK 99707
(907) 457-7834

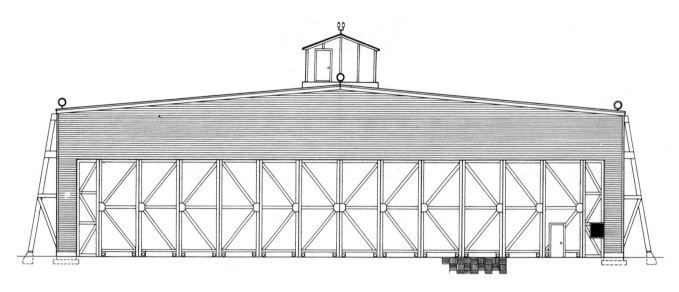

Kodiak T-Hangar, Ladd Field, Fairbanks, Alaska. *(I. N. Thomas, HABS)*

KETCHIKAN

Historic Ketchikan
P.O. Box 3364
Ketchikan, AK 99901
(907) 225-5515
FAX (907) 225-5515

PALMER

Matanuska-Susitna Borough
Historic Preservation Commission
350 East Dahlia Avenue
Palmer, AK 99645-6488
(907) 745-9681
FAX (907) 745-9845

SKAGWAY

City of Skagway
P.O. Box 521
Skagway, AK 99840
(907) 983-2420
FAX (907) 983-3420

Arizona

STATE HISTORIC PRESERVATION OFFICE

Arizona State Parks
1300 West Washington
Phoenix, AZ 85007
(602) 542-4174
FAX (602) 542-4180
E-mail: jgarrison@pr.state.az.us
Web Site: http://www.com.pr.
com.az
James W. Garrison, SHPO

STATEWIDE PRESERVATION ORGANIZATION

Arizona Preservation Foundation
P. O. Box 13492
Phoenix, AZ 85002
(602) 386-2466
Debbie Abele, President
Annette Napolitano, Executive
Director

NATIONAL TRUST REGIONAL OFFICE

Western Regional Office
One Sutter Street, Suite 707
San Francisco, CA 94104
(415) 956-0610
FAX (415) 956-0837
E-mail: nero@nthp.org
Web Site: http://www.nthp.org
Elizabeth Goldstein, Director

NATIONAL TRUST ADVISORS

James E. Babbit
Flagstaff, AZ

Grady Gammage, Jr.
Phoenix, AZ

STATEWIDE MAIN STREET COORDINATOR

Steve Schaefer, Coordinator
Arizona Main Street Program
Department of Commerce and
Community Development
3800 North Central, Suite 1400
Phoenix, AZ 85012
(602) 280-1350
FAX (602) 280-1305
Web Site: http://state.ax.us/
commerce

AMERICAN INSTITUTE OF ARCHITECTS CONTACTS

Tina Gobbel, Executive Director
AIA Arizona
AIA Central Arizona
AIA Rio Salado
802 North 5th Avenue
Phoenix, AZ 85003-1316
(602) 252-4200
FAX (602) 257-9661
Web Site: http://www.primenet.
com/aiaarizona

Brent Davis, Executive Director
AIA Southern Arizona
10 North Norton, Suite 120
Tuscon, AZ 85719
(502) 622-6248, (520) 622-6546
FAX (520) 622-6246
E-mail: aiasac@theriver.com
Web Site: http://www.theriver.
com/public/ciasac

Local Contacts

FLAGSTAFF

Flagstaff Historic Sites Commission
Community Development
City of Flagstaff
211 West Aspen Avenue
Flagstaff, AZ 86001
(620) 779-7685
FAX (520) 779-7696

FLORENCE

Florence Preservation Foundation
P.O. Box 962
Florence, AZ 85232
(520) 868-5409

PHOENIX

Rosson House Heritage Square Foundation
113 North 6th Street
Phoenix, AZ 85004
(602) 261-8948
(602) 534-1786
E-mail: foxaz1@aol.com
Web Site: http://members.aol.com/
foxaz1/historicheritagesquare

Mission San Xavier del Bac, Tucson, Arizona. *(W. M. Collier, Jr., L. Williams, HABS)*

TEMPE

Those Were the Days
516 South Mill Avenue
Tempe, AZ 85281
(602) 967-4729
FAX (602) 967-1428

TOMBSTONE

City Clerk
City of Tombstone
City Hall
P.O. Box 339
Tombstone, AZ 85638
(520) 457-2202
FAX (520) 457-3516

TUBA CITY

Tuba City Cultural Projects
P.O. Box 1570
Tuba City, AZ 86045
(520) 283-6321
(520) 283-4590

TUSCON

Armory Park Historic Zoning Advisory Board
445 South 4th Avenue
Tucson, AZ 85701
(520) 791-7905

Armory Park Neighborhood Association
P.O. Box 2132
Tuscon, AZ 85702
(520) 629-0270

Stone Avenue Temple Project
822 North Forgeus Avenue
Tucson, AZ 85716
(520) 327-2424
E-mail: tasydney@aol.com

WINDOW ROCK

Navajo Nation Historic Preservation Department
P.O. Box 4950
Window Rock, AZ 86515
(520) 871-6437
(520) 871-7886

Arkansas

STATE HISTORIC PRESERVATION OFFICE

Arkansas Historic Preservation Program
323 Center Street, Suite 1500
Little Rock, AR 72201
(501) 324-9150
FAX (501) 324-9184
E-mail: cathy@dah.state.ar.us
Cathryn H. Slater, SHPO

STATEWIDE PRESERVATION ORGANIZATION

Historic Preservation Alliance of Arkansas
P.O. Box 305
Little Rock, AR 72203
(501) 372-4757
FAX (501) 565-2805
Travis Walls, President
Marie Cassady, Executive Director

NATIONAL TRUST REGIONAL OFFICE

Southern Regional Office
456 King Street
Charleston, SC 29403
(803) 722-8552
FAX (803) 722-8652
E-mail: sro@nthp.org
Web Site: http://www.nthp.org
David Brown, Director

NATIONAL TRUST ADVISORS

Carl H. Miller
Little Rock, AR

Cyrus A. Sutherland
Fayetteville, AR

STATEWIDE MAIN STREET COORDINATOR

Marian Boyd, Coordinator
Main Street Arkansas
1500 Tower Building
323 Center Street
Little Rock, AR 72201
(501) 324-9880
FAX (501) 324-9184

AMERICAN INSTITUTE OF ARCHITECTS CONTACT

G. Frank Ivey, Jr., CAE, Executive Director
AIA Arkansas
University Tower Building
1123 South University, Penthouse Suite
Little Rock, AR 72204
(501) 663-8820
FAX (501) 663-9148

Local Contacts

BENTON

Benton County Preservation Project
400 South Walton Boulevard
Bentonville, AR 72712
(501) 273-9664

CAMDEN

Main Street Camden
P.O. Box 734
Camden, AR 71701
(501) 836-6426

GURDON

Gurdon Historic Preservation Association Inc.
P.O. Box 193
Gurdon, AR 71743
(501) 353-4435

HOT SPRINGS

Taylor Kempkes Architects
210 Central, Suite 2A
Hot Springs, AR 71901
(501) 624-5679

LITTLE ROCK

Friends of the Carousel, Inc.
P.O. Box 166802
Little Rock, AR 72216
(501) 375-5556

Historic Preservation Alliance of Arkansas
P.O. Box 305
Little Rock, AR 72203
(501) 372-4757

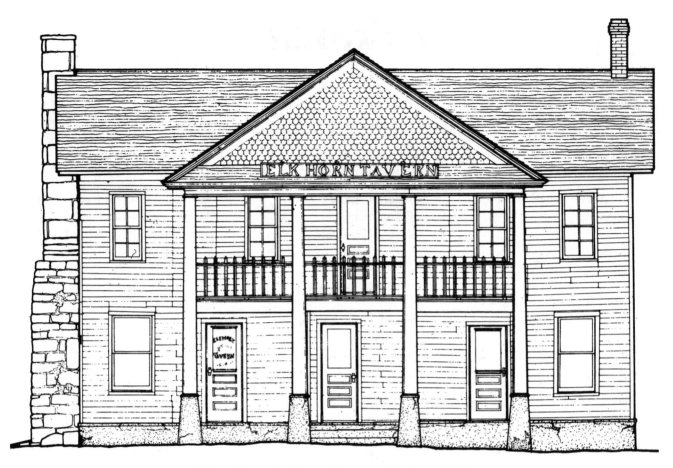

Elkhorn Tavern, Pea Ridge, Arkansas. *(D. T. Jones, HABS)*

Quapaw Quarter Association
P.O. Box 165023
Little Rock, AR 72216-5023
(501) 371-0075
FAX (501) 374-8142

WASHINGTON

**Pioneer Washington Restoration
Foundation**
P.O. Box 127
Washington, AR 71862
(501) 983-2828

California

STATE HISTORIC PRESERVATION OFFICE

Office of Historic Preservation
Department of Parks and Recreation
P.O. Box 942896
Sacramento, CA 94296-0001
(916) 653-5789
FAX (916) 653-9824
E-mail: calshpo@mail2.quiknet.com
Cherilyn Widdell, SHPO

STATEWIDE PRESERVATION ORGANIZATION

California Preservation Foundation
405 14th Street, Suite 1010
Oakland, CA 94612
(510) 763-0972
FAX (510) 763-4724
Michael Crowe, President
Jeff Eichenfield, Executive Director

NATIONAL TRUST REGIONAL OFFICE

Western Regional Office
One Sutter Street, Suite 707
San Francisco, CA 94104
(415) 956-0610
FAX (415) 956-0837
E-mail: wro@nthp.com
Web Site: http://www.nthp.org
Elizabeth Goldstein, Director

NATIONAL TRUST ADVISORS

Linda Dishman
Los Angeles, CA

Christine McAvoy
Hollywood, CA

ADVISORY COUNCIL ON HISTORIC PRESERVATION DIVISION

Western Office of Project Review
730 Simms Street, Room 401
Golden, CO 80401
(303) 231-5320

NATIONAL PARK SERVICE CONTACTS

Superintendent
Pacific Great Basin SSO
Pacific West Field Area, National Park Service
600 Harrison Street, Suite 600
San Francisco, CA 94107
(415) 427-1436
FAX (415) 744-4043

Field Director
Pacific West Field Area, National Park Service
600 Harrison Street, Suite 600
San Francisco, CA 94107
(415) 427-1301
FAX (415) 427-1485

STATEWIDE MAIN STREET COORDINATOR

Keith Kjelstrom, Coordinator
California Main Street Program
California Trade and Commerce Agency
801 K Street, Suite 1700
Sacramento, CA 95814
(916) 322-3536
FAX (916) 322-3524

AMERICAN INSTITUTE OF ARCHITECTS CONTACTS

Paul W. Welch, Jr., Hon. AIA, Executive Vice President
AIA/California Council
1303 J Street, Suite 200
Sacramento, CA 95814
(916) 448-9082
FAX (916) 442-5346
Web Site: http://www.aiacc.org

Bry Myown, Executive Director
AIA Long Beach/South Bay
210 East Ocean Boulevard, #A
Long Beach, CA 90802
(310) 495-1469
FAX (310) 491-1061

Gini Roundtree, Hon. AIA, Executive Director
AIA Central Valley
1025 19th Street, Suite 8
Sacramento, CA 95814
(916) 444-3658
FAX (916) 444-3005

Sally L. Phillips, Executive Director
AIA East Bay
City Square, 499 14th Street, #210
Oakland, CA 94612
(510) 464-3600
FAX (510) 464-3616
E-mail: aiaeb@aol.com

Executive Director
AIA Golden Empire
1712 19th Street, #207
Bakersfield, CA 93301

Florence Holt, Executive Director
AIA Inland California
10391 Corporate Drive
Redlands, CA 92374
(909) 799-7213
FAX (909) 799-7243

**Nicola Simmons, Executive
Director**
AIA Los Angeles
8687 Melrose Avenue, Suite #M-3
Los Angeles, CA 90069
(310) 785-1809
FAX (310) 785-1814
E-mail: aialosang@aol.com
Web Site: http://members.aol.
com/aialosang

**Eugene W. Bayol, Executive
Director**
AIA Emeritus
AIA Monterey Bay
P.O. Box 310
Monterey, CA 93940
(408) 372-6527
FAX (408) 372-6035

**Carolyn Newsom, Executive
Director**
AIA Orange County
Great Western Bank Tower
3200 Park Center Drive, #110
Costa Mesa, CA 92926

(714) 557-7796
FAX (714) 557-2639
E-mail: carolyn660@aol.com
Web Site: http://www.aiaoc.
org/aiaoc/

**Kimberly Anderson, Executive
Director**
AIA Redwood Empire
P.O. Box 4178
Santa Rosa, CA 95402
(707) 576-7799
FAX (707) 576-7819
E-mail: exec@aiare.org
Web Site: http://www.aire.org

**David A. Crawford, Executive
Director**
AIA San Diego
233 A Street, Suite 200
San Diego, CA 92101
(619) 232-0109
FAX (619) 232-4542

**Cheryl Di Donato, Executive
Director**
AIA San Fernando Valley
P.O. Box 261279
Encinco, CA 91426-1279
(818) 907-7151
FAX (818) 907-7152

**Robert Jacobvitz, Executive
Director**
AIA San Francisco
130 Sutter Street, Suite 600
San Francisco, CA 94104
(415) 362-7397

FAX (415) 362-4802
E-mail: aiabrdaol.com
Web Site: http://www.aiaonline.
com

Judy Nast, Executive Director
AIA San Joaquin
764 P Street
Fresno, CA 93721
(209) 266-0389
FAX (209) 266-9414

**Connie Barton, Executive
Director**
AIA San Mateo County
60 East Third Avenue, #130
San Mateo, CA 94401
(415) 348-5133
FAX (415) 348-7427

Jill Yeomans, Executive Director
AIA Santa Barbara
229 East Victoria Street
Santa Barbara, CA 93101
(805) 965-6307
FAX (805) 966-5861

**Kathryn R. Davis, Executive
Director**
AIA Santa Clara Valley
34 South First Street
San Jose, CA 95113
(408) 298-0611
FAX (408) 298-0619

Local Contacts

ALAMEDA

BCE
3210 Madison Street
Alameda, CA 94501
(510) 523-0906

City of Alameda
2250 Central Avenue
Planning Department, Room 160
Alameda, CA 94501
(510) 748-4554
FAX (510) 748-4593

ALTADENA

Altadena Heritage
P.O. Box 218
Altadena, CA 91003
(818) 798-1268

AUBURN

Placer County Department of
Museums
101 Maple Street
Auburn, CA 95603
(916) 885-9570

BERKELEY

Berkeley Architectural Heritage
Association
P.O. Box 1137
Berkeley, CA 94701
(510) 841-2242
FAX (510) 841-7421

BURBANK

Burbank Historical Society
1015 West Olive Avenue
Burbank, CA 91506
(818) 848-4721
FAX (818) 848-4739

CALABASAS

Leonis Adobe Association
23537 Calabasas Road
Calabasas, CA 91302

CAMPBELL

Campbell Historical Museum
51 North Central
Campbell, CA 95008
(408) 866-2119
FAX (408) 379-6349
Web Site: http://www.nvcom.
com/chm/

CARMEL

Carmel Heritage
P.O. Box 701
Carmel, CA 93921
(408) 624-4447
FAX (408) 624-1970

Web site: http://www.carmelnet.
com/heritage

Robinson Jeffers Tor House
Foundation
P.O. Box 2713
Carmel, CA 93921
(408) 624-1813

CLAREMONT

Claremont Heritage
590 West Bonita Avenue
P.O. Box 742
Claremont, California 91711
(909) 621-0848
FAX (909) 621-9995

COLOMA

Marshall Gold Discovery State
Historic Park
310 Back Street
P.O. Box 265
Coloma, CA 95613
(916) 622-3470
FAX (916) 622-3472

DANVILLE

Museum of the San Ramon Valley
P.O. Box 39
Danville, CA 94526
(510) 866-4900

ESCONDIDO

Escondido Historical Society
P.O. Box 263
Escondido, CA 92033
(619) 743-8207

FULLERTON

California State University
Fullerton Arboretum
P.O. Box 34080
Fullerton, CA 92634
(714) 773-8357

FRESNO

City of Fresno Historic Preservation
Commission
Department of Planning Inspection
2326 Fresno Street, City Hall
Fresno, CA 93726

Johnson Architecture
942 East Olive Avenue
Fresno, CA 93728
(209) 497-9620
FAX (209) 497-9812
E-mail: johnsarch@aol.com

GLENDALE

The Glendale Historical Society
P.O. Box 4173
Glendale, CA 91202

HOLLISTER

City of Hollister
375 5th Street
Hollister, CA 95023
(408) 637-8221

HOLLYWOOD

Design AID, Architecture Planning
Preservation
1722 North Whitley Avenue
Hollywood, CA 90028
(213) 962-4585
FAX (213) 962-8380
E-mail: daid@pacbell.net

HUNTINGTON BEACH

Huntington Beach Historical Society
19820 Beach Boulevard
Huntington Beach, CA 92648
(714) 962-5777

INDEPENDENCE

Eastern California Museum
P.O. Box 206
Independence, CA 93526
(619) 878-2411

INDUSTRY

Workman and Temple Family Homestead Museum
15415 East Don Julian Road
Industry, CA 91745
(818) 968-8492
FAX (818) 968-2048
E-mail: homesteadmuseum.org

LA QUINTA

City of La Quinta
78-495 Calle Tampico
P.O. Box 1504
La Quinta, CA 92253

LEUCADIA

Encinitas Historical Society
P.O. Box 232293
Leucadia, CA 92023

LONG BEACH

Long Beach Heritage Coalition
P.O. Box 92521
Long Beach, CA 90809-2521
(310) 493-7019

Rancho Los Cerritos
4600 Virginia Road
Long Beach, CA 90807
(562) 570-1775
FAX (562) 570-1893

RMS Foundation Inc.
The Queen Mary
1126 Queens Highway
Long Beach, CA 90802
(562) 435-3511
FAX (562) 437-4531

LOS ALTOS

Los Altos Historical Commission
One North San Antonio Road
Los Altos, CA 94022

LOS ANGELES

Englekirk and Sabol Inc.
2116 Arlington Avenue
Los Angeles, CA 90018

J. Paul Getty Research Institute
1200 Getty Center Drive
Suite 1100
Los Angeles, CA 90049
(310) 458-9811
Web Site: http://www.getty.edu

The Freeman House
1962 Glencoe Way
Los Angeles, CA 90068

St. James Club
8400 De Longpre Avenue
Suite 203
Los Angeles, CA 90069

MALIBU

Pepperdine University
Law Library
Malibu, CA 90263

MAMMOTH LAKES

Town of Mammoth Lakes
P.O. Box 1609
Mammoth Lakes, CA 93546
(619) 934-8983
FAX (619) 934-7066

MILPITAS

City of Milpitas
Parks Recreation and Cultural
Resources Commission
457 East Calaveras Boulevard
Milpitas, CA 95035
(408) 942-2379

MORGAN HILL

Historical Society of Morgan Hill
18240 Ransen Court
Morgan Hill, CA 95037

NAPA

City of Napa
Cultural Heritage Commission
P.O. Box 660
Napa, CA 94559

Napa County Landmarks
P.O. Box 702
Napa, CA 94559
(707) 255-1836
FAX (707) 255-2164
Web Site: http://www.wine.
com/net

OAKDALE

Oakdale Museum
280 North 3rd Avenue
Oakdale, CA 95361
(209) 847-3031
FAX (209) 847-6834
E-mail: oakdale@25sonnet.com

OAKLAND

Dunsmuir House and Gardens
2960 Peralta Oaks Court
Oakland, CA 94605
(510) 562-0328
FAX (510) 562-8294

Kahn Mortimer Associates
4623 Davenport Avenue
Oakland, CA 94619
(510) 482-1031
FAX (510) 482-1032
E-mail: vk@kmort.com

Oakland Heritage Alliance
P.O. Box 12425
Oakland, CA 94604
(510) 763-9218
FAX (510) 763-9218

Oakland Landmarks Preservation Advisory Board
Planning Department
1330 Broadway, Second Floor
Oakland, CA 94612

ONTARIO

City of Ontario
Planning Department
303 East B Street
Ontario, CA 91764

PACIFIC GROVE

Heritage Society of Pacific Grove
P.O. Box 1007
Pacific Grove, CA 93950

PACIFIC PALISADES

CA State Parks Angeles/Topanga
1501 Will Rogers Park Road
Pacific Palisades, CA 90272
(310) 454-8212
FAX (310) 459-2031

PALO ALTO

Palo Alto Stanford Heritage
P.O. Box 308
Palo Alto, CA 94302

PASADENA

City of Pasadena Design and Historic
Preservation Section
175 North Garfield Avenue, Room
254
Pasadena, CA 91109
(818) 405-4228
FAX (818) 405-3958

Pasadena Heritage
80 West Dayton Street
Pasadena, CA 91105
(818) 793-0617
FAX (818) 578-1007

PETALUMA

Heritage Homes of Petaluma
P.O. Box 2152
Petaluma, CA 94953
(707) 762-3456

PLACERVILLE

Tahoe-Comstock Heritage Area
The Heritage Areas Association
3177 Clark Street
Placerville, CA 95667
(916) 626-8697

PLEASANT HILL

Friends of Rodgers Ranch
P.O. Box 23381
Pleasant Hill, CA 94523
(510) 939-8436

REDLANDS

Kimberly Crest House and Gardens
P.O. Box 206
Redlands, CA 92373
(909) 792-2111

REDWOOD

City of Redwood City
P.O. Box 391
Redwood City, CA 94064
(415) 485-1971

Redwood City Heritage Association
P.O. Box 1273
Redwood City, CA 94064
(415) 365-5564

RICHMOND

Richmond Museum Association, Inc.
Box 1267
Richmond, CA 94802
(510) 235-7387
FAX (510) 235-4345

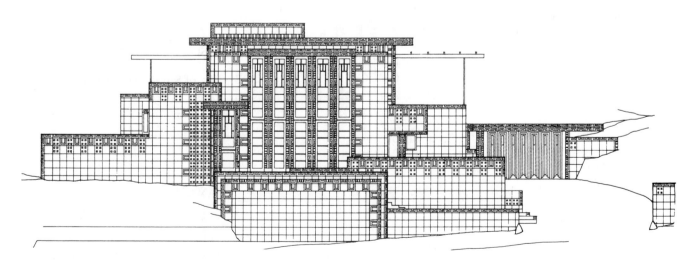

Storer House, Hollywood, California. *(J. R. Bateman, HABS)*

RIVERSIDE

Mission Inn Foundation
3639 6th Street
Riverside, CA 92501
(909) 781-8241

Old Riverside Foundation
P.O. Box 601
Riverside, CA 92502

University of California
Department of History
Riverside, CA 92521

SACRAMENTO

Department of Transportation
c/o Environmental Program (MS-27)
P.O. Box 942874
Sacramento, CA 94724-0001
(916) 322-9548

SAN DIEGO

Gaslamp Quarter Foundation
410 Island Avenue
San Diego, CA 92101
(619) 233-4692

Historical Site Board
City of San Diego
202 C Street, MS-4A
San Diego, CA 92101-4411
(619) 235-5224

San Diego State University
College of Arts & Letters, IA-100
5500 Campanile Drive
San Diego, CA 92182
(619) 594-5431
FAX (619) 594-6281

Save Our Heritage Organization
P.O. Box 3571
San Diego, California 92103
(619) 297-9327
FAX (619) 692-0944

SAN FRANCISCO

American Youth Hostels
Golden Gate Council
425 Divisadero Street, Suite 307
San Francisco, CA 94117
(415) 863-1444
FAX (415) 863-3865
E-mail: hiayh@norealhostels.org

Architectural Resources Group
Pier 9—The Embarcadero
San Francisco, CA 94111
(415) 421-1680
FAX (415) 421-0127

H. J. Degenkolb Associates
225 Bush Street, Suite 1000
San Francisco, CA 94104
(415) 392-6952
(415) 981-3157

Dolores Street Community Center
Hope House Project Cooperation
938 Valencia Street
San Francisco, CA 94110
(415) 282-6209
FAX (415) 282-2826

**Foundation for San Francisco's
Architectural Heritage**
2007 Franklin Street
San Francisco, CA 94109
(415) 441-3000
FAX (415) 441-3015

National Liberty Ship Memorial
SS Jeremiah O'Brian
Building A, Fort Mason Center
San Francisco, CA 94123-1382
(415) 441-3101
FAX (415) 441-3712

**The National Maritime Museum
Association**
P.O. Box 470310
San Francisco, CA 94147
(415) 929-0202
FAX (415) 673-5381

Page and Turnbull, Inc.
724 Pine Street
San Francisco, CA 94108
(415) 362-5154

San Francisco Historical Society
2601 17th Avenue
San Francisco, CA 94116
(415) 731-2187

SAN JOSE

Fox California Theatre
The Theatre Foundation Inc.
970 South 2nd Street
San Jose, CA 95112
(408) 293-2000
FAX (408) 294-2000
E-mail: foxcorp970@aol.com

Mieger, Mineweaser & Associates
1154 Park Avenue
San Jose, CA 95126
(408) 947-1900

**Preservation Action Council of San
Jose**
P.O. Box 2287
San Jose, CA 95109-2287
(408) 947-8025

Renasci
P.O. Box 28338
San Jose, CA 95159-8338
(408) 297-4084

San Jose Historic Landmarks
801 North First Street, Room 400
San Jose, CA 95110
(408) 277-4576
FAX (408) 277-3250

SAN JUAN CAPISTRANO

City of San Juan Capistrano
32400 Paseo Adelanto
San Juan Capistrano, CA 92675
(714) 493-1171
FAX (714) 493-1053

SAN LEANDRO

Basin Research Associates
Cultural Resource Services
1933 Davis Street, Suite 210
San Leandro, CA 94577
(510) 430-8441

San Leandro Historical Railway
Society
1302 Orchard Avenue
San Leandro, CA 94577
(415) 785-0778

SAN MATEO

San Mateo County Historic
Association
1700 West Hillsdale Boulevard
San Mateo, CA 94402
(415) 574-6441
FAX (415) 574-6468

SAN RAMON

Parks and Community Services
Commission
12501 Alcosta Boulevard
San Ramon, CA 94583
(510) 275-2300
FAX (510) 830-5162

SAN SIMEON

California Department of Parks and
Recreation
750 Hearst Castle Road
San Simeon, CA 93452
(805) 927-2075

SANTA BARBARA

Lenvik and Minor Associates
315 West Haley Street
Santa Barbara, CA 93101
(805) 963-3357
FAX (805) 963-2785
E-mail: lenvik@aol.com

SANTA CLARA

Historical and Landmarks
1500 Warburton Avenue
Santa Clara, CA 95050
(408) 984-3111

SARATOGA

City of Saratoga Heritage
Preservation Commission
Warner Hutton House
c/o City Hall
13777 Fruitvale Avenue
Saratoga, CA 95070
(408) 868-1233
FAX (408) 868-1280

SIMI VALLEY

Simi Valley Historical Society
P.O. Box 351
Simi Valley, CA 93062
(805) 526-0879

SOUTH PASADENA

South Pasadena Chamber of
Commerce
1610 Mission Street
South Pasadena, CA 91030
(818) 799-7161
FAX (818) 799-3008

STANFORD

Green Library
Serials Department
Stanford University
Stanford, CA 94305-6044
(415) 723-9108
FAX (415) 725-6874
Web Site: http://www.stanford.edu

TIBURON

Belvedere-Tiburon Landmarks
Society
1920 Paradise Drive
Box 134
Tiburon, CA 94920
(415) 435-1853

TRUCKEE

Truckee-Donner Historical Society,
Inc.
P.O. Box 893
Truckee, CA 95734
(916) 582-0893

TUJUNGA

National Historic Route 66
Federation
P.O. Box 423
Tujunga, CA 91043
(818) 352-7232
E-mail: national66@themail.net
Web Site: http://www.national66.
com/~natl66

WEAVERVILLE

Trinity County Historical Society
P.O. Box 333
Weaverville, CA 96093
(916) 623-5211

YUBA CITY

Community Memorial Museum
P.O. Box 1555
Yuba City, CA 95992
(916) 822-7141

Colorado

STATE HISTORIC PRESERVATION OFFICE

Colorado Historical Society
1300 Broadway
Denver, CO 80203
(303) 866-3395
FAX (303) 866-4464
Web Site: http://www.aclin.org/
other/historic/chs/index.html
James E. Hartmann, SHPO

STATEWIDE PRESERVATION ORGANIZATION

Colorado Preservation, Inc.
910 16th Street, Suite 1100
Denver, CO 80202
(303) 893-4260
FAX (303) 623-1508
E-mail: mld780@aol.com
Web Site: http://www.aclin.org/
code/cti
Ellen Ittelson, President
Monta Lee Dakin, Executive
Director

NATIONAL TRUST REGIONAL OFFICE

Mountains/Plains Regional Office
910 16th Street, Suite 1100
Denver, CO 80202
(303) 623-1504
FAX (303) 623-1508
E-mail: mpro@nthp.org
Web Site: http://www.nthp.org
Barbara Pahl, Director

NATIONAL TRUST ADVISORS

Betty M. Chronic
Boulder, CO

Ellen Kingman Fisher
Denver, CO

NATIONAL PARK SERVICE CONTACTS

Superintendent
Rocky Mountain SSO, National
Park Service
P.O. Box 25287
Denver, CO 80225-0287

Superintendent
Colorado Plateau SSO, National
Park Service
12795 West Almeda Parkway
P.O. Box 25287
Denver, CO 80225-0287

Field Director
Intermountain Field Area,
National Park Service
12795 West Alameda Parkway
P.O. Box 25287
Denver, CO 80225-0287

AMERICAN INSTITUTE OF ARCHITECTS CONTACTS

**Joseph M. Jackson, Associate AIA,
Executive Vice President**
AIA Colorado
1526 15th Street
Denver, CO 80202
(303) 446-2266
FAX (303) 446-0066
E-mail: aiadenco@aol.com

**Daphne Scott-Monroe, Associate
AIA, Executive Director**
AIA Denver
1526 15th Street
Denver, CO 80202
(303) 446-2266
FAX (303) 446-0066

Local Contacts

AURORA

Aurora History Museum
15001 East Alameda Drive
Aurora, CO 80012
(303) 739-6660
FAX (303) 739-6657

BOULDER

**Boulder County Land Use
Department**
P.O. Box 471
Boulder, CO 80306
(303) 441-3930
FAX (303) 441-4856

Web Site: http://www.boco.co.
gov/lu/

Historic Boulder
646 Pearl Street
Boulder, CO 80302
(303) 444-5192
FAX (303) 444-5309

COLORADO SPRINGS

Local History
Penrose Library
P.O. Box 1579
Colorado Springs, CO 80901
(719) 531-6333
FAX (719) 632-5744

CRESTED BUTTE

Board of Zoning and Architecture Review
P.O. Box 39
Crested Butte, CO 81224
(970) 349-5338
FAX (970) 349-6626
E-mail: townofcb@rmi.net

CRIPPLE CREEK

The City of Cripple Creek
337 East Bennett

P.O. Box 430
Cripple Creek, CO 80813
(719) 689-2502
FAX (719) 686-2502

DELTA

City of Delta Historic Preservation Board
360 Main Street
Delta, CO 81416
(970) 874-7566
FAX (970) 874-8776

DENVER

Central City Opera House Association
621 17th Street, Suite 1601
Denver, CO 80293
(303) 292-6500
(303) 292-4958

Community First Partners
2088 Jasmine Street
Denver, CO 80207
(303) 393-7623
FAX (303) 394-9876
E-mail: tesk@csn.net
Web Site: http://www.cns.net/~tesk

Gensler and Associate Architects
1616 Glenarm Place, Suite 200
Denver, CO 80202
(303) 595-8585
FAX (303) 825-6823

Historic Denver, Inc.
821 17th Street, Suite 500
Denver, CO 80202
(303) 296-9887
FAX (303) 296-2778
Web Site: http://www.mollybrown.com

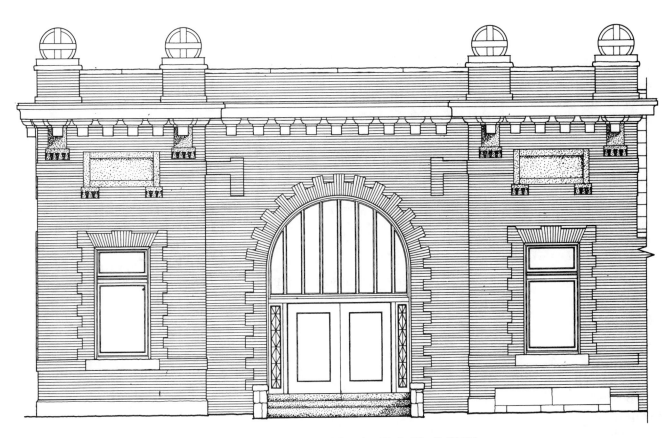

Moffatt Station, Denver, Colorado. *(D. R. Migell, HABS)*

Preservation Partnership
1540 Cook Street
Denver, CO 80206
(303) 399-4550
FAX (303) 329-9287
E-mail: wjdemaio@aol.com

Queen Anne Inn
2147 Tremont Place
Denver, CO 80205
(303) 296-6666
FAX (303) 296-2151
E-mail: queenanne@worldnet.att.net
Web Site: http://bedandbreakfastinns.
org/queenanne

ENGLEWOOD

**Modern Architecture Preservation
League**
3058 South Cornell Circle
Englewood, CO 80110
(303) 761-8979
FAX (303) 761-1178

FORT COLLINS

**Cache La Poudre River Heritage
Area**
City of Fort Collins
P.O. Box 580
Fort Collins, CO 80522
(970) 229-1525

FRISCO

Frisco Historical Society
P.O. Box 820
Frisco, CO 80443
(970) 668-3428

GEORGETOWN

Georgetown Mining Corridor
Georgetown Loop Railroad
1111 Rose Street
P.O. Box 217
Georgetown, CO 80444
(303) 569-2403

FAX (303) 569-2894
E-mail: markg@gtownloop.com
Web Site: http://www.gtownloop.
com

Historic Georgetown, Inc.
P.O. Box 667
Georgetown, CO 80444
(303) 569-2840
FAX (303) 674-2625
E-mail: histgtwn@sprynet.com

GRAND JUNCTION

**City of Grand Junction Community
Development**
250 North 5th Street
Grand Junction, CO 81501
(970) 244-1437
FAX (970) 224-4599
E-mail: kristenA@ci.grandjct.co.us

IDAHO SPRINGS

Historical Idaho Springs
P.O. Box 1318
Idaho Springs, CO 80452
(303) 567-4709

LAMAR

City of Lamar
102 East Parmenter
Lamar, CO 81052
(719) 336-4376
FAX (719) 336-2787

LAS ANIMAS

**Pioneer Historical Society of Bent
County**
P.O. Box 68
Las Animas, CO 81054
(719) 456-0220

MANITOU SPRINGS

City of Manitou Springs
Historic Preservation Commission
606 Manitou Avenue
Manitou Springs, CO 80829
(719) 685-4398
FAX (719) 685-5233

PUEBLO

Pueblo Regional Library
100 East Abriendo Avenue
Pueblo, CO 81004
(719) 543-9600
FAX (719) 543-9610

SILVER PLUME

Town of Silver Plume
Drawer F
Silver Plume, CO 80476
(303) 569-2363
FAX (303) 569-2363

SILVERTON

San Juan County Historical Society
P.O. Box 154
Silverton, CO 81433
(970) 387-5838

TELLURIDE

**Town of Telluride Planning
Department**
P.O. Box 397
Telluride, CO 81435
(970) 728-3071
FAX (970) 728-3078

Connecticut

STATE HISTORIC PRESERVATION OFFICE

Connecticut Historical
Commission
59 South Prospect Street
Hartford, CT 06106
(860) 566-3005
FAX (860) 566-5078
John W. Shannahan, SHPO

STATEWIDE PRESERVATION ORGANIZATION

Connecticut Trust for Historic
Preservation
940 Whitney Avenue
Hamden, CT 06517-4002
(203) 562-6312
FAX (203) 773-0107
Laura Weir Clarke, Executive
Director

NATIONAL TRUST REGIONAL OFFICE

Northeast Regional Office
Seven Faneuil Hall Marketplace
Boston, MA 02109
(617) 523-0885
FAX (617) 523-1199
E-mail: nero@nthp.org
Web Site: http://www.nthp.org
Wendy Nicholas, Executive
Director

NATIONAL TRUST ADVISORS

Nancy O. Alderman
North Haven, CT

Terry J. Tondro
Hartford, CT

STATEWIDE MAIN STREET COORDINATOR

Lisa Bumbera, Coordinator
Northeast Utilities Service
Company
107 Seldon Street
Berlin, CT 06037
(860) 665-5168
FAX (860) 665-5755

AMERICAN INSTITUTE OF ARCHITECTS CONTACT

Judy A. C. Edwards, Hon. AIA,
Executive Vice President
AIA Connecticut
87 Willow Street
New Haven, CT 06511-2627
(203) 865-2795
FAX (203) 562-5378

Local Contacts

BROOKFIELD

Tour De Force Designs
148 Whisconier Road, Route 25
Brookfield, CT 06804
(203) 775-4249

COS COB

Historical Society of the Town of
Greenwich
39 Strickland Road
Cos Cob, CT 06807
(203) 869-6899
FAX (203) 869-6727

DANBURY

Danbury Scott-Fanton Museum and
Historical Society
43 Main Street
Danbury, CT 06810
(203) 743-5200

DAYVILLE

Quinebaug and Shetucket Rivers
Valley National Heritage Corridor
c/o Northeastern Connecticut
Council of Governments
P.O. Box 161
Putnam, CT 06260
(860) 963-7226
FAX (860) 928-4720

FARMINGTON

C.D.C. Financial Corporation
17 Talcott Notch Road
Farmington, CT 06032
(203) 236-6234

GROTON

Town of Groton
Building Inspector
45 Fort Hill Road
Groton, CT 06340
(860) 441-6730
FAX (860) 448-3217

First Church of Christ, Congregational,
New Haven, Connecticut. *(L. Robinson,
W. Morton, HABS)*

GUILFORD

Faulkner's Light Brigade
P.O. Box 199
Guilford, CT 06437
(203) 453-8400

HAMDEN

Hamden Historical Society
P.O. Box 5512
Hamden, CT 06518

HARTFORD

Antiquarian and Landmarks Society
66 Forest Street
Hartford, CT 06103-9857
(860) 247-8996
FAX (860) 249-4907
E-mail: al5@hartnet.org

**Greater Hartford Architectural
Conservancy**
278 Farmington Avenue
Hartford, CT 06105
(203) 525-0279
FAX (203) 525-1907

Mark Twain Memorial
351 Farmington Avenue
Hartford, CT 06105
(203) 247-0998

Stowe-Day Foundation
77 Forest Street
Hartford, CT 06105
(860) 522-9258
FAX (860) 522-9259
E-mail: jo-blatti@hartnet.org

HARWINTON

**Harwinton Historic District
Commission**
Town of Harwinton
100 Bentley Drive
Harwinton, CT 06791
(860) 485-1381
FAX (860) 485-1381

IVORYTON

**Connecticut Trust for Historic
Preservation**
29 Summit Street
Ivoryton, CT 06442

LITCHFIELD

Litchfield Historical Society, Inc.
P.O. Box 385
Litchfield, CT 06759
(860) 567-4501
FAX (860) 567-3565

MIDDLETOWN

**Greater Middletown Preservation
Trust**
27 Washington Street
Middletown, CT 06457
(860) 346-1646

NEW HAVEN

**Neighborhood Housing Services of
New Haven, Inc.**
333 Sherman Avenue
New Haven, CT 06511
(203) 562-0598
FAX (203) 772-2876
E-mail: paley@netcon.com

New Haven Preservation Trust
P.O. Box 1671
New Haven, CT 06507-1671
(203) 562-5919
FAX (203) 562-2923

NEW MILFORD

**New Milford Trust for Historic
Preservation**
11 Whittlesey Avenue
New Milford, CT 06776

NEWTON

Heritage Preservation Trust
P.O. Box 3082
Newtown, CT 06470
(203) 748-6517
FAX (203) 792-0296

NORWALK

**Lockwood-Mathews Mansion
Museum, Inc.**
295 West Avenue
Norwalk, CT 06850
(203) 838-1434

NORWICH

Norwich Heritage Trust
P.O. Box 185
Norwich, CT 06360
(860) 892-5301

REDDING

Connecticut Firemen's Historical Society
230 Pine Street
Manchester, CT 06040
(860) 649-9436

SALISBURY

Salisbury Historic District Committee
P.O. Box 429
Salisbury, CT 06068

SIMSBURY

East Weatogue Historic District
57 East Weatogue Street
Simsbury, CT 06070
(860) 658-1190

STORRS

University of Connecticut Library
405 Babbidge Road U-205
Storrs, CT 06626-1205
(860) 486-2524
FAX (860) 486-4521
Web Site: http://www.spirit.lib.
uconn.edu/DoddCenter

TORRINGTON

Torrington Historical Society
192 Main Street
Torrington, CT 06790
(860) 482-8260

WALLINGFORD

Farrell and Leslie
P.O. Box 362
Wallingford, CT 06492
(203) 269-7756
FAX (203) 269-1927

WINCHESTER

Town of Winchester
338 Main Street
Winsted, CT 06098
(860) 379-2713
FAX (860) 738-7053
Web Site: http://www.state.ct.us/
munic/winchester

WEST HARTFORD

Town of West Hartford
Town Hall Common
West Hartford, CT 06107-2428
(860) 236-3231

WESTPORT

Westport Historical Society
25 Avery Place
Westport, CT 06880
(203) 222-1424
FAX (203) 222-0981

Delaware

STATE HISTORIC PRESERVATION OFFICE

Division of Historical and Cultural Affairs
P.O. Box 1401
Dover, DE 19903
(302) 739-5313
FAX (302) 739-6711
Web Site: http://www.lib.de.us/archives
Daniel Griffith, SHPO

STATEWIDE PRESERVATION ORGANIZATION

Preservation Delaware
Goodstay Center
2600 Pennsylvania Avenue
Wilmington, DE 19806

(302) 651-9617
FAX (302) 651-9603
Mary Jane Elliott, President
Dee Durnham, Executive Director

NATIONAL TRUST REGIONAL OFFICE

Mid-Atlantic Regional Office
One Penn Center at Suburban Station, Suite 1520
1617 John F. Kennedy Boulevard
Philadelphia, PA 19103-1815
(215) 568-8162
FAX (215) 568-9251
E-mail: maro@nthp.org
Web Site: http://www.nthp.org
Patricia Wilson Aden, Director

NATIONAL TRUST ADVISORS

Kim Rodgers Burdick
Wilmington, DE

Eldon duP. Homsey
Wilmington, DE

STATEWIDE MAIN STREET COORDINATOR

Violet Chilcoat, Coordinator
Delaware Main Street Program
Delaware Development Office
99 Kings Highway
P.O. Box 1401
Dover, DE 19903
(302) 739-4271
FAX (302) 739-5749
Web Site: http://www.state.de.us

Local Contacts

DOVER

Coastal Heritage Greenway
Division of Parks and Recreation
89 Kings Highway
P.O. Box 1401
Dover, DE 19903
(302) 739-5285
FAX (302) 739-3817
Web Site: http://www.state.de.us/govern/agencies/dnrec/parks/dsp1st.htm

Delaware Department of Transportation Environmental Studies Office
P.O. Box 778
Dover, DE 19903
(302) 739-4644
FAX (302) 739-2251
Web Site: http://www. mhahn@smtp.dot.state.dc.us

Hall of Records, Delaware Public Archives
P.O. Box 1401
Dover, DE 19903
(302) 739-3021

FAX (302) 739-6710
Web Site: http://archives@state.dc.us

NEWARK

National Council for Preservation Education
College of Urban Affairs
University of Delaware
Newark, DE 19716
(302) 831-1050
FAX (302) 831-3587
E-mail: david.ames@mus.udel.edu

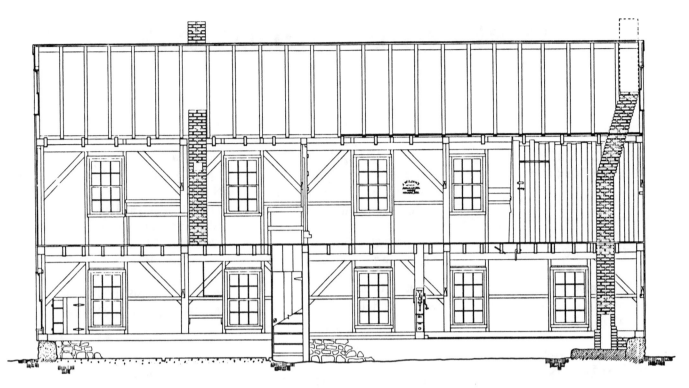

Alexander Wilson Agricultural Works, New Castle County, Delaware *(M. Fike, HABS)*

SMYRNA

Smyrna-Clayton Heritage Association
Box 611
Smyrna, DE 19977
(302) 653-8312

WILMINGTON

Hagley Museum and Library
Acquisitions Department
P.O. Box 3630

Buck Road
Wilmington, DE 19807
(302) 658-2400
FAX (302) 658-0568
Web Site: http://www.hagley.
lib.de.us

International Group for Historic Aircraft Recovery
2812 Fawkes Drive
Wilmington, DE 19808
(302) 994-4410

Mayor's Office
Planning Division
800 North French Street, Seventh
Floor
Wilmington, DE 19801
(302) 571-4030

District of Columbia

STATE HISTORIC PRESERVATION OFFICE

614 H Street, N.W., Suite 1120
Washington, DC 20001
(202) 727-7120
FAX (202) 727-8073
Web Site: http://www.ci.
washington.dc.us
Hampton Cross, SHPO, Director
DCRD/OD

STATEWIDE PRESERVATION ORGANIZATION

District of Columbia Preservation League
1511 K Street, N.W., Suite 739
Washington, DC 20005
(202) 737-1519
FAX (202) 737-1823
Sally Berk, President

NATIONAL TRUST REGIONAL OFFICE

Mid-Atlantic Regional Office
One Penn Center at Suburban
Station, Suite 1520
1617 John F. Kennedy Boulevard
Philadelphia, PA 19103-1815
(215) 568-8162

FAX (215) 568-9251
E-mail: maro@nthp.org
Web Site: http://www.nthp.org
Patricia Wilson Aden, Director

NATIONAL TRUST ADVISORS

Charles Cassell
Washington, DC

Carol Thompson-Cole
Washington, DC

NATIONAL PARK SERVICE FIELD CONTACTS

National Capital Field Area, National Park Service
1100 Ohio Drive, S.W.
Washington, DC 20242
(202) 619-7223
FAX (202) 619-7062
Web Site: http//www.cr.nps.gov

Superintendent
National Capital Area SSO,
National Park Service
1100 Ohio Drive, S.W.
Washington, DC 20242
(202) 619-7223
FAX (202) 619-7223

Field Director
National Capital Field Area,
National Park Service
1100 Ohio Drive, S.W.
Washington, DC 20242
(202) 619-7223
FAX (202) 619-7223

AMERICAN INSTITUTE OF ARCHITECTS CONTACT

Julienne A. Nelson, Executive Director
Washington Chapter/AIA
1777 Church Street, N.W.
Washington, DC 20036
(202) 667-1798
FAX (202) 667-4327
E-mail: aia-dc@ari.net
Web Site: http://www2.ari.
net/aia-dc

Local Contacts

DISTRICT OF COLUMBIA

African American Heritage Preservation Foundation
420 Seventh Street, N.W.
Suite 501

Washington, DC 20004
(202) 879-9779
FAX (202) 347-2617
Web Site: http://www.preservenet.
cornell.edu/aahpf/homepage.htm/

American Planning Association
1776 Massachusetts Avenue, N.W.
Washington, DC 20036
(202) 872-0611
FAX (202) 872-0643
Web Site: http://www.planning.org

American Society of Interior Designers
608 Massachusetts Avenue, N.E.
Washington, DC 20002
(202) 546-3480
FAX (202) 546-3240
E-mail: network@asid.noli.com

Association of Collegiate Schools of Architecture, Inc.
1735 New York Avenue, N.W.
Washington, DC 20006
(202) 785-2324

Capitol Hill Restoration Society
1002 Pennsylvania Avenue, S.E.
Washington, DC 20003
(202) 543-0425
E-mail: CapHRS@aol.com

CEHP, Inc.
1627 K Street, N.W.
Washington, DC 20036
(202) 293-1774

Colonial Dames of America
Charter III
6200 Oregon Avenue, N.W.
Suite 236
Washington, DC 20015
(202) 244-0199

Community Assistance and Partnership Parks
National Park Service
P.O. Box 37127
Washington, DC 20013

Crowell and Moring
1001 Pennsylvania Avenue, N.W.
Washington, DC 20004-2595
(202) 624-2592

Foundation for the Preservation of Historic Georgetown
P.O. Box 3603
Georgetown Station
Washington, DC 20007
(202) 628-5093
FAX (202) 628-5932

Grace Church, Georgetown, Washington, D.C. *(E. Villatoro, G. Rueblinger, HABS)*

General Services Association (WPT)
7th and D Streets, S.W., Room 7600
Washington, DC 20407
(202) 708-5334
FAX (202) 708-7671

GSA—PTS
Cultural/Environmental Affairs
18th and F Streets, N.W.
Room 7308
Washington, DC 20405
(202) 219-1088

H Street Community Development Corporation
501 H Street, N.E.
Washington, DC 20002

(202) 544-8353
FAX (202) 544-3051
E-mail: oomhscdc@aol.com

International Masonry Institute
823 15th Street, N.W.
Washington, DC 20005
(202) 783-3908
FAX (202) 783-0433

Jewish Historical Society
701 Third Street, N.W.
Washington, DC 20001
(202) 789-0900
FAX (202) 789-0485

The U Street Theatre Foundation
1215 U Street, N.W.
Washington, DC 20009
(202) 328-9177
FAX (202) 328-9245

National Association for Human Development
1424 16th Street, N.W., Suite 102
Washington, DC 20036
(202) 328-2191
FAX (202) 265-6682

National Capital Planning Commission
Technical Planning Services
801 Pennsylvania Avenue, N.W.
Washington, DC 20576
(202) 482-7200
FAX (202) 482-7272

National Center for Architecture and Urbanism
P.O. Box 32314
Washington, DC 20007
(202) 387-7600

National Conference of State Historic Preservation Officers
444 North Capitol Street, N.W.
Suite 342

Washington, DC 20001
(202) 624-5465
FAX (202) 624-5419

National Park Service
Archeological Assistance Division
P.O. Box 37127
Washington, DC 20013

National Park Service
Heritage Preservation Services
Program
P.O. Box 37127
Washington, DC 20013
(202) 343-9585
FAX (202) 343-3803
Web Site: http://www.cr.nps.gov

North American Society for Oceanic History
P.O. Box 18108
Washington, DC 20036

NPCA
1776 Massachusetts Avenue, N.W.
Washington, DC 20036
(202) 223-6722
FAX (202) 659-0650
Web Site: http://www.npca.org

Partners for Livable Places
1429 21st Street, N.W.
Washington, DC 20036
(202) 887-5990
FAX (202) 466-4845
E-mail: plcomms@concentric.net

Public Building Service, General Services Administration, Courthouse Management Division
1800 F Street, N.W.
Washington, DC 20405
(202) 219-1088
FAX (202) 501-3393
E-mail: rolando.rivas-camp@gsa.gov

St. John's Episcopal Church
Third Century Campaign
3240 O Street, N.W.
Washington, DC 20007
(202) 966-5129

Save the Tivoli, Inc.
P.O. Box 44930
Washington, DC 20026-4930
(202) 462-2792

Sheridan-Kalorama Historic Association, Inc.
2144 California Street, N.W., #812
Washington, DC 20008
(202) 483-4866

Society for American Archaeology
900 Second Street, N.E., #12
Washington, DC 20002
(202) 789-8200
FAX (202) 789-0284
E-mail: info@saa.org
Web Site: http://www.saa.org

The Trust for Public Land
666 Pennsylvania Avenue, S.E.
Suite 401
Washington, DC 20003
(202) 543-7552
(202) 544-4723

Tudor Place Foundation
1605 32nd Street, N.W.
Washington, DC 20007
(202) 956-2262

United States Mint
633 3rd Street, N.W.
Washington, DC
(202) 874-3134
FAX (202) 874-4083
Web Site: http://www.usmint.gov

Florida

STATE HISTORIC PRESERVATION OFFICE

Department of State, Division of Historical Resources
R. A. Gray Building
500 South Bronough Street
Tallahassee, FL 32399-0250
(904) 488-1480
FAX (904) 488-3353
E-mail: fldhr@mail.dos.state.fl.us
George Percy, SHPO

STATEWIDE PRESERVATION ORGANIZATION

Florida Trust for Historic Preservation
P. O. Box 11206
Tallahassee, FL 32302
(904) 224-8128
FAX (904) 921-0150
Web Site: http://hmitchell@
mail.dos.state.fl.us
Sylvia Vega Smith, President
Judith Carpenter, Executive Director

NATIONAL TRUST REGIONAL OFFICE

Southern Regional Office
456 King Street
Charleston, SC 29403
(803) 722-8552
FAX (803) 722-5652
E-mail: sor@nthp.org
Web Site: http://www.nthp.org
David Brown, Director

NATIONAL TRUST ADVISORS

Nancy Liebman
Miami Beach, FL

Janet Snyder Matthews
Sarasota, FL

STATEWIDE MAIN STREET COORDINATOR

Robert Trescott, Coordinator
Florida Main Street Program
Bureau of Historic Preservation
Division of Historical Resources
500 South Bronough Street
Fourth Floor, Room 411
Tallahassee, FL 32399-0250
(904) 487-2333
FAX (904) 922-0496
Web Site: http://trescott@
mail.dos.state.fl.us

AMERICAN INSTITUTE OF ARCHITECTS CONTACTS

George A. Allen, Hon. AIA, CAE, Executive Vice President
AIA Florida
104 East Jefferson Street
Tallahassee, FL 32301
(904) 222-7590
FAX (904) 224-8048

Andrea Geller, Interim Executive
AIA Ft. Lauderdale
227 S.W. 2nd Avenue
Ft. Lauderdale, FL 33301
(954) 728-9690
FAX (954) 728-9790

Evelyn B. McGrath, Hon. AIA
Executive Director
AIA Tampa Bay
200 North Tampa Street, Suite 100
Tampa, FL 33602
(813) 286-7225
FAX (813) 288-8247

Joyce Ridenour, Executive Director
AIA Florida Gulf Coast
P.O. Box 48986
Sarasota, FL 34230-5986
(941) 955-5063
FAX (941) 366-4101
E-mail: jrridenour@aol.com

Barbara L. Prado, Executive Secretary
AIA Miami
800 Douglas Entrance, #119
Coral Gables, FL 33134
(305) 448-7488
FAX (305) 448-0136

Lisa K. Foley, Executive Director
AIA Orlando
930 Woodcock Road, #226
Orlando, FL 32803
(407) 898-7006
FAX (407) 898-3399

Martha Smythe, Executive Director
AIA Palm Beach
504 Pinto Circle
Wellington, FL 33414
(407) 790-2514
FAX (407) 798-4905
E-mail: aiapalmbeach@aol.com

Local Contacts

BRADENTON

Manatee County Government
P.P.I.
1112 Manatee Avenue West
P.O. Box 1000, Fourth Floor
Bradenton, FL 34206
(941) 749-3070
FAX (941) 749-3071

CHOKOLOSKEE

Ted Smallwood's Store, Inc.
P.O. Box 367
Chokoloskee, FL 33925
(813) 695-2989

CORAL GABLES

City of Coral Gables Historic Preservation Division
Coral Gables City Hall
405 Biltmore Way
Coral Gables, FL 33134
(305) 460-5216
FAX (305) 460-5371

DELAND

Volusia County Growth Management Department
123 West Indiana Avenue
DeLand, FL 32720
(904) 736-5959
FAX (904) 822-5727
E-mail: tscofield@co.volusia.fl.us
Web Site: http://www.volusia.org

DELRAY BEACH

Historic Palm Beach County Preservation Board
P.O. Box 1221
Delray Beach, FL 33447
(561) 279-1475
FAX (561) 279-1476

FORT LAUDERDALE

Fort Lauderdale Historical Society
219 S.W. 2nd Avenue
Fort Lauderdale, FL 33301
(954) 463-4431
FAX (954) 463-4434

Sailboat Bend Historic Trust
P.O. Box 914
729 Middle Street
Ft. Lauderdale, FL 33312
(954) 467-0523

GAINESVILLE

Architecture and Fine Arts Library
201 AFA
University of Florida
Gainesville, FL 32611
(352) 392-0222
FAX (352) 392-7251
Web Site: http://caroline.eastlib.usl.edu:80/afa

GREEN COVE SPRINGS

City of Green Cove Springs
229 Walnut Street
Green Cove Springs, FL 32043
(904) 529-2200
FAX (904) 529-2208

HOLLYWOOD

City of Hollywood
2600 Hollywood Boulevard
Room 315
Hollywood, FL 33020
(954) 921-3471

JACKSONVILLE

Beaches Area Historical Society
P.O. Box 50646
Jacksonville, FL 32250
(904) 246-0093

Clara White Mission
613 West Ashley Street
Jacksonville, FL 32202
(904) 354-4162
FAX (904) 791-4360

National Society of Colonial Dames in America in the State of Florida
4114 Herschel Street, Suite #109
Jacksonville, FL 32210-2200
(904) 388-4223

Riverside-Avondale Preservation, Inc.
2623 Herschel Street
Jacksonville, FL 32204
(904) 389-2449
FAX (904) 389-0431

Springfield Preservation and Restoration
P.O. Box 3192
Jacksonville, FL 32206-3192
(904) 353-7727

KEY WEST

Audubon House and Tropical Gardens
205 Whitehead Street
Key West, FL 33040
(305) 294-2116
FAX (305) 294-4513

Friends of Fort Taylor
P.O. Box 58
Key West, FL 33041
(305) 292-6713
FAX (305) 292-6881

Historic Florida Keys Preservation Board
510 Greene Street
Key West, FL 33040
(305) 292-6718
FAX (305) 293-6348

Key West Art and Historical Society
3501 South Roosevelt Boulevard
Key West, FL 33040
(305) 296-3913
FAX (305) 296-6206

Key West Historic Architectural
Review Commission
P.O. Box 1409
Key West, FL 33041

Key West Maritime Historical
Society
P.O. Box 695
Key West, FL 33040
(305) 292-7903

Old Island Restoration Foundation,
Inc.
P.O. Box 689
Key West, FL 33041
(305) 294-9501
FAX (305) 294-4509

LAKELAND

Florida Southern College
111 Lake Hollinsworth Drive
Lakeland, FL 33801
(941) 680-4111
FAX (941) 680-4112
Web Site: http://ldennis@flsouthern.
edu

LARGO

Heritage Village
11909 125th Street, North
Largo, FL 33774
(813) 582-2123
FAX (813) 582-2455

MIAMI

Black Archives History and Research
Foundation of South Florida, Inc.
Joseph Caleb Community Center
5400 N.W. 22nd Avenue
Miami, FL 33142
(305) 636-2390
FAX (305) 636-2391

Dade Heritage Trust
190 S.E. 12th Terrace
Miami, FL 33131
(305) 358-9572
FAX (305) 358-1162

Development Management Services
13500 S.W. 104th Avenue
Miami, FL 33176
(305) 854-9812

The Foundation for Villa Vizcaya
3251 South Miami Avenue
Miami, FL 33129
(305) 857-3388
FAX (305) 857-6894

Miami Design Preservation League
P.O. Box 190180
Miami Beach, FL 33119-0180
(305) 672-2014
FAX (305) 672-4319

New Birth Corporation, Inc.
18330 N.W. 86th Avenue
Miami, FL 33015
(305) 823-4123

MIAMI BEACH

Miami Design Preservation League
P.O. Box 190180
Miami Beach, FL 33119-0180
(305) 672-2014
FAX (305) 672-4319

MICANOPY

Micanopy Historical Society
P.O. Box 462
Micanopy, FL 32667
(352) 466-3200

MONTICELLO

Jefferson Historical Association
P.O. Box 496
Monticello, FL 32345

OCALA

Historic Ocala Preservation Society
P.O. Box 3123
Ocala, FL 34478
(352) 351-1861

ORLANDO

Historic Preservation Office
400 South Orange Avenue
Sixth Floor
Orlando, FL 32801
(407) 246-2300
FAX (407) 246-2895

Preservation of Miles Park
7875 Canyon Lake Circle
Orlando, FL 32835
(813) 325-9774

PALM BEACH

Henry Morrison Flagler Museum
Whitehall Way and Coconut Row
P.O. Box 969
Palm Beach, FL 33480
(561) 655-2833
FAX (561) 655-2826
E-mail: flagler@emi.net
Web Site: http://www.flagler.org

Preservation Foundation of Palm
Beach, Inc.
356 South County Road
Palm Beach, FL 33480-4442
(561) 832-0731
FAX (561) 832-7174

PENSACOLA

Historic Pensacola Preservation
Board
120 East Church Street
Pensacola, FL 32501
(904) 444-8905
FAX (904) 444-8641

Pensacola Heritage Foundation
P.O. Box 12424
Pensacola, FL 32582
(904) 438-6505
FAX (904) 438-6505

PONCE INLET

Ponce de Leon Inlet Lighthouse
Preservation Association, Inc.
4931 South Peninsula Drive
Ponce Inlet, FL 32019
(904) 761-1821
FAX (904) 761-1821
E-mail: lighthouse@ponceinlet.org
Web Site: http://www.ponceinlet.
org

PUNTA GORDA

City of Punta Gorda Historical
Advisory Board
326 West Marion Avenue
Punta Gorda, FL 33950
(913) 639-1924

ST. AUGUSTINE

Lightner Museum
75 King Street, P.O. Box 334
St. Augustine, FL 32085-0334
(904) 824-2874

ST. CLOUD

City of St. Cloud
St. Cloud Historical Preservation
2901 17th Street
St. Cloud, FL 34769
(407) 957-7256
FAX (407) 892-5337

SANIBEL

Island Historic Museum
800 Dunlap
Sanibel, FL 33957
(813) 472-3373

SANTA ROSA BEACH

The Seaside Institute
P.O. Box 4730
Santa Rosa Beach, FL 32459
(904) 231-2421
FAX (904) 231-1884

SARASOTA

JRC Foundation Inc.
P.O. Box 3935
Sarasota, FL 34236

TALLAHASSEE

African American Heritage Trail
Bureau of Historic Preservation
500 South Bronough
Tallahassee, FL 32399-0250
(904) 487-2333
FAX (904) 922-0496
E-mail: bhp@mail.dos.state.fl.us

Historic Tallahassee Preservation
Board
329 North Meridian Street
Tallahassee, FL 32301

(904) 488-3901
FAX (904) 488-3903
Web Site: http://www.dos.state.fl.us

Red Hills Region
Red Hills Conservation
Program/Tall Timbers Research
Route 1, Box 678
Tallahassee, FL 32312
(904) 893-4153

Tall Timbers Research Inc.
Route 1, Box 678
Tallahassee, FL 32312
(904) 893-4153

TAMPA

Historic Tampa/Hillsborough
County Preservation Board
2009 North 18th Street
Tampa, FL 33605
(813) 272-3843

Tampa Preservation, Inc.
2007 North 18th Street
Tampa, FL 33605
(813) 248-5437
FAX (813) 248-2340

Tampa Union Station Preservation
and Redevelopment
2009 North 18th Street
Tampa, FL 33605
(813) 272-3843

TARPON SPRINGS

Tarpon Springs Cultural Center
101 South Pinellas Avenue
Tarpon Springs, FL 34689
(813) 942-5605
FAX (813) 938-2429

VENICE

Venice Archives and Area Historical
Collection
351 South Nassau Street
Venice, FL 34285
(941) 486-2487

Ralph Munroe Boathouse, Miami, Florida. *(S. Feller, HABS)*

Georgia

STATE HISTORIC PRESERVATION OFFICE

Historic Preservation Division
57 Forsyth Street, N.W.
Suite 500
Atlanta, GA 30303
(404) 656-2840
FAX (404) 651-8739
E-mail: mark_edwards@mail.dnr.
state.ga.us
Mark Edwards, SHPO

STATEWIDE PRESERVATION ORGANIZATION

Georgia Trust for Historic Preservation
1516 Peachtree Street, N.W.
Atlanta, GA 30309
(404) 881-9980
FAX (404) 875-2205
E-mail: gatrust@bellsouth.net
Gregory B. Paxton, President

NATIONAL TRUST REGIONAL OFFICE

Southern Regional Office
456 King Street
Charleston, SC 29403
(803) 722-8552
FAX (803) 722-8652
E-mail: sro@nthp.org
Web Site: http://www.nthp.org
David Brown, Director

NATIONAL TRUST ADVISORS

H. Ben Grace
Thomasville, GA

Roy Mann
Rome, GA

NATIONAL PARK SERVICE CONTACTS

Superintendent
Atlantic Coastal Plains SSO
Southeast Field Area, National
Park Service
100 Alabama Street, N.W.
1924 Building
Atlanta, GA 30303
(404) 331-4998
FAX (404) 563-3263

Superintendent
Appalachian SSO
Southeast Field Area, National
Park Service
100 Alabama Street, N.W.
1924 Building
Atlanta, GA 30303
(404) 331-4998
FAX (404) 563-3263

Superintendent
Gulf Coast SSO
Southeast Field Area, National
Park Service
75 Spring Street, S.W.
Atlanta, GA 30303

Field Director
Southeast Field Area, National
Park Service
100 Alabama Street, N.W.
1924 Building
Atlanta, GA 30303
(404) 331-4998
FAX (404) 563-3263

STATEWIDE MAIN STREET COORDINATOR

Mary Anne Thomas, Coordinator
Georgia Main Street Program
Center for Business and
Economic Development
Georgia Southwestern State
University
800 Whealey Street
Americus, GA 31709
(912) 931-2124
FAX (912) 931-2092
E-mail: gamanst@gsw1500.gsw.
peachnet.edu

AMERICAN INSTITUTE OF ARCHITECTS CONTACT

Eleanor McNamara
231 Peachtree Street, N.E.
Suite B-04
Atlanta, GA 30303
(404) 222-0099
FAX (404) 222-9916

Local Contacts

ALBANY

Thronateeska Heritage Foundation
100 Roosevelt Avenue
Albany, GA 31701
(912) 432-6955
FAX (912) 435-1572

AMERICUS

Sumter Historic Trust, Inc.
P.O. Box 1416
Americus, GA 31709
(912) 924-9051

ATHENS

Athens-Clarke Heritage Foundation
489 Prince Avenue, Fire Hall #2
Athens, GA 30601
(706) 353-1801

National Alliance of Preservation Commissions
609 Caldwell Hall/University of Georgia

Athens, GA 30602
(404) 542-4731

University of Georgia School of Environmental Design
Caldwell Hall
Athens, GA 30602
(404) 542-3030

ATLANTA

American College
3330 Peachtree Road, N.E.
Atlanta, GA 30326-1001
(404) 231-9000

Atlanta History Center
130 West Paces Ferry Road N.W.
Atlanta, GA 30305-1366
(404) 814-4000
FAX (404) 814-4186
Web Site: http://www.atl.hist.org

Atlanta Preservation Center
156 Seventh Street, N.E., Suite 3
Atlanta, GA 30308
(404) 876-2041
FAX (404) 876-2618

Atlanta Urban Design Commission
55 Trinity Avenue
Suite 3400
Atlanta, GA 30335-0331
(404) 330-6200
FAX (404) 658-7491

Georgia African American Historic Preservation Committee and Network
c/o Office of the President
Morris Brown College
643 Martin Luther King, Jr. Drive
Atlanta, GA 30314
(404) 220-0102
FAX (404) 659-4315

Georgia State University
Department of History
100 Decatur Street, S.E.
Atlanta, GA 30303
(404) 651-2000

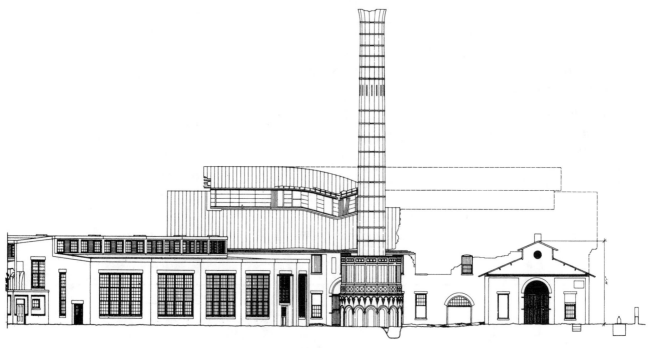

Central of Georgia Railway Repair Shops, Savannah, Georgia. *(P. Dubin, HAER)*

AUGUSTA

Augusta Canal Heritage Corridor
Augusta Canal Authority
801 Broad Street, Suite 507
Augusta, GA 30901-1225
(706) 722-1071

Historic Augusta
P.O. Box 37
Augusta, GA 30903-0037
(706) 724-0436
FAX (706) 724-3083

Summerville Neighborhood Association
P.O. Box 12212
Augusta, GA 30904
(404) 738-7527

AVONDALE

City of Avondale Estates
Historic Preservation Commission
21 North Avondale Plaza
Avondale Estates, GA 30002
(404) 294-5400
FAX (404) 299-8137

BRUNSWICK

Downtown Development Authority
P.O. Box 684
Brunswick, GA 31521
(912) 265-4032
FAX (912) 265-8181

Mainstreet Brunswick
P.O. Box 684
Brunswick, GA 31521
(912) 265-4032
FAX (912) 265-8181

BUCHANAN

Haralson County Historical Society
P.O. Box 585
Buchanan, GA 30113
(404) 646-3509

CAIRO

Grady County Historical Society, Inc.
P.O. Box 586
Cairo, GA 31728
(912) 226-2927

CAMILLA

Southwest GA Regional Development Center
P.O. Box 346
Camilla, GA 31730
(912) 336-5616
FAX (912) 430-4337

CARTERSVILLE

Noble Hill-Wheeler Memorial
Heritage Center
105 Fite Street
Cartersville, GA 30120
(770) 382-3392

COLUMBUS

Woodruff Museum of Civil War Naval History
P.O. Box 1022
Columbus, GA 31902
(706) 327-9798

Historic Columbus Foundation, Inc.
P.O. Box 5312
Columbus, GA 31906
(706) 322-0756
FAX (706) 576-4760

DECATUR

Downtown Development Authority
P.O. Box 220
Decatur, GA 30030
(404) 371-8386
FAX (404) 378-2678

EATONTON

Eatonton-Putnam County Historical Society, Inc.
104 Church Street
Eatonton, GA 31024
(404) 485-4532

FORTSON

Mountain Hill School Foundation Inc.
4216 Georgia Highway 219
Fortson, GA 31808
(706) 687-0303
FAX (706) 687-0306

FORT VALLEY

Fort Valley Main Street
P.O. Box 1864
Fort Valley, GA 31030
(912) 825-5986

GAINESVILLE

Beulah Rucker Museum and Educational Foundation, Inc.
P.O. Box 587
2101 Athens Highway
Gainesville, GA 30507
(770) 287-0500
FAX (770) 531-4713

HOMER

Banks County Historical Society
P.O. Box 473
Homer, GA 30547
(404) 778-1900

JEKYLL ISLAND

Jekyll Island Museum
375 Riverview Drive
Jekyll Island, GA 31527
(912) 635-2119
FAX (912) 635-4420

LA GRANGE

Troup County Archives
136 Main Street
P.O. Box 1051
La Grange, GA 30241
(912) 884-1828

MACON

Macon Heritage Foundation
P.O. Box 6092
Macon, GA 31208
(912) 742-5084
FAX (912) 742-2008

MARIETTA

City of Marietta
205 Lawrence Street
Marietta, GA 30060
(770) 528-0500

Cobb Landmarks and Historical Society, Inc.
145 Denmead Street
Marietta, GA 30060
(770) 426-4982

METTA

Candler County Historical Society
P.O. Box 325
Metter, GA 30439
(912) 685-6375

ST. SIMONS ISLAND

Fort Frederica National Monument
Route 9, Box 286-C
St. Simons Island, GA 31522
(912) 638-3639

SAVANNAH

Historic Railroad Shops
601 W. Harris Street
Savannah, GA 31401
(912) 651-6840

Historic Savannah Foundation
P.O. Box 1733
Savannah, GA 31402
(912) 233-7787
FAX (912) 233-7706
Web Site: http://www.
historicsavannah.org

Municipal Research Library
City of Savannah
P.O. Box 1027
Savannah, GA 31402
(912) 651-6412
FAX (912) 233-1992

The Ossabaw Island Foundation
402 East Bryan Street
Savannah, GA 31401
(912) 233-5104

THOMASVILLE

Thomasville Landmarks
P.O. Box 1285
Thomasville, GA 31792
(912) 226-6016
FAX (912) 226-6672

TOCCOA

Main Street Toccoa
P.O. Box 579
Toccoa, GA 30577
(706) 886-8451
FAX (706) 886-7766

TYBEE ISLAND

Tybee Island Historical Society Inc.
30 Meddin Drive
P.O. Box 366
Tybee Island, GA 31328
(912) 786-5801
FAX (912) 786-6538

VALDOSTA

Regional South Georgia Development Center
P.O. Box 1223
Valdosta, GA 31603
(912) 333-5277
FAX (912) 333-5312

Valdosta State University
1500 North Pattersol Street
Valdosta, GA 31698
(912) 333-5800
FAX (912) 245-3891

Hawaii

STATE HISTORIC PRESERVATION OFFICE

Department of Land and Natural Resources
P.O. Box 621
Honolulu, HI 96809
(808) 587-0401
Michael D. Wilson, SHPO

STATEWIDE PRESERVATION ORGANIZATION

Historic Hawai'i Foundation
P. O. Box 1658
Honolulu, HI 96806
(808) 523-2900
FAX (808) 523-0800
E-mail: hhfd@lava.net
David Scott, Executive Director

NATIONAL TRUST REGIONAL OFFICE

Western Regional Office
One Sutter Street, Suite 707
San Francisco, CA 94104
(415) 956-0610
FAX (415) 956-0837
E-mail: wro@nthp.org
Web Site: http://www.nthp.org
Elizabeth Goldstein, Director

NATIONAL TRUST ADVISORS

Mary Moragne Cooke
Honolulu, HI

Russell Kokubun
Volcano, HI

NATIONAL PARK SERVICE CONTACT

Superintendent
Pacific Islands SSO, National Park Service
300 Ala Moana Boulevard, Room 6305
Box 50165
Honolulu, HI 96850
(808) 541-2693
FAX (808) 541-3696

STATEWIDE MAIN STREET COORDINATOR

Coordinator
Main Street Hawai'i
Department of Land and Natural Resources
33 South King Street, Sixth Floor
Honolulu, HI 96813
(808) 587-0003
FAX (808) 587-0018

AMERICAN INSTITUTE OF ARCHITECTS CONTACTS

Beverly McKeague, Executive Vice President
Hawaii State Council/AIA
1128 Nuuanu Avenue
Honolulu, HI 96817
(808) 545-4242
FAX (808) 537-1463

Shirley L. Cruthers, Executive Vice President
AIA Honolulu
1128 Nuuanu Avenue
Honolulu, HI 96817
(808) 545-4242
FAX (808) 537-1463

Nanette T. Kwon, Executive Secretary
AIA Maui
P.O. Box 929
Wailuku Maui, HI 96796
(808) 244-9574
FAX (808) 244-9574

Local Contacts

HILO

Hilo/Plantation Heritage Corridor
Hilo Main Street Program
252 Kamehameha Avenue,
Hilo, HI 96720
(808) 935-8850
FAX (808) 935-3899

The Lyman Museum and Mission House
276 Haili Street
Hilo, HI 96720
(808) 935-5021
FAX (808) 969-7685
E-mail: lymanwks@inteepac.net

HONOLULU

Friends of Iolani Palace
P.O. Box 2259
Honolulu, HI 96804
(808) 522-0824
FAX (808) 532-1051

Hawaii Maritime Center
Pier Seven
Honolulu, HI 96813
(808) 523-6151
FAX (808) 536-1579

Mission Houses Museum
553 South King Street
Honolulu, HI 96813
(808) 531-0481
FAX (808) 545-2280

University of Hawaii at Manoa
American Studies Department
1890 East-West Road

Moore 324
Honolulu, HI 96822
(808) 956-8570
FAX (808) 956-4733
E-mail: amstuh@hawaii.edu

LAHAINA

The Lahaina Restoration Foundation
120 Dickenson Street
Lahaina, HI 96761
(808) 661-3262
FAX (808) 661-9309

LIHUE

The Hanalei Project
Museum Grove Farm Homestead
P.O. Box 1631

Lihue, HI 96766
(808) 245-3202
FAX (808) 245-7988

Kauai Historic Preservation Review Commission
County of Kauai Planning Department
4396 Rice Street, Suite 101
P.O. Box 1778
Lihue, HI 96766
(808) 245-3373
FAX (808) 245-8693

WAILUKU

Maui Historical Society
2375-A Main Street
Wailuku, HI 96793
(808) 244-3326
FAX (808) 244-3920

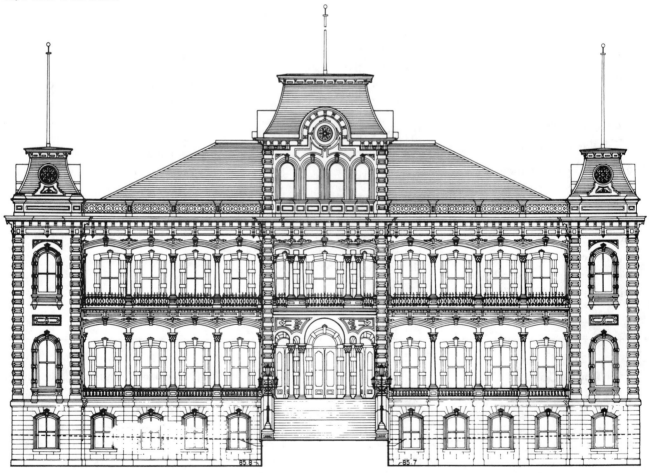

'Iolani Palace, Honolulu, Hawai'i. *(E. D. Chauviere, HABS)*

Idaho

STATE HISTORIC PRESERVATION OFFICE

Idaho State Historical Society
1109 Main Street, Suite 250
Boise, ID 83702-5642
(208) 334-3847
FAX (208) 334-2775
E-mail: rmyohe@aol.com
Robert M. Yohe II, SHPO

STATEWIDE PRESERVATION ORGANIZATION

Idaho Historic Preservation Council
P. O. Box 1495
Boise, ID 83701
(208) 386-9124

Tricia Canaday, President
Donna Hartmans, Acting
Executive Director

NATIONAL TRUST REGIONAL OFFICE

Western Regional Office
One Sutter Street, Suite 707
San Francisco, CA 94104
(415) 956-0610
FAX (415) 956-0837
E-mail: wor@nthp.org
Web Site: http://www.nthp.org
Elizabeth Goldstein, Director

NATIONAL TRUST ADVISORS

Sheri Freemuth
Boise, ID

Jerry T. Myers
Pocatello, ID

AMERICAN INSTITUTE OF ARCHITECTS CONTACT

Connie Searles, Executive Director
AIA Idaho
2419 W. State Street, Suite 5
Boise, ID 83702-3167
(208) 345-3072
FAX (208) 343-8046

Local Contacts

CALDWELL

Canyon County Parks and Recreation
P.O. Box 44
1115 Albany Street
Caldwell, ID 83605
(208) 454-7435

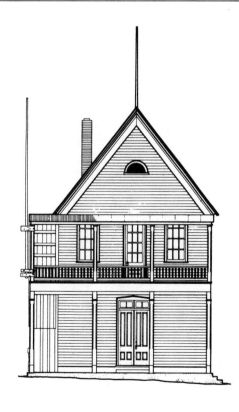

Pioneer Lodge No.1, International Order of Odd Fellows Hall, Idaho City, Idaho. *(M. Wellen, J. Schafer, HABS)*

HAILEY

Ezra Pound Association
P.O. Box 1400
Hailey, ID 83333
(208) 788-4700

POCATELLO

Pocatello Historic Preservation Commission
P.O. Box 4169
Pocatello, ID 83205
(208) 234-6184
FAX (208) 234-6296

Illinois

STATE HISTORIC PRESERVATION OFFICE

Illinois Historic Preservation Agency
One Old State Capitol Plaza
Springfield, IL 62701-1512
(217) 785-1153
FAX (217) 524-7525
William L. Wheeler, SHPO

STATEWIDE PRESERVATION ORGANIZATION

Landmarks Preservation Council of Illinois
53 West Jackson Boulevard
Suite 752
Chicago, IL 60604
(312) 922-1742
FAX (312) 922-8112
E-mail: nsn.nscs/il.us.org/regio/lpcl
David Keene, President
Donna Harris, Executive Director

NATIONAL TRUST REGIONAL OFFICE

Midwest Regional Office
53 West Jackson Boulevard,
Suite 1135
Chicago, IL 60604
(312) 939-5547
FAX (312) 939-5651
E-mail: mwro@nthp.org
Web Site: http://www.nthp.org
Jim Mann, Director

NATIONAL TRUST ADVISORS

Amy R. Hecker
Chicago, IL

Susan S. Schanlaber
Aurora, IL

STATEWIDE MAIN STREET COORDINATORS

Laurie Scott, Regional Coordinator
Main Street Partnership
220 South State Street, Suite 1880
Chicago, IL 60604
(312) 427-3688
FAX (312) 427-6251

Valecia Crisafulli, State Coordinator
Illinois Main Street Program
612 Stratton Building
Springfield, IL 62706
(217) 524-6869
FAX (217) 782-7589

Nick Kalogeresis, Suburban Main Street Coordinator
Illinois Main Street Suburban Program
Office of Lieutenant Governor
100 West Randolph, Suite 15-200
Chicago, IL 60601
(312) 814-8760
FAX (312) 814-4862

AMERICAN INSTITUTE OF ARCHITECTS CONTACTS

Shirley J. Norvell, Hon. AIA, Executive Vice President
AIA Illinois
520 South Second Street, #802
Springfield, IL 62701
(217) 522-2309
FAX (217) 522-5370

Tracy Owens, Executive Assistant
AIA Central Illinois
520 South Second Street, #802
Springfield, IL 62071
(217) 525-0981
FAX (217) 522-5370

Alice Sinkevitch, Director
AIA Chicago
222 Merchandise Mart
Suite 1049
Chicago, IL 60654
(312) 670-7770
FAX (312) 670-2422

Corda Murphy, Executive Director
AIA Northeast Illinois
412 Green Valley Drive
Naperville, IL 60540
(630) 527-8550
FAX (630) 357-4818

Local Contacts

ALTON

Alton Lake Heritage Parkway Commission
Box 821
Alton, IL 62002
(618) 498-2829

Alton Market Place Association
100 East Broadway
Alton, IL 62002
(618) 463-1016
FAX (618) 463-1091

AURORA

Aurora Historical Museum
P.O. Box 905
Aurora, IL 60506
(630) 897-9029
FAX (630) 897-9029

BELVIDERE

Belvidere Historic Preservation Commission
c/o Belvidere/Boone Planning Department
601 North Main, Suite 103
Belvidere, IL 61008
(815) 544-5271
FAX (815) 547-8701

BISHOP HILL

Bishop Hill State Historic Site
P.O. Box D
Bishop Hill, IL 61419
(309) 927-3890

BLOOMINGTON

McClean County Historical Society
200 North Main Street
Bloomington, IL 61701
(309) 827-0418
FAX (309) 827-0100

BROOKFIELD

Grossdale Depot
Brookfield Historical Society
8820½ Brookfield Avenue
Brookfield, IL 60513-1670
(773) 384-4000, Ext. 562

CARBONDALE

Carbondale Preservation Commission
City of Carbondale
200 S. Illinois Avenue
P.O. Box 2047
Carbondale, IL 62902-2047
(618) 549-5302
FAX (618) 457-3283

CARROLLTON

Illinois Valley Heritage Area
Illinois Valley Cultural Heritage Association
Route 3, Box 46
Carrollton, IL 62016
(217) 942-3859

CHAMPAIGN

Ohio River Corridor
City of Champaign
City Building
102 North Neil Street
Champaign, IL 61820
(217) 351-4417
FAX (217) 351-6910

Preservation and Conservation Association
P.O. Box 2555, Station A
Champaign, IL 61825
(217) 328-7222

CHICAGO

American Planning Association
122 South Michigan Avenue, Suite 1600
Chicago, IL 60603
(312) 431-9100
FAX (312) 431-9985

Auditorium Theatre
50 East Congress
Chicago, IL 60605
(312) 431-2395
FAX (312) 922-0347

Baldwin Development
209 South La Salle Street, #403
Chicago, IL 60604-1203
(312) 553-6150
FAX (312) 553-6151

Frank Lloyd Wright Building Conservancy
343 South Dearborn Street
Suite 1701
Chicago, IL 60604-3815
(312) 663-1786
FAX (312) 663-1683
E-mail: bldgcons@aol.com

Illinois and Michigan Canal National Heritage Corridor
Canal Corridor Association
220 S. State Street, Suite 1880
Chicago, IL 60604
(312) 427-3688
FAX (312) 427-6251

Illinois Historic Preservation Agency
160 North La Salle, Suite South 916
Chicago, IL 60601
(312) 814-1409

Inspired Partnerships
53 West Jackson Boulevard
Suite 852
Chicago, IL 60604
(312) 294-0077
FAX (312) 294-0085

KPMG Peat Marwick
303 East Wacker Drive
Chicago, IL 60601
(312) 938-1000
FAX (312) 938-0449

Mayer Jeffers Gillespie
1017 West Webster Avenue
Chicago, IL 60614
(773) 935-3011
FAX (773) 935-9230

National Association of Realtors
430 North Michigan Avenue
Chicago, IL 60611
(312) 329-8200
FAX (312) 329-8576

Norwood Park Historical Society
5831 North Nickerson
Chicago, IL 60631
(773) 774-7440

School of the Art Institute of Chicago
John M. Flexman Library
37 South Wabash
Chicago, IL 60603
(312) 899-5099

Three Arts Club of Chicago
1300 North Dearborn Street
Chicago, IL 60610
(312) 944-6250
FAX (312) 944-6284

Vintage Realty
1001 North Winchester Avenue
Chicago, IL 60622
(773) 235-1200
FAX (773) 235-3694

EAST MOLINE

Nixalite of America
1025 16th Avenue
East Moline, IL 61244
(309) 755-8771
FAX (309) 755-0777
E-mail: nixalite@qconline.com

EDWARDSVILLE

Edwardsville Historic Preservation Commission
14 Eagle Court
Edwardsville, IL 62025
(618) 656-0239

Republic Building, Chicago, Illinois. *(P. Gardner, HABS)*

ELGIN

Elgin Heritage Commission
150 Dexter Court
Elgin, IL 60120-5555
(847) 931-6100
FAX (847) 931-5610

ELMHURST

Elmhurst Historical Society
P.O. Box 1291
Elmhurst, IL 60126-1291
(630) 530-0776

ELSAH

Historic Elsah Foundation
P.O. Box 117
Elsah, IL 62028
(618) 374-1059

EVANSTON

Evanston Preservation Commission
2100 Ridge Avenue
Evanston, IL 60201
(847) 866-2928
FAX (847) 328-4905

GALENA

Galena State Historic Sites
307 Decatur Street
P.O. Box 333
Galena, IL 61036
(815) 777-3310
FAX (815) 777-3300

GLENCOE

Historic Preservation Commission
Village of Glencoe
675 Village Court
Glencoe, IL 60022
(847) 835-4111

GLEN ELLYN

Village of Glen Ellyn
Assistant to the Village
Administration
Historical Sites Commission
535 Duane Street
Glen Ellyn, IL 60137
(630) 469-5000
FAX (630) 469-8849

HINSDALE

Hinsdale Historical Society
P.O. Box 336
Hinsdale, IL 60521
(630) 789-2600

JACKSONVILLE

Jacksonville Historic Preservation
Commission
Municipal Building
200 West Douglas
Jacksonville, IL 62650
(217) 479-4627

JOLIET

City of Joliet
150 West Jefferson Street
Joliet, IL 60432
(815) 740-2433
FAX (815) 740-1221

KANKAKEE

Riverview Historic District
P.O. Box 571
Kankakee, IL 60901
(815) 935-8534

LAKE FOREST

First Presbyterian Church
700 North Sheridan Road
Lake Forest, IL 60045
(847) 234-6250
FAX (847) 234-6283

MOLINE

City of Moline Planning Department
619 16th Street
Moline, IL 61265
(309) 797-0491
FAX (309) 797-0479

Rock Island County Historic Society
822 11th Avenue
P.O. Box 632
Moline, IL 61266
(309) 764-8590

OAK PARK

Historical Society of Oak Park and
River Forest
P.O. Box 771
Oak Park, IL 60303
(708) 848-6755

OTTAWA

Ottawa Historic Preservation League
P.O. Box 295
Ottawa, IL 61350
(815) 434-4016

PEOTONE

Historical Society of Greater
Peotone
Box 87
Peotone, IL 60468
(312) 747-7500

QUINCY

Gardner Museum of Architecture
and Design
332 Maine Street
Quincy, IL 62301
(217) 224-6873
FAX (217) 224-6873

Quincy Preservation Commission
706 Maine Street, Third Floor
Quincy, IL 62301
(217) 228-4514
FAX (217) 221-2288
E-mail: chuckb@bcc.net

ROCKFORD

Rockford Historic Preservation Commission
425 East State Street
Rockford, IL 61104
(815) 987-5600
FAX (815) 967-6933

Tinker Swiss Cottage
411 Kent Street
Rockford, IL 61102
(815) 964-2424
FAX (815) 964-2466
Web Site: http://www.tinkercottage.com

ROCK ISLAND

City Rock Island Preservation Commission
Commission and Economic
Development Department
1528 Third Avenue
Rock Island, IL 61201
(309) 793-3442
FAX (309) 793-0655

SPRINGFIELD

Dana Thomas House Foundation
P.O. Box 7123
Springfield, IL 62791
(217) 782-6776
FAX (217)788-9450

Illinois Department of Natural Resources
Division of Planning
524 South 2nd Street
Springfield, IL 62701-1787
(217) 782-6320
FAX (217) 524-4177

Illinois Main Street
612 Stratton Building
Springfield, IL 62706
(217) 524-6869
FAX (217) 782-7589
Web Site: http://www.state.il.us/
Hgov/mainst.html

Lincoln Home National Historic Site
413 South 8th Street
Springfield, IL 62701
(217) 492-4241
FAX (217) 497-4673

URBANA

Lachlan Furgerson Blair
506 West Illinois Street
Urbana, IL 61801-3928
(217) 344-7526
FAX (217) 344-7535

VILLA PARK

Historic Villa Park Preservation Commission
Village of Villa Park
20 South Ardmore Avenue
Villa Park, IL 60181
(630) 834-2010

WEST CHICAGO

City of West Chicago Historical Museum
132 Main Street
West Chicago, IL 60185
(630) 231-3376

WHEATON

Conservation Foundation
703 Warrenville Road
Wheaton, IL 60187
(630) 682-3505
FAX (630) 682-5087

Wheaton History Center—WHPC
P.O. Box 373
Wheaton, IL 60189
(630) 682-9472
FAX (630) 682-9913

WOOD DALE

Wood Dale Historical Society
Yesterday's Farm Museum
P.O. Box 13
7N040 Wood Dale Road
Wood Dale, IL 60191
(708) 595-8777

WOODSTOCK

City of Woodstock
P.O. Box 190
Woodstock, IL 60098
(815) 338-4300
FAX (815) 334-2269

Indiana

STATE HISTORIC PRESERVATION OFFICE

Department of Natural Resources
402 West Washington Street
Indiana Government Center
South, Room W274
Indianapolis, IN 46204
(317) 232-1646
FAX (317) 232-0693
Larry D. Macklin, SHPO

STATEWIDE PRESERVATION ORGANIZATION

Historic Landmarks Foundation
of Indiana
340 West Michigan Street
Indianapolis, IN 46202-3204
(317) 639-4534
FAX (317) 639-6734
J. Reid Williamson, Jr.,
President/CEO

NATIONAL TRUST REGIONAL OFFICE

Midwest Regional Office
53 West Jackson Boulevard,
Suite 1135
Chicago, IL 60604
(312) 939-5547
FAX (312) 939-5651
E-mail: mwro@nthp.org
Web Site: http://www.nthp.org
Jim Mann, Director

NATIONAL TRUST ADVISORS

Kent Schuette
Lafayette, IN

J. Reid Williamson, Jr.
Indianapolis, IN

STATEWIDE MAIN STREET COORDINATOR

Margaret Lawrence, Coordinator
Indiana Main Street Program
Indiana Department of
Commerce
One North Capitol, Suite 700
Indianapolis, IN 46204-2288
(317) 232-8910
FAX (317) 233-6887
Web Site: http://www.indiana.
tourism

AMERICAN INSTITUTE OF ARCHITECTS CONTACT

Kenneth A. Englund, Executive
Director
AIA Indiana
47 South Pennsylvania Street
Indianapolis, IN 46204
(317) 634-6993
FAX (317) 266-0515

Local Contacts

BEDFORD

Bedford College Center
Branch of Oakland City College
405 I Street
P.O. Box 455
Bedford, IN 47421
(812) 279-8126
FAX (812) 279-6210

CAMBRIDGE CITY

Historic Landmarks Foundation of
Indiana
P.O. Box 284
Eastern Regional Office
Cambridge City, IN 47327
(765) 478-3172
FAX (765) 478-3410

Indiana National Road Association
Huddleston Farm House
P.O. Box 284
Cambridge City, IN 47327
(317) 478-3172
(765) 478-3410

ELKHART

Ruthmere Museum
302 East Beardsley Avenue
Elkhart, IN 46514
(219) 264-0330
FAX (219) 266-0474

EVANSVILLE

Historic Southern Indiana
University of Indiana
8600 University Boulevard
Evansville, IN 47712
(812) 465-7014
FAX (812) 465-7061

North Manchester Public Library, North Manchester, Indiana. *(P.D. Adams, HAER)*

Reitz Home Preservation Society
P.O. Box 1322
Evansville, IN 47706
(812) 426-1871
FAX (812) 426-2179

**Vanderburgh County Historical
Society**
113 East Diamond Avenue
Evansville, IN 47711-3203
(812) 465-7014
FAX (812) 465-7061

FISHERS

Conner Prairie
13400 Allisonville Road
Fishers, IN 46038
(317) 776-6000
FAX (317) 776-6014

FORT WAYNE

Arch, Inc.
437 E. Berry Street, Suite 204
Fort Wayne, IN 46802
(219) 426-5117
FAX (219) 422-8712

**Community Development and
Planning**
One Main Street, Room 800
City of Fort Wayne, Indiana
Fort Wayne, IN 46802
(219) 427-1140
FAX (219) 427-1140

GOSHEN

Face of the City
232 South Main Street
Goshen, IN 46526

(219) 533-3538
FAX (219) 533-2103
E-mail: coyne.gte.net

GREENFIELD

City of Greenfield
P.O. Box 456
Greenfield, IN 46140
(317) 462-8552
FAX (317) 462-8552

INDIANAPOLIS

**Hammond Historic Preservation
Commission**
649 Conkey Street
Hammond, IN 46324
(219) 853-6398
FAX (219) 853-6628

Historic Preservation and Archaeology
402 West Washington Street
Room W 274
Indianapolis, IN 46204
(317) 232-1646
FAX (317) 232-0693

Indianapolis Historic Preservation Commission
2060 City-County Building
200 East Washington Street
Indianapolis, IN 46204
(317) 327-4406
FAX (317) 327-4407

Village Community Development Corporation
8888 Keystone Crossing, Suite 900
Indianapolis, IN 46240
(317) 581-4370
FAX (317) 587-0340

JEFFERSONVILLE

Howard Steamboat Museum, Inc.
P.O. Box 606
Jeffersonville, IN 47131-0606
(812) 283-3728
FAX (812) 283-6049

Historic Landmarks Foundation of Indiana
113 West Chestnut Street
Jeffersonville, IN 47130
(812) 284-4534
FAX (812) 285-9923
E-mail: sregion@unix.adept.net

LAFAYETTE

Tippecanoe County Public Library
627 South Street
Lafayette, IN 47901
(765) 429-0100
FAX (765) 429-0150

Wabash Valley Trust for Historic Preservation
P.O. Box 1354

Lafayette, IN 47902
(317) 474-4505

MADISON

Cornerstone Society, Inc.
P.O. Box 92
Madison, IN 47250
(812) 265-6507

Historic Madison, Inc.
500 West Street
Madison, IN 47250
(812) 265-2967
FAX (812) 273-3941
E-mail: hmihmfi@seidate.com

MARION

Grant County Convention
Recreation and Visitors Commission
215 South Adams Street
Marion, IN 46952
(765) 668-5435
FAX (765) 668-5443

MUNCIE

College of Architecture and Planning
Ball State University
2000 University Ave.
Muncie, IN 47306
(765) 289-1241

NEW HARMONY

Historic New Harmony
Box 579
New Harmony, IN 47631
(812) 682-4488
FAX (812) 682-4313

PLAINFIELD

Guilford Township Historical Collection
Plainfield Public Library
1120 Stafford Road

Plainfield, IN 46168
(317) 839-6602
FAX (317) 839-4044

RICHMOND

Wayne County Convention and Tourism Bureau
5701 National Road, East
Richmond, IN 47374
(765) 935-8687
FAX (765) 935-0440

RUSHVILLE

Rush County Heritage, Inc.
Rural Route 4, Box 121
Rushville, IN 46173
(317) 629-2386

SOUTH BEND

Historic Preservation Commission of South Bend and St. Joseph County
Room 1123
County City Building
South Bend, IN 46601
(219) 235-9798
FAX (219) 235-9030

Northern Indiana Historic Society
808 West Washington
South Bend, IN 46601
(219) 284-9664

South Bend Heritage Foundation
914 Lincolnway West
South Bend, IN 46616
(219) 289-1066
FAX (219) 289-4550

Southhold Preservation
516 E. South Street
South Bend, IN 46601
(219) 234-3441
FAX (219) 234-3441

Iowa

STATE HISTORIC PRESERVATION OFFICE

State Historical Society of Iowa
600 East Locust Street
Des Moines, IA 50319
(515) 281-8837
FAX (515) 242-6498
Web Site: http://www.uiowa.
edu/~shsi/index.htm
Tom Morain, SHPO

STATEWIDE PRESERVATION ORGANIZATION

Iowa Historic Preservation
Alliance
P. O. Box 814
Mount Pleasant, IA 52641-0814
(319) 337-3514
Cooper Norman, President
Joyce Barrett, Executive Director

NATIONAL TRUST REGIONAL OFFICE

Midwest Regional Office
53 West Jackson Boulevard,
Suite 1135
Chicago, IL 60604
(312) 939-5547
FAX (312) 939-5651
E-mail: mwro@nthp.org
Web Site: http://www.nthp.org
Jim Mann, Director

NATIONAL TRUST ADVISORS

David L. Cordes
Mount Pleasant, IA

Curt Heidt
Clive, IA

STATEWIDE MAIN STREET COORDINATOR

Thomas D. Guzman, Coordinator
Main Street Iowa
Iowa Department of Economic
Development
200 East Grand Avenue
Des Moines, IA 50309
(515) 242-4733
FAX (515) 242-4859

AMERICAN INSTITUTE OF ARCHITECTS CONTACT

Suzanne K. Schwengles, Hon.
AIA, CAE, Executive Vice
President
AIA Iowa
1000 Walnut Street, #101
Des Moines, IA 50309
(512) 244-7502
FAX (515) 244-5347

Local Contacts

AMANA

Amana Heritage Society
P.O. Box 81
Amana, IA 52203
(319) 622-3567
FAX (319) 622-6481

AMES

Department of Planning and
Housing
P.O. Box 811

City of Ames
Ames, IA 50010
(515) 239-5400

BURLINGTON

Art Guild of Burlington, Inc.
P.O. Box 5
Burlington, IA 52601
(319) 754-8069
FAX (319) 754-4731

COUNCIL BLUFFS

Historic General Dodge House
621 Third Street
Council Bluffs, IA 51503-6614
(712) 322-2406

DES MOINES

American Institute of Architects
Iowa Chapter
1000 Walnut Street, #101
Des Moines, IA 50309
(515) 244-7502
FAX (515) 244-5347

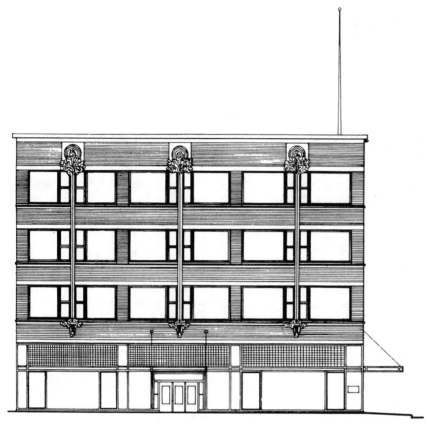

Van Allen and Son Store, Clinton, Iowa. *(HABS)*

Iowa Department of Economic Development
Division of Tourism
200 East Grand Avenue
Des Moines, IA 50309
(515) 242-4705
FAX (515) 242-4719

RDG Bussard/Dikis, Inc.
303 Locust Street
Des Moines, IA 50309
(515) 288-3141
FAX (515) 288-8631

Sherman Hill Association
756 16th Street
Des Moines, IA 50314
(515) 284-5717

Wallace House Foundation
756 16th Street
Des Moines, IA 50314-1601
(515) 243-7063

DUBUQUE

Dubuque County Historical Society
P.O. Box 266
Dubuque, IA 52004-0266
(319) 557-9545
(319) 583-1241

Main Street Dubuque
909 Main Street, Suite 22LL
Dubuque, IA 52001
(319) 588-4400
FAX (319) 588-0645

FORT MADISON

Fort Madison Historic Preservation Commission
City Hall
811 Avenue East
Fort Madison, IA 52627
(319) 372-7700
FAX (319) 372-7750

KEOSAUQUA

Villages of Van Buren, Inc.
P.O. Box 9
Keosauqua, IA 52565
(319) 293-7111
FAX (319) 293-6258
E-mail: villages@netins.net

LAPORTE CITY

LaPorte City Historic Preservation Commission
507 Locust Street
LaPorte City, IA 50651
(319) 342-2707

WATERLOO

Silos and Smokestacks
P.O. Box 2845
Waterloo, IA 50704
(319) 234-4567
FAX (319) 234-8228

Kansas

STATE HISTORIC PRESERVATION OFFICE

Dr. Ramon S. Powers, SHPO,
Executive Director
Kansas State Historical Society
6425 Southwest 6th Avenue
Topeka, KS 66615-1099
(913) 272-8681 x 205
FAX (913) 272-8682
E-mail: cmagnus@hspo.wpo.
state.ks.us
Web Site: http://www.history.
cc.ukans.edu/heritage/kshs/
kshshhtml

STATEWIDE PRESERVATION ORGANIZATION

Kansas Preservation Alliance
700 SW Jackson, Suite 209
Topeka, KS 66603-3731
(913) 235-6163
FAX (913) 357-6450
Bob Marsh, President

NATIONAL TRUST REGIONAL OFFICE

Mountains/Plains Regional Office
910 16th Street, Suite 1100
Denver, CO 80202
(303) 623-1504
FAX (303) 623-1508
E-mail: mpro@nthp.org
Web Site: http://www.nthp.org
Barbara Pahl, Director

NATIONAL TRUST ADVISORS

Joan E. Adam
Atchinson, KS

Joan B. Cole
Wichita, KS

STATEWIDE MAIN STREET COORDINATOR

Jeanne Stinson, Coordinator
Kansas Main Street Program
Kansas Department of
Commerce and Housing
700 S.W. Harrison Street
Suite 1300
Topeka, KS 66603-3712
(913) 296-3485
FAX (913) 296-0186

AMERICAN INSTITUTE OF ARCHITECTS CONTACT

Trudy M. Aron, Hon. AIA, CAE,
Executive Director
AIA Kansas
700 Jackson Street, #209
Topeka, KS 66603-3757
(913) 357-5308
FAX (913) 357-6450
E-mail: aiaks@kspress.com

Local Contacts

COLBY

Prairie Museum of Art and History
1905 South Franklin Avenue
Colby, KS 67701
(785) 462-4590
E-mail: prairiem@colby.ixks.com

KANSAS CITY

Kansas City
City of Kansas City
Kansas Planning and Zoning
Division
701 North 7th Street, Room 421
Kansas City, KS 66101
(913) 573-5750
FAX (913) 573-5745

LAWRENCE

Lawrence City Historic Resources
Administration
City Hall, First Floor
6 East 6th Street
Lawrence, KS 66044-0708
(913) 832-3151
FAX (913) 832-3160

Lawrence Preservation Alliance
P.O. Box 1073
Lawrence, KS 66044

Eisenhower House, Abilene, Kansas. *(T. Simmons, HABS)*

TOPEKA

Historic Topeka
3127 S.W. Hunton, Suite 6
Topeka, KS 66604
(913) 354-8982

WICHITA

Wichita-Sedgwick County
Metropolitan Area Planning
Department
City Hall
455 North Main Street, Tenth floor
Wichita, KS 67202
(316) 268-4421
FAX (316) 268-4390

PITTSBURG

Stillwell Heritage and Educational
Foundation
P.O. Box 1904
Pittsburg, KS 66762
(316) 235-1997

SHAWNEE MISSION

Johnson County Museums
6305 Lackman Road
Shawnee Mission, KS 66217
(913) 631-6709
FAX (913) 631-6359

Kentucky

STATE HISTORIC PRESERVATION OFFICE

Kentucky Heritage Council
300 Washington Street
Frankfort, KY 40601
(502) 564-7005
FAX (502) 564-5820
E-mail: morgan2@mail.state.ky.us
David L. Morgan, SHPO

STATEWIDE PRESERVATION ORGANIZATION

Commonwealth Preservation Advocates, Inc.
P. O. Box 387
Frankfort, KY 40602-0378
(606) 292-2111
FAX (606) 292-2106
E-mail: covecon@fuse.net
Web Site: http://www.covington.uscenet.com
Leah Konicki, President

NATIONAL TRUST REGIONAL OFFICE

Southern Regional Office
456 King Street
Charleston, SC 29403
(803) 722-8552
FAX (803) 722-8652
E-mail: sro@nthp.org
Web Site: http:///www.nthp.org
David Brown, Director

NATIONAL TRUST ADVISORS

Barbara Hulette
Lexington, KY

Ann Early Sutherland
Bardstown, KY

STATEWIDE MAIN STREET COORDINATOR

Roger Stapleton, Coordinator
Kentucky Main Street Program
Kentucky Heritage Council
300 Washington Street
Frankfort, KY 40601
(502) 564-7005
FAX (502) 564-5820
E-mail: rstapleton@mail.state.ky.us

AMERICAN INSTITUTE OF ARCHITECTS CONTACT

Janet Pike, Executive Director
AIA Kentucky
209 East High Street
Lexington, KY 40507
(606) 233-7671
FAX (606) 233-1716
E-mail: aiakyjanet@aol.com

Local Contacts

BARDSTOWN

CLG Preservation Program
115 East Stephen Foster Avenue
Bardstown, KY 40004
(502) 348-1808
FAX (502) 348-1818

Wetherby's Antiques and Gallery
97 West Flaget Avenue
Bardstown, KY 40004-1439
(502) 349-0139

BELLEVUE

City of Bellevue Preservation Office
616 Poplar Street
Bellevue, KY 41073
(606) 431-8866
FAX (606) 261-0436

BOWLING GREEN

Bowling Green Historic Preservation Board
c/o City County Planning
Commission
1141 State Street

Bowling Green, KY 42101
(502) 842-1953
FAX (502) 842-1282

Riverview House Musuem
1100 West Main Avenue
P.O. Box 10059
Bowling Green, KY 42102-4859
(502) 843-5565
FAX (502) 843-5557

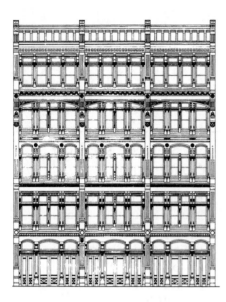

Hart Block, Louisville, Kentucky. *(C. Alexander, HABS)*

Western Kentucky University
Department CFS Academic Complex
Bowling Green, KY 42101
(502) 745-3999
FAX (502) 745-2084
E-mail: cfs@wku.edu
Web Site: http://www.wkuweb1.
wku.edu/Dept/Acedemic/
Education/cfs

BURLINGTON

Boone County Historic Preservation Review Board
2995 Washington Street
Burlington, KY 41005
(606) 334-2111
FAX (606) 334-2264

Dinsmore Homestead Foundation, Inc.
P.O. Box 453
Burlington, KY 41005
(606) 586-6117
FAX (606) 586-6117

COVINGTON

Economic Development Department and Commonwealth Preservation Advocates
City of Covington
638 Madison Avenue
Covington, KY 41011
(606) 292-2111
E-mail: covecom@fuse.net
Web Site: http://www.covington.
uscenet.com

DANVILLE

Boyle Landmark Trust
Campus-Kenneth
P.O. Box 215
Danville, KY 40423
(606) 236-6568
FAX (606) 236-7611

LEXINGTON

African American Heritage Commission
545 Chestnut Street
Lexington, KY 40508
(502) 564-3940
FAX (502) 564-8992

Bluegrass Trust for Historic Preservation
253 Market Street
Lexington, KY 40507
(606) 253-0362
FAX (606) 259-9210

Drystone Masonry Conservancy, Inc.
3533 Winding Drive
Lexington, KY 40517
(606) 272-4807
FAX (606) 245-2251
E-mail: drystoneus@aol.com

Kentucky Mansions Preservation Foundation, Inc.
P.O. Box 132
Lexington, KY 40501
(606) 233-9999

Lexington-Frankfort Scenic Corridor
Donamire Farm
Box 12850
Lexington, KY 40583
(606) 233-3824
FAX (606) 255-8020

LOUISVILLE

Historic Homes Foundation, Inc.
3110 Lexington Road
Louisville, KY 40206-3046
(502) 899-5079
FAX (502) 899-5079

Jefferson County Historic Preservation and Archives
810 Barrett Avenue
Louisville, KY 40204
(502) 574-5761
FAX (502) 574-6886

Louisville Development Authority
Landmarks Commission
600 West Main, Suite 300
Louisville, KY 40202
(502) 574-4141
FAX (502) 574-4143

Portland Museum
2308 Portland Avenue
Louisville, KY 40212
(502) 776-7678

RICHMOND

Interior Design Program
102 Burrier Building
Richmond, KY 40475
(606) 622-3445

Louisiana

STATE HISTORIC PRESERVATION OFFICE

Department of Culture, Recreation and Tourism
P.O. Box 44247
Baton Rouge, LA 70804
(504) 342-8200
FAX (504) 342-8173
Gerri Hobdy, SHPO

STATEWIDE PRESERVATION ORGANIZATION

Louisiana Preservation Alliance
P. O. Box 1587
Baton Rouge, LA 70821
(504) 928-9304
FAX (504)926-2534
Ed Dubuisson, President
Jennifer Maul, Executive Director

NATIONAL TRUST REGIONAL OFFICE

Southern Regional Office
456 King Street
Charleston, SC 29403
(803) 722-8552
FAX (803) 722-8652
E-mail: sro@nthp.org
Web Site: http://www.nthp.org
David Brown, Director

NATIONAL TRUST ADVISORS

Winifred Byrd
Baton Rouge

Joseph F. Newell
New Orleans

STATEWIDE MAIN STREET STATE COORDINATOR

Kathy Morgan, Coordinator
Louisiana Main Street Program
Division of Historic Preservation
P. O. Box 44247
Baton Rouge, LA 70804
(504) 342-8160
FAX (504) 342-8173
E-mail: kmorgan@crt.state.la.us
Web Site: http://www.crt.state.la.us/crt/ocd/hp/msmain.htm

AMERICAN INSTITUTE OF ARCHITECTS CONTACT

Richard C. Thevenot, Hon. AIA, Executive Director
AIA Louisiana
521 America Street
Baton Rouge, LA 70802
(504) 387-5579
FAX (504) 387-2743
E-mail: hg@aiala.com
Web Site: http://www.aiala.com

Local Contacts

ABBEVILLE

Abbeville Main Street Program
P.O. Box 1170
Abbeville, LA 70511
(318) 898-4110
FAX (318) 898-4298

BATON ROUGE

Foundation for Historical Louisiana
900 North Boulevard
Baton Rouge, LA 70802
(504) 387-2464
FAX (504) 343-3989
E-mail: fhistorica@aol.com
Web Site: http://www.explorebr.com/ffhl

Magnolia Mound Plantation
2161 Nicholson Drive
Baton Rouge, LA 70802
(504) 343-4955
FAX (504) 343-6739

Mississippi River Heritage Corridor
P.O. Box 41380
Baton Rouge, LA 70835-1380
(504) 272-1825

DESTREHAN

Destrehan Manor
13034 River Road
P.O. Box 5
Destrehan, LA 70047
(504) 764-9315
FAX (504) 725-1929

Louis Lanoix House, New Orleans, Louisiana. *(G. Embry, HABS)*

HOUMA

Terrebonne Historical and Cultural Association, Southdown Plantation House/The Terrebonne Museum
LA Highway 311 and St. Charles Street
P.O. Box 2095
Houma, LA 70361
(504) 851-0154

LAFAYETTE

Downtown Development Authority
735 Jefferson Street, Suite 204
Lafayette, LA 70501
(318) 291-5566
(318) 291-5573

MARKSVILLE

City of Marksville
440 North Main Street
Marksville, LA 71351

(318) 253-9500
FAX (318) 253-0457

NATCHITOCHES

Cane River National Heritage Area
P.O. Box 537
Natchitoches, LA 71457
(318) 357-0447
FAX (318) 357-8341

Natchitoches Historic Foundation, Inc.
P.O. Box 2351
Natchitoches, LA 71457
(318) 352-0990

NEW ORLEANS

Eskew Filson Architects
1008 North Peters Street
New Orleans, LA 70116
(504) 561-8686

Historic District Landmarks Commission
830 Julia Street
New Orleans, LA 70113
(504) 565-7440
FAX (504) 565-6269

Jean Lafitte National Historical Park and Preserve
365 Canal Street, Suite 2400
New Orleans, LA 70130
(504) 589-3882
FAX (504) 589-3851

Louisiana Landmarks Society, Pitot House and Museum
1440 Moss Street
New Orleans, LA 70119
(504) 482-0312
FAX (504) 482-0312
Web Site: http://www.neworleans.com/museum/pitot

Preservation Resource Center of New Orleans
604 Julia Street
New Orleans, LA 70130
(504) 581-7032
FAX (504) 522-9275
E-mail: prc@lamerica.net
Web Site: http://www.brecht.com/prc

Save Our Cemeteries, Inc.
P.O. Box 58105
New Orleans, LA 70158
(504) 525-3377
FAX (504) 525-6677
E-mail: soc@gnofn.org
Web Site: http://www.gnofn.org/soc.

VACHERIE

Oak Alley Foundation
3645 Louisana Highway 18
Vacherie, LA 70090
(504) 265-2151 or 1-800-442-5539
FAX (504) 265-7035
E-mail: oalley@aol.com

Maine

STATE HISTORIC PRESERVATION OFFICE

Maine Historic Preservation Commission
55 Capitol Street, Station 65
Augusta, ME 04333
(207) 287-2132
FAX (207) 278-2335
E-mail: sheshet@state.me.us
Web Site: http://www.state.me.us/mhpc/homepag1.htm
Earle G. Shettleworth, Jr., SHPO

STATEWIDE PRESERVATION ORGANIZATION

Maine Preservation
P. O. Box 1198
500 Congress Street
Portland, ME 04104
(207) 775-3652
Ann Niles, President
Janet Roberts, Executive Director

NATIONAL TRUST REGIONAL OFFICE

Northeast Regional Office
Seven Faneuil Hall Marketplace
Boston, MA 02109
(617) 523-0885
FAX (617) 523-1199
E-mail: nero@nthp.org
Web Site: http://www.nthp.org
Wendy Nicholas, Director

NATIONAL TRUST ADVISOR

Eleanor "Noni" Ames
Cumberland Foreside, ME

AMERICAN INSTITUTE OF ARCHITECTS CONTACT

Judith W. Harvie, Executive Director
Maine AIA
3 Sylvan Way
Manchester, ME 04351
(207) 623-1218
FAX (207) 623-1218

Local Contacts

BAR HARBOR

Maine Acadian Heritage Center
Acadia National Park
P.O. Box 177
Bar Harbor, ME 04609
(207) 288-5472
FAX (207) 288-5507
E-mail: bruce_jacobson@nps.gov

Town of Bar Harbor
P.O. Box 337
Bar Harbor, ME 04609-0337
(207) 288-4098
FAX (207) 288-4461

BATH

Maine Maritime Museum
Washington Street
Bath, ME 04530
(207) 443-1316
FAX (207) 443-1665
Web Site: http://www.bathmaine.com

BETHEL

The Bethel Historical Society
P.O. Box 12
Bethel, ME 04217
(207) 824-2908 or (800) 824-2910

DAMARISCOTTA

Damariscotta River Association
P.O. Box 333
Damariscotta, ME 04543
(207) 563-1393
FAX (207) 563-1393
E-mail: dra@maine.maine.edu

GREENVILLE

Moosehead Marine Museum
P.O. Box 1151
Greenville, ME 04441
(207) 695-2716

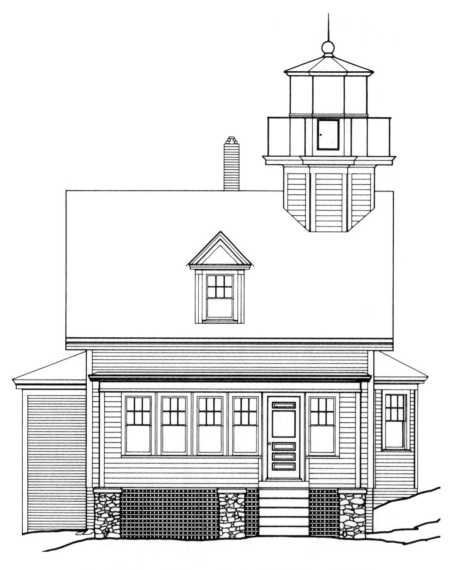

St. Croix River Lighthouse, Dochet Island, Maine. *(HABS)*

New England Electric Railway Historical Society, Inc.
Drawer A
Seashore Trolley Museum
Kennebunkport, ME 04046
(207) 967-2712
FAX (207) 967-2800
E-mail: carshop@gwi.net
Web Site: http://www.swi.net/
trolley

KINGFIELD

The Stanley Museum, Inc.
P.O. Box 280
Kingfield, ME 04947
(207) 265-2729

LEWISTON

Historic Preservation Review Board
City Building
Lewiston, ME 04240
(207) 784-2951
FAX (207) 784-2959

LIVERMORE FALLS

Washburn-Norlands Foundation
290 Norlands Rd
Livermore, ME 04253
(207) 897-4366

NEW GLOUCESTER

New Gloucester Public Library
P.O. Box 105
New Gloucester, ME 04260
(207) 926-4840
FAX (207) 926-2717

NORTHEAST HARBOR

Schoolhouse Ledge
Northeast Harbor, ME 04662
(207) 276-3266

KENNEBUNK

Brick Store Museum
P.O. Box 177
Kennebunk, ME 04043
(207) 985-4802
FAX (207) 985-6887
E-mail: brickstore@cybertours.com
Web Site: http://www.cybertours.
com/~brickstore

Kennebunk Historic Preservation Commission
1 Summer Street
Kennebunk, ME 04046
(207) 962-3675
FAX (207) 985-4609

KENNEBUNKPORT

Kennebunkport Historical Society
P.O. Box 1173
Kennebunkport, ME 04046
(207) 967-2751
FAX (207) 967-1205

PORTLAND

City of Portland Historic Preservation Committee
City Hall—389 Congress Street, Room 404
Portland, ME 04101
(207) 874-8300, EXT. 8726
FAX (207) 756-8258

Greater Portland Landmarks
165 State Street
Portland, ME 04101
(207) 774-5561
FAX (207) 774-2509

Maine Preservation
P.O. Box 1198
Portland, ME 04104
(207) 775-3652

Mohr and Seredin Landscape Architects
18 Pleasant Street
Portland, ME 04101
(207) 871-0003
FAX (207) 871-1419
E-mail: msla@gwi.net

ROCKPORT

Maine Coast Artists
P.O. Box 147
Rockport, ME 04856
(207) 236-2875
FAX (207) 236-2490

SACO

Saco Historic Preservation Commission
City Hall
300 Main Street
Saco, ME 04072
(207) 282-3487
FAX (207) 282-8209
E-mail: develop@sacomaine.org
Web Site: http://www.sacomaine.org

TOPSHAM

Town of Topsham Planning Office
22 Elm Street
Topsham, ME 04086
(207) 725-2454

WELLS

Laudholm Trust
P.O. Box 1007
Wells, ME 04090
(207) 646-4521
FAX (207) 641-2036
E-mail: 103203.1462@compuserve.com

YARMOUTH

Yarmouth Historical Society
P.O. Box 107
Yarmouth, ME 04096
(207) 846-6259
FAX (207) 846-2422

YORK

Old York Historical Society
P.O. Box 312
York, ME 03909
(207) 363-4974
FAX (207) 363-4021
Web Site: http://www.nentug.org/museums/oldyork

Maryland

STATE HISTORIC PRESERVATION OFFICE

Maryland Historical Trust
100 Community Place
Third Floor
Crownsville, MD 21032-2023
(410) 514-7600
FAX (410) 514-7678
E-mail: mdshpo@ari.net
Web Site: http://www2.ari.net/mdshpo
Rodney J. Little, SHPO

STATEWIDE PRESERVATION ORGANIZATIONS

Maryland Association of Historic District Commissions
602 Pleasant Hill Road
Ellicott City, MD 21043
(410) 514-7616
Donald Kann, President
Lisa Jensen Wingate, Executive Director

Maryland Heritage Alliance
Historic Magruder House
4703 Annapolis Road
Bladensburg, MD 20710
(301) 927-7150
FAX (301) 927-5407
Eric Hertfelder, President

Preservation Maryland
24 West Saratoga Street
Baltimore, MD 21201

(410) 685-2886
FAX (410) 539-2182
Rene Gunning, President
Tyler Gearhart, Executive Director

NATIONAL TRUST REGIONAL OFFICE

Mid-Atlantic Regional Office
One Penn Center at Suburban Station, Suite 1520
1617 John F. Kennedy Boulevard
Philadelphia, PA 19103-1815
(215) 568-8162
FAX (215) 568-9251
E-mail: maro@nthp.org
Web Site: http://www.nthp.org
Patricia Wilson Aden, Director

NATIONAL TRUST ADVISORS

Grant Dehart, AICP
Annapolis, MD

Michael F. Trostel, FAIA
Baltimore, MD

STATEWIDE MAIN STREET COORDINATOR

Cindy Stone
Maryland Main Street Center
100 Community Place, CAA
Crownsville, MD 21032
(410) 514-7256

AMERICAN INSTITUTE OF ARCHITECTS CONTACTS

Karen Lewand, Executive Director
AIA Baltimore
11½ West Chase Street
Baltimore, MD 21201
(410) 625-2585
FAX (410) 727-4620
E-mail: aiabalt@erols.com

Lloyd Unsell, Jr., Executive Director
AIA Maryland
AIA Potomac Valley
1426 Fenwick Lane
Silver Spring, MD 20910
(310) 588-7095
FAX (310) 589-4016

Ann Stacy, Hon. AIA, Executive Director
Chesapeake Bay Chapter
2109 East Baltimore Street
Baltimore, MD 21231
(410) 522-3050
FAX (410) 522-1380
E-mail: annsl@erols

Local Contacts

ACCOKEEK

Potomac River Heritage Project
The Accokeek Foundation
3400 Brian Point Road
Accokeek, MD 20607
(301) 283-2113
FAX (301) 283-2049
E-mail: accofound@aol.com
Wilton Corkern, President

ANNAPOLIS

Charles Carroll House of Annapolis, Inc.
107 Duke of Gloucester Street
Annapolis, MD 21401
(410) 269-1737
FAX (410) 269-1740

City of Annapolis Historic District Commission
160 Duke of Gloucester Street
Annapolis, MD 21401
(410) 263-7961
FAX (410) 263-1129

Historic Annapolis Foundation
18 Pinkney Street
Annapolis, MD 21401

(410) 267-7619
FAX (410) 267-6189
Web Site: http://www.annapolis.org

Historic Naval Ships Association of North America, Inc.
c/o U.S. Naval Academy Museum
118 Maryland Avenue
Annapolis, MD 21402-5034
(410) 293-2108
FAX (410) 293-5220

BALTIMORE

Allegany County Historical Society
218 Washington Street
Cumberland, MD 21502
(301) 777-8678

Church Restoration Services
811 Rolyn Avenue
Baltimore, MD 21237
(410) 444-7616
FAX (410) 325-9072

Commission for Historical and Architectural Preservation
Charles L. Benton, Jr. Building
417 East Fayette Street
Suite 1037

Baltimore, MD 21202-3431
(410) 396-4866
FAX (410) 396-5662

Friends of the President Street Station Baltimore Civil War Museum
President Street Station, Inc.
601 President Street
Baltimore, MD 21202
(410) 385-5188
FAX (410) 385-5189
E-mail: museum@
civilwarinbaltimore.org

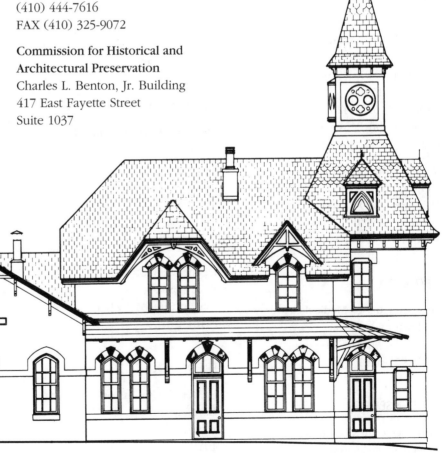

Baltimore and Ohio Railway Station, Point of Rocks, Maryland. *(T. Wolosz, HAER)*

League of Historic American Theatres
34 Market Place, Suite 320
Baltimore, MD 21202
(410) 659-9533
FAX (410) 837-9664

Penza Associates Architects, Inc.
2203 North Charles Street
Baltimore, MD 21218
(301) 467-7741

Society for the Preservation of Federal Hill and Fells Point
812 South Ann Street
Baltimore, MD 21231
(410) 675-6750
FAX (410) 675-6769

Star-Spangled Banner Flag House
844 East Pratt Street
Baltimore, MD 21202
(410) 837-1793
FAX (410) 837-1812

Constellation Foundation, Inc.
Pier One, East Pratt Street
Baltimore, MD 21202-3134
(410) 539-1797
FAX (410) 625-1426
Web Site: http://www.constellation.org

Whitney Bailey Cox and Magnani
849 Fairmont Avenue, Suite 100
Baltimore, MD 21286
(410) 512-4500
FAX (410) 324-4100

BETHESDA

Howard Hughes Medical Center
1 Cloister Court
Bethesda, MD 20814-1460
(301) 951-6711

BLADENSBURG

Prince George's Heritage, Inc.
4703 Annapolis Road
Bladensburg, MD 20710

(301) 927-7150
FAX (301) 927-5407

CHESTERTOWN

Historical Society of Kent County
P.O. Box 665
Chestertown, MD 21620
(410) 778-3499

CHEVY CHASE

Traceries
5420 Western Avenue
Chevy Chase, MD 20815
(301) 656-5283
FAX (301) 656-5420

CLINTON

Surratt Society
P.O. Box 427
Clinton, MD 20735-0427
(301) 868-1121
FAX (301) 868-8177

CROWNSVILLE

Maryland Environmental Trust
100 Community Place, First Floor
Crownsville, MD 21032-2023
(410) 514-7900
FAX (410) 514-7919

ELLICOTT CITY

Historic Ellicott City, Inc.
P.O. Box 244
Ellicott City, MD 21043
(410) 461-6908

FREDERICK

Frederick City Historic District Commission
c/o City Hall
101 North Court Street
Frederick, MD 21701
(301) 694-1655
FAX (301) 696-0925

R. Christopher Goodwin and Associates, Inc.
241 East 4th Street, Suite 100
Frederick, MD 21701
(301) 694-6428
FAX (301) 695-5327

GRANTSVILLE

Spruce Forest Artisan Village
117 Casselman Road
Grantsville, MD 21536
(301) 895-3332

GREENBELT

Greenhorne and O'Mara, Inc.
9001 Edmonston Road
Greenbelt, MD 20770
(301) 982-2800

JESSUP

Plastmo, Inc.
8246 Sandy Court
Jessup, MD 20794
(301) 776-0200 or 1-800-899-0992
FAX (410) 792-8047
Web Site: http://www.rio.com/~plastmo/plast@web.html

OXON HILL

Oxon Hill Manor/MNCPPC
6901 Oxon Hill Road
Oxon Hill, MD 20745
(301) 839-7782
FAX (301) 839-4867

PRINCESS ANNE

Lower Eastern Shore Heritage Area
Lower Eastern Shore Heritage Committee
P.O. Box 148
Princess Anne, MD 21853
(410) 651-6345
FAX (410) 651-6207

ROCKVILLE

City of Rockville
111 Maryland Avenue
Rockville, MD 20850
(301) 309-3000
FAX (301) 762-7153

Peerless Rockville Historic Preservation, Ltd.
P.O. Box 4262
Rockville, MD 20849-4262
(301) 762-0096
FAX (301) 762-0961
E-mail: peerless@millkern.com
Web Site: http://www.millkern.com/peerless

ST. MARY'S CITY

Historic St. Mary's City Commission
P.O. Box 39
St. Mary's City, MD 20686
(301) 862-0960 or (301) 862-0990
FAX (301) 862-0968
Web Site: http://www.webgraphic.com/hfmc/

SNOW HILL

Beach to Bay Indian Trail
Furnace Town Foundation, Inc.
Box 207
Snow Hill, MD 21863
(410) 632-2032

TOWSON

Baltimore County Historical Trust
P.O. Box 10067
Towson, MD 21285-0067
(401) 832-1812

Historic Towson, Inc.
P.O. Box 10072
Towson, MD 21285-0072
(401) 832-1776
FAX (410) 321-6340

THURMONT

Catoctin Furnace Historical Society, Inc.
12320 Auburn Road
Thurmont, MD 21788
(301) 271-2306

UPPER MARLBORO

Historic Preservation Commission
Prince George's County Planning Department
14741 Governor Oden Bowie Drive, CAB, Fourth Floor
Upper Marlboro, MD 20772
(301) 952-3520
FAX (301) 952-4121

WESTMINSTER

Union Mills Homestead Foundation
3311 Littlestown Pike
Westminster, MD 21158
(410) 848-2288

Massachusetts

STATE HISTORIC PRESERVATION OFFICE

Massachusetts Historical Commission
220 Morrissey Boulevard
Boston, MA 02125
(617) 727-8470
TDD 1-800-392-6090
FAX (617) 727-5128
E-mail: mhc.sec.state.ma.us
Web Site: http://www.magnet.
state.ma.us/sec/mhc
Judith McDonough, SHPO

STATEWIDE PRESERVATION ORGANIZATION

Historic Massachusetts, Inc.
45 School Street
Boston, MA 02108
(617) 723-3383
FAX (617) 523-3782
Marcia Molay, Executive Director

NATIONAL TRUST REGIONAL OFFICE

Northeast Regional Office
Seven Faneuil Hall Marketplace
Boston, MA 02109
(617) 523-0885
FAX (617) 523-1199
E-mail: nero@nthp.org
Web Site: http://www.nthp.org
Wendy Nicholas, Director

NATIONAL TRUST ADVISORS

Philip B. Herr
Newton, MA

Thomas M. Menino
Boston, MA

NATIONAL PARK SERVICE CONTACT

Superintendent
New England SSO, National Park
Service
15 State Street
Boston, MA 02109-3572
(617) 223-5200
FAX (617) 223-5022

STATEWIDE MAIN STREET COORDINATOR

Emmy Hahn, Assistant Director
Downtown Revitalization
Program
The Commonwealth of
Massachusetts
Executive Office of Communities
and Development
100 Cambridge Street
Boston, MA 02202
(617) 727-7180
FAX (617) 727-4259

AMERICAN INSTITUTE OF ARCHITECTS CONTACTS

Richard Fitzgerald, Executive Director
AIA Massachusetts
Boston Society of Architects/AIA
52 Broad Street
Boston, MA 02109
(617) 951-1433 x232
FAX (617) 951-0845
E-mail: bsarch@architects.org
Web Site: http://www.architects.
org

Dorothy A. Fassett, Executive Secretary
AIA Central Massachusetts
14 East Worcester Street
Worcester, MA 01604
(508) 753-8903
FAX (508) 757-7769

Alexandra Lee, Executive Director
AIA Western Massachusetts
52 Broad Street
Boston, MA 02109
(617) 951-1433
(617) 951-0845

Local Contacts

ALLSTON

St. Luke's and St. Margaret's Episcopal Church
5 St. Luke's Road
Allston, MA 02134
(617) 782-1577

ANDOVER

Andover Historical Society
97 Main Street
Andover, MA 01810
(508) 475-2236
FAX (508) 470-2741

ARLINGTON

Arlington Historical Society
7 Jason Street
Arlington, MA 02174
(617) 648-4300

Simpson, Gumpert and Heger Inc.
297 Broadway
Arlington, MA 02174
(617) 643-2000
FAX (617) 643-2009

ATTLEBORO

Smyth Associates
8 North Main Street
P.O. Box 4141
Attleboro, MA 02703
(508) 226-4135
FAX (508) 226-5578

AYER

Ayer Historical Commission
Town of Ayer
P.O. Box 924
Ayer, MA 01432
(508) 772-2597

BARNSTABLE

Cape Cod Heritage Program
Cape Cod Commission
3225 Main Street
P.O. Box 226
Barnstable, MA 02630
(508) 362-3828
FAX (508) 362-3136
E-mail: capecommission@
compuserve.com
Web Site: http://www.vsa.cape.
com/~cccom

BEVERLY

The Trustees of Reservations
572 Essex Street
Beverly, MA 01951
(508) 921-1944
FAX (508) 921-1948

BOSTON

Architectural Heritage Foundation
Old City Hall
45 School Street
Boston, MA 02108
(617) 523-8678
FAX (617) 523-3782

Boston Affiliates, Inc.
156 Milk Street
Boston, MA 02109
(617) 451-9450
FAX (617) 451-6475
E-mail: smass52583@aol.com

The Bostonian Society
The Old State House
206 Washington Street
Boston, MA 02109
(617) 720-1713
FAX (617) 720-3289

Boston Preservation Alliance
45 School Street
Boston, MA 02108
(617) 367-2458
FAX (617) 227-1886

Boston University American and New England Studies
704 Commonwealth Avenue,
Second Floor
Boston, MA 02215
(617) 353-2948

The Community Preservation Project
P.O. Box 8381
Boston, MA 02114
(617) 455-1950
E-mail: tccp@aol.com

The First Church of Christ Scientist
Church History
175 Huntington Avenue
Boston, MA 02115
(617) 450-3505
FAX (617) 450-3415

First Partners Group, Inc.
400 Commonwealth Avenue
Boston, MA 02215
(617) 266-3400

Goody, Clancy and Associates
334 Boylston Street
Boston, MA 02116
(617) 262-2760
FAX (617) 262-9512
E-mail: arch@gcassoc.com
Web Site: http://www.gcassac.com

Historic Boston, Inc.
3 School Street
Boston, MA 02108
(617) 227-4679
FAX (617) 742-7431

Law Office of Stephen Small
75 Federal Street, Suite 1100
Boston, MA 02110
(617) 357-4012
FAX (617) 357-1857

North Bennet Street School
39 North Bennet Street
Boston, MA 02113
(617) 227-0156
FAX (617) 227-9292

186

PRESERVATION PHONE BOOK

Paul Revere Memorial Association
19 North Square
Boston, MA 02113
(617) 523-2338
FAX (617) 523-1775

Perry Dean Rogers and Partners
177 Milk Street
Boston, MA 02109
(617) 423-0100
FAX (617) 426-2274

Preservation Technology Association
1 Washington Mall, 16th Floor
Boston, MA 02108
(617) 227-0900
FAX (617) 227-5535

Shepley Bulfinch Richardson and Abbott
40 Broad Street
Boston, MA 02109
(617) 423-1700
FAX (617) 451-2420

Society for the Preservation of New England Antiquities
141 Cambridge Street
Boston, MA 02114
(617) 227-3956
FAX (617) 227-9204

South End Historical Society, Inc.
532 Massachusetts Avenue
Boston, MA 02118
(617) 536-4445

SPNEA—Museums Department
141 Cambridge Street
Boston, MA 02114
(617) 227-3956
FAX (617) 227-9204

BRAINTREE

Braintree Historical Society, Inc.
31 Tenney Road
Braintree, MA 02184-6512
(617) 848-1640
FAX (617) 380-0731

BROOKLINE

Longyear Museum
120 Seaver Street
Brookline, MA 02146
(617) 277-8943

Olmsted Center for Landscape Preservation
National Park Service
99 Warren Street
Brookline, MA 02146
(617) 566-1689
FAX (617) 232-3964

CAMBRIDGE

Cambridge Historical Commission
57 Inman Street
City Hall Annex
Cambridge, MA 02139
(617) 498-9040 or (617) 394-4683
FAX (617) 349-6165

Cambridge Historical Society
159 Brattle Street
Cambridge, MA 02138
(617) 547-4252
FAX (617) 661-1623

Mount Auburn Cemetery
580 Mount Auburn Street
Cambridge, MA 02138
(617) 547-7105

CHARLESTOWN

Charlestown Preservation Society
P.O. Box 201
Charlestown, MA 02129
(617) 241-7500
FAX (617) 242-3756

CHESTERFIELD

Hilltown Community Development Corporation
P.O. Box 17
Chesterfield, MA 01012
(413) 296-4536
FAX (413) 296-4020
E-mail: hcdc@external.umass.edu

CONCORD

Fannin/Lehner
Preservation Consultants
271 Lexington Road
Concord, MA 01742
(508) 369-6703
FAX (508) 371-9883
E-mail: dentils@aol.com

Louisa May Alcott Memorial Association
P.O. Box 343
Concord, MA 01742
(508) 369-4118
FAX (508) 369-1367

DEERFIELD

Historic Deerfield, Inc.
P.O. Box 321
Deerfield, MA 01342
(413) 774-5581
FAX (413) 773-7415

Pocumtuck Valley Memorial Association
10 Memorial Street
Deerfield, MA 01342
(413) 774-7476
FAX (413) 774-5400
E-mail: puma@shaysnet.com

EDGARTOWN

Edgartown Historic District Commission
P.O. Box 5158
Edgartown, MA 02539
(508) 627-6155
FAX (508)627-6123

Martha's Vineyard Preservation Trust
P.O. Box 5277
Edgartown, MA 02539
(508) 627-4440
FAX (508) 627-8017

GLOUCESTER

Cape Ann Historical Association
27 Pleasant Street
Gloucester, MA 01930
(508) 283-0455

HARVARD

Fruitlands Museums, Inc.
102 Prospect Hill Road
Harvard, MA 01451
(508) 456-3924
FAX (508) 456-9393
E-mail: frutland@usa1.com
Web Site: http://www1.usa1.com/
frutland

HINGHAM

Hingham Historical Commission
570 Main Street
Hingham, MA 02043
(617) 749-0612
FAX (617) 749-1795
E-mail: amacmil570@aol.com

HYANNIS

Barnstable Historical Commission
Town Hall
Hyannis, MA 02601
(508) 790-6270
FAX (508) 775-3344

LENOX

Edith Wharton Restoration, Inc
P.O. Box 974
Lenox, MA 01240
(413) 637-1899
FAX (413) 637-0619

LOWELL

Lowell Historic National Park
67 Kiek Street
Lowell, MA 01852
(508) 458-7653
FAX (508) 458-9502

Muckle and Associates
354 Andover Street
Lowell, MA 01852
(508) 937-2747

U.S. Department of the Interior
Canal Way Division of National
Park
222 Merrimack Street, Suite 400
Lowell, MA 01852
(508) 458-7653
FAX (508) 458-9502

MENDON

Preservation Services, Inc.
59 North Avenue
P.O. Box 18
Mendon, MA 01756
(508) 473-4884

NANTUCKET

Nantucket Historical Association
P.O. Box 1016
Nantucket, MA 02554
(508) 228-1894
FAX (508) 228-5618

**Nantucket Historic District
Commission**
37 Washington Street
Nantucket, MA 02554
(508) 228-7231

South Family Dwelling and Washshed, Harvard Shakers, Worcester, Massachusetts. *(R. T. Newman, HABS)*

NATICK

Natick Center Association, Inc.
2 Summer Street, Suite 304
Natick, MA 01760
(508) 650-8848
FAX (508) 655-0032

NEW BEDFORD

Downtown New Bedford, Inc.
106 William Street
New Bedford, MA 02740
(508) 990-2777
FAX ((508) 997-7969

New Bedford Historical Commission
City Hall
133 Williams Street
New Bedford, MA 02740
(508) 979-1400

Schooner Ernestina Commission
P.O. Box 2010
New Bedford, MA 02741
(508) 992-4900
FAX (508) 984-7719
Web Site: http://www.ernestina.org

Waterfront Historic Area League
(WHALE)
33 William Street
New Bedford, MA 02740
(508) 997-1776
FAX (508) 984-1250

NEWBURYPORT

Historical Society of Old Newbury
98 High Street
Newburyport, MA 01950
(508) 462-2681

NORTH ADAMS

Cummings Studios
P.O. Box 427
North Adams, MA 01247
(413) 664-6578
FAX (413) 664-6570
E-mail: stglst@aol.com

NORTH ATTLEBORO

North Attleboro Historical Society
P.O. Box 1102
North Attleboro, MA 02760
(508) 695-6680

SALEM

Essex Heritage Area
Essex Heritage Commission
6 Central Street
Salem, MA 01970
(508) 741-8100
FAX (508) 745-6130

Historic Salem, Inc.
P.O. Box 865
Salem, MA 01970
(508) 745-0799

Peabody Essex Museum
East India Square
Salem, MA 01970
(508) 745-1876
FAX (508) 744-6776
E-mail: pem@pem.org

The Salem Partnership
6 Central Street
Salem, MA 01970
(508) 741-8100
(508) 745-6131
E-mail: partnership@cove.com

SANDWICH

Heritage Cape Cod
P.O. Box 2105
Sandwich, MA 02563
(508) 888-1233
FAX (508) 888-4318

SOUTH BOSTON

St. Augustine's Save the Chapel
Committee
9 F Street
South Boston, MA 02127
(617) 268-1230 or (617) 269-3831

SPRINGFIELD

Springfield Preservation Trust
979 Main Street
Springfield, MA 01103
(413) 747-0656

TRURO

Truro Historical Society, Inc.
P.O. Box 486
Truro, MA 02666
(508) 349-2809

WATERTOWN

Historical Commission of
Watertown
Administration Building
Watertown, MA 02172
(617) 972-6417

WORCESTER

East Side Community Development
Corporation
20 Envelope Terrace
Worcester, MA 01604
(508) 799-6942
FAX (508) 799-0110

Oak Hill Community Development
74 Providence Street
Worcester, MA 01604-4204
(508) 754-2858
FAX (508) 754-0138

Preservation Worcester
10 Cedar Street
Worcester, MA 01609
(508) 754-8760
FAX (508) 792-6818

Michigan

Local Contacts

ADRIAN

Siena Heights College Library
1247 East Siena Heights Drive
Adrian, MI 49221
(517) 264-7150
FAX (517) 264-7711

ALBION

Albion Public Library
501 South Superior
Albion, MI 49224

ALLEGAN

Allegan Historic District Commission
Allegan City Hall
112 Locust Street
Allegan, MI 49010
(616) 673-5511

ALLEN PARK

Great Lakes Lighthouse Keeper's Association
4901 Evergreen Road
Dearborn, MI 48128-1491
(313) 436-9150

ALPENA

Jesse Besser Museum
491 Johnson Street
Alpena, MI 49707
(517) 356-2202
FAX (517) 356-3133
E-mail: jbmuseum@northland.
lib.mi.us

ANN ARBOR

Ann Arbor Historic District Commission
100 North Fifth Avenue
Ann Arbor, MI 48104
(313) 996-3008

BATTLE CREEK

Historical Society of Battle Creek
196 Capital Avenue, N.E.
Battle Creek, MI 49017
(616) 965-2613

Preservation Action Alliance
47 North Washington Avenue
Battle Creek, MI 49017
(616) 968-1113
FAX (616) 963-7022

BIRMINGHAM

City of Birmingham
P.O. Box 3001
Birmingham, MI 48012
(810) 644-1800

CALUMET

Keweenaw National Historical Park
P.O. Box 471
100 Redjacket Road, Second Floor
Calumet, MI 49913
(906) 337-3168

CHARLOTTE

**Eaton County Historical
Commission**
P.O. Box 25
Charlotte, MI 48813
(517) 543-6999

DEARBORN

Henry Ford Estate
University of Michigan at Dearborn
4901 Evergreen Road
Dearborn, MI 48128-1491
(313) 436-9150

DETROIT

Preservation Wayne
The David MacKenzie House
4735 Cass Avenue

Detroit, MI 48202
(313) 577-3559
FAX (313) 577-7666

**Southwest Detroit Business
Association**
1601 Clark Street
Detroit, MI 48209
(313) 842-0986
FAX (313) 842-6350

Steamer Columbia Foundation
1020 Iroquois Avenue
Detroit, MI 48214
(313) 224-3487

EAGLE HARBOR

**Keweenaw County Historical
Museum**
HC1, Box 265L
Eagle Harbor, MI 49951
(906) 289-4990

EAST POINT

City Manager
23200 Gratiot Avenue
East Point, MI 48021
(810) 445-5026

EAST LANSING

Michigan State University
East Lansing, MI 48824
(517) 353-8723

FARMINGTON HILLS

Farmington Hills Historic District
Commission
31555 Eleven Mile Road
Farmington Hills, MI 48336
(810) 347-4611

GRAND RAPIDS

Dwelling Place of Grand Rapids
339 South Division Avenue
Grand Rapids, MI 49503
(616) 454-0928

Heritage Hill Foundation
126 College Avenue, S.E.
Grand Rapids, MI 49503
(616) 459-8950

**Kent County Council for Historic
Preservation**
247 Morris, S.E.
Grand Rapids, MI 49503
(616) 454-5373
FAX (616) 459-5360

GROSSE POINT SHORES

Edsel and Eleanor Ford House
1100 Lake Shore Road
Grosse Point Shores, MI 48236
(313) 884-4222
FAX (313) 884-5977

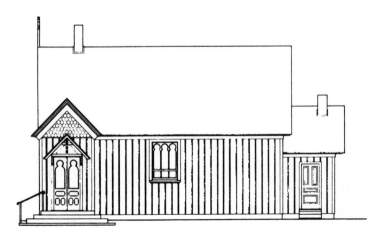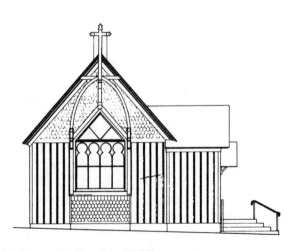

St. Katherine's Episcopal Church, Williamstown, Michigan. *(M. Trumbo, HABS)*

HOUGHTON

Western Upper Peninsula Heritage Reserve
Regional Planning Commission
P.O. Box 365
Houghton, MI 49931
(906) 482-7205

KALAMAZOO

Stuart Area Restoration Association
530 Douglas Avenue
Kalamazoo, MI 49007
(616) 344-7432
FAX (616) 344-7346

Vine Neighborhood Association
511 West Vine Street
Kalamazoo, MI 49008
(616) 349-8463
FAX (616) 343-3243

LANSING

Capitol Facility Operations
100 North Capitol
P.O. Box 30036
Lansing, MI 48909
(517) 373-0184

LOWELL

Fallasburg Historical Society
10889 52nd Street
Lowell, MI 49331
(616) 897-6430

MARSHALL

Marshall Historical Society
107 North Kalamazoo
P.O. Box 68
Marshall, MI 49068
(616) 781-8544

MASON

Mason Historic District Commission
201 West Ash Street
Mason, MI 48854

MIDLAND

Midland County Historical Society
1801 West St. Andrews Road
Midland, MI 48640
(517) 835-7401

MONROE

Community Development
120 East First Street
Monroe, MI 48161
(313) 243-0700

MOUNT CLEMENS

Mount Clemens Historic
c/o Frankie Kendrick Marcou
98 Gallup Avenue
Mount Clemens, MI 48043

MUSKEGON

Muskegon County Museum
430 West Clay
Muskegon, MI 49440
(616) 722-0278

ROMEO

Romeo Downtown Development Authority
P.O. Box 52
Romeo, MI 48065
(810) 752-0527

SALINE

Saline Historic District Commission
P.O. Box 40
Saline, MI 48176
(313) 996-3008

SOUTH LYON

South Lyon Area Historical Society
P.O. Box 263
South Lyon, MI 48178
(313) 437-9279

TRAVERSE CITY

Opera House City Heritage Association
P.O. Box 2005
Traverse City, MI 49685

WASHINGTON

Friends of the Octagon House
P.O. Box 94118
Washington, MI 48094
(313) 795-3587

WESTLAND

Ford Heritage Trail
Wayne County Park Division
33175 Ann Arbor Trail
Westland, MI 48185
(313) 261-2034

UNIVERSITY CENT

Delta College
Delta Road
University Cent, MI 48710

VASSAR

Cork Pine Preservation Association
205 North West
Vassar, MI 48768
(517) 823-3442

ZEELAND

Zeeland Historical Society
P.O. Box 165
37 East Main Avenue
Zeeland, MI 49464
(616) 772-4079

Minnesota

STATE HISTORIC PRESERVATION OFFICE

Minnesota Historical Society
345 Kellogg Boulevard West
St. Paul, MN 55102
(612) 296-6126
FAX (612) 297-3343
E-mail: robert.garcia@mnhs.org
Web Site: http://www.mnhs.org
Dr. Nina Archabal, SHPO

STATEWIDE PRESERVATION ORGANIZATION

Preservation Alliance of Minnesota
International Market Square
275 Market Street, Suite 54
Minneapolis, MN 55405-1621
(612) 338-6763
FAX (612) 338-7981
Web Site: http://www.umn.
edu/n/home/m121/brook024/
pam.htm
Roger Brooks, President

NATIONAL TRUST REGIONAL OFFICE

Midwest Regional Office
53 West Jackson Boulevard,
Suite 1135
Chicago, IL 60604
(312) 939-5547
FAX (312) 939-5651
E-mail: mwro@nthp.org
Web Site: http://www.nthp.org
Jim Mann, Director

NATIONAL TRUST ADVISORS

Jodi Lynn Phelps
Virginia, MN

Charlene Roise
Minneapolis, MN

AMERICAN INSTITUTE OF ARCHITECTS CONTACTS

Beverly Hauschild, Hon. AIA, Executive Vice President
AIA Minneapolis/AIA St. Paul
AIA Nothern Minnesota
International Market Square
275 Market Street, Suite 54
Minneapolis, MN 55404
(612) 338-6763
FAX (612) 338-7981

Peter A. Rand, FAIA, Executive Vice President
AIA Minneapolis/AIA St. Paul
AIA Nothern Minnesota
International Market Square
275 Market Street, Suite 54
Minneapolis, MN 55404
(612) 338-6763
FAX (612) 338-7981

Local Contacts

BAYPORT

Anderson Windows Inc.
Research & Development
100 Fourth Avenue, North
Bayport, MN 55003
(612) 439-5150

BECKER

Sherburne County Historical Society
13122 First Street
Becker, MN 55308

(612) 261-4433
FAX (612) 261-5048

DULUTH

Duluth Public Library
520 West Superior Street
Duluth, MN 55802
(218) 723-3821
FAX (218) 723-3822

Glensheen/University of Minnesota
3300 London Road
Duluth, MN 55804

(218) 724-8864
FAX (218) 724-3779
E-mail: glen@d.umn.edu

EDEN PRAIRIE

City of Eden Prairie
8080 Mitchell Road
Eden Prairie, MN 55344
(612) 937-2262

EDINA

Edina Heritage Preservation Board
4801 West 50th Street
Edina, MN 55424
(612) 927-8861
FAX (612) 927-7645

Friends of the Basilica
6507 Ridgeview Circle
Edina, MN 55439
(612) 944-0443

EMBARRASS

Sisu Heritage Inc.
Box 127
Embarrass, MN 55732
(218) 984-3402

FERGUS FALLS

City of Fergus Falls
P.O. Box 868
112 West Washington
Fergus Falls, MN 56538-0868
(218) 739-2251
FAX (218) 739-0149

GREENWOOD

P. R. Johnson Construction, Inc
21770 Fairview Street
Greenwood, MN 55331
(612) 474-2227

HASTINGS

**Hastings Heritage Preservation
Commission**
Hastings City Hall
101 4th Street East
Hastings, MN 55033
(612) 437-4127
FAX (612) 437-7082

MINNEAPOLIS

MacDonald and Mack Arichitects
712 Grain Exchange Building
Minneapolis, MN 55415
(612) 341-4051
FAX (612) 337-5843

Pillsbury "A" Mill, Minneapolis, Minnesota. *(D. Jacobson, HABS)*

Martha H. Frey Historic Preservation Consultant
2445 34th Avenue, South
Minneapolis, MN 55406
(612) 729-3407
FAX (612) 729-4910
E-mail: martfrey.aol.com

Minneapolis Heritage Preservation Commission
City Hall, Room 210
350 South 5th Street
Minneapolis, MN 55415-1385
(612) 673-2422
FAX (612) 673-2728

RED WING

Red Wing Heritage Preservation Commission
City Hall
P.O. Box 34
Red Wing, MN 55066
(612) 388-6734

ST. PAUL

Great River Road Mississippi River Parkway Commission
336 Robert Street, Suite 1513
St. Paul, MN 55101
(612) 224-9903

Historic Dayton's Bluff Association
732 Margaret Street
St. Paul, MN 55106
(612) 776-3414
FAX (612) 776-2694

Lowertown Redevelopment Corporation
175 5th Street, East
Box 104
St. Paul, MN 55101-2901
(612) 227-9131
FAX (612) 223-5708

Minnesota Historical Society
Capitol Historic Site
Minnesota State Capitol, Room B59
75 Constitution Avenue
St. Paul, MN 55155
(612) 296-6808
Web Site: http://www.mnhs.org

St. Paul Heritage Preservation Commission
c/o LIEP
350 St. Peter Street
Suite 300
St. Paul, MN 55102
(612) 266-9087
FAX (612) 266-9099

WALKER

Mississippi Headwaters
Mississippi Headwaters Board
Cass County Courthouse
P.O. Box 3000
Walker, MN 56484
(218) 547-7248
FAX (218) 547-7376
Web Site: http://www.
mhbriverwatch.dst.mn.us

WARROAD

Marvin Windows
P.O. Box 100
Warroad, MN 56763
(218) 386-1430
FAX (218) 386-2925

Mississippi

STATE HISTORIC PRESERVATION OFFICE

Mississippi Department of Archives and History
P.O. Box 571
Jackson, MS 39205-0571
(601) 359-6850
FAX (601) 359-6975
Elbert Hilliard, SHPO

STATEWIDE PRESERVATION ORGANIZATION

Mississippi Heritage Trust
P.O. Box 577
Jackson, MS 39205-0577
(601) 354-0200
FAX (601) 354-0220
Al Hollingsworth, President

Stella Gray Bryant, Executive Director

NATIONAL TRUST REGIONAL OFFICE

Southern Regional Office
456 King Street
Charleston, SC 29403
(803) 722-8552
FAX (803) 722-8652
E-mail: sro@nthp.org
Web Site: http://www.nthp.org
David Brown, Director

NATIONAL TRUST ADVISORS

Alferdteen Brown Harrison
Jackson, MS

Samuel H. Kaye
Columbus, MS

STATEWIDE MAIN STREET COORDINATOR

Beverly Meng, Coordinator
Mississippi Downtown
Development Association
P.O. Box 2719
Jackson, MS 39207
(601) 948-0404
FAX (601) 353-0402
E-mail: mdda@misnet.com

Local Contacts

BILOXI

City of Biloxi
P.O. Box 775
Biloxi, MS 39533
(601) 435-6254
FAX (601) 435-6181

CANTON

Canton Redevelopment Authority
P.O. Box 192
226 East Peace
Canton, MS 39046
(601) 859-3815

HATTIESBURG

Hattiesburg Area Historical Society
P.O. Box 1573
Hattiesburg, MS 39401
(601) 545-4594

JACKSON

Farish Street Historic District Neighborhood Foundation
300 North Farish Street, Suite C
Jackson, MS 39201
(601) 944-1600

Foundation for the Mid South
308 East Pearl Street, Fourth Floor
Jackson, MS 39201
(601) 355-8167
FAX (601) 355-6499

E-mail: lilly@fndmidsouth.org
Web Site: http://www.fndmidsouth.org

Museum of the Southern Jewish Experience
P.O. Box 16528
Jackson, MS 39236
(601) 362-6357
FAX (601) 366-6293

MERIDIAN

Grand Opera House of Mississippi, Inc.
P.O. Box 5792
Meridian, MS 39302
(601) 693-5239

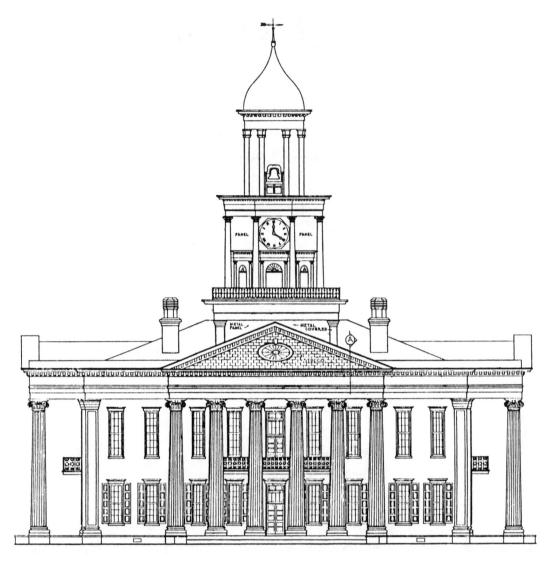

Warren County Courthouse, Vicksburg, Mississippi. *(F. Deboe, S. Tuminello, E. Murphy, HABS)*

MOUND BAYOU

African American Historic Preservation Committee— Mississippi Heritage Trust
c/o Town of Mound Bayou
P.O. Box 680
Mound Bayou, MS 38762
(601) 741-2193
FAX (601) 741-2195

NATCHEZ

Historic Natchez Foundation
P.O. Box 1761
Natchez, MS 39121
(601) 442-2500
FAX (601) 442-2525

Preservation Society of Ellicott Hill
215 South Pearl Street
Natchez, MS 39120

VICKSBURG

Vicksburg Foundation for Historic Preservation
P.O. Box 254
Vicksburg, MS 39181
(601) 636-5010
FAX (601) 636-5010

WOODVILLE

Wilkinson County Museum
Woodville Civic Club
P.O. Box 902
Woodville, MS 39669
(601) 888-4808

Missouri

STATE HISTORIC PRESERVATION OFFICE

State Department of Natural Resources
100 Jefferson
P.O. Box 176
Jefferson City, MO 65102
(573) 751-7858
FAX (573) 526-2852
E-mail: mmiles@mail.more.net
David A. Shorr, SHPO

STATEWIDE PRESERVATION ORGANIZATION

Missouri Alliance for Historic Preservation
P.O. Box 895
Jefferson City, MO 65102
(573) 635-6877
Jeanine Cook, President

NATIONAL TRUST REGIONAL OFFICE

Midwest Regional Office
53 West Jackson Boulevard, Suite 1135
Chicago, IL 60604
(312) 939-5547
FAX (312) 939-5651
E-mail: mwro@athp.org
Web Site: http://www.nthp.org
Jim Mann, Director

NATIONAL TRUST ADVISORS

Greg Allen
Kansas City, MO

Janice J. Mattews
Sikeston, MO

STATEWIDE MAIN STREET COORDINATOR

Randy Gray, Coordinator
Missouri Main Street Program
Missouri Department of Economic Development
301 West High Street
Truman Building, Room 770
P.O. Box 118
Jefferson City, MO 65102
(573) 751-7939
FAX (573) 526-8999

AMERICAN INSTITUTE OF ARCHITECTS CONTACTS

Pat Amick, Executive Director
AIA Missouri
204 A East High Street
Jefferson City, MO 65101
(573) 635-8555
FAX (573) 636-5783

Anita Valdivia, Executive Director
AIA Kansas City
104 West Ninth Street
Kansas City, MO 64105
(816) 221-3485
FAX (816) 221-5653

Patricia Bausch, Administrative Director
AIA St. Louis
911 Washington Avenue, #225
St. Louis, MO 63101
(314) 621-3484
FAX (314) 621-3489

Local Contacts

INDEPENDENCE

Jackson County Historical Society
129 West Lexington
Independence, MO 64050
(816) 461-1897
FAX (816) 461-1510
E-mail: jchs@crn.org
Web Site: http://www.crn.org/

JAMESTOWN

Missouri River Heritage Corridor
Missouri River Communities Network
Route 1, Box 4030
Jamestown, MO 65046
(816) 849-2589
FAX (816) 849-2589

JEFFERSON CITY

Cole County Historical Society
109 Madison Street
Jefferson City, MO 65101-3015
(573) 635-1850

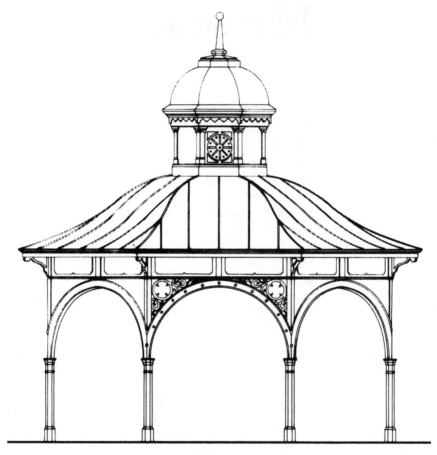

Summerhouse, Tower Grove Park, St. Louis, Missouri. *(S. Bauer, HABS)*

KANSAS CITY

Historic Kansas City Foundation
712 Broadway, #404
Kansas City, MO 64105
(816) 471-3391
FAX (816) 471-3915

ST. JOSEPH

St. Joseph Preservation, Inc.
P.O. Box 8541
St. Joseph, MO 64508
(816) 232-8300

ST. LOUIS

**The Greater Ville Historic
Development Corporation**
4206 West Kennerly
St. Louis, MO 63113
(314) 534-8015
FAX (314) 534-6440

Landmarks Association of St. Louis
917 Locust, 7th Floor
St. Louis, MO 63101-1413
(314) 421-6474

Montana

STATE HISTORIC PRESERVATION OFFICE

State Historic Preservation Office
1410 8th Avenue
P.O. Box 201202
Helena, MT 59620-1202
(406) 444-7715
FAX (406) 444-6575
Paul M. Putz, SHPO

STATEWIDE PRESERVATION ORGANIZATION

Montana Preservation Alliance
P. O. Box 1872
Bozeman, MT 59771-1872
(406) 585-9551
FAX (406) 585-0468
B. Derek Strahn, President

NATIONAL TRUST REGIONAL OFFICE

Mountains/Plains Regional Office
910 16th Street, Suite 1100
Denver, CO 80202
(303) 623-1504
FAX (303) 623-1508
E-mail: mpro@nthp.org
Web Site: http://www.nthp.org
Barbara Pahl, Director

NATIONAL TRUST ADVISORS

Jeanette McKee
Hamilton, MT

Judy McNally
Billings, MT

AMERICAN INSTITUTE OF ARCHITECTS CONTACT

C. Joann Harris, Executive
Director
AIA Montana
P.O. Box 20996
Billings, MT 59104
(406) 259-7300
FAX (406) 259-4211
E-mail: assocmgt@wtp.net

Local Contacts

BILLINGS

Billings Preservation Society, Inc
914 Division Street
Billings, MT 59101
(406) 252-5100
(406) 252-0091

Yellowstone River Valley Heritage
Area
Western Heritage Center
2822 Montana Avenue
Billings, MT 59101
(406) 256-6809

BUTTE

Southwest Montana Heritage and
Recreation Area
(Butte-Anaconda Mining Heritage
Park)
Community Development Services
of Montana
954 West Caledonia Street
Butte, MT 59701
(406) 723-7993
FAX (406) 723-7993
E-mail: janallyce@aol.com

GREAT FALLS

Cascade County Historical Society
1400 First Avenue, North
Great Falls, MT 59401
(406) 452-3462
FAX (406) 452-3462

Great Falls City County Planning
Board
Box 5021
Great Falls, MT 59403
(406) 727-5881

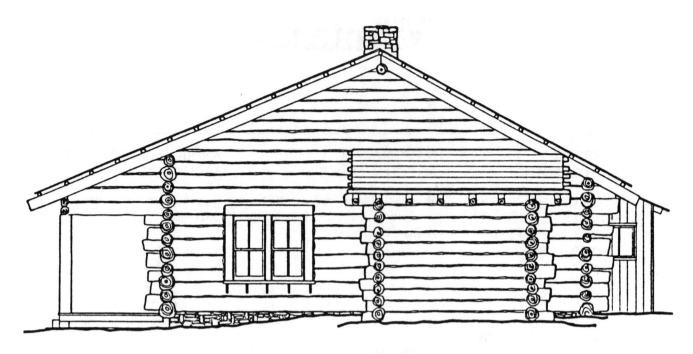

Lubuc Ranger Station, East Glacier, Montana. *(K. Speece, HABS)*

HAVRE

Memorial Museum (Clack Museum)
H. Earl and Margaret Turner Clack
306 3rd Street
Havre, MT 59501
(406) 265-4000

HELENA

City of Helena
Planning Department
316 North Park Avenue
Helena, MT 59623
(406) 447-8437

VIRGINIA CITY

Virginia City Preservation Alliance
P.O. Box 55
Virginia City, MT 59755
(406) 843-5300

Nebraska

STATE HISTORIC PRESERVATION OFFICE

Nebraska State Historical Society
P.O. Box 82554
Lincoln, NE 68501
1-800-833-6747
(402) 471-4787
FAX (402) 471-3100
Lawrence Sommer, SHPO

STATEWIDE PRESERVATION ORGANIZATION

Nebraska Preservation Council Network
1014 Boswell
Crete, NE 68333
(402) 826-8234
FAX (402) 826-8600
Janet Jeffries, President

NATIONAL TRUST REGIONAL OFFICE

Mountains/Plains Regional Office
910 16th Street, Suite 1100
Denver, CO 80202
(303) 623-1504
FAX (303) 623-1508
E-mail: mpro@nthp.org
Web Site: http://www.nthp.org
Barbara Pahl, Director

NATIONAL TRUST ADVISORS

Nancy Hoch
Nebraska City, NE

Perry L. Poyner
Omaha, NE

NATIONAL PARK SERVICE CONTACTS

Superintendent
Great Plains SSO
Midwest Field Area, National
Park Service
1709 Jackson Street
Omaha, NE 68102
(402) 221-3471
FAX (402) 221-2039

Field Director
Midwest Field Area, National
Park Service
1709 Jackson Street
Omaha, NE 68102
(402) 221-3431
FAX (402) 221-2039

Local Contacts

KEARNEY

The Frank House
c/o Mrs. Virginia L. Lund
2010 West 24th Street
Kearney, NE 68847
(308) 237-4275

LINCOLN

Preservation Association of Lincoln
c/o Rogers House
2145 B Street
Lincoln, NE 68502
(402) 476-6961

University of Nebraska
205 HE University of Nebraska
Lincoln, NE 68583-0802
(402) 472-6319

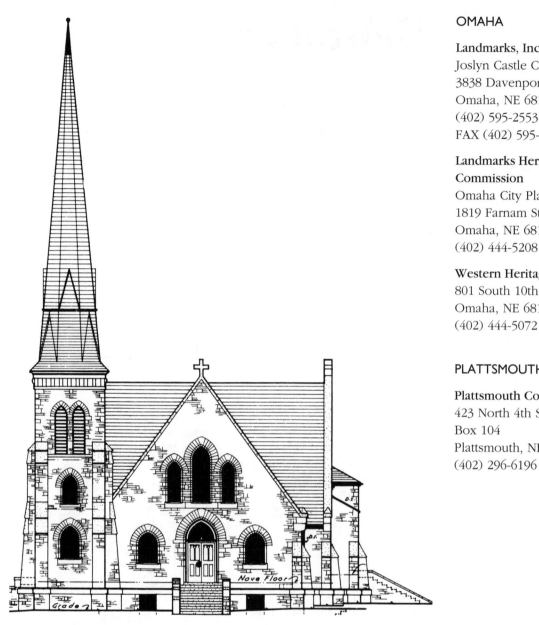

Church of the Holy Trinity (Episcopal), Lincoln, Nebraska. *(F. Mooberry, HABS)*

OMAHA

Landmarks, Inc.
Joslyn Castle Carriage House
3838 Davenport Street
Omaha, NE 68131
(402) 595-2553
FAX (402) 595-2556

Landmarks Heritage Preservation Commission
Omaha City Planning Department
1819 Farnam Street, Suite 1100
Omaha, NE 68183
(402) 444-5208

Western Heritage Society
801 South 10th Street
Omaha, NE 68108
(402) 444-5072

PLATTSMOUTH

Plattsmouth Conservancy
423 North 4th Street
Box 104
Plattsmouth, NE 68048
(402) 296-6196

Nevada

STATE HISTORIC PRESERVATION OFFICE

Historic Preservation Office
101 South Stewart Street
Capitol Complex
Carson City, NV 89710
(702) 687-6360
Ronald James, SHPO

NATIONAL TRUST REGIONAL OFFICE

Western Regional Office
One Sutter Street, Suite 707
San Francisco, CA 94104
(415) 956-0610
FAX (415) 956-0837
E-mail: wro@nthp.org

Web Site: http://www.nthp.org
Elizabeth Goldstein, Director

NATIONAL TRUST ADVISORS

Andria S. Daley-Taylor
Virginia City

Gene Sergerblom
Boulder City, NV

AMERICAN INSTITUTE OF ARCHITECTS CONTACTS

Randy Lavigne, Executive
Director
AIA Las Vegas
UNLV Box 454018

4505 South Maryland Parkway
Las Vegas, NV 89154
(702) 895-0936
FAX (702) 895-4417
E-mail: aialasvegas.org

Penny Robison, Executive
Secretary
AIA Northern Nevada
P.O. Box 607
Reno, NV 89504-0607
(702) 827-6600
FAX (702) 827-6692

Local Contacts

RENO

Nevada Historical Society
1650 North Virginia Street
Reno, NV 89503
(702) 688-1190

Truckee Meadows Community
College
7000 Dandini Boulevard
Reno, NV 89512
(702) 673-7000

WINNEMUCCA

North Central Nevada Historical
Society
Humboldt Museum
P.O. Box 819
Winnemucca, NV 89445
(702) 623-2912

James D. Roberts House, Carson City,
Nevada. *(J. T. McCreery, HABS)*

New Hampshire

STATE HISTORIC PRESERVATION OFFICE

New Hampshire Division of
Historical Resources
P.O. Box 2043
Concord, NH 03302-2043
(603) 271-6435
FAX (603) 271-3433
Nancy Muller, Director and
SHPO

STATEWIDE PRESERVATION ORGANIZATION

Inherit New Hampshire, Inc.
264 North Main Street
P. O. Box 268
Concord, NH 03302-0268
(603) 224-2281
FAX (603) 226-4466
Don Leavitt, President
Eugene Kincaid, Executive
Director

NATIONAL TRUST REGIONAL OFFICE

Northeast Regional Office
Seven Faneuil Hall Marketplace
Boston, MA 02109
(617) 523-0885
FAX (617) 523-1199
E-mail: nero@nthp.org
Web Site: http://www.nthp.org
Wendy Nicholas, Director

NATIONAL TRUST ADVISORS

Alice DeSouza
Bedford, NH

Michael C. Harvell
Portsmouth, NH

STATEWIDE MAIN STREET COORDINATOR

Kathy LaPlante, Coordinator
New Hampshire Main Street
Center
New Hampshire Community
Development Authority
14 Dixon Avenue, Suite 102
Concord, NH 03301
(603) 223-9942
(603) 226-2816

AMERICAN INSTITUTE OF ARCHITECTS CONTACT

Deirdre Brotherson, Executive
Director
AIA New Hampshire
P.O. Box 247
Concord, NH 03302-0247
(603) 226-4550
FAX (603) 226-4550

Local Contacts

ALSTEAD

Historic Window and Door
Corporation
Junction 123A and 123
P.O. Box 138
Alstead, NH 03602
(603) 835-2918

BETHLEHEM

North Country Council
107 Glessner Road
Bethlehem, NH 03574
(603) 444-6303

CHARLESTOWN

Connecticut River Valley
Connecticut River Joint
Commissions
P.O. Box 1182
Charlestown, NH 03603
(603) 826-4800

CONCORD

New Hampshire Heritage Trail
New Hampshire State Parks
P.O. Box 1856
Concord, NH 03302-1856
(603) 271-3255

DEERFIELD

Town of Deerfield
8 Raymond Road
P.O. Box 159
Deerfield, NH 03037
(603) 463-8811

Shaker Church Family Cow Barn, Enfield, New Hampshire. *(P. M. Burkhart, HABS)*

ENFIELD

Enfield Shaker Museum
2 Lower Shaker Village
Enfield, NH 03748
(603) 632-4346

HARRISVILLE

Historic Harrisville, Inc.
Box 79
Harrisville, NH 03450
(603) 827-3333
FAX (603) 827-3722

MANCHESTER

Manchester Historic Association
129 Amherst Street
Manchester, NH 03101
(603) 622-7531
FAX (603) 622-0822

NASHUA

Nashua Historic District Commission
City Hall
229 Main Street
Nashua, NH 03061
(603) 883-0015

NEWPORT

Town Offices
15 Sunapee Street
Newport, NH 03773
(603) 863-2224

SWANZEY

Swanzey Preservation Society Inc.
P.O. Box 10323
Swanzey, NH 03446
(603) 352-6156

New Jersey

STATE HISTORIC PRESERVATION OFFICE

Department of Enviromental Protection
CN-402, 401 East State Street
Trenton, NJ 08625
(609) 292-2885
FAX (609) 292-7695
Robert C. Shinn, SHPO

STATEWIDE PRESERVATION ORGANIZATION

New Jersey Historic Trust
CN 404, 506–508 East State Street
Trenton, NJ 08625
(609) 984-0473
FAX (609) 984-7590
Harriette Hawkins, Executive Director

Preservation New Jersey, Inc.
The Proprietary House
149 Kearny Avenue, Second Floor
Perth Amboy, NJ 08861-4700
(908) 442-1100
FAX (908) 442-2442

E-mail: presnj@aol.com
Janice Wilson Stridick, President
Mary Delaney Krugman, Executive Director

NATIONAL TRUST REGIONAL OFFICE

Mid-Atlantic Regional Office
One Penn Center at Suburban Station
Suite 1520
1617 John F. Kennedy Boulevard
Philadelphia, PA 19103-1815
(215) 568-8162
FAX (215) 568-9251
E-mail: maro@nthp.org
Web Site: http://www.nthp.org
Patricia Wilson Aden, Director

NATIONAL TRUST ADVISORS

Flavia Alaya
Paterson, NJ

Michael C. Henry, AIA
Bridgeton, NJ

STATEWIDE MAIN STREET COORDINATOR

Barbara Swanda, Coordinator
CN 806
Trenton, NJ 08625
(609) 292-9798
FAX (609) 633-6266

AMERICAN INSTITUTE OF ARCHITECTS CONTACT

Joseph Simonetta, CAE, Executive Director
AIA New Jersey
196 West State Street
Trenton, NJ 08608
(609) 393-5690
FAX (609) 396-5361

Local Contacts

ALLAIRE

Allaire Village, Inc.
Allaire Road
P.O. Box 220
Allaire, NJ 07727
(201) 930-2253

BURLINGTON

Burlington County Historical Society
457 High Street
Burlington, NJ 08016
(609) 386-4773

CAPE MAY

Mid-Atlantic Center for the Arts
P.O. Box 340
Cape May, NJ 08204

(609) 884-5404
FAX (609) 884-2006

CAPE MAY

Cape May Court Cultural and Heritage Commission
DN 101
Library Office Building
Cape May, NJ 08210
(609) 465-1005

CRANBURY

**Cranbury Historical and
Preservation Society**
P.O. Box 77
Cranbury, NJ 08512
(609) 655-3736

FLEMINGTON

**Hunterdon County Cultural and
Heritage Commission**
Administration Building
Flemington, NJ 08822
(908) 788-1256

FREEHOLD

**Freehold Township Historic
Preservation Commission**
Municipal Hall
Municipal Plaza
Freehold, NJ 07728
(908) 294-2000

HADDONFIELD

Haddonfield Preservation Society
120 Warwick Road
Haddonfield, NJ 08033
(609) 429-5486

HO-HO-KUS

Friends of the Hermitage
335 North Franklin Turnpike
Ho-Ho-Kus, NJ 07423
(201) 445-8311

LISBON

Pinelands Federal Natural Reserve
The Pineland Commission
P.O. Box 7
New Lisbon, NJ 08604
(609) 894-9344

JERSEY CITY

**Barrow Mansion Development
Corporation**
83 Wayne Street
Jersey City, NJ 07302
(201) 432-6979

Columbus Line, Inc.
Plaza 2
Harborside Financial Center
Jersey City, NJ 07311
(201) 432-0900

**Lindemon, Winckelmann, Deupree
Martin AIA/Associates**
295 Newark Avenue
Jersey City, NJ 07302
(201) 333-5017

LAKEWOOD

**Municipal Building Heritage
Commission**
231 Third Street
Lakewood, NJ 08701
(908) 364-2500

MARGATE

Save Lucy Committee, Inc.
P.O. Box 3000
Margate, NJ 08402
(609) 822-6519

MARLTON

Historic Preservation Commission
125 East Main Street
Marlton, NJ 08053
(609) 983-2914

MORRIS PLAINS

Craftsman Farms Foundation
2352 Route 10 West
Box 5
Morris Plains, NJ 07950
(201) 540-1165

MORRISTOWN

Fosterfields Living Historical Farm
Morris County Park Commission
73 Kahdena Road
Morristown, NJ 07960

(201) 326-7645

Historic Speedwell
333 Speedwell Avenue
Morristown, NJ 07960
(201) 540-0211

MMT Local History Department
Free Public Library
1 Miller Road
Morristown, NJ 07960
(201) 538-3473
FAX (201) 267-4064

Morristown National Historical Park
Washington Place
Morristown, NJ 07960
(201) 539-2085

NEWARK

**Newark Preservation and Landmarks
Committee**
P.O. Box 1066
Newark, NJ 07101
(201) 622-4910

New Jersey Historical Society
230 Broadway
Newark, NJ 07104
(201) 483-3939

New Jersey Transit Corporation
One Penn Plaza East
Newark, NJ 07105
(201) 491-7199

NEWPORT

New Jersey Coastal Heritage Trail
P.O. Box 568
Newport, NJ 08345
(609) 447-0103

NUTLEY

Historic Restoration Trust of Nutley
3 Kingsland Street
Nutley, NJ 07110
(201) 661-3410

OCEAN GROVE

Ocean Grove Camp Meeting
Association
54 Pitman Avenue
P.O. Box 126
Ocean Grove, NJ 07756
(908) 988-5533

PATERSON

**City of Paterson Historic
Preservation Commission**
65 McBride Avenue
Paterson, NJ 07501
(201) 279-5980

PRINCETON

Historic Preservation Officer
Township of Princeton
369 Witherspoon Street
Princeton, NJ 08540
(609) 921-1359

Nassau Architects
164 Nassau Street
Princeton, NJ 08542
(609) 924-4446

RIDGEFIELD

Brisk Waterproofing Company, Inc.
720 Grand Avenue
Ridgefield, NJ 07657
(212) 532-4430

SOMERS POINT

**Risley Homestead Committee of the
Atlantic County Historical Society**
P.O. Box 301
Somers Point, NJ 08244
(609) 927-5218

STOCKTON

**Delaware and Raritan Canal Heritage
Corridor**
Delaware and Raritan Canal
Commission
P.O. Box 539
Stockton, NJ 08559-0539
(609) 397-2000

TENAFLY

Tenafly Historic Preservation
Commission
100 River Edge Road
Tenafly, NJ 07670
(201) 568-6100

TRENTON

Free Public Library
120 Academy Street
Trenton, NJ 08608
(609) 392-7188

Historic Preservation Office New
Jersey Department
CN404 501 East State Street
Fourth Floor
Trenton, NJ 08625-0404
(609) 292-2023

Isles Incorporated
10 Wood Street
Trenton, NJ 08608
(609) 393-5656

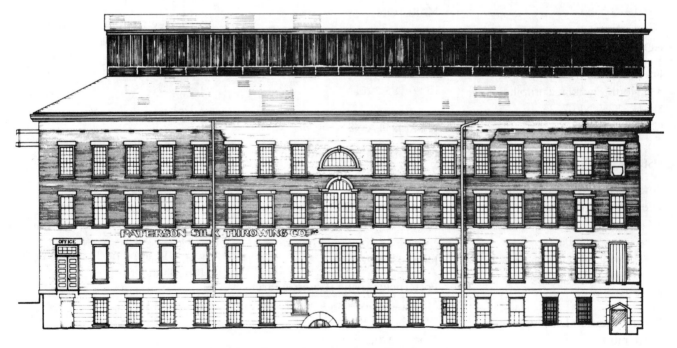

Phoenix Mill, Paterson, New Jersey. *(W. Gavzy, HAER)*

New Mexico

STATE HISTORIC PRESERVATION OFFICE

Historic Preservation Division, Office of Cultural Affairs
228 East Palace Avenue
Santa Fe, NM 87503
(505) 827-6320
FAX (505) 827-6338
E-mail: nmshpo@arms.state.nm.us
Lynne Sebastian, Director

STATEWIDE PRESERVATION ORGANIZATION

New Mexico Preservation Heritage Alliance
P. O. Box 2490
Santa Fe, NM 87504-2490
(505) 983-2645
FAX (505) 983-1464
Tom Merlan, President

NATIONAL TRUST REGIONAL OFFICE

Southwest Regional Office
500 Main Street, Suite 1030
Fort Worth, TX 76102
(817) 332-4398
FAX (817) 332-4512
E-mail: swro@nthp.org
Web Site: http://www.nthp.org
Jane Jenkins, Director

NATIONAL TRUST ADVISORS

Barbara A. Perea Casey
Roswell, NM

Mary Pietsch Davis
Corrales, NM

NATIONAL PARK SERVICE CONTACT

Superintendent
Southwest SSO, National Park Service
1100 Santa Fe Trail
Santa Fe, NM 87501-0728

STATEWIDE MAIN STREET COORDINATOR

Elmo Baca, Coordinator
New Mexico Main Street Program
Economic Development
1100 St. Francis Drive
Santa Fe, NM 87503
(505) 827-0200
FAX (505) 827-1645

AMERICAN INSTITUTE OF ARCHITECTS CONTACT

Mary Thomas, Executive Director
AIA Albuquerque
215 Gold S.W., #102
Alberquerque, NM 87102
(505) 244-3737
FAX (505) 244-3756

Local Contacts

ABIQUIU

Georgia O'Keeffe Foundation
P.O. Box 40
Abiquiu, NM 87510
(505) 685-4539

ALBUQUERQUE

City of Albuquerque Economic Division
P.O. Box 1293
Albuquerque, NM 87103
(505) 768-3270

Mariah Associates, Inc.
4221-B Balloon Park Road N.E.
Albuquerque, NM 87109
(505) 761-0099
FAX (505) 761-0208

Menaul Historical Library of the Southwest
301 Menaul Boulevard, N.E.
Albuquerque, NM 87107
(505) 343-7480

El Cerrito, Upper Pecos River Valley, New Mexico. *(M. Lewis, HABS)*

Petroglyph National Monument
6001 Unser Boulevard N.W.
Albuquerque, NM 87120
(505) 899-0205

CORRALES

Corrales Historic Preservation Committee
P.O. Box 704
Corrales, NM 87048
(505) 898-5017

LAS VEGAS

Citizens Committee for Historic Preservation
P.O. Box 707
Las Vegas, NM 87701
(505) 425-8803
FAX (505) 454-1020

ROSWELL

Historical Society for Southeast New Mexico
200 North Lea Avenue
Roswell, NM 88201
(505) 622-8333

SANTA FE

City of Santa Fe Planning Division
P.O. Box 909
Santa Fe, NM 87504-0909
(505) 984-6808
FAX (505) 986-6910

Cornerstones Community Partnership
227 Otero Street
Santa Fe, NM 87501
(505) 982-9521
FAX (505) 982-2516

Historic Santa Fe Foundation
P.O. Box 2535
Santa Fe, NM 87504-2535
(505) 983-2567
FAX (505) 983-2567

National Park Service Conservation Program
P.O. Box 728
Santa Fe, NM 87504
(505) 988-6797
FAX (505) 988-6709

SILVER CITY

Silver City Museum
312 West Broadway
Silver City, NM 88061
(505) 538-5921
FAX (505) 388-1096

TAOS

Kit Carson Historic Museums
P.O. Drawer CCC
Taos, NM 87571
(505) 758-0505
FAX (505) 758-0330

New York

STATE HISTORIC PRESERVATION OFFICE

Parks, Recreation and Historic Preservation
Agency Building #1, Empire State Plaza
Albany, NY 12238
(518) 474-0443
FAX (518) 474-4492
Bernadette Castro, SHPO

STATEWIDE PRESERVATION ORGANIZATION

Preservation League of New York State
44 Central Avenue
Albany, NY 12206-3002
(518) 462-5658
FAX (518) 462-5684
E-mail: plnys@worldnet.att.net
Darlene McCloud, President

NATIONAL TRUST REGIONAL OFFICE

Northeast Regional Office
Seven Faneuil Hall Marketplace
Boston, MA 02109
(617) 523-0885
FAX (617) 523-1199
E-mail: nero@nthp.org
Web Site: http://www.nthp.org
Wendy Nicholas, Director

NATIONAL TRUST ADVISORS

Henry McCartney
Rochester, NY

Anthony C. Wood
New York, NY

STATEWIDE MAIN STREET COORDINATOR

Mr. David Church, President
New York Main Street Alliance
488 Broadway, Suite 506
Albany, NY 12207
(518) 432-4094
FAX (518) 427-8625
E-mail: nyps@wizvax.net

AMERICAN INSTITUTE OF ARCHITECTS CONTACTS

Barbara Rodriguez, Hon. AIA, Executive Vice President
AIA New York State
235 Lark Street
Albany, NY 12210
(518) 449-3334
FAX (518) 426-8176
E-mail: aiahys.org

Michael Felschow, Executive Director
AIA Buffalo/Western New York
c/o School of Architecture and Planning
SUNY Buffalo
Buffalo, NY 14214-3087
(716) 829-2008
FAX (716) 829-2297

Roberta Rodriguez-Bacchus, Component Executive
AIA Eastern New York
235 Lark Street
Albany, NY 12210

(518) 465-3191
FAX (518) 426-8176

Ann LoMonte, Executive Director
AIA Long Island
330 Old Country Road
Mineola, NY 11501
(516) 294-0971
FAX (516) 294-0973

Carol Clark, Executive Director
AIA New York Chapter
200 Lexington Avenue, Sixth Floor
New York, NY 10016
(212) 683-0023
FAX (212) 696-5022

Nancy Macon, Executive Director
AIA Rochester
Eastman Place, #100
387 East Main Street
Rochester, NY 14604
(716) 232-7650
FAX (716) 262-2525

Judith A. Rudikoff, Executive Director
AIA Westchester/Mid-Hudson
P.O. Box 462
South Salem, NY 10590
(914) 533-6240
FAX (914) 533-6240

Local Contacts

ALBANY

City of Albany Planning Office
City Hall, Fourth Floor
Albany, NY 12207
(518) 434-5190
FAX (518) 434-5193

Historic Albany Foundation
44 Central Avenue
Albany, NY 12206
(518) 465-2987

Shaker Heritage Society
1848 Shaker Meeting House
Albany Shaker Road
Albany, NY 12211
(518) 456-7890

John G. Waite Associates, Architects
388 Broadway
Albany, NY 12207
(518) 449-5440
FAX (518) 449-5828

AMAGANSETT

Amagansett Historical Association
P.O. Box 7077
Amagansett, NY 11930
(516) 267-3020

ARKVILLE

The Catskill Center for Conservation and Development
Arkville, NY 12406
(914) 586-2611
FAX (914) 586-3044
E-mail: cccd@catskill.net

BRONX

City Island Historical Society
City Island Museum
190 Fordham Street
Bronx, NY 10464
(718) 885-0008

Longwood Historic District Commission Association, Inc.
965 Longwood Avenue, Room 214
Bronx, NY 10459
(718) 328-4500
FAX (718) 328-4789

National Museum of the American Indian Repatriation Office
3401 Bruckner Boulevard
Bronx, NY 10461
(212) 825-4467
FAX (212) 825-4489
E-mail: nmai-rb.white@ic.si.edu

BROOKLYN

Brooklyn Heights Association
55 Pierrepont Street
Brooklyn, NY 11201
(718) 858-9193
FAX (718) 875-5607

Pratt Institute Center for Community and Environmental Development
379 Dekalb Avenue, Second Floor
Brooklyn, NY 11205
(718) 636-3486
FAX (718) 636-3709
E-mail: picced.org

Prospect Park Alliance, Inc.
95 Prospect Park West
Brooklyn, NY 11215
(718) 965-8951
FAX (718) 965-8972
E-mail: prospect1@juno.com

BUFFALO

Buffalo Olmstead Parks Conservancy
84 Parkside Avenue
Buffalo, NY 14214
(716) 838-1249

International Chimney
P.O. Box 260
Buffalo, NY 14231
(716) 634-3967
FAX (716) 634-3983

Preservation Coalition of Erie County
P.O. Box 768
Buffalo, NY 14213
(716) 837-8858

CANASTOTA

Canastota Canal Town Museum
122 Canal Street
P.O. Box 51
Canastota, NY 13032
(315) 697-3451
FAX (315) 697-3769

CARMEL

Putnam County
110 Old Route 6
Carmel, NY 10512
(914) 225-2641

CAZENOVIA

Cazenovia Preservation Foundation
Box 627
Cazenovia, NY 13035-0627
(315) 655-9009

CLINTON

Historic Preservation Commission
Village of Clinton
7 Marvin Street
Clinton, NY 13323
(914) 266-5740

COHOES

Great Northern Frontier Heritage Area
Hudson-Mohawk Urban Cultural Park Commission (RiverSpark)
97 Mohawk Street
Cohoes, NY 12047
(518) 237-7999/0072 FAX

COLD SPRING

The Garden Conservancy
Box 219
Cold Spring, NY 10516
(914) 265-2029
FAX (914) 265-9620

COOPERSTOWN

Friends of Hyde Hall, Inc.
P.O. Box 721
Cooperstown, NY 13326
(607) 547-5098
FAX (607) 547-8462

CROWN POINT

Champlain Valley Heritage Network
c/o Lake Placid/Essex County
Visitors Bureau
RR1, Box 220
Crown Point, NY 12928
(518) 597-4646

CUTCHOGUE

Old House Society
P.O. Box 361
Cutchogue, NY 11935
(516) 734-5989

EAST MEADOW

Miraclean Systems, Inc.
268 East Meadow Avenue
East Meadow, NY 11554
(516) 794-5800
FAX (516) 794-5895

ELMIRA

Chemung County Historic Society
415 East Water Street
Elmira, NY 14901
(607) 734-4167
(607) 734-1565

Near Westside Neighborhood
Association
353 Davis Street

Elmira, NY 14901
(607) 733-4924
FAX (607) 734-1207

ESSEX

Essex Community Heritage
Organization, Inc. (ECHO)
P.O. Box 250
Essex, NY 12936
(518) 963-7088
FAX (518) 963-4615

FLUSHING

Bowne House Historical Society
37-01 Bowne Street
Flushing, NY 11354
(718) 359-0528

FREDONIA

Fredonia Preservation Society
P.O. Box 422
Fredonia, NY 14063
(716) 672-5341

GERMANTOWN

Friends of the Palatine Parsonage
641 CTY, Route 8
Germantown, NY 12526
(518) 537-4727
E-mail: alybooks@epix.net

GREENPORT

Village of Greenport
236 Third Street
Greenport, NY 11944
(516) 477-2385
FAX (516) 477-1877

ITHACA

Historic Ithaca and Tompkins County
120 North Cayuga Street
Ithaca, NY 14850
(607) 273-6633

FAX (607) 273-4816
E-mail: hi@lightlink.com

National Council of Preservation
Education
212 West Sibley
Cornell University
Ithaca, NY 12853
(607) 255-7261
E-mail: mat4@cornell.edu

Vertical Access
P.O. Box 4135
Ithaca, NY 14852
(607) 257-4049
FAX (607) 257-2129

JAMAICA

Greater Jamaica Development
Corporation
90-04 161st Street
Jamaica, NY 11432
(718) 291-0282
FAX (718) 291-0492

KEESEVILLE

Adirondack Architectural Heritage
1759 Main Street
Keeseville, NY 12944
(518) 834-9328

Friends of the North Country
1A Mills Street
P.O. Box 446
Keeseville, NY 12944
(518) 834-9606
FAX (518) 834-9687

LARCHMONT

Building Renovation
18 Elm Avenue
Larchmont, NY 10538
(914) 834-4349

LONG ISLAND CITY

Arteco Center
3020 49th Street
Long Island City, NY 11103

MASPETH

Towne House Restorations
58-15 49th Place
Maspeth, NY 11378
(718) 326-4210
FAX (718) 326-1344

MILLBROOK

Land Trust Alliance—NY
R.R. 2, Box 13
Millbrook, NY 12545
(914) 677-0084

MOUNT KISCO

Westchester Preservation League
42 McLain Street
Mount Kisco, NY 10549
(914) 242-9890

NEW PALTZ

Huguenot Historical Society of New Paltz, Inc.
P.O. Box 339
New Paltz, NY 12561
(914) 255-1660
FAX (914) 255-0376
E-mail: hugenothistoricalsociety
@worldnet.att.net

NEW YORK

Abigail Adams Smith Museum
421 East 61st Street
New York, NY 10021
(212) 838-6878
FAX (212) 838-7390

American Express Company
American Express Tower
World Financial Center
New York, NY 10285
(212) 640-5609

American Society of Mechanical Engineers
345 East 47th Street
New York, NY 10017
(212) 705-7722

Central Park
Administrative Office
830 Fifth Avenue
New York, NY 10021
(212) 360-8111

Claremont Riding Academy
175 West 89th Street
New York, NY 10024
(212) 724-5100
FAX (212) 799-3568

Fraunces Tavern Museum
54 Pearl Street
New York, NY 10004
(212) 425-1778
FAX (212) 509-3467

Greenwich Village Society for Historic Preservation
47 Fifth Avenue
New York, NY 10003
(212) 924-3895

Heritage Trails New York
61 Broadway
New York, NY 10006
(212) 269-1500

Historic Districts Council
45 West 67th Street
New York, NY 10023
(212) 799-5837
FAX (212) 875-0209
E-mail: franny@hdc.org

Historic House Trust of NYC
The Arsenal, 203 Central Park
New York, NY 10021
(212) 360-8123
FAX (212) 360-8201

The Historic Society of Rockland County
20 Zukor Road
New City, NY 10956
(914) 634-9629
FAX (914) 634-8690

Mitchell Kurtz
Architect PC
611 Broadway, Room 542
New York, NY 10012
(212) 598-4367

Orin Lehman
Orin Lehman Foundation, Inc.
20 East 69th Street
New York, NY 10021-4922
(212) 734-6450

Gordon Lorenz Design, Inc.
P.O. Box 560 Village Station
New York, NY 10014
(212) 777-8368

Metropolitan Historic Structures Association
15 Gramercy Park
New York, NY 10003
(212) 473-6045
FAX (212) 475-3692

Mottola-Poet Associates
51 West 14th Street
New York, NY 10011
(212) 627-7299
FAX (212) 627-1567
E-mail: mottola@aol.com

Municipal Art Society
457 Madison Avenue
New York, NY 10022
(212) 935-3960
FAX (212) 753-1816

Natural Resources Defense Council
40 West 20th Street
New York, NY 10011-4211
(212) 727-2700
FAX (212) 727-1773
Web Site: http://www.nrdc.org

New York City Landmarks Preservation Commission
100 Old Slip
New York, NY 10005
(212) 487-6800

New York Landmarks Conservancy
141 Fifth Avenue, Third Floor
New York, NY 10010
(212) 995-5260
FAX (212) 995-5268

The New York Public Library
Division G
P.O. Box 2237
Grand Central Station
New York, NY 10017
(212) 930-0800

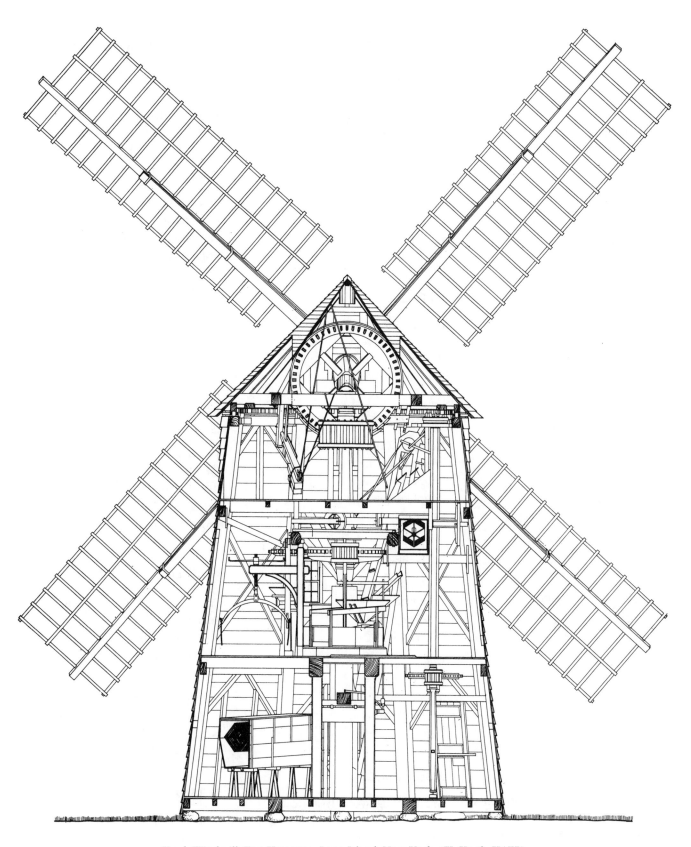

Hook Windmill, East Hampton, Long Island, New York. *(K. Hoeft, HAER)*

New York Public Library
Division P
Grand Central Station
P.O. Box 2240
New York, NY 10163
(212) 930-0800

Riverside Park Fund
475 Riverside Drive, Room 249
New York, NY 10115
(212) 870-3070
FAX (212) 870-3079

School of Architecture
Cooper Union
7 East Seventh Street
Cooper Square
New York, NY 10003
(212) 353-4220

WANT Publishing Company
420 Lexinton Avenue, Suite 300
New York, NY 10170
(212) 687-3774
E-mail: rwant@msn.com
Web Site: http://www.courts.com

World Monuments Fund
949 Park Avenue
New York, NY 10028
(212) 517-9367
FAX (212) 517-9494
Web Site: http://www.
worldmonuments.org

NORTH TONAWANDA

**Carousel Society of the Niagara
Frontier**
P.O. Box 672
180 Thompson Street
North Tonawanda, NY 14120
(716) 693-1885
FAX (716) 743-9018

OSSINING

Ossining Historical Society Museum
196 Croton Avenue
Ossining, NY 10562
(914) 941-0001

OSWEGO

**The Heritage Foundation of
Oswego, Inc.**
156 West Second Street
P.O. Box 405
Oswego, NY 13126
(315) 342-3354

OYSTER BAY

Raynham Hall Museum
20 West Main Street
Oyster Bay, NY 11771
(516) 922-6808

PITTSFORD

Historic Pittsford
18 Monroe Avenue
Pittsford, NY 14534
(716) 381-3799

POUGHKEEPSIE

**Dutchess County Landmarks
Association, Inc.**
P.O. Box 944
Poughkeepsie, NY 12602
(914) 471-1638

RHINEBECK

Hudson River Heritage, Inc.
Box 287
Rhinebeck, NY 12572
(914) 876-2472

Wilderstein Preservation
P.O. Box 383
Rhinebeck, NY 12572
(914) 876-4818
E-mail: wilder@pojonews.infi.net

RIDGEWOOD

**Greater Ridgewood Historical
Society**
1820 Flushing Avenue
Ridgewood, NY 11385
(718) 456-1776

ROCHESTER

Susan B. Anthony Memorial, Inc.
17 Madison Street
Rochester, NY 14608
(716) 235-6124
Web Site: http://www.frontiernet.
net/~hurst/sbahouse/sbahome.htm

ROME

**City of Rome's Historic and Scenic
Preservation Commission**
Planning Department
Rome City Hall
Rome, NY 13440
(315) 339-7643

RYE

Jay Heritage Center
210 Boston Post Road
P.O. Box 661
Rye, NY 10580
(914) 698-9275

Rye Historical Society
One Purchase Street
Rye, NY 10580
(914) 967-7588
FAX (914) 967-4604

SAG HARBOR

**Eastville Community Historical
Society**
P.O. Box 2036
Sag Harbor, NY 11963
(516) 725-0011

Village of Sag Harbor
55 Main Street, P.O. Box 660
Sag Harbor, NY 11963
(516) 725-0222

SARANAC

Historic Saranac Lake
132 River Street
P.O. Box 1030

Saranac Lake, NY 12983
(518) 891-0971

SARATOGA SPRINGS

The Saratoga Associates
443 Broadway
Saratoga Springs, NY 12866
(518) 587-2550
FAX (518) 587-2564

**Saratoga Springs Preservation
Foundation**
P.O. Box 442
Saratoga Springs, NY 12866
(518) 587-5030
FAX (518) 587-0470

SENECA FALLS

Village of Seneca Falls
Planning Department
60 State Street
P.O. Box 108
Seneca Falls, NY 13148
(315) 568-6894
FAX (315) 568-2336

SETAUKET

**Society for the Preservation of Long
Island Antiquities**
93 North Country Road
Setauket, NY 11733
(516) 941-9444
FAX (516) 941-9184

SMITHTOWN

Smithtown Historical Society
P.O. Box 69
Smithtown, NY 11787
(516) 265-6768
FAX (516) 265-6768

STATEN ISLAND

Preservation League of Staten Island
P.O. Box 10071

Staten Island, NY 10301
(718) 447-2036
FAX (718) 876-8068

Snug Harbor Cultural Center, Inc.
1000 Richmond Terrace
Staten Island, NY 10301
(718) 448-2500
FAX (718) 442-8534

STONY BROOK

Stony Brook Community Fund
111 Main Street
P.O. Box 572
Stony Brook, NY 11790
(516) 751-2244
FAX (516) 751-2024

SYRACUSE

City of Syracuse
Department of Community
Development
233 East Washington
Syracuse, NY 13202
(315) 448-8100
FAX (315) 448-8036

The Heritage Coalition, Inc.
Teall Avenue Station
P.O. Box 6233
Syracuse, NY 13217
(315) 471-2162

TAPPAN

Tappantown Historical Society
Box 71
Tappan, NY 10983
(914) 359-1149

TARRYTOWN

Historic Hudson Valley
150 White Plains Road
Tarrytown, NY 10591
(914) 631-8200
FAX (914) 631-0089

Web Site: http://www.
hudsonvalley.org

TROY

Hartgen Archeological Association
27 Jordan Road
Troy, NY 12180
FAX (518) 283-6276

UTICA

City of Utica Bureau of Planning
1 Kennedy Plaza
Utica, NY 13502
(315) 792-0187
FAX (315) 797-6607

Landmarks of Greater Utica
1124 State Street
Utica, NY 13502
(315) 732-7376

WATERFORD

**New York State Historic
Preservation Office**
Peebles Island
P.O. Box 189
Waterford, NY 12188-0189
(518) 237-8643
FAX (518) 233-9049

WATER MILL

Water Mill Museum
Old Mill Road
P.O. Box 63
Water Mill, NY 11976
(516) 726-4625

YONKERS

Hudson River Museum
511 Warburton Avenue
Yonkers, NY 10701
(914) 963-4550
FAX (914) 963-8558

North Carolina

STATE HISTORIC PRESERVATION OFFICE

Division of Archives and History
109 East Jones Street
Raleigh, NC 27601-2807
(919) 733-7305
FAX (919) 733-8807
E-mail: jcrow@ncsl.dcr.state.nc.us
Web site: http://www.hpo.dcr.state.nc.us/
Dr. Jeffrey J. Crow Jr, SHPO

STATEWIDE PRESERVATION ORGANIZATION

Preservation North Carolina
P.O. Box 27644
Raleigh, NC 27611-7644
(919) 832-3652
FAX (919) 832-1651
E-mail: presnc@mindspring.com
Web Site: http://www.presnc.org
Samuel W. Johnson, President
J. Myrick Howard, Executive Director

NATIONAL TRUST REGIONAL OFFICE

Southern Regional Office
456 King Street
Charleston, SC 29403
(803) 722-8552
FAX (803) 722-8652
E-mail: sro@nthp.org
Web Site: http://www.nthp.org
David Brown, Director

NATIONAL TRUST ADVISORS

Margaret Kluttz
Salisbury, NC

Richard A. Matthews
Asheville, NC

STATEWIDE MAIN STREET COORDINATOR

Rodney Swink, Coordinator
North Carolina Main Street Center
North Carolina Department of Commerce
Division of Community Assistance
P.O. Box 12600
Raleigh, NC 27605-2600
(919) 733-2850
FAX (919) 733-5262
E-mail: rswink@dcg.commerce.state.nc.us

AMERICAN INSTITUTE OF ARCHITECTS CONTACTS

Timothy D. Kent, CAE, Executive Vice President
AIA North Carolina
115 West Morgan Street
Raleigh, NC 27601
(919) 833-6656
FAX (919) 833-2015

Lynette Rinker, Executive Director
AIA Charlotte
P.O. Box 561065
Charlotte, NC 28256
(704) 895-0422
FAX (704) 895-0422

Local Contacts

ALBEMARLE

Stanley County Preservation Commission
245 East Main Street
Albemarle, NC 28001
(704) 983-7316
FAX (704) 983-7296

ASHEVILLE

Albemarle Park-Manor Grounds Association, Inc.
P.O. Box 2231
Asheville, NC 28802-2231
(704) 258-1283

Coalition for the Blue Ridge Parkway
c/o Bob Shepherd
Land of Sky Regional Council
25 Heritage Drive
Asheville, NC 28806
(704) 251-6622
FAX (704) 251-6353
E-mail: bob@landofsky.org

Historic Resources Commission of
Asheville and Buncombe County
P.O. Box 7148
Asheville, NC 28802
(704) 259-5836
FAX (704) 259-5428

Preservation Society of Asheville
and Buncombe County
P.O. Box 2806
Asheville, NC 28802
(704) 254-2343
FAX (704) 254-2343

The YMI Cultural Center, Inc.
P.O. Box 7301
Asheville, NC 28802
(704) 252-4614
FAX (704) 257-4539

BADIN

The Yadkin/Pee Dee Lakes Project
P.O. Box 338
Badin, NC 28009
(704) 422-3215
FAX (704) 422-5860
E-mail: acousins@uwharrie.org
E-mail: bbohling@uwharrie.org

BEAUFORT

Beaufort Historical Association
P.O. Box 1709
Beaufort, NC 28516
(919) 728-5225
FAX (919) 728-4966

BREVARD

Transylvania County Historical
Society
P.O. Box 2061
Brevard, NC 28712
(704) 884-5137

BROADWAY

Longstreet Memorial Fund
414 North Main Street

Broadway, NC 27505
(919) 258-3156

CATAWBA

Town of Catawba Historical
Association, Inc.
P.O. Box 147
Catawba, NC 28609
(704) 241-4077

CHAPEL HILL

Chapel Hill Preservation Society
610 East Rosemary Street
Chapel Hill, NC 27514
(919) 942-7818
FAX (919) 942-7845

CHARLOTTE

Charlotte Historic District
Commission
600 East 4th Street
Charlotte, NC 28202-2853
(704) 336-2302
FAX (704) 336-5123
E-mail: pewsb@mail.charmeck.nc.us

CONCORD

Concord Downtown
Redevelopment Corporation
P.O. Box 62
Concord, NC 28026
(704) 784-4208
FAX (704) 784-2421
E-mail: cddc@popnet.net

DALLAS

Gaston County Museum
P.O. Box 429
Dallas, NC 28034
(704) 922-7681
FAX (704) 922-7683

DURHAM

Durham City/County Planning
101 City Hall Plaza
Durham, NC 27701
(919) 560-4137
FAX (919) 560-4641

Historic Preservation Society of
Durham
P.O. Box 61581
Durham, NC 27715
(919) 682-3036

GREENSBORO

Greensboro Preservation Society,
Inc.
447 West Washington Street
Greensboro, NC 27401
(919) 272-5003

Historic Greensboro District
Commission
Housing/Commumity Development
P.O. Box 3136
Greensboro, NC 27402
(910) 373-2144
FAX (910) 412-6315

Preservation Greensboro, Inc.
P.O. Box 13136
Greensboro, NC 27415
(910) 272-5003

HICKORY

Hickory Historic Preservation
Commission
P.O. Box 398
Hickory, NC 28603
(704) 323-7422
FAX (704) 323-7550
E-mail: treynolds@cihickory.nc.us

Hickory Landmarks Society
P.O. Box 2341
Hickory, NC 28603
(704) 322-4731
FAX (704) 327-9096

HILLSBOROUGH

Alliance for Historic Hillsborough
150 East King Street
Hillsborough, NC 27278
(919) 732-7741
FAX (919) 732-6322
E-mail: ahhillsboro@visionet.org

JAMESTOWN

Historic Jamestown Society
P.O. Box 512
Jamestown, NC 27282
(910) 454-3819

LENOIR

City of Lenoir Planning Department
P.O. Box 958
Lenoir, NC 28645
(910) 757-2200
FAX (910) 757-2162

LEXINGTON

Davidson County Historical Museum
2 South Main Street
Old Courthouse
Lexington, NC 27292
(910) 242-2035

LUMBERTON

Carolina Civic Center
P.O. Box 844
Lumberton, NC 28359
(910) 738-4339
FAX (910) 738-4339

MORGANTON

Historic Burke Foundation
P.O. Box 915
Morganton, NC 28680
(704) 437-4104
FAX (704) 433-6715

MURFREESBORO

Murfreesboro Historical Association, Inc.
P.O. Box 3
Murfreesboro, NC 27855
(919) 398-5922
FAX (919) 398-4886

NEW BERN

New Bern Historical Society Foundation, Inc.
P.O. Box 119
New Bern, NC 28563
(919) 638-8558
FAX (919) 638-5773

New Bern Preservation Foundation
P.O. Box 207
New Bern, NC 28563
(919) 633-6448
FAX (919) 633-6448

Tryon Palace Historic Sites and Gardens
P.O. Box 1007
610 Pollock Street
New Bern, NC 28563
(919) 638-1560
FAX (919) 514-4876

RALEIGH

Capital Area Preservation, Inc.
Mordecai Historic Park
109 South Bloodworth Street
Raleigh, NC 27601
(919) 833-6404
FAX (919) 834-7314

Department of the Secretary of State
300 North Salisbury Street
Raleigh, NC 27611
(919) 733-4201

Raleigh Historic Districts Commission
P.O. Box 829 Century Station
Raleigh, NC 27602
(919) 832-7238
FAX (919) 890-3690
E-mail: rhdc@rhdc.org

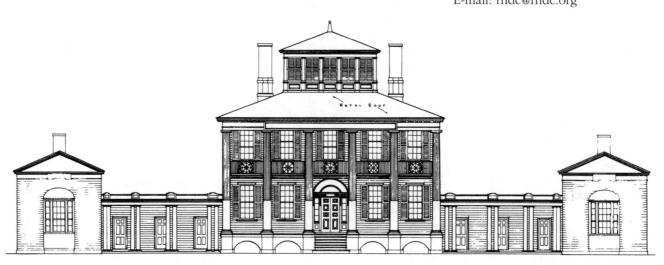

Hayes Manor, Edenton, North Carolina. *(F. Nichols, HABS)*

Stained Glass Associates
P.O. Box 1531
Raleigh, NC 27602
(919) 266-2493

Wake County Historic Preservation
Commission
P.O. Box 550 Planning Department
Raleigh, NC 27602
(919) 856-6327
FAX (919) 856-6184
E-mail: rquinn@co.wake.nc.us

ROCKY MOUNT

Rocky Mount/Edgecombe
Community Development
Corporation
148 South Washington Street
Rocky Mount, NC 27801
(919) 442-5178
FAX (919) 442-1675
E-mail: rmecdccommdeye@
msn.com

RODANTHE

Chicamacomico Historical
Association, Inc.
P.O. Box 5
Rodanthe, NC 27963
(919) 987-2203

RUTHERFORDTON

Rutherfordton Town Revitalization,
Inc.
Downtown Rutherfordton
134 North Washington Street
Rutherfordton, NC 28139
(704) 287-2071
FAX (704) 286-8054

SALISBURY

Historic Salisbury Foundation
P.O. Box 4221
Salisbury, NC 28145
(704) 636-0103
FAX (704) 636-2522

Rowan Museum, Inc.
2029 Robin Road
Salisbury, NC 28144
(704) 633-5946

Salisbury Historic Preservation
Commission
P.O. Box 479
Salisbury, NC 28145
(704) 638-5207
FAX (704) 638-8438
E-mail: hgala@ci.salisbury.nc.us

SANFORD

Revitalize Downtown
City of Sanford
P.O. Box 3729
Sanford, NC 27331-3729
(919) 775-8244
FAX (919) 775-8207

SHELBY

Historic Shelby Foundation
P.O. Box 2321
Shelby, NC 28151
(704) 481-1842

STATESVILLE

Iredell Historical Properties
Commission
P.O. Box 788
Statesville, NC 28687
(704) 878-5384

WELDON

Tacoma Steckley—NC and
Associates
312 Washington Avenue
P.O. Box 741
Weldon, NC 27890
(919) 536-2700
FAX (919) 536-3300
E-mail: tsnc@3rddoor.com

WILMINGTON

Historic Wilmington Foundation,
Inc.
209 Dock Street
Wilmington, NC 28401
(910) 762-2511
FAX (910) 762-2525

Lower Cape Fear Historical Society,
Inc.
126 South Third Street
Wilmington, NC 28401
(910) 762-0492

WINSTON-SALEM

Historic Bethabara Park
2147 Bethabara Road
Winston-Salem, NC 27106
(910) 924-8191
FAX (910) 924-0535

Old Salem, Inc.
VP Restoration
Box F, Salem Station
Winston-Salem, NC 27108-0346
(910) 721-7300
FAX (910) 721-7335
Web Site: http://www.oldsalem.org

Winslow—Considine, Inc.
P.O. Box 10973
Winston-Salem, NC 27108
(910) 722-7982
FAX (910) 722-8671
E-mail: winslow@ols.net
Web Site: http://www.philanthropy-
journal.org

Winston-Salem/Forsyth
County/Kernersville Historic
Properties Commission
P.O. Box 2511
Winston-Salem, NC 27102
(919) 727-2087

North Dakota

STATE HISTORIC PRESERVATION OFFICE

State Historical Society of North Dakota
612 East Boulevard Avenue
Bismark, ND 58505
(701) 328-2667
FAX (701) 328-3710
James E. Sperry, SHPO
E-mail: ccmail.hist.soc@ranch.
state.nd.us

STATEWIDE PRESERVATION ORGANIZATION

Preservation North Dakota
#221 Jamestown Mall
Jamestown, ND 58401
(701) 251-1855
FAX (701) 252-2101

Jane Edwards, President

NATIONAL TRUST REGIONAL OFFICE

Mountains/Plains Regional Office
910 16th Street, Suite 1100
Denver, CO 80202
(303) 623-1504
FAX (303) 623-1508
E-mail: mpro@nthp.org
Web Site: http://www.nthp.org
Barbara Pahl, Director

NATIONAL TRUST ADVISORS

Joan Galleger
Devils Lake, ND

Barbara Lang
Jamestown, ND

AMERICAN INSTITUTE OF ARCHITECTS CONTACT

Odin Dahl, Executive Secretary
AIA North Dakota
P.O. Box 1403
Fargo, ND 58107
(701) 232-6571
FAX (701) 235-8020

Local Contacts

GRAND FORKS

Grand Forks Preservation Commission
1114 Chestnut Street
Grand Forks, ND 58201
(701) 780-1155

Hospital, Fort Totten, North Dakota. *(K. L. Anderson, HABS)*

Ohio

STATE HISTORIC PRESERVATION OFFICE

Ohio Historic Preservation Office
567 East Hudson Street
Columbus, OH 43211-1030
(614) 297-2470
FAX (614) 297-2496
E-mail: ajloveday@aol.com
Amos J. Loveday, SHPO

STATEWIDE PRESERVATION ORGANIZATION

Ohio Preservation Alliance, Inc.
65 Jefferson Avenue
Columbus, OH 43215
(614) 221-0227
FAX (614) 228-7445
Sarah Goss Norman, President

NATIONAL TRUST REGIONAL OFFICE

Midwest Regional Office
53 West Jackson Boulevard,
Suite 1135
Chicago, IL 60604
(312) 939-5547
FAX (312) 939-5651
E-mail: mwro@nthp.org
Web Site: http://www.nthp.org
Jim Mann, Director

NATIONAL TRUST ADVISOR

Sandra Hull
Wooster, OH

Gregory Lashutka
Columbus, OH

AMERICAN INSTITUTE OF ARCHITECTS CONTACTS

David W. Field, Hon. AIA, CAE, Executive Vice President
AIA Ohio
17 South High Street
Twelfth Floor
Columbus, OH 43215
(614) 221-0338
FAX (614) 221-1989

Becky Boyce, Executive Secretary
AIA Akron
13512 Sugarbush Avenue NW
Mogadone, OH 44260
(330) 699-9788
FAX (330) 699-9788
E-mail: aiakron@aol.com

Pat Daugherty, Executive Director
AIA Cincinnati
Longworth Hall Design Center
700 West Pete Rose Way
Cincinnati, OH 45203
(513) 421-4661
FAX (513) 421-4661

Dianne Hart, Executive Director
AIA Cleveland
The Park Building
140 Public Square, #502
Cleveland, OH 44114
(216) 771-1240
FAX (216) 771-3218

Inez Kirby, Hon. AIA, Executive Director
AIA Columbus
1631 N.W. Professional Plaza
Columbus, OH 43220
(614) 451-7654
FAX (614) 459-0855

Paula Williams, Executive Director
AIA Dayton
5816 Daffodil Circle
Dayton, OH 45449
(513) 291-1913
FAX (513) 436-4994

Tina Fejes, Executive Secretary
AIA Toledo
136 North Summit Street
First Floor
Fort Industry Square
Toledo, OH 43604-1057
(419) 255-9222
FAX (419) 241-8636

Local Contacts

AKRON

Ohio and Erie Canal Heritage Corridor
Ohio and Erie Canal Corridor Coalition
520 S. Main Street, Suite 2541-F
Akron, OH 44311
(330) 434-5657
FAX (330) 434-5657

Progress Through Preservation
641 West Market Street
Akron, OH 44303
(330) 762-1411
FAX (330) 762-1449

Stan Hywet Hall and Gardens Inc.
714 North Portage Path
Akron, OH 44303
(330) 836-5533
FAX (330) 836-2680

Summit County Historical Society
550 Copley Road
Akron, OH 44320
(330) 535-1120
(330) 535-5164

CINCINNATI

Blue Chip Builders Inc.
896 Kieley Place
Cincinnati, OH 45217
(513) 242-1300
FAX (513) 242-2338

Cincinatti Preservation Association
342 West Fourth Street
Cincinnati, OH 45202
(513) 721-4506
FAX (513) 721-6832

Little Miami Scenic River
Little Miami, Inc.
3012 Section Road
Cincinnati, OH 45237
(513) 351-6400

Miami Purchase Preservation Fund
8132 Freeman Avenue
Cincinnati, OH 45214
(513) 241-0504

Mt. Auburn Good Housing Foundation
2003 Auburn
Cincinnati, OH 45219
(513) 241-6292
FAX (513) 241-8937

CLEVELAND

Cleveland Restoration Society
Statler Office Tower
1127 Euclid Avenue, Suite 458
Cleveland, OH 44115-1601
(216) 621-1498
FAX (216) 621-5228

Historic Warehouse District Development
614 Superior Avenue, N.W.
Suite 714
Cleveland, OH 44113
(216) 344-3937
FAX (216) 344-3962

Mid State Restoration
2609 Monroe Avenue
Cleveland, OH 44113
(216) 771-2112
FAX (216) 771-0508

Columbia St. Vincent Charity Hospital
2351 East 22nd Street
Cleveland, OH 44115
(216) 861-6200

YMCA of Greater Cleveland
2200 Prospect Avenue
Cleveland, OH 44115
(216) 344-0095
FAX (216) 334-3901

CLEVELAND HEIGHTS

City of Cleveland Heights
Planning and Development Department
40 Severance Circle
Cleveland Heights, OH 44118
(216) 291-4847
FAX (216) 291-3761

COLUMBUS

The Columbus Landmarks Foundation
61 Jefferson Avenue
Columbus, OH 43215
(614) 221-0227
FAX (614) 221-0227

German Village Society
German Village Preservation
588 South Third Street
Columbus, OH 43215
(614) 221-8888
FAX (614) 221-4747

Kappa Kappa Gamma Heritage Museum
P.O. Box 38
530 East Town Street
Columbus, OH 43216
(614) 228-6515
FAX (614) 228-7809

Marble Institute of America
30 Eden Alley, Suite 201
Columbus, OH 43215
(614) 228-6194

Ohio Arts Council
727 East Main Street
Columbus, OH 43205-1796
(614) 466-2613
FAX (614) 466-4494
Web Site: http://www.oac.ohio.gov/www/eac/oac.html

The Ohio State University
190 North Oval Mall, Room 108
Columbus, OH 43210
(614) 292-7970
FAX (614) 292-2820
E-mail: klebeg.1@osu.edu

CORNING

Sunday Creek Associates
P.O. Box 400
Corning, OH 43730
(614) 394-1171

CUYAHOGA FALLS

JDJ and A, Inc.
2250 6th Street
Cuyahoga Falls, OH 44221
(330) 923-4756

DAYTON

City of Dayton
Department of Planning
101 West Third Street
P.O. Box 22
Dayton, OH 45401
(513) 443-3685
FAX (513) 443-4281

Dayton Aviation Heritage National Historical Park
P.O. Box 9280
Wright Brothers Station
Dayton, OH 45409
(937) 225-7705
FAX (937) 225-7706

Montgomery County Historical Society
7 North Main Street
Dayton, OH 45402
(937) 228-6271
FAX (937) 331-7160

Preservation Dayton, Inc.
P.O. Box 3614
Dayton, OH 45401
(347) 775-2815

HAMILTON

Citizens for Historic and Preservation Services
365 South B Street
Hamilton, OH 45013
(513) 863-1716

Fitton Center for Creative Arts
101 South Monument Avenue
Hamilton, OH 45011
(513) 863-8873
FAX (513) 863-8865

HUDSON

Hudson Heritage Association
P.O. Box 2218
Hudson, OH 44236
(216) 653-9817

KETTERING

Kettering-Morraine Museum and Historical Society
35 Moraine Circle, South
Kettering, OH 45439
(937) 299-2722

LIMA

American House
P.O. Box 5283
Lima, OH 45802
(419) 224-6873

MANSFIELD

City of Mansfield, Ohio
Community Development
Department
30 North Diamond Street
Mansfield, OH 44902
(419) 755-9795
FAX (419) 755-9465

MENTOR

City of Mentor
8500 Civic Center Boulevard
Mentor, OH 44060
(216) 974-5740
FAX (216) 974-5708

MIDDLEFIELD

Middlefield Historical Society
P.O. Box 1100
Middlefield, OH 44062-1100
(216) 632-0400

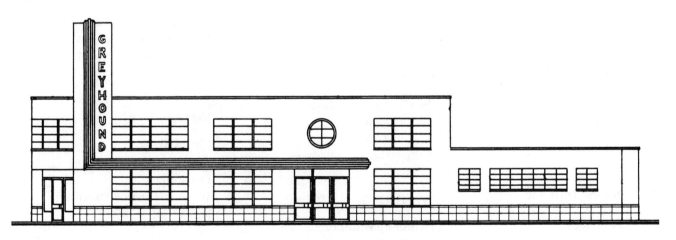

Greyhound Terminal, Dayton, Ohio. *(S. Bauer, HABS)*

NELSONVILLE

Hocking Valley Museum of Theatrical History, Inc.
34 Public Square
Nelsonville, OH 45764
(614) 753-1924

OBERLIN

Oberlin Historical and Improvement Organization
MPO Box 0455
Oberlin, OH 44074
(216) 774-1700

Oberlin Historic Preservation Commission
525 East College
Oberlin, OH 44074
(216) 775-8457

PERRYSBERG

Historic Perrysburg, Inc.
P.O. Box 703
Perrysburg, OH 43552

STEUBENVILLE

City of Steubenville Historic Landmarks Commission
308 Market Street
Steubenville, OH 43952
(614) 283-6076
FAX (614) 283-6082

TALLMADGE

Tallmadge Historical Society
P.O. Box 25
Tallmadge, OH 44278
(330) 630-9760

TIFFIN

Tiffin Historic Trust, Inc.
P.O. Box 333
Tiffin, OH 44883
(419) 447-4789

TOLEDO

Housing Commissioner
One Government Center
Suite 1800
Toledo, OH 43604-2275
(419) 245-1416
FAX (419) 245-1413

Maumee Valley Heritage Corridor
Maumee Heritage Corridor, Inc.
2036 North Kennison Drive
Toledo, OH 43609
(419) 385-7200

Neighborhoods in Partnership
2272 Collingwood Boulevard
Toledo, OH 43620
(419) 241-9682
FAX (419) 243-1100
E-mail: nipcovaes@aol.com

North River Development Corporation
725 LaGrange Street
Toledo, OH 43604
(419) 243-3204
FAX (419) 243-7918

Toledo Warehouse District Association
27 Broadway
Toledo, OH 43602
(419) 255-7100
FAX (419) 255-6636

Women of the Old West End
P.O. Box 4745
Toledo, OH 43610-0745
(419) 246-4612

TROY

Overfield Tavern Museum
201 East Water Street
Troy, OH 45373
(937) 335-4019

TWINSBURG

Twinsburg Historical Society
P.O. Box 7
Twinsburg, OH 44087
(216) 487-5565

WARREN

City of Warren
Community Development Department
418 South Main Street
Warren, OH 44481
(330) 841-2595
FAX (330) 841-2643

WILMINGTON

Clinton County Historical Society
P.O. Box 529
Wilmington, OH 45177
(513) 382-4684

WOODSFIELD

Monroe County Historical Society
P.O. Box 538
Woodsfield, OH 43793
(614) 472-1933

Monroe County Park District
101 North Main Street, Room 24
Woodsfield, OH 43793
(614) 472-1328
FAX (614) 472-5156

WORTHINGTON

Worthington Historical Society
50 West New England Avenue
Worthington, OH 43085
(614) 885-1247

XENIA

City of Xenia
Community Development Department
101 North Detroit Street
Xenia, OH 45385-2926
(937) 376-7232
FAX (973) 374-1818

Oklahoma

STATE HISTORIC PRESERVATION OFFICE

Oklahoma Historical Society
2704 Villa Prom, Shepherd Mall
Oklahoma City, OK 73107
(405) 521-6249
FAX (405) 947-2918
J. Blake Wade, SHPO

STATEWIDE PRESERVATION ORGANIZATION

Preservation Oklahoma, Inc.
P. O. Box 25043
Oklahoma City, OK 73125-0043
(405) 232-5747
FAX (405) 232-5816
E-Mail: presvok@aol.com
Martin L. J. Newman, President
Robert Erwin, Executive Director

NATIONAL TRUST REGIONAL OFFICE

Southwest Regional Office
500 Main Street, Suite 1030
Fort Worth, TX 76102
(817) 332-4398
FAX (817) 332-4512
E-mail: swro@nthp.org

Web Site: http://www.nthp.org
Jane Jenkins, Director

NATIONAL TRUST ADVISORS

Cathy Keating
Oklahoma City, OK

Martin Newman
Tulsa, OK

STATEWIDE MAIN STREET COORDINATOR

Melody Kellogg, Coordinator
Oklahoma Main Street Program
Oklahoma Department of
Commerce
P.O. Box 26980
Oklahoma City, OK 73126-0980
(405) 815-5115
FAX (405) 815-5234
E-mail: melody_kellogg@odoc.
state.ok.us
Web Site: http://www.odoc.state.
ok.us

AMERICAN INSTITUTE OF ARCHITECTS CONTACTS

Jan Gilmore Edwards, Executive
Director
AIA Oklahoma
P.O. Box 18714
Oklahoma City, OK 73154-1305
(405) 236-0295
FAX (405) 232-1415

Melissa Hunt, Component
Executive
AIA Central Oklahoma
3000 Gen. Pershing Boulevard
Studio 4
Oklahoma City, OK 73107
(405) 948-7174
FAX (405) 948-7397
E-mail: jeff_mel_hunt@
worldnet.att.net
Web Site: http://www.astr.com/
aiacoc

Elaine Bergman, Executive
Director
AIA Eastern Oklahoma
2210-R South Main Street
Tulsa, OK 74114-1153
(918) 583-0013
FAX (918) 583-0026

Local Contacts

DUNCAN

Association of South Central
Oklahoma Governments
802 Main
P.O. Box 1647

Duncan, OK 73534
(405) 252-0595
FAX (405) 252-6170
E-mail: assog@texhoma.com

FORT SUPPLY

Oklahoma Historical Society
Fort Supply Military Park
P.O. Box 247
Fort Supply, OK 73841
(405) 766-3767

MUSKEGOEE

City of Muskegoee Planning Department
P.O. Box 1927
Muskogee, OK 74402
(918) 684-6232
FAX (918) 684-6233

NEWKIRK

Newkirk Community Historic Society
500 West 8th Street
Newkirk, OK 74647
(405) 362-2377
FAX (405) 362-3724
Web Site: http://brigadoon.com/
~rlobsing/NKHomepage.html

OKLAHOMA CITY

City of Oklahoma
City Planning Department

420 West Main Street, Suite 900
Oklahoma City, OK 73102
FAX (405) 232-8317

Oklahoma City Urban Renewal Authority
204 North Robinson, Suite 2400
Oklahoma City, OK 73102
(405) 235-3771
FAX (405) 232-8317

Preservation Oklahoma
P.O. Box 25043
Oklahoma City, OK 73125
(405) 232-5747

OKMULGEE

Creek Council House
Town Square
Okmulgee, OK 74447
(918) 756-1167
FAX (918) 758-1122

PONCA CITY

City of Ponca City
P.O. Box 1450
Ponca City, OK 74602
(405) 767-0334
FAX (405) 767-0325

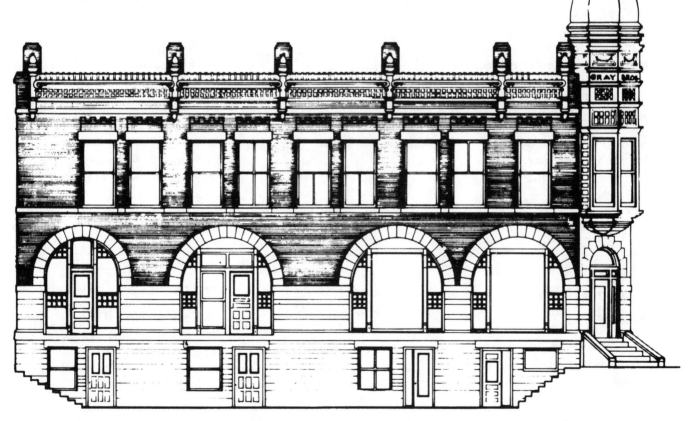

Gray Brothers Block, Guthrie, Oklahoma. *(J. Robbins, HABS)*

Oregon

STATE HISTORIC PRESERVATION OFFICE

State Parks and Recreation
Department
1115 Commercial Street, N.E.
Salem, OR 97310-1001
(503) 378-5019
FAX (503) 378-6447
Bob Meinen, SHPO

STATEWIDE PRESERVATION ORGANIZATION

Historic Preservation League of
Oregon
P.O. Box 40053
Portland, OR 97240
(503) 243-1923
FAX (503) 224-2311
Mike Byrnes, President
Lisa Burcham, Executive Director

NATIONAL TRUST REGIONAL OFFICE

Western Regional Office
One Sutter Street, Suite 707
San Francisco, CA 94104
(415) 956-0610
FAX (415) 956-0837
E-mail: wro@nthp.org

Web Site: http://www.nthp.org
Elizabeth Goldstein, Director

NATIONAL TRUST ADVISORS

George Kramer
Ashland, OR

Judith Rees
Portland, OR

STATEWIDE MAIN STREET COORDINATOR

Andree Tremoulet, VP of
Programs
Oregon Main Street Program
Oregon Downtown
Development Association
Livable Oregon, Inc.
921 S.W. Morrison Street
Suite 508
Portland, OR 97205
(503) 222-2182
FAX (503) 222-2359

AMERICAN INSTITUTE OF ARCHITECTS CONTACTS

Stephen Kafoury, Executive
Director
Architects Council of
Oregon/AIA
1207 S.W. 6th Avenue
Portland, OR 97204
(503) 223-2330
FAX (503) 228-4529

Saundra Stevens, Hon. AIA,
Executive Director
AIA Portland
315 S.W. Fourth Avenue
Portland, OR 97204
(503) 223-8757
(503) 220-0254

Douglas Beauchamp, Executive
Director
AIA Southwest Oregon
164 West Broadway
Eugene, OR 97401-3004
(541) 485-2278
FAX (541) 485-2478

Local Contacts

ALBANY

City of Albany—Planning
c/o Pam Seitz
P.O. Box 490
Albany, OR 97321
(541) 917-7550
FAX (541) 917-7573

ASTORIA

Columbia River Maritime Museum
1792 Marine Drive
Astoria, OR 97103
(503) 325-2323

AURORA

Aurora Colony Historical Society
Box 202
Aurora, OR 97002
(503) 678-5754

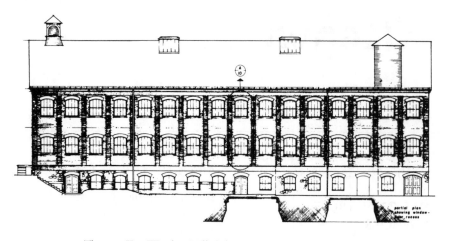

Thomas Kay Woolen Mill, Salem, Oregon. *(Hanns, HABS)*

City of Aurora
Historic Review Board
P.O. Box 100
Aurora, OR 97002

EUGENE

O'Ryan Antiques
1030 Tillmore
Eugene, OR 97402
(541) 984-0047

GRESHAM

Historic Columbia River Highway
Historic Preservation League of
Oregon
1333 N.W. Eastman Parkway
Gresham, OR 97030
(503) 669-2378

MEDFORD

Southern Oregon Historical Society
106 North Central Avenue
Medford, OR 97501-5926
(541) 773-6536
FAX (541) 776-7994

NEWPORT

Lincoln County Historical Society
545 S.W. 9th Street
Newport, OR 97365
(541) 265-7509
FAX (541) 265-3992
E-mail: coasthistory@newportnet.
com

PORTLAND

Bosco-Milligan Foundation
P.O. Box 14157
Portland, OR 97214
(503) 231-7264
FAX (503) 231-7311

**Historic Preservation League of
Oregon**
P.O. Box 40053
Portland, OR 97240
(503) 243-1923

Livable Oregon, Inc.
Downtown Development
Association
921 S.W. Morrison Street, Suite 508
Portland, OR 97205
(503) 222-2182
FAX (503) 222-2359

Portland Planning Bureau
1120 S.W. 5th Avenue, #1002
Portland, OR 97204

PRINEVILLE

**City of Prineville Planning
Department**
400 East Third Street
Prineville, OR 97754
(541) 447-5726
FAX (541) 447-5628

ROSEBURG

**Douglas County Planning
Department**
Justice Building, Room 106
Roseburg, OR 97470
(541) 440-4289
FAX (541) 440-6266
Web Site: http://206.100.190.19/
dougco/

SALEM

Stage Incorporated
170 High Street, S.E.
Salem, OR 97301-3608
(503) 375-3574
FAX (503) 375-0284
E-mail: stage@wvi.com

Pennsylvania

STATE HISTORIC PRESERVATION OFFICE

Pennsylvania Historical and Museum Commission
P.O. Box 1026
Harrisburg, PA 17108
(717) 787-2891
FAX (717) 783-9924

STATEWIDE PRESERVATION ORGANIZATION

Preservation Pennsylvania
257 North Street
Harrisburg, PA 17101
(717) 234-2310
FAX (717) 234-2522
Margaret Wallis, President
Caroline E. Boyce, Executive Director

NATIONAL TRUST REGIONAL OFFICE

Mid-Atlantic Regional Office
One Penn Center at Suburban Station, Suite 1520
1617 John F. Kennedy Boulevard
Philadelphia, PA 19103-1815
(215) 568-8162
FAX (215) 568-9251
E-mail: maro@nthp.org
Web Site: http://www.nthp.org
Patricia Wilson Aden, Director

NATIONAL TRUST ADVISORS

Randy Cooley
Hollidaysburg, PA

Mary Werner DeNadai, AIA
Chadds Ford, PA

NATIONAL PARK SERVICE CONTACTS

Northeast Regional Director
Northeast Regional Office
National Park Service
U.S. Custom House
200 Chestnut Street
Philadelphia, PA 19106
(215) 597-7013
FAX (617) 223-5199

Superintendent
Chesapeake Allegheny
Northeast Field Area
National Park Service
U.S. Custom House
200 Chestnut Street,
Philadelphia, PA 19106
(215) 597-7013
FAX (617) 223-5199

STATEWIDE MAIN STREET COORDINATOR

Diana Kerr, Coordinator
Pennsylvania Main Street Program
Department of Community and Economic Development
504 Forum Building, Room 372
Harrisburg, PA 17120
(717) 783-3068
FAX (717) 234-4560

AMERICAN INSTITUTE OF ARCHITECTS CONTACTS

Lela Shultz, Executive Director
Pennsylvania Society of Architects/AIA
P.O. Box 5570
Harrisburg, PA 17110-0570
(717) 236-4055
FAX (717) 236-5407
E-mail: lelapsa@ptd.net

Joan Newbury, Executive Secretary
AIA Central Pennsylvania
P.O. Box 1001
Harrisburg, PA 17108-1001
(717) 234-1455
FAX (717) 737-4314

Sandra L. Garz, Executive Director
AIA Philadelphia
117 South 17th Street
Philadelphia, PA 19103
(215) 569-3186
FAX (215) 569-9226
E-mail: aiaphila@voicenet.com

Anne Swager, Executive Director
AIA Pittsburgh
211 Ninth Street
Pittsburgh, PA 15222
(412) 471-9548
FAX (412) 471-9501
E-mail: sbtraub@aol.com

Local Contacts

ALTOONA

Allegheny Ridge State Heritage Park
Midstate Bank Building
P.O. Box 348
Altoona, PA 16603
(814) 942-8288

Womans Club of Altoona
3400 Crescent Road
Altoona, PA 16602
(814) 943-6804
FAX (814) 943-4003

AMBLER

Wissahickon Valley Historical Society
P.O. Box 96
Ambler, PA 19002
(215) 646-6541

Wissahickon Valley Watershed Association
12 Morris Road
Ambler, PA 19002-5499
(215) 646-8866
FAX (215) 654-7489
E-mail: info@wvwa.org
Web Site: http://www.wvwa.org

AVONDALE

Modern Mushroom Farms, Inc.
P.O. Box 340
Avondale, PA 19311
(610) 268-3535
FAX (610) 268-3099

BEDFORD

Lincoln Highway Heritage Park Corridor
Bedford County Planning Commission
203 South Juliana Street
Bedford, PA 15522
(814) 623-4827

BETHLEHEM

Delaware and Lehigh Navigation Canal National Heritage Cooridor Commission
10 East Church Street, Room P-208
Bethlehem, PA 18018
(610) 861-9345
FAX (610) 861-9347

BROOMALL

Delaware County Historical Society
Malin and James Roads
Broomall, PA 19008
(215) 874-6444

BRYN MAWR

Lower Merion Conservancy
9 South Bryn Mawr Avenue
Bryn Mawr, PA 19010
(610) 520-9895
FAX (610) 520-9894

BUSHKILL

Delaware Water Gap National Recreational Area
River Road
Bushkill, PA 18324
(717) 588-2418
FAX (717) 588-2780
E-mail: dewa_superintendent@
nps.gov

BUTLER

Butler County Historical Society
P.O. Box 414
Butler, PA 16003
(412) 283-8116

CHADDS FORD

Chadds Ford Historical Society
P.O. Box 27
Chadds Ford, PA 19317
(610) 388-7376
FAX (610) 388-7480

CHESTER SPRINGS

Historic Yellow Springs, Inc.
1685 Art School Road
P.O. Box 62
Chester Springs, PA 19425
(610) 827-7414
FAX (610) 827-1336

COATESVILLE

The Graystone Society, Inc.
76 South First Avenue
Coatesville, PA 19320
(610) 384-9282
FAX (610) 384-3396

CONSHOHOCKEN

Eastern National Park and Monument Association
446 North Lane
Conshohocken, PA 19428
(610) 832-0555
FAX (610) 832-0242
E-mail: eastnatl@ix.netcom.com

DOUGLASSVILLE

Historic Preservation Trust of Berks County
P.O. Box 245
Douglassville, PA 19518
(610) 385-4762

DOYLESTOWN

Heritage Conservancy
85 Old Dublin Pike
Doylestown, PA 18901
(215) 345-7020
FAX (215) 345-4328
E-mail: hconserv@aol.com

DREXEL HILL

Alumni Association
Delta Omicron Chapter
Theta Chi Fraternity, Inc.

719 Anderson Avenue
Drexel Hill, PA 19026
(215) 565-2896

EASTON

Easton Heritage Alliance
643 Ferry Street
P.O. Box 994
Easton, PA 18044
(610) 258-1612
FAX (610) 253-1608

ERIE

Crowner King Architects
11 East 4th Street
Erie, PA 16507
(814) 452-4522
FAX (814) 452-2251
E-mail: bojocrown@aol

Erie County Historical Society
417 State Street
Erie, PA 16501
(814) 454-1813
FAX (841) 452-1744

EXTON

West Whiteland Historical
Commission
222 North Pottstown Pike
Exton, PA 19341
(215) 363-8091

FARMINGTON

National Road Heritage Park
3543 National Road and Nelson
Road
Box 528
Farmington, PA 15437
(412) 329-1560
FAX (412) 329-1561

FRANKLIN

Oil Region Heritage Park
Venango County Planning
Commission
1283 Liberty Street
P.O. Box 1130
Franklin, PA 16323
(814) 432-9531

FORT WASHINGTON

Highlands Historical Society
7001 Sheaff Lane
Fort Washington, PA 19034
(215) 641-2687
FAX (215) 641-2556

FRANKLIN

**Venango County Planning
Commission**
Courthouse Annex
1174 Elk Street
Franklin, PA 16323
(814) 432-9531

GREENSBURG

Lincoln Highway Heritage Cooridor
P.O. Box 386
Greensburg, PA 15601
(412) 668-8330

HARRISBURG

**PA Historical and Museum
Commission**
Bureau for Historic Preservation
Box 1026
Harrisburg, PA 17108-1026
(717) 783-9927
FAX (717) 772-0920

Pennsylvania Heritage Society
Box 11466
Harrisburg, PA 17108
(717) 787-2407
FAX (717) 783-9924

Harrisburg Community and
Economic Affairs, Inc.
32 Evergreen Street,
Harrisburg, PA 17104
(717) 238-3185
FAX (717) 232-8396

Historic Harrisburg Association
1230 North 3rd Street
Harrisburg, PA 17102
(717) 233-4646
FAX (717) 233-0635

HATBORO

The Millbrook Society
P.O. Box 506
Hatboro, PA 19040
(215) 675-0119

HERSHEY

Antique Auto Club of America
501 West Governor Road
P.O. Box 417
Hershey, PA 17033
(717) 534-1910
FAX (717) 534-9101

HOMESTEAD

Steel Industry Heritage Corporation
338 East Ninth Avenue, First Floor
Homestead, PA 15120
(412) 464-4020
FAX (412) 464-4417
E-mail: sihe@aol.com
Web Site: http://www.trfn.clpgh.
org/sihe

HUNTINGDON

Huntingdon County Planning and
Development
c/o 223 Penn Street
Huntingdon, PA 16652
(814) 643-5091
FAX (814) 643-8152

JOHNSTOWN

Johnstown Area Heritage Association
P.O. Box 1889
Johnstown, PA 15907
(814) 539-1889
FAX (814) 535-1931
E-mail: jaha@ctcnet.net
Web Site: http://www.ctcnet.net/jaha

LANCASTER

Historic Preservation Trust of Lancaster County
123 North Prince Street
Lancaster, PA 17603
(717) 291-5861
FAX (717) 291-5861

Lancaster County Planning Commission
50 North Duke Street
P.O. Box 3480
Lancaster, PA 17608
(717) 299-8333
FAX (717) 295-3659
E-mail: planning@co.lancaster.pa.us
Web Site: http://www.co.lancaster.pa.us

LANSDALE

Lansdale Borough Hall
One Vine Street
Lansdale, PA 19446
(215) 368-1691
FAX (215) 361-8399

MEADVILLE

Redevelopment Authority
R.D. 2 Dunham Road
Meadville, PA 16335
(814) 337-8200
FAX (814) 333-9032

MEDIA

Delaware County Planning Department
Toal Building
2nd and Orange Streets
Media, PA 19063
(610) 891-5200
FAX (610) 891-5203

MEYERSDALE

Meyersdale Area Historical Society
P.O. Box 134
Meyersdale, PA 15552
(814) 443-1431
FAX (814) 445-3632

MONT CLARE

Schuylkill Canal Association
P.O. Box 3
Mont Clare, PA 19452
(610) 983-9999

MORGANTOWN

Tri-County Heritage Society
P.O. Box 352
Morgantown, PA 19543
(610) 286-7477
FAX (610) 286-6588
E-mail: cwepler@postoffice.ptd.net

NEWTOWN

Friends of the Farmstead, Inc.
P.O. Box 844
Newtown, PA 18940-0844
(215) 968-3085

Newtown Historic Association, Inc.
P.O. Box 303
Newtown, PA 18940
(215) 968-4004

PHILADELPHIA

Chestnut Hill Historical Society
8708 Germantown Avenue
Philadelphia, PA 19118
(215) 247-0417
FAX (215) 247-9329

Fairmont Park Commission
Memorial Hall/West Park
P.O. Box 21601
Philadelphia, PA 19131
(215) 685-0046

G.A.R. Memorial Museum
4278 Griscom Street
Philadelphia, PA 19124
(215) 673-1688

Henry George Birthplace
413 South 10th Street
Philadelphia, PA 19147
(215) 922-4278

Laurel Hill Mansion
East Edgely Drive
Fairmont Park East
Philadelphia, PA 19121
(215) 235-1776

Multicultural Affairs Congress
1515 Market Street, Suite 2020
Philadelphia, PA 19102
(215) 636-3316
FAX (215) 636-3327

National Society of the Colonial Dames of America
Stenton Mansion
1630 Latimer Street
Philadelphia, PA 19103
(215) 735-6737

Partners for Sacred Places
1616 Walnut Street, Suite 2310
Philadelphia, PA 19103
(215) 546-1288
FAX (215) 546-1180

Philadelphia Historical Commission
1401 Arch Street, Suite 1301
Philadelphia, PA 19102
(215) 686-4583
FAX (215) 686-4593

Philadelphia Historic Preservation
Corporation
1616 Walnut Street, Suite 2310
Philadelphia, PA 19103
(215) 546-1146
FAX (215) 546-1180

Philadelphia Society for the
Preservation of Landmarks
321 South Fourth Street
Philadelphia, PA 19106
(215) 925-2251
FAX (215) 925-7909

Preservation Alliance for Greater
Philadelphia
1616 Walnut Street, Suite 2310
Philadelphia, PA 19103
(215) 546-1146
FAX (215) 546-1180
E-mail: historic@libertynet.org

Reading Terminal Market
Preservation Fund
234 Spruce Street
Philadelphia, PA 19106
(215) 627-4910
FAX (212) 627-4031

Technical Assistance Branch
c/o Rebecca Shiffer
U.S. Customs House
Room 251
Second and Chestnut Streets
Philadelphia, PA 19106

University City Historical Society
The Woodlands
4000 Woodland Avenue
Philadelphia, PA 19104
(215) 386-2181
FAX (215) 387-3019
E-mail: thewoods@libertynet.org
Web Site: http://www.libertynet.
org/~thewoods

University of Pennsylvania
Historic Preservation Program
115 Meyerson Hall
210 South 34th Street
Philadelphia, PA 19104-6311

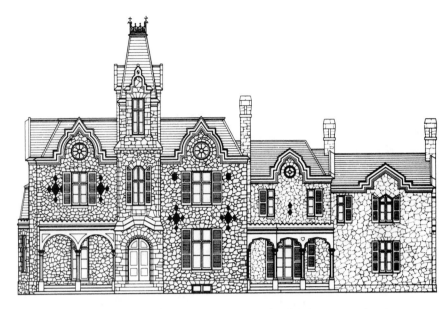

Ebenezer Maxwell House, Germantown, Philadelphia, Pennsylvania.
(A. C. Morrison, HABS)

(215) 898-3169
FAX (215) 573-6326
E-mail: hyndman@pobox.upenn.
edu

Naomi Wood Collection at
Woodford Mansion
33rd and Dauphin Street
Philadelphia, PA 19132
(215) 229-6115

PITTSBURG

Frick Art and Historical Center
7227 Reynolds Street
Pittsburgh, PA 15206
(412) 371-0600
FAX (412) 241-5393

Historical Society of Western
Pennsylvania
1212 Smallman Street
Pittsburgh, PA 15222
(412) 454-6000
FAX (412) 454-6031

Pittsburgh History and Landmarks
Foundation
450 The Landmarks Building
One Station Square
Pittsburgh, PA 15219
(412) 471-5808
FAX (412) 471-1633

Preservation Pittsburgh
601 Wood Street, Fourth Floor
Pittsburgh, PA 15222
(412) 456-2233

Society for the Preservation of the
Duquesne Heights Incline
1220 Grandview Avenue
Pittsburgh, PA 15211
(412) 381-1665

S.T.V., Inc.
4 Gateway Center, Suite 325
Pittsburgh, PA 15222
(412) 392-3500
FAX (412) 392-3501
Web Site: http://www.stvinc.com

Western Pennsylvania Conservancy
209 Fourth Avenue
Pittsburgh, PA 15222
(412) 288-2777
FAX (412) 281-1792

PLYMOUTH MEETING

Conservancy of Montgomery
County
P.O. Box 314
Plymouth Meeting, PA 19462
(215) 283-0383
FAX (215) 283-0383

Plymouth Meeting Historical Society
Box 167
Plymouth Meeting, PA 19462
(610) 828-8111

READING

Central Park Historic District
P.O. Box 13325
Reading, PA 19612
(610) 372-4019
FAX (610) 376-2401

SCRANTON

Lackawanna Heritage Valley
200 Adams Avenue
Scranton, PA 18503
(717) 963-6826

Lackawanna Historical Society
232 Monroe Avenue
Scranton, PA 18510-2104
(717) 344-3841

TRAPPE

Historical Society of Trappe
P.O. Box 828
Trappe, PA 19426
(215) 489-2624

UPLAND

The Friends of The Caleb Pusey
House, Inc.
15 Race Street
P.O. Box 1183
Upland, PA 19015
(610) 876-0516

VANDERGRIFT

Victorian Vandergrift Museum and
Historical Society, Inc.
P.O. Box 183
Vandergrift, PA 15690
(412) 568-1990

WASHINGTON

Washington County History and
Landmarks Foundation
P.O. Box 274
Washington, PA 15301
(412) 225-2350

WAYMART

Waymart Area Historical Society
Box 255 South Street
Waymart, PA 18472
(717) 488-6134

WEST CHESTER

Chester County Historical Society
225 North High Street
West Chester, PA 19380
(610) 692-4800
FAX (610) 692-4357
E-mail: cchs@chesco.com

East Goshen Historical Commission
1580 Paoli Pike
West Chester, PA 19380
(610) 692-7171

West Chester Historical and
Architectural Review Board
c/o Department of Building and
Housing
401 East Gay Street
West Chester, PA 19380
(610) 696-1773

WHITEHALL

Whitehall Historical Preservation
Society
P.O. Box 39
Whitehall, PA 18052
(610) 776-7166

WYOMISSING

Berks County Conservancy
960 Old Mill Road
Wyomissing, PA 19610
(610) 372-4992

Schuylkill River Heritage Park
Corridor
Schuylkill River Greenway
Association
960 Old Mill Road
Wyomissing, PA 19610
(610) 372-3916
FAX (610) 372-8264

YORK

Historic York, Inc.
224 North George Street
P.O. Box 2312
York, PA 17405
(717) 843-0320
FAX (717) 845-6050

Rhode Island

<table>
<tr><td>

STATE HISTORIC PRESERVATION OFFICE

Rhode Island Historical
Preservation and Heritage
Commission
Old State House
150 Benefit Street
Providence, RI 02903
(401) 277-2678
FAX (401) 277-2968
Frederick C. Williamson, SHPO

</td><td>

NATIONAL TRUST REGIONAL OFFICE

Northeast Regional Office
Seven Faneuil Hall Marketplace
Boston, MA 02109
(617) 523-0885
FAX (617) 523-1199
E-mail: nero@nthp.org
Web Site: http://www.nthp.org
Wendy Nicholas, Director

</td><td>

NATIONAL TRUST ADVISORS

Sean O. Coffey
Providence, RI
Keith W. Stokes
Middletown, RI

</td></tr>
</table>

Local Contacts

BLOCK ISLAND

Block Island Historical Society
P.O. Box 79
Block Island, RI 02807
(401) 466-2481

BRISTOL

Roger Williams College
Old Ferry Road
Bristol, RI 02809-2921
(401) 253-1040
FAX (401) 254-3480

CENTRAL FALLS

Historic Central Falls, Inc.
12 Clinton Street
Central Falls, RI 02863
(401) 723-8730

EAST GREENWICH

Town of East Greenwich
Department of Planning
125 Main
P.O. Box 111
East Greenwich, RI 02818
(401) 886-8645
FAX (401) 886-8625

EAST PROVIDENCE

Les Haworth
694 North Broadway
East Providence, RI 02914
(401) 434-1430
FAX (401) 434-4430

MIDDLETOWN

Middletown Historical Society
P.O. Box 4196

Middletown, RI 02840
(401) 849-1870

NARRAGANSETT

Town of Narragansett
25 Fifth Avenue
Narragansett, RI 02882
(401) 789-1044
FAX (401) 783-9637

NEWPORT

The Preservation Society of Newport County
424 Bellevue Avenue
Newport, RI 02840-6924
(401) 847-1000
FAX (401) 847-1361

Chateau-sur-Mer, Newport, Rhode Island. *(P. Veeder, HABS)*

PAWTUCKET

Preservation Society of Pawtucket, Inc.
P.O. Box 735
Pawtucket, RI 02862
(401) 725-9581

PROVIDENCE

City of Providence
Providence City Archives
25 Dorrance Street
Providence, RI 02903
(401) 421-7740

Heritage Trust of Rhode Island
199 Hope Street
Providence, RI 02906
(401) 253-2707
FAX (401) 253-0412

Providence Preservation Society
21 Meeting Street
Providence, RI 02903
(401) 831-7440
FAX (410) 831-8583

Providence Preservation Society (PPS) Revolving Fund
24 Meeting Street
Providence, RI 02903
(401) 272-2760
FAX (401) 273-9190

WOONSOCKET

Blackstone River Valley NHC
One Depot Square
Woonsocket, RI 02895
(401) 762-0250
FAX (401) 762-0530

South Carolina

STATE HISTORIC PRESERVATION OFFICE

Department of Archives and History
P.O. Box 11669
Columbia, SC 29211
(803) 734-8609
FAX (803) 734-8820
Richard Runnels, Acting SHPO

STATEWIDE PRESERVATION ORGANIZATION

The Palmetto Trust for Historic Preservation
P.O. Box 12547
Columbia, SC 29211
(803) 771-6132
FAX (803) 765-9316
Sarah Spruill, President

NATIONAL TRUST REGIONAL OFFICE

Southern Regional Office
456 King Street
Charleston, SC 29403
(803) 722-8552
FAX (803) 722-8652
E-mail: sro@nthp.org
Web Site: http://www.nthp.org
David Brown, Director

NATIONAL TRUST ADVISOR

Evelyn (Patti) M. McGee
Charleston, SC

STATEWIDE MAIN STREET COORDINATOR

Ben Boozer, Coordinator
South Carolina Downtown
Development Association

P.O. Box 11637
1529 Washington Street
Columbia, SC 29211
(803) 256-3560
FAX (803) 799-9520
E-mail: bboozer@masc.state.sc.us
Bill Steiner, ASC

AMERICAN INSTITUTE OF ARCHITECTS CONTACT

Executive Director
AIA South Carolina
1522 Richland Street
Columbia, SC 29201
(803) 252-6050
FAX (803) 256-0546

Local Contacts

ABBEVILLE

Abbeville County Historical Society
P.O. Box 12
Abbeville, SC 29620
(864) 459-2466

ADAMS RUN

Oak Hall Plantation
8654 Savannah Highway
Adams Run, SC 29426
(803) 881-6344

BEAUFORT

Board of Architectural Review
152 Middle Road
Beaufort, SC 29902
(803) 524-4304
FAX (803) 524-3269

City of Beaufort
P.O. Drawer 1167
Beaufort, SC 29901
(803) 525-7010
FAX (803) 525-7013

Historic Beaufort Foundation
P.O. Box 11
Beaufort, SC 29901
(803) 524-6334
FAX (803) 524-6240

CHARLESTON

Drayton Hall
3380 Ashley River Road
Charleston, SC 29414
(803) 766-0188
FAX (803) 766-0878

Charleston Affordable Housing Inc.
180 Meeting Street, #205
Charleston, SC 29401
(803) 577-4060
FAX (803) 577-5326

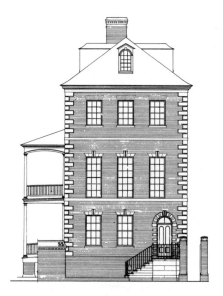

Gadsden House, Charleston, South Carolina. *(J. Burnett, HABS)*

Charleston Citywide Local Development Corporation
75 Calhoun Street, Third Floor
Charleston, SC 29401
(803) 724-3796
FAX (803) 724-7354

Charleston County Planning Department
3870 Leed's Avenue, Suite 110
North Charleston, SC 29405
(803) 740-3200
FAX (803) 740-3222

Historic Charleston Foundation
11 Fulton Street
Charleston, SC 29401
(803) 723-1623
FAX (803) 577-2067

Old Exchange Building
City of Charleston
P.O. Box 304
Charleston, SC 29401
(803) 727-2165
FAX (803) 727-2163

Preservation Society of Charleston
P.O. Box 521
Charleston, SC 29402
(803) 722-4630
FAX (803) 723-4381

COLUMBIA

Chicora Foundation, Inc.
P.O. Box 8664
Columbia, SC 29202
(803) 787-6910
FAX (803) 787-6910

Historic Columbia Foundation
1601 Richland Street
Columbia, SC 29201
(803) 252-7742
FAX (803) 252-5001

Richland County Historic Preservation Commission
1616 Blanding Street
Columbia, SC 29201
(803) 252-3964

South Carolina Heritage Corridor
South Carolina Department of Parks, Recreation and Tourism
Heritage and Tourism Development
1205 Pendleton Street
Columbia, SC 29201
(803) 734-1654
FAX (803) 734-0670

State Historic Preservation Office
1430 Senate Street
P.O. Box 11669
Columbia, SC 29211
(803) 734-8577
FAX (803) 734-8820

EDGEFIELD

Old Edgefield Dirtrict Museum
P.O. Box 174
Edgefield, SC 29824
(803) 637-5304
FAX (803) 637-6066

MT. PLEASANT

African American Heritage Council
1106 Port Harbor Court
Mt. Pleasant, SC 29464
(803) 881-5516
FAX (803) 881-7070

Boone Hill Plantation
P.O. Box 1554
Mt. Pleasant, SC 29465
(803) 884-4371

PENDLETON

Pendleton District Historical and Recreational Commission
125 East Queen Street
P.O. Box 565
Pendleton, SC 29670
(864) 646-3782 or 1-800-862-1795
FAX (864) 646-2506
E-mail: tendture@innova.net

SUMMERVILLE

Plantation Painters Inc.
103 Quail Lane
Summerville, SC 29485
(803) 873-6400

Town of Summerville
104 Civic Center
Summerville, SC 29483
(803) 871-6000
FAX (803) 871-6954

South Dakota

STATE HISTORIC PRESERVATION OFFICE

State Historical Preservation Center
Cultural Heritage Center
900 Governors Drive
Pierre, SD 57069
(605) 773-3458
FAX (605) 773-6041
Jay Vogt, Acting SHPO

STATEWIDE PRESERVATION ORGANIZATION

Historic South Dakota Foundation

P.O. Box 113
Pierre, SD 50501
(605) 224-9398
FAX (605) 224-6815
Mark Wolfe, President
Jeane Wharton, Acting Executive Director

NATIONAL TRUST REGIONAL OFFICE

Mountains/Plains Regional Office
910 16th Street, Suite 1100
Denver, CO 80202
(303) 623-1504
FAX (303) 623-1508

E-mail: mpro@nthp.org
Web Site: http://www.nthp.org
Barbara Pahl, Director

AMERICAN INSTITUTE OF ARCHITECTS CONTACT

Ward B. Whitwam, AIA, Executive Secretary
AIA South Dakota
P.O. Box 1596
Sioux Falls, SD 57101
(605) 334-2422
FAX (605) 333-0243

Old Fort Randall Church, Gregory County, South Dakota. *(H. E. Anderson, HABS)*

Local Contacts

DEADWOOD

Deadwood Historic Preservation
City of Deadwood
108 Sherman Street
Deadwood, SD 57732
(605) 578-2082
FAX (605) 578-2084
E-mail: hpc@deadwood.net

MITCHELL

Friends of the Middle Border Museum of American Indian and Pioneer Life
1311 South Duff Street
P.O. Box 1071
Mitchell, SD 57301
(605) 996-2122
FAX (605) 996-0323

RAPID CITY

City of Rapid City
Historic Preservation
300 6th Street
Rapid City, SD 57701
(605) 394-4120
FAX (605) 394-6636

Tennessee

STATE HISTORIC PRESERVATION OFFICE

Department of Environment and Conservation
401 Church Street, L & C Tower, 21st Floor
Nashville, TN 37243-0435
(615) 532-0109
FAX (615) 532-0120
Ollie Keller, SHPO

STATEWIDE PRESERVATION ORGANIZATION

Association for the Preservation of Tennessee Antiquities
110 Leake Avenue
Nashville, TN 37205
(615) 352-8247
FAX (615) 352-8247
Joan H. Vollmer, President

Tennessee Heritage Alliance
Upper Cumberland Institute
Box 5183
Tennessee Tech University
Cookeville, TN 38505
(615) 372-3338
FAX (615) 372-6142
Homer Kemp, President

NATIONAL TRUST REGIONAL OFFICE

Southern Regional Office
456 King Street
Charleston, SC 29403
(803) 722-8552
FAX (803) 722-8652
E-mail: sro@nthp.org
Web Site: http://www.nthp.org
David Brown, Director

NATIONAL TRUST ADVISORS

Victor Ashe
Knoxville, TN

Mimi Phillips
Memphis, TN

STATEWIDE MAIN STREET COORDINATOR

Coordinator
Tennessee Main Street Project
Department of Economic and Community Development
320 6th Avenue North, Sixth Floor
Nashville, TN 37243-0405
(615) 741-2373
FAX (615) 741-5070

AMERICAN INSTITUTE OF ARCHITECTS CONTACTS

Connie Wallace, Hon. AIA, CAE, Executive Vice President
AIA Tennessee
209 10th Avenue South #506
Nashville, TN 37203
(615) 255- 3860
FAX (615) 254-1186

Carolyn R. Miller, Executive Secretary
AIA Chattanooga
4407 South Choctaw Drive
Chattanooga, TN 37411
(423) 698-3048
FAX 1-800-807-7961

Ann White, Executive Director
AIA East Tennessee
10 Emory Place
Knoxville, TN 37917
(423) 637-5003
FAX (423) 637-2046

Alison Melton, Executive Director
AIA Memphis
22 North Front Street #840
Memphis, TN 38103
(901) 525-3818
FAX (901) 527-7566

Carol Pedigo, Executive Director
AIA Middle Tennessee
209 10th Avenue South #415
Nashville, TN 37203
(615) 259-9664
FAX (615) 742-0954

Local Contacts

CHATTANOOGA

Chattanooga-Hamilton County Regional Planning Commission
200 City Hall Annex
Chattanooga, TN 37402
(423) 757-5216
FAX (423) 757-5532

CLARKSVILLE

Clarksville-Montgomery County Museum
200 South Second Street
P.O. Box 383
Clarksville, TN 37040
(615) 648-5780
FAX (615) 553-5179

COOKEVILLE

Depot Museum
City of Cookeville
P.O. Box 998
Cookeville, TN 38503
(615) 528-8570

ETOWAH

Tennessee Overhill Heritage Association
Tennessee Overhill
P.O. Box 143
Etowah, TN 37331
(423) 263-7232
FAX (423) 263-1670
E-mail: cldwll@cococo.net

FRANKLIN

The Carter House
P.O. Box 555
Franklin, TN 37064
(615) 791-1861
FAX (615) 794-1327
E-mail: julep19@mail.idt.nct

Heritage Foundation of Franklin and Williamson County
P.O. Box 723
Franklin, TN 37065
(615) 591-8500
FAX (615) 591-8502

Historic Carnton Plantation
1345 Carnton Lane
Franklin, TN 37064
(615) 794-0903
FAX (615) 794-4275

HERMITAGE

The Ladies' Hermitage Association
4580 Rachel's Lane
Hermitage, TN 37076
(615) 889-2941

HOHENWALD

Tennessee Natchez Trace
Tennessee Natchez Trace Corridor Association
Hohenwald Depot
112 East Main Street
Hohenwald, TN 38462
(615) 794-5555

JACKSON

Jackson Historic Zoning Commission
105 North Church Street
Jackson, TN 38301
(901) 425-8275
FAX (901) 425-8281
E-mail: planning@usit.net

JONESBOROUGH

America's First Frontier
Northeast Tennessee Tourism Association
P.O. Box 415
Jonesborough, TN 37659
1-(800) 468-6882

KINGSPORT

Allandale Mansion
City of Kingsport
225 West Center Street
Box A-2
Kingsport, TN 37660
(423) 229-9422
FAX (423) 224-2479

KNOXVILLE

East Tennesee Development District
P.O. Box 19806
Knoxville, TN 37939
(423) 584-8553
FAX (423) 584-5159

Tennessee Valley Authority River Systems Operations
WT 10B-K
400 West Summit Hill Drive
Knoxville, TN 37902
(423) 632-6065
FAX (423) 632-4607

MEMPHIS

Memphis Heritage Inc.
P.O. Box 3143
Memphis, TN 38173
(901) 529-9828

Memphis Landmarks Commission
City Hall
125 North Main Street, Room 443
Memphis, TN 38103-2017
(901) 576-7191
FAX (901) 576-7188

MURFREESBORO

Friends of the Stones River National Battlefield
2115 Shannon Drive
Murfreesboro, TN 37129
(615) 890-1400
FAX (615) 893-5362

Public History and Historic Preservation
Department of History
P.O. Box 23
Middle Tennessee State University
Murfreesboro, TN 37132
(615) 898-2544
FAX (615) 898-5881

Tennessee Civil War Heritage Area
c/o James K. Huhta
Center for Historic Preservation
Middle Tennessee State University
Box 80
Murfreesboro, TN 37132
(615) 898-2947
FAX (615) 898-5614

NASHVILLE

Belle Meade Mansion
5025 Harding Road
Nashville, TN 37205
(615) 356-0501
FAX (615) 356-2336

Historic Nashville, Inc.
P.O. Box 190516
Nashville, TN 37219
(615) 244-7835
FAX (615) 244-7838

Tennessee Historical Commission
2941 Lebanon Road
Nashville, TN 37214
(615) 742-6716

RUGBY

Historic Rugby
Box 8
Rugby, TN 37733
(423) 628-2441
FAX (423) 628-2266
E-mail: rugbytm@highland.net

SUMMERTOWN

The Farm Building Company
P.O. Box 149
Summertown, TN 38483
(615) 964-3579

St. Mary's Church, Nashville, Tennessee. *(D. Woodrum, HABS)*

TULLAHOMA

Tennessee's Backroads Heritage
300 South Jackson
Tullahoma, TN 37388
(615) 454-9446
FAX (615) 454-9986

E-mail: cherrycon@juno.com
Web Site: http://www.tenweb.com/
tnbkrds/ or http://www.cyber-time.
com/tnbkrds

Texas

STATE HISTORIC PRESERVATION OFFICE

Texas Historical Commission
P.O. Box 12276
Austin, TX 78711-2276
(512) 463-6100
FAX (512) 475-4872
Web Site: http://www.thc.state.
tx.us
Curtis Tunnell, SHPO

STATEWIDE PRESERVATION ORGANIZATION

Preservation Texas, Inc.
2300 Primrose
Fort Worth, TX 76111
(817) 838-2824
FAX (817) 838-2848
Betty Massey, President
Libby Willis, Executive Director

NATIONAL TRUST REGIONAL OFFICE

Southwest Regional Office
500 Main Street, Suite 1030
Fort Worth, TX 76102
(817) 332-4398
FAX (817) 332-4512
E-mail: swro@nthp.org
Web Site: http://www.nthp.org
Jane Jenkins, Director

NATIONAL TRUST ADVISOR

Paula Peters
Dallas, TX

STATEWIDE MAIN STREET COORDINATOR

Terry Colley, Coordinator
Texas Main Street Center
Texas Historical Commission
1511 Colorado Street
P.O. Box 12276
Austin, TX 78711
(512) 463-6092
FAX (512) 463-5862
Web Site: http://www.thc.state.
tx.us
Terry Colley, ASC

AMERICAN INSTITUTE OF ARCHITECTS CONTACTS

David Lancaster, CAE, Executive Vice President
Texas Society of Architects/AIA
816 Congress Avenue, Suite 970
Austin, TX 78701
(512) 478-7386
FAX (512) 478-0528
Web Site: http://www.txarch.
com

Sally Fly
Executive Director
AIA Austin
1206 West 38th Street, #205
Austin, TX 78705
(512) 452-4332
FAX (512) 452-2284
E-mail: aiaaustin@aol.com

Gloria Wise, Executive Director
AIA Dallas
2811 McKinney, Suite 20

Lock Box 104
Dallas, TX 75204
(214) 871-2788
FAX (214) 871-2324

Suzie S. Adams, Executive Director
AIA Fort Worth
675 N. Henderson, #800
Fort Worth, TX 76107
(817) 338-4668
FAX (817) 338-4695
E-mail: aiafw@flash.net

Martha C. Murphree, Hon. AIA, Executive Director
AIA Houston
20 Greenway Plaza, #246
Houston, TX 77046
(713) 622-2081
FAX (713) 621-0925
E-mail: aiahoutx@pdq.net

Carmen Perez-Garcia, Executive Director
AIA Lower Rio Grande Valley
312 North 6th Street
McAllen, TX 78501
(210) 682-7070
FAX (210) 686-3096

Torrey M. Stanley, Executive Director
AIA San Antonio
1149 East Commerce, #200
San Antonio, TX 78205
(210) 226-4979
FAX (210) 226-3062

Local Contacts

ABILENE

Abilene Preservation League
P.O. Box 3451
Abilene, TX 79604
(915) 676-3775
FAX (915) 676-4800

AMARILLO

The City of Amarillo
Planning Department
509 East 7th, Room 206
P.O. Box 1971
Amarillo, TX 79105
(806) 378-4222
FAX (806) 378-9388

AUSTIN

Austin Heritage Society
P.O. 2113
Austin, TX 78768
(512) 474-5198
FAX (512) 474-2125

Prewitt and Associates, Inc.
7701 North Lamar, Suite 104
Austin, TX 78752
(512) 459-3349
FAX (512) 459-3851
E-mail: 105435.2703@compuserve.com

St. Edward's University
3001 South Congress Avenue
Austin, TX 78704
(512) 448-8417
FAX (512) 448-8492

Texas Department of Transportation
125 East 11th Street
Austin, TX 78701-2483
(512) 416-2152

Texas Heritage Commission
P.O. Box 12276
Austin, TX 78711
(512) 463-5754
FAX (512) 475-4872

Texas Historical Foundation
P.O Box 50314
Austin, TX 78763
(512) 453-2154
FAX (512) 453-2164

Texas Neighborhood Conservation Fund
823 Harris Avenue
Austin, TX 78705
(512) 452-1103
E-mail: thf@texashf.org

University of Texas at Austin
Austin, TX 78701
(512) 471-3434

BEAUMONT

Beaumont Heritage Society
Community Account
2985 French Road
Beaumont, TX 77706
(409) 898-0348
FAX (409) 898-8487

City of Beaumont
Planning Division
P.O. Box 3827
Beaumont, TX 77704
(409) 880-3764
FAX (409) 880-3732

Jefferson County Historical Commission
1149 Pearl Street, Third Floor
Beaumont, TX 77701
(409) 835-8701
FAX (409) 784-5811

BEDFORD

Bedford Historical Foundation
P.O. Box 157
Bedford, TX 76095
(817) 952-2492
FAX (817) 952-2263

BROWNSVILLE

Brownsville Historical Association
P.O. Box 846
Brownsville, TX 78520
(210) 542-3929

BRYAN

City of Bryan
P.O. Box 1000
300 South Texas Avenue
Bryan, TX 77805
(409) 821-3409
FAX (409) 361-3882
E-mail: acrocket@cl.bryan.tx.us

BURTON

Operation Restoration, Inc.
P.O. Box 98
Burton, TX 77835
(409) 289-3378

CENTER

Shelby Foundation
321 Shelbyville Street
Center, TX 75935
(409) 598-3682
FAX (409) 598-8163

DALLAS

City of Dallas
Department of Planning and Development
1500 Marilla, Room 50N
Dallas, TX 75201
(214) 670-4118

Dallas Historical Society
P.O. Box 150038
Dallas, TX 75315
(214) 421-4500
FAX (214) 421-7500

Deep Ellum Development
3200 Main Street, Suite 1.3
Dallas, TX 75226
(214) 748-1999
FAX (214) 748-8643

Friends of Fair Park
P.O. Box 150248
Dallas, TX 75315
(214) 426-3400
FAX (214) 426-0737

Grace United Methodist Church
4105 Junius
Dallas, TX 75246
(214) 824-2533
FAX (214) 824-2279

Majestic Theatre
1925 Elm Street, Suite 300
Dallas, TX 75201
(214) 880-0137

Preservation Dallas
2922 Swiss Avenue
Dallas, TX 75204
(214) 821-3290
FAX (214) 821-3573

Web Site: http://www.
preservationdallas.org

DENTON

Denton County Historical Commission
P.O. Box 2184
Denton, TX 76202
(817) 383-8073
FAX (817) 565-8693

DRIPPING SPRING

Friends of the Poundhouse Foundation
P.O. Box 589
Dripping Spring, TX 78620
(512) 858-4659
FAX (512) 858-5285

EDCOUCH

City of Edcouch
P.O. Box 86
Edcouch, TX 78538
(210) 262-2140
FAX (210) 262-4953

EDINBURG

City of Edinburg
Main Street
P.O. Box 1079
Edinburg, TX 78540
(210) 383-5661
FAX (210) 383-7111

EL PASO

El Paso Mission Trail Association
1 Civic Center Plaza

Col. Walter Gresham House, Galveston, Texas. *(L. Johnston, HABS)*

El Paso, TX 79901
(915) 534-0630
FAX (915) 532-2963
1-800-351-6024

FORT STOCKTON

Fort Stockton Historical Society
Annie Riggs Memorial Museum
301 South Main Street
Fort Stockton, TX 79735
(915) 336-2167

FORT WORTH

Historic Fort Worth, Inc.
1110 Penn Street
Fort Worth, TX 76102
(817) 332-5875
FAX (817) 332-3902

Historic Preservation Council for
Tarrant County
1111 Foch Street, Suite 101
Fort Worth, TX 76107
(817) 338-0267
FAX (817) 335-SAVE

Southside Preservation Association
1519 Lipscomb Street
Fort Worth, TX 76104
(817) 926-2800

Southside Preservation League
P.O. Box 3039
Fort Worth, TX 76113
(817) 926-2800

Texas Heritage, Inc.
1509 Pennsylvania Avenue
Fort Worth, TX 76104
(817) 336-1212
FAX (817) 335-5338

GAINESVILLE

Cooke County Heritage Society
Morton Museum
P.O. Box 150
Gainesville, TX 76241
(817) 668-8900

GEORGETOWN

Georgetown Heritage Society
P.O. Box 1265
101 West 7th
Georgetown, TX 78626
(512) 863-5598

GRAPEVINE

Grapevine Heritage Foundation
One Liberty Park Plaza
Grapevine, TX 76051
(817) 481-0454
FAX (817) 488-1048

HILLSBORO

Hillsboro Heritage League, Inc.
P.O. Box 2
Hillsboro, TX 76645
(817) 582-2825

HOUSTON

Greater Houston Preservation
Alliance
712 Main, Suite 110
Houston, TX 77002
(713) 216-5000
(713) 216-2143

KYLE

Antiquities Planning and Consulting
831 Petra's Way
Kyle, TX 78640
(512) 398-2946
FAX (512) 398-2946

LAREDO

Azteca Economic Development and
Preservation Organization
20 Iturbide Street
Laredo, TX 78040
(210) 726-4462
FAX (210) 726-9014

Los Caminos del Rio, Inc.
P.O. Box 415
Laredo, TX 78042

(210) 791-4300
FAX (210) 724-9039

Webb County Heritage Foundation
P.O. Box Drawer 446
Laredo, TX 78042
(210) 727-0977
FAX (210) 727-0577

LUBBOCK

Ranching Heritage Center
Texas Tech University
P.O. Box 43191
Lubbock, TX 79409-3191
(806) 742-0498
FAX (806) 742-1136

MARSHALL

Harrison County Historic
Commission
Peter Whitstone Square
Marshall, TX 75670
(903) 938-2680

McALLEN

McAllen Chamber of Commerce
P.O. Box 790
McAllen, TX 78505
(210) 682-2871
FAX (210) 631-8571

MESQUITE

Historic Mesquite, Inc.
P.O. Box 850137
Mesquite, TX 75185-0137
(214) 216-6468
FAX (972) 216-8109
E-mail: charlene_orr@msn.com

MT. VERNON

Franklin County Historical
Association
P.O. Box 289
Mt. Vernon, TX 75457
(903) 537-2264
FAX (903) 537-4315

NAVASOTA

The Cotton Republic: Texas Origins and Echoes
Harlock History Center
1215 East Washington Avenue
Navasota, TX 77868
(409) 825-7055

NEW BRAUNFELS

New Braunfels Conservation Society
P.O. Box 310933
New Braunfels, TX 78131
(210) 629-2943

PLANO

Heritage Farmstead
1900 West 15th Street
Plano, TX 75075
(214) 881-0140
FAX (972) 422-6481

RICHMOND

Fort Bend Museum Associates
P.O. Drawer 460
Richmond, TX 77406
(713) 342-6478
FAX (281) 282-2407

ROUND TOP

Winedale Historical Center
P.O. Box 11
Round Top, TX 78954
(409) 278-3530
FAX (409) 278-3531

SAN ANTONIO

Alamo-La Bahia Corridor
Alamo Area Council of
Governments
118 Broadway, Suite 400
San Antonio, TX 78205
(210) 225-5201
FAX (210) 225-5937

City of San Antonio
Planning Department
P.O. Box 839966
San Antonio, TX 78283-3966
(210) 207-7951
FAX (210) 207-4441

Institute of Texas Cultures
University of Texas
801 South Bowie Street
San Antonio, TX 78205
(210) 458-2337
FAX (210) 458-2219

King William Association
1032 South Alamo Street
San Antonio, TX 78210
(210) 227-8786
FAX (210) 277-8038

Market Trail
Alamo Area Council of Government
118 Broadway
San Antonio, TX 78205
(210) 225-5201
(210) 225-5937

Monte Vista Historical Association
P.O. Box 12386
San Antonio, TX 78212
(210) 737-8212

San Antonio Conservation Society
107 King William Street
San Antonio, TX 78204-1399
(210) 224-6163
FAX (210) 224-6168

Williams, Schneider, Calvetti, Inc.
2955 Nacogdoches Road
San Antonio, TX 78217
(210) 828-6419
FAX (210) 828-4414

SAN MARCOS

The Heritage Asssociation of San Marcos, Inc.
P.O. Box 1806
San Marcos, TX 78666
(512) 392-4295

SHERMAN

Main Street Sherman
111 A North Travis
Sherman, TX 75090
(903) 892-8576

TEMPLE

Railroad and Pioneer Museum
P.O. Box 5126
Temple, TX 76501
(817) 298-5172

TYLER

Historic Tyler, Inc.
P.O. Box 6774
Tyler, TX 75711
(903) 595-1960
FAX (903) 593-1543
E-mail: histyler@gower.net

VICTORIA

Victoria Preservation, Inc.
P.O. Box 1486
Victoria, TX 77902
(512) 573-1878
FAX (512) 573-5247
E-mail: vpi@vpitx.net

WACO

Historic Waco Foundation, Inc.
810 South Fourth Street
Waco, TX 76706
(817) 753-5166
FAX (817) 753-5166

WOODVILLE

Tyler County Heritage Society
DBA Heritage Village Museum
P.O. Box 888
Woodville, TX 75979
(409) 283-2272
FAX (409) 283-2194

Utah

STATE HISTORIC PRESERVATION OFFICE

Utah State Historical Society
300 Rio Grande
Salt Lake City, UT 84101
(801) 533-3500
FAX (801) 533-3503
Max Evans, SHPO

STATEWIDE PRESERVATION ORGANIZATION

Utah Heritage Foundation
Memorial House in Memory
Grove Park
P.O. Box 28
Salt Lake City, UT 84110-0028
(801) 533-0858
FAX (801) 537-1245
Don Stromquist, President

Lisbeth Henning, Executive
Director

NATIONAL TRUST REGIONAL OFFICE

Western Regional Office
One Sutter Street, Suite 707
San Francisco, CA 94104
(415) 956-0610
FAX (415) 956-0837
E-mail: wro@nthp.com
Web Site: http://www.nthp.org
Elizabeth Goldstein, Director

NATIONAL TRUST ADVISORS

Tina Stahlke Lewis
Park City, UT

Rob White
Salt Lake City, UT

STATEWIDE MAIN STREET COORDINATOR

Coordinator
Utah Main Street Program
Department of Community and
Economic Development
324 South State Street, Suite 500
Salt Lake City, UT 84111
(801) 538-8638
FAX (801) 538-8888

AMERICAN INSTITUTE OF ARCHITECTS CONTACT

**Elizabeth Mitchell, Executive
Director**
AIA Utah/Salt Lake
75 East Broadway
Salt Lake City, UT 84111
(801) 532-1727
FAX (801) 532-4576

Local Contacts

OGDEN

City of Ogden
Department of Community
Development
2484 Washington Boulevard,
Second Floor
Ogden, UT 84401
(801) 629-8921
FAX (801) 629-8902

Egyptian Theatre Foundation
P.O. Box 4
Ogden, UT 84402
(801) 394-2730

Weber County Heritage Foundation
Eccles Community Arts Center
2589 Jefferson Avenue
Ogden, UT 84401
(801) 392-3231

PAYSON

People Preserving Peteetneet
51 North 100 West
Payson, UT 84651
(801) 465-2253

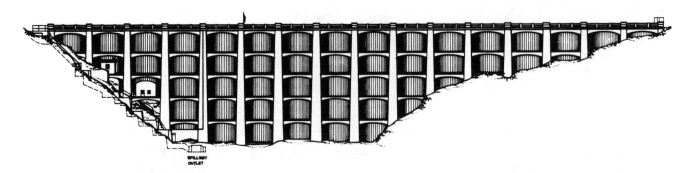

Mountain Dell Dam, Parleys Canyon, Salt Lake County, Utah. *(T. Ristau, Magden, HAER)*

ST. GEORGE

City of St. George
Community Development Office
175 East 200 North
St. George, UT 84770
(801) 634-5800
FAX (801) 674-4261

SALT LAKE CITY

Cooper/Roberts Architects
202 West 300 North
Salt Lake City, UT 84103
(801) 355-5915
FAX (801) 355-9885

Salt Lake City Historic Landmarks Commission
451 South State Street
City and County Building
Room 406
Salt Lake City, UT 84111
(801) 535-7757
FAX (801) 535-6174

Vermont

STATE HISTORIC PRESERVATION OFFICE

Vermont Division for Historic Preservation
135 State Street, Drawer 33
Montpelier, VT 05633-1201
(802) 828-3056
Townsend Anderson, SHPO

STATEWIDE PRESERVATION ORGANIZATION

Preservation Trust of Vermont
104 Church Street
Burlington, VT 05401
(802) 658-6647
FAX (802) 860-1191
Judy Hayward, President
Paul Bruhn, Executive Director

NATIONAL TRUST REGIONAL OFFICE

Northeast Regional Office
Seven Faneuil Hall Marketplace
Boston, MA 02109
(617) 523-0885
FAX (617) 523-1199
E-mail: nero@nthp.org
Web Site: http://www.nthp.org
Wendy Nicholas, Director

NATIONAL TRUST ADVISORS

Paul Bruhn
Burlington, VT

Elizabeth Courtney
Chittenden, VT

NATIONAL MAIN STREET COORDINATOR

Jane Lendway, Co-Coordinator
Vermont Downtown Program
Department for Historic Preservation
135 State Street, Drawer 33
Montpelier, VT 05633-1201
(802) 828-3226
FAX (802) 828-3206
E-mail: dhp@gatedca.state.vt.us

AMERICAN INSTITUTE OF ARCHITECTS CONTACT

Hanne N. Williams, Executive Director
AIA Vermont
RFD #1, Box 67
Waitsfield, VT 05673
(802) 496-3761
FAX (802) 496-5124

Local Contacts

BELLOWS FALLS

Historic Preservation Commission CLG
P.O. Box 370
Bellows Falls, VT 05101
(802) 463-3456
FAX (802) 463-1227

BRATTLEBORO

The Landmark Trust (U.S.A), Inc
R.R. 1, Box 510
Kipling Road

Brattleboro, VT 05301
(802) 254-6868
FAX (802) 257-7783

Town of Brattleboro
230 Main Street, Room 202
Brattleboro, VT 05301
(802) 254-4541 Ext. 111

BURLINGTON

City of Burlington
135 Church Street, Suite 3
Burlington, VT 05401-8415
(802) 865-7194

FAX (802) 865-7195
E-mail: whiteyvt@aol.com

University of Vermont
Burlington, VT 05405
(802) 656-2646
FAX (802) 656-4038
E-mail: smower@zoo.uvm.edu

COLCHESTER

Arnold and Scangas Architects
29 Ethan Allan Avenue
Colchester, VT 05446
(802) 655-1061
FAX (802) 655-1068

State of Vermont Capital Complex, Montpelier, Vermont. *(P. Borchers, M. Melragon, M. Fazlo, HABS)*

LUDLOW

Black River Academy Museum
High Street
P.O. Box 73
Ludlow, VT 05149
(802) 228-5050

MANCHESTER

Friends of Hildene, Inc.
P.O. Box 377
Manchester, VT 05254
(802) 362-1788
FAX (802) 362-1564

MIDDLEBURY

Fire Safety Institute
P.O. Box 674
Middlebury, VT 05753
(802) 462-2663
E-mail: firesafe@panther.
middlebury.edu

MORETOWN

Gap Management Company, Inc.
RD #1, Box 860
Moretown, VT 05660
(802) 828-3056
FAX (802) 244-5095

NORWICH

Douglas Gest Restorations
Box 832
Norwich, VT 05055
(802) 649-2928

ORLEANS

Orleans County Historical Society
Old Stone House Museum
RR #1, Box 500
Orleans, VT 05860
(802) 754-2022

WINDSOR

Historic Windsor, Inc.
Windsor House
P.O. Box 1777
Windsor, VT 05089-0021
(802) 674-6752
FAX (802) 674-6179

Village Design Review Board
Town of Woodstock
31 The Green
Woodstock, VT 05091
(802) 457-3456
FAX (802) 457-2329
E-mail: wa2p@valley.net

Virginia

STATE HISTORIC PRESERVATION OFFICE

Department of Historic Resources
221 Governor Street
Richmond, VA 23219
(804) 786-3143
FAX (804) 225-4261
H. Alexander Wise, Jr., SHPO

STATEWIDE PRESERVATION ORGANIZATIONS

Association for the Preservation of Virginia Antiquities
204 West Franklin Street
Richmond, VA 23220-5012
(804) 648-1889
FAX (804) 775-0802
Robert Benton Giles, President
Peter Dun Grover, Executive Director

Preservation Alliance of Virginia
700 Harris Street, Suite 106
Charlottesville, VA 22903
(804) 984-4484
FAX (804) 984-5947
E-mail: pav@c2w.com
Bessie B. Carter, President
Kat Imhoff, Executive Director

NATIONAL TRUST REGIONAL OFFICE

Mid-Atlantic Regional Office
One Penn Center at Suburban Station, Suite 1520
1617 John F. Kennedy Boulevard
Philadelphia, PA 19103-1815
(215) 568-8162
FAX (215) 568-9251
E-mail: maro@nthp.org
Web Site: http://www.nthp.org
Patricia Wilson Aden, Director

NATIONAL TRUST ADVISORS

Robert B. Lambeth, Jr.
Bedford, VA

Partricia L. Zontine
Winchester, VA

STATEWIDE MAIN STREET COORDINATOR

Louellen Brumgard, Program Manager
Virginia Main Street Program
Department of Housing and Community Development
Third Floor
501 North Second Street
Richmond, VA 23219
(804) 371-7030
FAX (804) 371-7093

AMERICAN INSTITUTE OF ARCHITECTS CONTACTS

John W. Braymer, Ph.D, Executive Vice President
Virginia Society/AIA
15 South Fifth Street
Richmond, VA 23219
(804) 644-3041
FAX (804) 643-4607
E-mail: jbraymer@aiava.org

Bertha Hess, Executive Director
AIA Hampton Roads
7 Koger Center # 127
Norfolk, VA 23503
(757) 461-2899
FAX (757) 461-2899

Ann Thompson, Executive Director
AIA Northern Virginia
205 South Patrick Street
Alexandria, VA 22314
(703) 549-9747
FAX (703) 549-9783
E-mail: aianova@aol.com

Local Contacts

ALEXANDRIA

Alexandria Board of Architectural Review
Department of Planning and Zoning
301 King Street, Room 2100
Alexandria, VA 22314
(703) 838-4666
FAX (703) 838-6393

Alexandria Library (Lloyd House)
220 North Washington Street
Alexandria, VA 22314
(703) 838-4578
FAX (703) 706-3912

Historic Alexandria Foundation
P.O. Box 19252
Alexandria, VA 22320-0252
(703) 549-5811

Office of Historic Alexandria
City Hall
Box 178
Alexandria, VA 22313
(703) 838-4554
FAX (703) 838-6451

AMHERST

Amherst County Historical Museum
P.O. Box 741
Amherst, VA 24521
(804) 946-9068
FAX (804) 946-9348

ARLINGTON

Arlington County Community Planning Housing and Development
Community Improvement Division
2100 Clarendon Boulevard, #701
Arlington, VA 22201
(703) 358-3804
FAX (703) 358-3834

BOYDTON

The Boyd Tavern Foundation
P.O. Box 183
Boydton, VA 23917
(804) 738-6226

BRANDY STATION

Brandy Station Foundation
Box 165
Brandy Station, VA 22714
(540) 825-0433

BROOKNEAL

Patrick Henry Memorial Foundation
Red Hill
Route 2, Box 127
Brookneal, VA 24528
(804) 376-2044
FAX (804) 376-2647

CHARLOTTESVILLE

Thomas Jefferson Memorial Foundation, Inc.
Monticello
P.O. Box 316
Charlottesville, VA 22902
(804) 894-9800
FAX (804) 977-7757

FAIRFAX

City of Fairfax
Department of Community Development and Planning
10455 Armstrong Street
Fairfax, VA 22030
(703) 385-7930
FAX (703) 385-7977

FALLS CHURCH

Fairfax County History Commission
Heritage Resources
2855 Annandale Road
Falls Church, VA 22042
(703) 324-3185

FOREST

Corporation for Jefferson's Poplar Forest
P.O. Box 419
Forest, VA 24551
(804) 525-1806
FAX (804) 525-7252
Web Site: http://www.poplarforst.
org

FREDERICKSBURG

Center for Historic Preservation
1301 College Avenue, Suite B40
Fredericksburg, VA 22401
(540) 654-1041
FAX (540) 654-1068

Historic Fredericksburg Foundation
P.O. Box 8327
Fredericksburg, VA 22404
(540) 371-4504
FAX (540) 371-4505

HANOVER

Hanover County Planning Department
P.O. Box 470
Hanover, VA 23069
(804) 537-6171

Hanover Tavern Foundation
P.O. Box 487
Hanover, VA 23069
(804) 537-5050
FAX (804) 537-5823

HEATHSVILLE

Hughletts Tavern Foundation
Rices Hotel
P.O. Box 579
Heathsville, VA 22473
(804) 529-6224

Northumberland Preservation, Inc.
P.O. Box 88
Heathsville, VA 22473
(804) 580-8581

LEXINGTON

Historic Lexington Foundation
P.O. Box 901
10 East Washington Street
Lexington, VA 24450
(540) 463-6832

Washington and Lee University
Lee Chapel
Lexington, VA 24450
(540) 463-8768

LYNCHBURG

Lynchburg Historical Foundation
P.O. Box 248
Lynchburg, VA 24505
(804) 528-5353
FAX (804) 528-9413

Lynchburg Historical Foundation
Revolving Fund, Inc.
900 Fifth Street
Lynchburg, VA 24504
(804) 283-4451

MANASSAS

Culbertson Company of Virginia
12923 Balls Ford Road
Manassas, VA 22109
(703) 631-0502
FAX (703) 631-0615

McLEAN

Oldham Historic Properties, Inc
904 Turkey Run Road
McLean, VA 22101
(703) 893-3219
FAX (703) 847-2911
E-mail: tloldham@ad.com

MIDDLEBURG

The John Singleton Mosby Heritage Area
Janet Whitehouse
P.O. Box 1178
Middleburg, VA 22117
(540) 687-6681

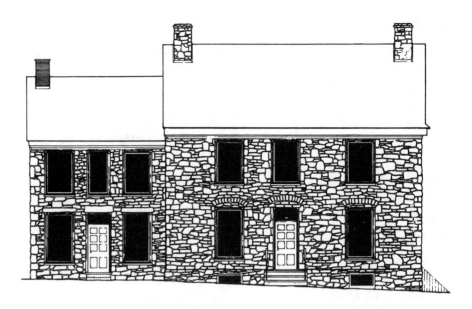

Hollingsworth House (Abram's Delight), Winchester, Virginia. *(R. Rogers, HABS)*

NEWPORT NEWS

City of Newport News
Department of Planning and
Development
2400 Washington Avenue
Newport News, VA 23607
(757) 247-8428
FAX (757) 926-3504

NORFOLK

Cavalier Land, Inc.
P.O. Box 3175
Norfolk, VA 23514
(757) 625-3502
FAX (757) 625-8235

Hampton Roads Naval Museum
Norfolk Naval Base
1 Waterside Drive, Suite 248
Norfolk, VA 23510-1607
(757) 444-8971

ORANGE

Orange County Historical Society
P.O. Box 591
Orange, VA 22960
(540) 672-5366

PETERSBURG

Historic Blandford Cemetery Foundation, Inc.
250 South Sycamore Street
Petersburg, VA 23803
(804) 733-2397

Historic Petersburg Foundation
P.O. Box 691
Petersburg, VA 23804
(804) 732-2096
FAX (804) 733-0867

Planning and Community Development
City Hall, Room 304
Petersburg, VA 23803
(804) 733-2308

RICHMOND

Historic Richmond Foundation
707-A East Franklin Street
Richmond, VA 23219-2313
(804) 643-7407
FAX (804) 788-4244

Lower James River Association
P.O. Box 110
Richmond, VA 23218
(804) 730-8297
FAX (804) 730-8297
E-mail: jra@i2020.net

Old Dominion Chapter, NRHS
P.O. Box 8583
Richmond, VA 23226
(804) 231-4324

SALEM

Salem Historical Society
801 East Main Street
Salem, VA 24153
(540) 389-6760

SMITHFIELD

Historic St. Luke's Restoration
331 South Church Street
Smithfield, VA 23430
(757) 357-7107

STAUNTON

Frontier Culture Museum of Virginia
P.O. Box 810
Staunton, VA 24402-0810
(540) 332-7850
FAX (540) 332-9989

Historic Staunton Foundation
120 South Augusta Street
Staunton, VA 24401
(540) 885-7676
FAX (540) 885-5976
E-mail: hst@cfw.com

STRATFORD

Robert E. Lee Memorial Association, Inc.
Stratford Hall Plantation
Stratford, VA 22558
(804) 493-8038
FAX (804) 493-0333

VIENNA

Historic Vienna Inc.
P.O. Box 53
Vienna, VA 22183
(703) 281-3573

WARRENTON

Piedmont Environmental Council
45 Horner Street
P.O. Box 460
Warrenton, VA 20188
(540) 347-2334
FAX (540) 349-9003
Web Site: http://www.pec-va.org

WATERFORD

Waterford Foundation
P.O. Box 142
Waterford, VA 20197
(540) 882-3018
FAX (540) 882-3921

WILLIAMSBURG

Association for Preservation Technology International
P.O. Box 3511
Williamsburg, VA 23187
(703) 373-6050

Colonial Williamsburg Foundation
P.O. Box 1776
Architectural Collections
Williamsburg, VA 23187-1776
(757) 220-7432

Colonial Williamsburg Foundation Library
P.O. Box 1776
Williamsburg, VA 23187

James City and County Historical Commission
P.O. Box 8784
Williamsburg, VA 23187
(757) 566-0363
FAX (757) 566-8413

Yorktown Victory Center
P.O. Box 1607
Williamsburg, VA 23107-1607
(757) 887-1776
FAX (757) 887-1306

WINCHESTER

Preservation of Historic Winchester
2 North Cameron Street
Winchester, VA 22601
(540) 667-3577
FAX (540) 667-3583

Shenandoah Valley Battlefields
Winchester/Frederick County
Economic Development
Commission
45 East Boscawen Street
Winchester, VA 22601
(540) 665-0973
FAX (540) 722-0604
E-mail: wfcedc@shentel.net

Washington

STATE HISTORIC PRESERVATION OFFICE

Office of Archaeology and
Historic Preservation
111 21st Avenue S.W.
P.O. Box 48343
Olympia, WA 98504-8343
(360) 753-4011
FAX (360) 586-0250
David M. Hansen, Acting SHPO
E-mail: davidh@cted.wa.gov

STATEWIDE PRESERVATION ORGANIZATION

Washington Trust for Historic
Preservation
204 First Avenue, South
Seattle, WA 98104
(206) 624-7880
FAX (206) 622-1766
Leonard Garfield, President

NATIONAL TRUST REGIONAL OFFICE

Western Regional Office
One Sutter Street, Suite 707
San Francisco, CA 94104
(415) 956-0610
FAX (415) 956-0837
E-mail: wro@nthp.org
Web Site: http://www.nthp.org
Elizabeth Goldstein, Director

NATIONAL TRUST ADVISORS

Anthony H. Anderson
Spokane, WA

Karen Gordon
Seattle, WA

NATIONAL PARK SERVICE CONTACT

Superintendent
Columbia Cascades SSO
Pacific West Field Area, National
Park Service
909 First Avenue, Suite 546
Seattle, WA 98104-1060

STATEWIDE MAIN STREET COORDINATOR

Susan Kempf, Coordinator
Washington Downtown
Revitalization Services
906 Columbia S.W.
P.O. Box 48300
Olympia, WA 98504-8300
(360) 586-8977
FAX (360) 586-0873

AMERICAN INSTITUTE OF ARCHITECTS CONTACTS

Mary D. Mauerman, Executive
Director

AIA Washington
Capitol Court, Suite 237
1110 Capitol Way South
Olympia, WA 98501-2272
(360) 943-6012
FAX (360) 352-1870
E-mail: aiawacncl@aol.com

Marga Rose Hancock, Hon. AIA,
Executive Vice President
AIA Seattle
1911 First Avenue
Seattle, WA 98101
(206) 448-4938
FAX (206) 572-2634

Cynthia Peterson, Executive
Director
AIA Southwest Washington
502 South 11th Street
Tacoma, WA 98402
(206) 627-4006
FAX (206) 572-2634
E-mail: cpaiaswwa@aol.com

Evelyn T. Creager, Executive
Director
AIA Spokane
335 W. Sprague Avenue
Spokane, WA 99204-0210
(509) 747-5498
FAX (509) 747-5498

Local Contacts

CHENEY

Eastern Washington University
History Department
Patterson 2000
Cheney, WA 99004
(509) 359-2337
FAX (509) 359-4275

EVERETT

**City of Everett Planning and
Community Development**
2930 Wetmore Avenue, Suite 100
Everett, WA 98201
(206) 257-8731
FAX (206) 257-8742

LONGVIEW

**Longview Historic Preservation
Commission**
P.O. Box 128
Longview, WA 98632
(360) 577-3330
(360) 577-4018
E-mail: julie.hourck@ci.longview.
washwa.us

OLYMPIA

Office of Historic Preservation
111 West 21st Avenue
P.O. Box 48343
Olympia, WA 98504
(360) 753-4011
FAX (360) 586-0250

OYSTERVILLE

Oysterville Restoration Foundation
P.O. Box 71
Oysterville, WA 98641
(360) 665-5151

PORT TOWNSEND

Jefferson County Historical Society
210 Madison Street
Port Townsend, WA 98368
(206) 385-1003

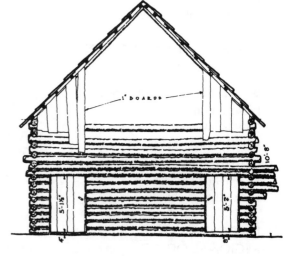

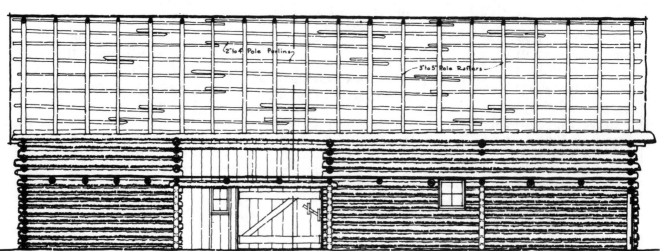

Clugston Barn, Colville, Washington. *(F. Dings, A. Welch, HABS)*

PUYALLUP

Ezra Meeker Museum
P.O. Box 103
Puyallup, WA 98371
(206) 848-1770

Puyallup Main Street
104 West Main Avenue, Suite 204
P.O. Box 476
Puyallup, WA 98371
(206) 840-2631

SEATTLE

Historic Seattle Preservation and Development Authority
605 First Avenue, Suite 100
Seattle, WA 98104
(206) 622-6952
FAX (206) 622-1197

KPFF Consulting Engineers
1201 Third Avenue, Suite 900
Seattle, WA 98101
(206) 622-5822
FAX (206) 622-8130

Urban Conservation Division
700 Third Avenue, Fourth Floor
Seattle, WA 98104
(206) 684-0228
FAX (206) 233-5142

SPOKANE

Historic Preservation Office
808 West Spokane Falls Boulevard, Room 627
Spokane, WA 99201
(509) 456-4378

TACOMA

Tacoma Historic Preservation
747 Market Street, Suite 836
Tacoma, WA 98402
(206) 591-5220
FAX (206) 591-5232

TOPPENISH

Yakama Nation Museum
P.O. Box 151
Toppenish, WA 98948
(509) 865-2800

VANCOUVER

City of Vancouver
1101 Officers Row
Vancouver, WA 98661
(360) 699-5288

Vancouver National Historic Reserve
City of Vancouver
Vancouver, WA 98668
(360) 696-2899

West Virginia

STATE HISTORIC PRESERVATION OFFICE

West Virginia Division of Culture and History
Historic Preservation Office
1900 Kanawha Boulevard East
Charleston, WV 25305-0300
(304) 558-0220
FAX (304) 558-2779
William M. Drennen, Jr., SHPO

STATEWIDE PRESERVATION ORGANIZATION

Preservation Alliance of West Virginia
P.O. Box 3371
Charleston, WV 25333-3371
(304) 342-6972
FAX (304) 342-6973
Billy Joe Peyton, President
Terrell Ellis, Executive Director

NATIONAL TRUST REGIONAL OFFICE

Mid-Atlantic Regional Office
One Penn Center at Suburban
Station, Suite 1520
1617 John F. Kennedy Boulevard
Philadelphia, PA 19103-1815
(215) 568-8162
FAX (215) 568-9251
E-mail: maro@nthp.org
Web Site: http://www.nthp.org
Patricia Wilson Aden, Director

NATIONAL TRUST ADVISORS

Terrell B. Ellis
Charleston WV

Walton Stowell
Harpers Ferry, WV

STATEWIDE MAIN STREET COORDINATOR

Monica Miller, Coordinator
West Virginia Main Street
Program
Capitol Complex, Building 6,
Room 553
Charleston, WV 25305
(304) 558-0121
FAX (304) 558-0449
E-mail: mmileemail.wvnet.edu
Web Site: http://www.wvdo.org

AMERICAN INSTITUTE OF ARCHITECTS CONTACT

Roberta J. Guffey, Hon. AIA, Executive Director
West Virginia Society of
Architects/AIA
P.O. Box 813
Charleston, WV 25323
(304) 344-9872
FAX (304) 343-0205

Local Contacts

ARTHURDALE

Arthurdale Heritage, Inc.
P.O. Box 850
Arthurdale, WV 26520
(304) 864-3959
FAX (304) 864-4602

BEVERLY

Rich Mountain
Battlefield Foundation

P.O. Box 227
Beverly, WV 26253
(304) 637-7424
E-mail: phyllisb@neumedia.net

FAIRMONT

Pricketts Fort Memorial Foundation
Route 3
P.O. Box 407
Fairmont, WV 26554
(304) 363-3030

GAULEY BRIDGE

Historic Midland Trail
The Midland Trail Scenic Highway
Association, Inc.
P.O. Box 568
Gauley Bridge, WV 25085
1-800-822-8760
(304) 632-1284

GLENVILLE

Patchwork in the Glen, Ltd.
102 South Lewis
Glenville, WV 26351
(304) 462-8698
FAX (304) 462-8698

LEWISBURG

Carnegie Hall Inc.
105 Church Street
Lewisburg, WV 24901
(304) 645-7917
FAX (304) 645-3228
E-mail: omaooo49@mail.wvnet.edu

MATEWAN

West Virginia Coal Heritage Area
Coal Country, Inc.
P.O. Box 368
Matewan, WV 25678
(304) 426-4239
FAX (304) 426-4230
E-mail: matewan@eastky.com

Thomas Shepherd's Grist Mill, Shepherdstown, West Virginia. *(B. Freeman, HABS)*

MORGANTOWN

Mon Valley Tri-State Network, Inc.
P.O. Box 4239
Morgantown, WV 26504-4239
(304) 293-2789
FAX (304) 293-2552

West Virginia University
Department of History
P.O. Box 6303
Morgantown, WV 26506
(304) 293-2421
FAX (304) 293-6858

SALEM

Fort New Salem
Salem-Teikyo University
P.O. Box 500
Salem, WV 26426
(304) 782-5245
FAX (304) 782-5395

WHEELING

Friends of Wheeling, Inc.
P.O. Box 889
Wheeling, WV 26003
(304) 232-7163

**Victorian Wheeling Landmarks
Foundation**
P.O. Box 667
Wheeling, WV 26003-0085
(304) 233-1600

Wheeling Heritage Area
Department of Development
City County Building, Room 305
Wheeling, WV 26003
(304) 234-3701
FAX (304) 234-3605

Wisconsin

STATE HISTORIC PRESERVATION OFFICE

State Historical Society of Wisconsin
816 State Street
Madison, WI 53706
(608) 264-6500
FAX (608) 264-6404
E-mail: jeff.dean@ccmail.adp.wisc.edu
Jeff Dean, SHPO

STATEWIDE PRESERVATION ORGANIZATION

Wisconsin Trust for Historic Preservation
646 West Washington Avenue, Suite D
Madison, WI 53703
(608) 255-0348
Shawn Graff, President

NATIONAL TRUST REGIONAL OFFICE

Midwest Regional Office
53 West Jackson Boulevard, Suite 1135
Chicago, IL 60604
(312) 939-5547
FAX (312) 939-5651
E-mail: mwro@nthp.org
Web Site: http://www.nthp.org
Jim Mann, Director

NATIONAL TRUST ADVISORS

Brian Rude
Madison, WI

Cate Zeuske
Madison, WI

STATEWIDE MAIN STREET COORDINATOR

Alicia Goehring, Coordinator
Wisconsin Main Street Program
Department of Development
123 West Washington
P.O. Box 7970
Madison, WI 53707
(608) 267-3855
FAX (608) 266-8969

AMERICAN INSTITUTE OF ARCHITECTS CONTACT

William M. Babcock, CAE, Executive Director
Wisconsin Society of Architects/AIA
321 South Hamilton Street
Madison, WI 53703
(608) 257-8477
FAX (608) 257-0242

Local Contacts

BARABOO

Al Ringling Theatre Friends
136 4th Avenue
P.O. Box 381
Baraboo, WI 53913
(608) 356-8864

CLEVELAND

Centreville Settlement, Inc.
P.O. Box 247
Cleveland, WI 53015
(414) 693-8558

FOND DU LAC

City of Fond Du Lac
Redevelopment Division
160 South Macy Street
P.O. Box 150
Fond Du Lac, WI 54936-0150
(414) 929-3311
FAX (414) 929-3291

GERMANTOWN

Germantown Historical Society
W148N12297 Pleasant View Drive
Germantown, WI 53022
(414) 628-3170

KENOSHA

Kenosha County Historical Society
6300 3rd Avenue
Kenosha, WI 53143
(414) 654-5770
FAX (414) 654-1730

LAC du FLAMBEAU

Lac du Flambeau Heritage Tourism Project
P.O. Box 67
Lac du Flambeau, WI 54538
(715) 588-9052
FAX (715) 588-9408

LA CROSSE

Architectural Researches, Inc.
2540 Sherwood Drive
La Crosse, WI 54601
(608) 788-5932

MADISON

Frank Lloyd Wright Heritage Tour
3100 Lake Mendota Drive, #606
Madison, WI 53705
(608) 238-1608

Wisconsin Heritage Tourism
123 West Washington Street
P.O. Box 7976
Madison, WI 53707
(608) 266-7299
FAX (608) 261-8213

MAZOMANIE

Mazomanie Historical Society Museum
118 Broadhead Street
Mazomanie, WI 53560
(608) 795-2992

MENASHA

Fox-Wisconsin Rivers Heritage Corridor
East Central Wisconsin Regional Planning Commission
132 Main Street
Menasha, WI 54952
(414) 751-4770
FAX (414) 751-4771

MEQUON

City of Mequon
Landmarks Commission
11333 North Cedarburg Road, 60 West
Mequon, WI 53092
(414) 242-3100
FAX (414) 242-9655

MILWAUKEE

Historic Milwaukee, Inc.
P.O. Box 93309
Milwaukee, WI 53203
(414) 277-7795

Wisconsin Ethnic Settlement Trail
5900 North Port Washington Road
Suite 146
Milwaukee, WI 53217
(414) 961-2110
Web Site: http://www.west.org

Wisconsin Heritage, Inc.
2000 West Wisconsin Avenue
Milwaukee, WI 53233
(414) 931-0808
FAX (414) 931-1005

ONEIDA

Oneida Tribe of Indians of Wisconsin
P.O. Box 365
Oneida, WI 54155
(414) 494-4362

PLATTEVILLE

City of Platteville
Office of Community Planning and Development
P.O. Box 780
75 North Bonson Street
Platteville, WI 53818
(608) 348-9741
FAX (608) 348-9145

James Fraser House, Honey Creek Falls, Wisconsin. *(E. Kusseraw, HABS)*

SHEBOYGAN

Sheboygan Area School District
830 Virginia Avenue
Sheboygan, WI 53081
(414) 459-3500
FAX (414) 459-6487

SUPERIOR

Douglas County Historical Society
Fairlawn Museum
906 East 2nd Street
Superior, WI 54880
(715) 394-5712
FAX (715) 394-2043

RACINE

Preservation Racine
P.O. Box 383
Racine, WI 53401
(414) 634-5748

RICHLAND CENTER

City of Richland Center
P.O. Box 230
Richland Center, WI 53581
(608) 647-3466
FAX (608) 647-8360

VIROQUA

Associates to Restore the Temple Theatre
220 South Main Street
Viroqua, WI 54665
(608) 637-8190
FAX (608) 637-8326

WAUSAU

Friends of Wausau Landmarks
711 Mcindoe Street
Wausau, WI 54403
(715) 845-7637

Wyoming

Local Contacts

BIG HORN

Bradford Brinton Memorial Museum
Box 460
Big Horn, WY 82833
(307) 672-3173
FAX (307) 672-3258

CASPAR

Natrona County Planning Department
120 West First Street, Suite 200
Casper, WY 82601
(307) 235-9435
FAX (307) 235-9436

EVANSTON

Tracks Across Wyoming Corridor
Evanston Urban Renewal Agency
1200 Main Street
Evanston, WY 82930
(307) 789-9690
FAX (307) 789-4109

RAWLINS

Old Pen Joint Powers Board
500 West Walnut Street
Rawlins, WY 82301
(307) 324-4422
FAX (307) 828-4004

SHERIDAN

Sheridan Heritage Center, Inc.
P.O. Box 6393
Sheridan, WY 82801
(307) 674-5440
FAX (307) 674-1556

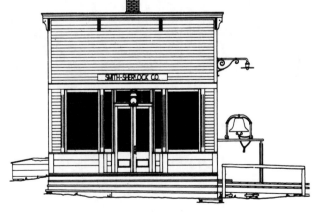

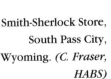

Smith-Sherlock Store, South Pass City, Wyoming. *(C. Fraser, HABS)*

Puerto Rico

STATE HISTORIC PRESERVATION OFFICE

Office of Historic Preservation
Box 82, La Fortaleza
San Juan, PR 00901
(787) 721-2676
FAX (787) 723-0957
Lilliane D. Lopez, SHPO

STATEWIDE PRESERVATION ORGANIZATION

Sociedad para la Preservación Historica de Puerto Rico
c/o Nestor Murray Irizarry
Casa Paoli
Calle Mayor 14
Ponce, PR 00731
(787) 840-4115

NATIONAL TRUST REGIONAL OFFICE

Mid-Atlantic Regional Office
One Penn Center at Suburban Station, Suite 1520
1617 John F. Kennedy Boulevard
Philadelphia, PA 19103-1815
(215) 568-8162
FAX (215) 568-9251
E-mail: maro@nthp.org
Web Site: http://www.nthp.org
Patricia Wilson Aden, Director

NATIONAL TRUST ADVISORS

Jose R. Coleman-Davis Pagan
Old San Juan, PR

Pablo Ojeda-O'Neill
Old San Juan, PR

STATEWIDE MAIN STREET COORDINATOR

Mr. Rafael Cerame, Coordinator
Corazón del Pueblo
P.O. Box S 4275
San Juan, PR 00905
(787) 728-5585
FAX (787) 728-5655

NATIONAL PARK SERVICE CONTACT

San Juan NHS
Fort San Cristobal
Norzagarray Street
San Juan, PR 00901

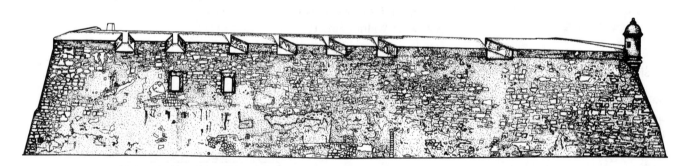

San Carlos Ravelin, San Juan National Historic Site, Old San Juan, Puerto Rico. *(J. Blanco, HABS)*

U.S. Virgin Islands

Local Contacts

ST. CROIX

T. K. Properties, Inc.
P.O. Box 5968
St. Croix, VI 00824
(809)778-5626

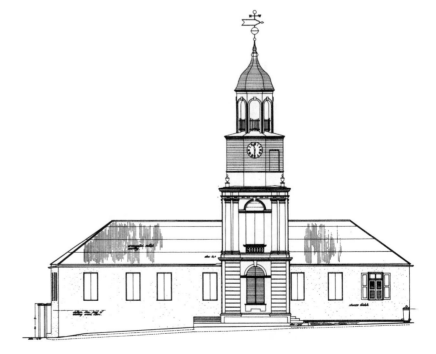

Former Lutheran Church of Our Lord of Zebaoth, Christiansted, St. Croix, Virgin Islands. *(F. C. Gjessing, HABS)*

Index

Page numbers in italic refer to illustrations.

Abandoned Shipwreck Act, 38, 40
Abilene, Kansas, Eisenhower House, *172*
Accessibility, resources and bibliography, 56
Adam brothers, 19
Adaptive use, resources and bibliography, 56–57
Advisory Council on Historic Preservation, 38
  contacts, 122
  described, 97–99
Advocacy:
  legal approaches, 41–42
  resources and bibliography, 57
Age, National Register of Historic Places eligibility, 12
Alabama:
  contacts in, 123–124
  degree programs in preservation, 43
Alaska, contacts in, 125–126
Alaska Coastal Management Program, 39
Alexander Wilson Agricultural Works (New Castle County, Delaware), *145*
Americans with Disabilities Act, 40
Amory Tickner House (Boston, Massachusetts), *19*
Annapolis, Maryland, Dr. Upton Scott House, *19*
Appraisals, resources and bibliography, 57
Archaeological Resource Protection Act of 1979, 38, 40
Archeology, resources and bibliography, 57

Archeology and Ethnography Program (NPS), 85
Architectural styles, 17, 18–26
  Art Deco (1925–1940), 25
  Beaux Arts (1890–1920), 23
  Chicago Style (1875–1910), 24
  Classical Revival (1900–1920), 24–25
  Early English Colonial (1600s–1700), 18–19
  exotic revivals (1830–1930), 21
  Federal Style (1780–1820), 19–20
  Georgian Style (1700–1776), 19
  Gothic Revival Style (1830–1890), 20–21
  Greek Revival Style (1820–1860), 20
  International Style (1920–1945), 25–26
  Italianate Style (1830–1880), 21
  Jeffersonian Style (1790–1830), 20
  overview, 18
  Prairie Style (1900–1920), 24
  Queen Anne (1880–1900), 22
  Richardsonian Romanesque (1870–1900), 23
  Second Empire (1860–1890), 21–22
  Shingle Style (1880–1900), 22–23
  Spanish Colonial (1565–1850), 19
  Stick Style (1860–1890), 22
  twentieth-century architecture, resources and bibliography, 76
  vernacular architecture, 26
Architecture:
  resources and bibliography, 57–58
  twentieth-century, resources and bibliography, 76

Arizona:
  contacts in, 127–128
  degree programs in preservation, 46
Arkansas:
  contacts in, 129–130
  degree programs in preservation, 46
Art Deco style (1925–1940), described, 25
Art Moderne, 25
Austin, Texas, John Houghton House, *22*

Baltimore and Ohio Railway Station (Point of Rocks, Maryland), *181*
Bank of San Mateo (Redwood City, California), *25*
Battlefields, resources and bibliography, 58
Beacon Hill courtyard (Boston, Massachusetts), *122*
Beaux Arts style (1890–1920), described, 23
Bibliography and resources, 56–77
Birmingham, Alabama, Sloss-Sheffield Steel and Iron Company, *124*
Boston, Massachusetts:
  Amory Tickner House, *19*
  Beacon Hill courtyard, *122*
  Union Oyster House, *11*
Breuer, Marcel, 25
Building codes, resources and bibliography, 58
Byways and trails, resources and bibliography, 75

California:
    contacts in, 131–137
    degree programs in preservation, 46
California Environmental Quality Act, 39
Carpenter Gothic, 21, 22
Carson City, Nevada, James D. Roberts House, *203*
Cast-iron technology, Italianate Style, 21
Centennial Celebrations (1876), 19
Central of Georgia Railway Repair Shops (Savannah, Georgia), *154*
Charleston, South Carolina, 12–13
    Gadsden House, *240*
Charlottesville, Virginia, Pavilion II, University of Virginia, *20*
Chateau-sur-Mer (Newport, Rhode Island), *238*
Chicago, Illinois:
    Field House, Garfield Park, *86*
    Frederick C. Robie House, *24*
    Museum of Science and Industry, *37*
    Reliance Building, *24*
    Republic Building, *163*
Chicago Style (1875–1910), described, 24
Children, resources and bibliography, 58–59
Christ Episcopal Church (Raleigh, North Carolina), *20*
Christiansted, St. Croix, Virgin Islands, Lutheran Church of Our Lord of Zebaoth, *269*
Chronological listing, 78–80
Church of the Holy Trinity (Lincoln, Nebraska), *202*
Civil War (U.S.), 21
Classical Revival style (1900–1920), described, 24–25
Clinton, Iowa, Van Allen and Son Store, *170*
Clugston Barn (Colville, Washington State), *260*
Colonel Walter Gresham House (Galveston, Texas), *248*
Colorado:
    contacts in, 138–140
    degree programs in preservation, 46
Colville, Washington State, Clugston Barn, *260*
Connecticut, contacts in, 141–143

Conservation, resources and bibliography, 59
Convention Concerning the Protection of the World Cultural and Natural Heritage, 117–118
Cultural diversity, resources and bibliography, 59

Dayton, Ohio, Greyhound Terminal, *225*
Degree programs in preservation, 43–49
Delaware:
    contacts in, 144–145
    degree programs in preservation, 46
Delaware Block building (Leadville, Colorado), *31*
Denver, Colorado, Moffatt Station, *139*
Department of Transportation Act, 38
Design review, resources and bibliography, 59–60
Detroit, Michigan, Grand Riviera Theatre, *23*
Directories, resources and bibliography, 60
Disasters, resources and bibliography, 60
District of Columbia, *see* Washington, D.C.
Dochet Island, Maine, St. Croix River Lighthouse, *178*
Documentation, resources and bibliography, 60–61
Downtown revitalization, resources and bibliography, 61–62
Dr. Upton Scott House (Annapolis, Maryland), *19*

Early English colonial (1600s–1700), described, 18–19
Easements:
    Historic Rehabilitation Tax Credit, 41
    resources and bibliography, 62
East Glacier, Montana, Lubuc Ranger Station, *200*
East Hampton, New York, Hook Windmill, *215*
Ebenezer Maxwell House (Germantown, Pennsylvania), *235*
Ecole des Beaux-Arts (Paris, France), 23

Economic Recovery Tax Act of 1982, 9
Economic revitalization, resources and bibliography, 62
Edenton, North Carolina, Hayes Manor, *220*
Education:
    degree programs in preservation, 43–49
    resources and bibliography, 76
Egyptian revival, described, 21
Eisenhower House (Abilene, Kansas), *172*
El Cerrito (Upper Pecos River Valley, New Mexico), *210*
Eligibility requirements, National Register of Historic Places, 11–12
Elkhorn Tavern (Pea Ridge, Arkansas), *130*
Enfield, New Hampshire, Shaker Church Family Cow Barn, *205*
Environmental issues, resources and bibliography, 62–63
Executive Branch, federal government, 100–102
Exotic revivals (1830–1930), described, 21
Exposition Internationale des Arts Decoratifs et Industriels Modernes, 25

Fairbanks, Alaska, Kodiak T-Hangar, Ladd Field, *126*
Fairfield, Connecticut, Old Ogden House, *18*
Federal government, 100–105
    Executive Branch, 100–102
    independent agencies, 102–103, 105
    legal approaches, 38
    Legislative Branch, 103
    offices, 103–104
Federal Rehabilitation Tax Credit, *see* Historic Rehabilitation Tax Credit
Federal Style (1780–1820), described, 19–20
Field House, Garfield Park (Chicago, Illinois), *86*
First Church of Christ (New Haven, Connecticut), *142*
First Presbyterian Church (Salisbury, North Carolina), *23*
Florida:
    contacts in, 149–152

degree programs in preservation, 47

Former Lutheran Church of Our Lord of Zebaoth (Christiansted, St. Croix, Virgin Islands), *269*

Fort Totten, North Dakota, Hospital, *222*

Frederick C. Robie House (Chicago, Illinois), *24*

Freemason Street Baptist Church (Norfolk, Virginia), *9*

French Quarter (New Orleans, Louisiana), *17*

Fund raising, resources and bibliography, 63–64

Gadsden House (Charlestown, South Carolina), *240*

Galveston, Texas, Colonel Walter Gresham House, *248*

Gaming, resources and bibliography, 64

Garden District home (New Orleans, Louisiana), *95*

Garfield Park (Chicago, Illinois), *86*

Georgetown, Washington, D.C., Grace Church, *147*

Georgia:
    contacts in, 153–156
    degree programs in preservation, 44, 47

Georgian style (1700–1776), described, 19

Germantown, Pennsylvania, Ebenezer Maxwell House, *235*

Gingerbread house (Tyringham, Massachusetts), *61*

Glossary of terms, 50–55

Gothic Revival style (1830–1890), described, 20–21

Goyer-Lee House (Memphis, Tennessee), *22*

Grace Church (Georgetown, Washington, D.C.), *147*

Grand Central Station (New York, New York), 14

Grand Riviera Theatre (Detroit, Michigan), *23*

Gray Brothers Block (Guthrie, Oklahoma), *228*

Greek Revival Style (1820–1860), described, 20

Greenough, Horatio, 6

Gregory County, South Dakota, Old Fort Randall Church, *241*

Greyhound Terminal (Dayton, Ohio), *225*

Gropius, Walter, 25

Growth management, resources and bibliography, 64

Guidebooks, resources and bibliography, 64

Guthrie, Oklahoma, Gray Brothers Block, *228*

Hancock Shaker Village (Pittsfield, Massachusetts), *51*

Hart Block (Louisville, Kentucky), *174*

Harvard Shakers, South Family Dwelling and Washshed (Worcester, Massachusetts), *187*

Hawaii:
    contacts in, 157–158
    degree programs in preservation, 47

Hayes Manor (Edenton, North Carolina), *220*

Hazardous materials, resources and bibliography, 64

Heritage corridors, resources and bibliography, 64

Heritage Preservation Services (NPS), 86

High Victorian Gothic Style, described, 21

Historical American Buildings Survey/Historic American Engineering Record (NPS), 85

Historic district, 10
    legal approaches, 37
    resources and bibliography, 64–65

Historic homes, resources and bibliography, 65

Historic preservation law, 17

Historic Rehabilitation Tax Credit, 14, 17, 40–41
    description and eligibility, 32–35

Historic Sites Act of 1935, 36

Historic trails/scenic byways, resources and bibliography, 75

Hollingsworth House (Abram's Delight) (Winchester, Virginia), *257*

Hollywood, California, Storer House, *135*

Honey Creek Falls, Wisconsin, James Fraser House, *265*

Honolulu, Hawaii, Iolani Palace, *158*

Hook Windmill (East Hampton, New York), *215*

Hospital (Fort Totten, North Dakota), *222*

Howard University Divinity School (Washington, D.C.), *55*

Hyman, Sidney, 7

Idaho, contacts in, 159–160

Idaho City, Idaho, Pioneer Lodge No. 1, International Order of Odd Fellows Hall, *159*

Identification, *see* Property identification

Illinois:
    contacts in, 161–165
    degree programs in preservation, 44, 47

Incentives, *see* Tax incentives

Independent agencies, federal government, 102–103, 105

Indiana:
    contacts in, 166–168
    degree programs in preservation, 44

Industrial sites, resources and bibliography, 66

Inspection, resources and bibliography, 66

Integrity, National Register of Historic Places eligibility, 11–12

Intermodal Surface Transportation Efficiency Act of 1991, 40

International Order of Odd Fellows Hall (Idaho City, Idaho), *159*

International organizations: listing of, 111–118

International Style (1920–1945), described, 25–26

Interstate highway system, 8

Iolani Palace (Honolulu, Hawaii), *158*

Iowa, contacts in, 169–170

Isaac Bell House (Newport, Rhode Island), *23*

Italianate style (1830–1880), described, 21

Jacksonville, Florida, Oriental Greek Orthodox Church, *21*

James D. Roberts House (Carson City, Nevada), *203*

James Fraser House (Honey Creek Falls, Wisconsin), *265*

Jefferson, Thomas, 20

Jeffersonian style (1790–1830), described, 20
Jewish Reform movement, 21
John Griswold House (Newport, Rhode Island), *22*
John Houghton House (Austin, Texas), *22*
Johnson, Lyndon B., 4

Kansas:
    contacts in, 171–172
    degree programs in preservation, 47
Kentucky:
    contacts in, 173–174
    degree programs in preservation, 47
Kodiak T-Hangar, Ladd Field (Fairbanks, Alaska), *126*

Ladd Field (Fairbanks, Alaska), *126*
Landscapes, resources and bibliography, 66
Land-use laws and preservation, resources and bibliography, 66
Land-use planning, resources and bibliography, 66
"Late medieval" style, 18
Law, *see* Legal approaches
Leadville, Colorado, Delaware Block building, *31*
Legal approaches, 36–42
    advocacy, 41–42
    federal laws, 38
    local designations, 37
    local laws, 39–40
    National Register of Historic Places, 36–37
    overview, 36
    ownership, 36
    property identification and listing, 36
    regulation and procedural protections, 37
    resources and bibliography, 66–67
    state laws, 38–39
    state registers, 37
    tax incentives, 40–41
Legislation, resources and bibliography, 66–67
Legislative Branch, federal government, 103
Lincoln, Nebraska, Church of the Holy Trinity, *202*
Local ordinances:

described, 12–14
legal approaches, 37, 39–40
resources and bibliography, 67
tax incentives, 41
Los Angeles, California, Richfield Oil Building, *25*
Louisiana:
    contacts in, 175–176
    degree programs in preservation, 47
Louisiana State Museum Cabildo (New Orleans, Louisiana), *84*
Louis Lanoix House (New Orleans, Louisiana), *176*
Louisville, Kentucky, Hart Block, *174*
Lovell Beach House (Newport Beach, California), *26*
Lubuc Ranger Station (East Glacier, Montana), *200*
Lutheran Church of Our Lord of Zebaoth (Christiansted, St. Croix, Virgin Islands), *269*

Maine, contacts in, 177–179
Maintenance, resources and bibliography, 67–69
Mansart, François, 22
Maritime issues, resources and bibliography, 69
Maryland:
    contacts in, 180–183
    degree programs in preservation, 44, 47
Massachusetts:
    contacts in, 184–188
    degree programs in preservation, 44
McKim, Mead and White, 23
Memphis, Tennessee, Goyer-Lee House, *22*
Miami, Florida, Ralph Munroe Boathouse, *152*
Michigan:
    contacts in, 189–191
    degree programs in preservation, 44–45, 48
Mies van der Rohe, Ludwig, 25
Military installations, resources and bibliography, 69
Minneapolis, Minnesota, Pillsbury "A" Mill, *193*
Minnesota, contacts in, 192–194
Minnesota Environmental Rights Act, 39

Mission Church (Santa Anna Pueblo, New Mexico), *19*
Mission San Xavier del Bac (Tucson, Arizona), *128*
Mississippi, contacts in, 195–196
Missouri:
    contacts in, 197–198
    degree programs in preservation, 43, 48
The Modern House, 25
Moffatt Station (Denver, Colorado), *139*
Montana, contacts in, 199–200
Montpelier, Vermont, State of Vermont Capital Complex, *254*
Moorish revival, described, 21
Mountain Dell Dam, Parleys Canyon (Salt Lake County, Utah), *252*
Multiple resource nomination, 10
Museum Management Program (NPS), 85
Museum of Science and Industry (Chicago, Illinois), *37*
Museum properties, resources and bibliography, 70

Napoleon III (e. of France), 22
Nashville, Tennessee:
    Public Square, *21*
    St. Mary's Church, *245*
National Environmental Policy Act, 38
National Historic Landmarks, 12, 29
National Historic Preservation Act of 1966, 8–9, 12, 28, 38, 97
National Main Street Center, contacts, 122
National organizations, 106–110
National Park Service, 84
    contacts, 122
    described, 84, 85–87
National Register, History, and Education Program (NPS), 86
National Register of Historic Places, 9–12, 17, 27–29
    benefits of, 12, 28–29
    eligibility requirements, 11–12, 27–28
    legal approaches, 36–37
    listing in, 10
    nomination process, 10–11, 27
    purpose of, 9–10
    resources and bibliography, 70
National Trust for Historic Preservation, vii, 41–42, 88–96, 121–122

Board of Advisors, 96
Board of Trustees, 95–96
described, 84
executive staff, 93
ex-officio trustees, 96
historic sites, 94–95
offices, programs, and services of, 88–93
regional offices, 93–94
Nebraska, contacts in, 201–202
Neighborhood revitalization, resources and bibliography, 70
Neutra, Richard, 25
Nevada:
contacts in, 203
degree programs in preservation, 48
New England:
Early English Colonial (1600s–1700), 18
Shingle Style (1880–1900), 22–23
New Hampshire, contacts in, 204–205
New Haven, Connecticut:
First Church of Christ, 142
Yale University, 45
New Jersey, contacts in, 206–208
New Mexico, contacts in, 209–210
New Mexico Prehistoric and Historic Sites Preservation Act, 39
New Orleans, Louisiana:
French Quarter, 17
Garden District home, 95
Louisiana State Museum Cabildo, 84
Louis Lanoix House, 176
Saint Charles Avenue mansions, 28
Newport, Rhode Island:
Chateau-sur-Mer, 238
Isaac Bell House, 23
John Griswold House, 22
Newport Beach, California, Lovell Beach House, 26
New York, New York, 5
Grand Central Station, 14
New York Public Library, 57
United States Sub-Treasury, 20
New York Public Library (New York, New York), 57
New York State:
contacts in, 211–217
degree programs in preservation, 45
Nomination process, National Register of Historic Places, 10–11

Norfolk, Virginia, Freemason Street Baptist Church, 9
North Carolina, contacts in, 218–221
North Dakota, contacts in, 222
North Manchester, Indiana, North Manchester Public Library, 167
North Manchester Public Library (North Manchester, Indiana), 167

Ohio:
contacts in, 223–226
degree programs in preservation, 43, 48
Oklahoma:
contacts in, 227–228
degree programs in preservation, 48
Old Fort Randall Church (Gregory County, South Dakota), 241
Old Ogden House (Fairfield, Connecticut), 18
Old San Juan, Puerto Rico, San Carlos Ravelin, San Juan National Historic Site, 268
Oral history, resources and bibliography, 70
Oregon:
contacts in, 229–230
degree programs in preservation, 45
Organizational development, resources and bibliography, 70–72
Organizations, 83–118
Advisory Council on Historic Preservation, 97–99
federal government, 100–105
international, 111–118
national and regional, 106–110
National Park Service, 85–87
National Trust for Historic Preservation, 88–96
overview, 83–84
state and territories, 121–122. See also entries under specific states and territories
Oriental Greek Orthodox Church (Jacksonville, Florida), 21
Ownership, legal approaches, 36

Palladio, Andrea, 19
Park Historic Structures and Cultural Landscapes Program (NPS), 86–87
Patterson, New Jersey, Phoenix Mill, 208

Pavilion II, University of Virginia (Charlottesville, Virginia), 20
Pea Ridge, Arkansas, Elkhorn Tavern, 130
Pennsylvania:
contacts in, 231–236
degree programs in preservation, 43, 45
Philosophy, resources and bibliography, 72–73
Phoenix Mill (Patterson, New Jersey), 208
Pillsbury "A" Mill (Minneapolis, Minnesota), 193
Pioneer Lodge No. 1, International Order of Odd Fellows Hall (Idaho City, Idaho), 159
Pittsfield, Massachusetts, Round barn, Hancock Shaker Village, 51
Planning, resources and bibliography, 72
Point of Rocks, Maryland, Baltimore and Ohio Railway Station, 181
Poppeliers, John, 18
Prairie Style (1900–1920), described, 24
Preservation:
bibliography and resources, 56–77
chronological landmarks, 78–80
organizations, 83–118. See also Organizations
rationale for, 4–7
Preservation philosophy, resources and bibliography, 72–73
President's Advisory Council on Historic Preservation, 9
Pressed metal technology, Italianate style, 21
Price, Bruce, 23
Private ownership, legal approaches, 36
Procedural protection, legal approaches, 37
Property identification and listing, legal approaches, 36
Property rights, resources and bibliography, 73
Public Buildings Cooperative Use Act, 38
Public ownership, legal approaches, 36
Public Square (Nashville, Tennessee), 21
Puerto Rico, contacts in, 268

Queen Anne style (1880–1900), described, 22

Railroads, resources and bibliography, 73
Raleigh, North Carolina, Christ Episcopal Church, *20*
Ralph Munroe Boathouse (Miami, Florida), *152*
Redwood City, California, Bank of San Mateo, *25*
Reference books, resources and bibliography, 73–74
Regional organizations, 106–110
Regulation, legal approaches, 37
Rehabilitation standards, U.S. Department of the Interior, 30–31
Reliance Building (Chicago, Illinois), *24*
Religious properties, resources and bibliography, 74
Republic Building (Chicago, Illinois), *163*
Reservoir Salvage Act, 38
Resources and bibliography, 56–77
Restoration, resources and bibliography, 74
Revolutionary War, 19
Revolving funds, resources and bibliography, 74
Rhode Island:
    contacts in, 237–238
    degree programs in preservation, 43
Richardson, H. H., 23
Richardsonian Romanesque style (1870–1900), described, 23
Richfield Oil Building (Los Angeles, California), *25*
Riggs Bank Building (Washington, D.C.), *105*
Round barn, Hancock Shaker Village (Pittsfield, Massachusetts), *51*
Rural preservation, resources and bibliography, 74–75
Ruskin, John, 6, 7

St. Charles Avenue mansions (New Orleans, Louisiana), *28*
St. Croix River Lighthouse (Dochet Island, Maine), *178*
St. Katherine's Episcopal Church (Williamstown, Michigan), *190*

St. Louis, Missouri, Summerhouse, Tower Grove Park, *198*
St. Mary's Church (Nashville, Tennessee), *245*
Salem, Oregon, Thomas Kay Woolen Mill, *230*
Salisbury, North Carolina, First Presbyterian Church, *23*
Salt Lake County, Utah, Mountain Dell Dam, Parleys Canyon, *252*
San Carlos Ravelin, San Juan National Historic Site (Old San Juan, Puerto Rico), *268*
San Juan, Puerto Rico, San Carlos Ravelin, San Juan National Historic Site, *268*
Santa Anna Pueblo, New Mexico, Mission Church, *19*
Savannah, Georgia, Central of Georgia Railway Repair Shops, *154*
Scenic byways/historic trails, resources and bibliography, 75
Second Empire style (1860–1890), described, 21–22
Secretary of the Interior, *see* U.S. Department of the Interior
Shaker Church Family Cow Barn (Enfield, New Hampshire), *205*
Shepherdstown, West Virginia, Thomas Shepherd's Grist Mill, *263*
Shingle Style (1880–1900), described, 22–23
Ship Captain's Steamboat House (New Orleans, Louisiana), *13*
Significance, National Register of Historic Places eligibility, 11
Sloss-Sheffield Steel and Iron Company (Birmingham, Alabama), *124*
Smith-Sherlock Store (South Pass City, Wyoming), *267*
South Carolina:
    contacts in, 239–240
    degree programs in preservation, 48
South Dakota, contacts in, 241–242
Southern Colonial style, 19
South Family Dwelling and Washshed, Harvard Shakers (Worcester, Massachusetts), *187*

South Pass City, Wyoming, Smith-Sherlock Store, *267*
Spanish Colonial style (1565–1850), described, 19
Special structure types, resources and bibliography, 75
State Historic Preservation Officer (SHPO), 9, 10, 14, 27, 38, 98, 121
State laws:
    legal approaches, 38–39
    resources and bibliography, 75
    tax incentives, 41
State of Vermont Capital Complex (Montpelier, Vermont), *254*
State registers, legal approaches, 37
Steamboat House (New Orleans, Louisiana), *13*
Steinbeck, John, 6
Stick Style (1860–1890), described, 22
Storer House (Hollywood, California), *135*
Structure types, resources and bibliography, 75
Sullivan, Louis, 24
Summerhouse, Tower Grove Park (St. Louis, Missouri), *198*
Surface Mining Control and Reclamation Act of 1977, 38

Tax incentives, 14, 17
    legal approaches, 40–41
    resources and bibliography, 65–66, 75
Tax Reform Act of 1976, 9, 14
Teaching, resources and bibliography, 76
Technology, resources and bibliography, 76
Tennessee:
    contacts in, 243–245
    degree programs in preservation, 46, 48
Texas:
    contacts in, 246–250
    degree programs in preservation, 49
Thomas Kay Woolen Mill (Salem, Oregon), *230*
Thomas Shepherd's Grist Mill (Shepherdstown, West Virginia), *263*
Tourism, resources and bibliography, 76
Tower Grove Park (St. Louis, Missouri), *198*

Trails and byways, resources and bibliography, 75

Transportation, resources and bibliography, 76

Truman Harry S, vii

Tucson, Arizona, Mission San Xavier del Bac, *128*

Twentieth-century architecture, resources and bibliography, 76

Tyringham, Massachusetts, Gingerbread house, *61*

Union Oyster House (Boston, Massachusetts), *11*

Union Station (Washington, D.C.), 14

U.S. Conference of Mayors, 8

U.S. Department of the Interior, 12, 17

  contacts, 122

  rehabilitation standards, 30–31

U.S. National Park Service, 12, 27, 28, 37

U.S. Sub-Treasury (New York, New York), *20*

U.S. Supreme Court, local ordinances, 14

U.S Virgin Islands, contacts in, 269

University of Virginia (Charlottesville, Virginia), *20*

Upton Scott House (Annapolis, Maryland), *19*

Urban environments, resources and bibliography, 76

Urban Renewal, 8

Utah:

  contacts in, 251–252

  degree programs in preservation, 49

Van Allen and Son Store (Clinton, Iowa), *170*

Vermont:

  contacts in, 253–254

  degree programs in preservation, 46

Vermont State Capital Complex (Montpelier, Vermont), *254*

Vernacular architecture, described, 26

Vicksburg, Mississippi, Warren County Courthouse, *196*

Virginia:

  contacts in, 255–258

  degree programs in preservation, 43–44, 49

Walter Gresham House (Galveston, Texas), *248*

Warren County Courthouse (Vicksburg, Mississippi), *196*

Washington, D.C.:

  contacts in, 146–148

  degree programs in preservation, 46–47

  Grace Church, *147*

  Howard University Divinity School, *55*

  Riggs Bank Building, *105*

  Union Station, 14

  Willard Hotel, 14

Washington State:

  contacts in, 259–261

  degree programs in preservation, 49

West Virginia, contacts in, 262–263

Willard Hotel (Washington, D.C.), 14

Williamstown, Michigan, St. Katherine's Episcopal Church, *190*

Winchester, Virginia, Hollingsworth House (Abram's Delight), *257*

Wisconsin:

  contacts in, 264–266

  degree programs in preservation, 49

With Heritage So Rich, 8, 9

Worcester, Massachusetts, South Family Dwelling and Washshed, Harvard Shakers, *187*

World Heritage Convention, 117–118

Wren, Sir Christopher, 19

Wright, Frank Lloyd, 23, 24

Wyoming, contacts in, 267

Yale University (New Haven, Connecticut), *45*

Young, Dwight, 4–7